Publications of the

CENTER FOR EDUCATION IN LATIN AMERICA
INSTITUTE OF INTERNATIONAL STUDIES

Teachers College, Columbia University

Lambros Comitas
General Editor

We Wish to Be Looked Upon
A Study of Aspirations of Youth in a Developing Society
VERA RUBIN AND MARISA ZAVALLONI

Guidelines to Problems of Education in Brazil
A Review and Selected Bibliography
MALVINA R. MCNEIL

Black Images
WILFRED G. CARTEY

The Middle Beat
A Correspondent's View of Mexico, Guatemala, and El Salvador
PAUL P. KENNEDY

Telling Tongues
Language Policy in Mexico, Colony to Nation
SHIRLEY B. HEATH

Telling Tongues

Language Policy
in Mexico

Colony
to Nation

SHIRLEY BRICE HEATH

Teachers College Press
Teachers College, Columbia University
New York and London

© 1972 by Teachers College, Columbia University
Library of Congress Catalogue Card Number 72-408

Manufactured in the United States of America

The Indian design shown on front and back covers of this book is Aztec and representative of those used by Nahuatl-speaking people. The cross is a composite from two photographs. Both churches which include parts of this cross in their architecture are in Indian regions of Mexico, one is Tlaxcala, the other in Puebla. The basic framework suggests the rugged crosses constructed during the early colonial period; the additional detail of design is similar to that used in some modern churches of Mexico. Cover design is by Martha A. Tomazic. The map on page 2 is by T. Norman Tomazic.

Editor's Note

As one who has followed with interest the academic progress of Shirley Brice Heath through her graduate student and early professional years, I am particularly pleased to welcome her monograph, *Telling Tongues,* as the fifth publication in this series. Sponsored by the Center for Education in Latin America, the series attempts not only to bring forth the specifics of formal education in this vast portion of the New World, but also to offer materials and analyses that place the educational process in a meaningful context. Dr. Heath, in this monograph, examines language policy, one of the most fundamental and vexsome educational issues in any polyglot society, within the framework of nearly half a millenium of Mexican experience. Her subject is not only of historical interest but of continuing theoretical importance and of practical consequence to educators and planners in other countries of Latin America or, for that matter, the world, that have linguistically diversified populations. As the author herself has put it, "Today nations such as Peru, Bolivia, Ecuador, and Guatemala face problems closely analogous to those Mexican anthropologists and political administrators confronted forty years ago." With Mexico as the mirror, *Telling Tongues* charts the complex use of language policy as the means to diverse social and ideological ends.

The series itself focuses on those political units, those nations, territories, and colonies south of the Rio Grande commonly referred to as Latin America and the Caribbean. These constituent societies form a complex sphere which, with considerable theoretical difficulty, can be ordered into three culturally distinctive segments, a tripartite scheme which illuminates the heterogeneity of the area. Within each subdivision, uniformities in historical development, similar patterns of economic exploitation, and indigenous populations of roughly equal size and complexity have led to structurally homologous forms of social organization and articulation. Social institutions in each of these subdivisions, including those related to education, have developed distinctively regional forms and carry specific social significance.

One subdivision includes the territories and countries of the Antilles and the Circum-Caribbean. Characteristically, these societies contain institutions that bear the imprint of a long colonial heritage and a social legacy from forced connection with the metropoles of Western Europe. The populations of many of these societies have been derived primarily from Africa, but they also include socially important pockets of people with origins in Europe, the Indian subcontinent, China, and the Middle East. *We Wish to Be Looked Upon* and *Black Images* are books in this series which concentrate on these island and coastal polities. A second subdivision includes those countries, most often located in the highlands of South and Central America, which contain large, culturally viable populations of Amerindians and in which the process of social and cultural integration of native peoples has dramatically influenced the course and form of nation-building. *The Middle Beat* and this present volume deal with nations in this subdivision, a region sometimes referred to as Indo-America. The third subdivision encompasses the societies of the southern, temperate zones of the Western Hemisphere, which demographically and culturally are dominated by the descendants of migrants from Europe. *Guidelines to Problems of Education in Brazil* focuses on this region.

Lambros Comitas

Foreword

This case study will be of considerable interest, because the ingredients of the case recur so widely. Official policy versus local interests; generalized values versus efficacy in some particular task; uniformity and integration versus respect for existing difference and identity—just such questions arise in many cases in which policy toward language is an issue. Dr. Heath sheds light on all these questions in one of the very few full studies of the working out of such problems that we have. She found herself impelled to tell the full story, after having begun with only the recent period in mind, and we can be grateful that she obeyed the impulse.

The longer time perspective enables us to grasp what may be said to be an historical experiment resolving each of the conflicts noted above: official policy cannot bring about change against the interests of those available to carry out policy; a language associated with broad but inaccessible values cannot eliminate one effective for immediate values and needs; uniformity and integration cannot be peacefully imposed at the expense of identity and self-respect.

It is striking to see these questions persist through five centuries. In the first period the center of official policy is in Spain, of local interests in the colony, Mexico. The conflict is between the royal goal of a Castilianized empire, more uniform and integrated, and the various colonial goals—for friars, religious conversion, but social and economic positions for native interpreters (*naguatlatos*), settlers (*encomenderos*), and colony-born religious personnel, all of whom find advantage in accepting the persistence of the Indian languages. Uniformity and integration fail, not from respect for existing difference and identity, but from concern to maintain a hierarchical structure—Indians who learn Spanish may be as quick to pursue their own advantages as the small corps of interpreters already are, or at least less humble, and the few Indians who have learned Latin are unable to avoid looking down on priests who know it less well.

In the period of national independence the center of official policy is the Mexican capital, local interests are in the governments and the educational systems of the regions, and among teachers themselves. The conflict of values is between an ideal national (first Hispanic, then Mexican) culture and the communicative realities of Indian communities. Uniformity and integration fail at first from lack of respect for existing difference and identity, and begin to succeed when the latter are taken appropriately into account.

The lesson that is learned toward the end of the story has been there all along in the country's own history. Early missionaries learned the Indian languages from necessity (there being so many languages and Indians, so few missionaries, that to teach the Indians Spanish as a prerequisite to teaching them Christianity would be to postpone conversion indefinitely; and if settlers could rely on native interpreters to exploit the Indians and manage a hierarchy, the friars could not rely on interpreters to ascertain the state of a soul and its knowledge of religion). The Indians became Christian to a greater or lesser degree; they did not know themselves part of a national or Hispanic culture. (Note in Chapter Five the shock caused government officials by Manuel Gamio's report "that a great many people in Teotihuacan had no broader concept of 'fatherland' than the village in which they had been born.")

The lesson is also there in the countryside, if one would expose oneself to it, but, Dr. Heath reports, it is only after decades of pronouncements and proposals, that in 1927 an Undersecretary of Education, Moises Sáenz, took a tour of federal schools that exposed the failure of the "direct method" (teaching only in Spanish) of teaching Spanish in rural schools:

He concluded that, despite rhetoric claiming the necessity of a national language for national unity, politicians and educators alike had not made a concerted effort to teach Spanish to the Indians. They left them to learn Spanish incidentally. Decision-makers in national language policy had not only failed to resolve the problems of teaching the national language; they had not even attacked the problem with any degree of realism. Sáenz' tour convinced him that daily classroom conflict between teachers who felt compelled to try to teach Spanish and Indian children who were determined to speak their mother tongue brought only frustration and bitterness which endangered the future of a rural school system (Chapter Six).

The lesson is demonstrated more than once again, by natural experiments and by a planned intervention. The 1930 census showed that among states with heavy Indian populations, the illiteracy rate was 77.11 in Oaxaca, 77.81 in Chiapas, but only 50.04 in Yucatan, where most primary-level teachers were teaching children in their native Mayan tongue. Then in 1939, during the presidency of Lázaro Cárdenas, himself part Tarascan Indian from the state of Michoacán, an experimental Tarascan Project was carried out under the direction of Mauricio (Morris) Swadesh, former student of Sapir and one of the great linguists of this century. Swadesh trained twenty youths, native speakers of Tarascan with some previous educational training, to transcribe spoken Tarascan into the alphabet accepted by the First Assembly of Philologists and Linguists (which Cárdenas had suggested be called by the Department of Indian Affairs). The twenty teachers prepared texts and materials for use by Tarascan children and adults, and then taught literacy in Tarascan, introducing Spanish only after the students had learned to read and write in their own language. Within a period of thirty days some of the Indians in the project learned to read and write, and within forty days, all had done so. The result was undeniable proof that the Indians could learn to read more rapidly in their own tongue than in Spanish.

The lesson is, of course, a general one: in order to bring about change, one must first accept people for what and who they are. In particular, one must come to understand the social meaning of ways of speaking—whether it is a question of a wholly different language, as with the Indian languages of Mexico, and many Indians and Chicanos in the United States, or a question of a distinctive dialect or style, as with many blacks in the United States. (See my introduction, and many of the papers, in Cazden,

John, and Hymes, 1972 *). The Mexican case is an important lesson in a related sense—concern for national unity, fear of separatism, motivated much of the hostility to Indian languages, misinformed and misguided as it was. In the event, national integration was found to require, not uniformity, but an appropriate organization of diversity. This is a somewhat dialectic lesson, but the dialectic has a further twist: respect for local integrity and languages can not be taken for granted, and where present, is not enough.

During the Cortinez presidency, bilingual education emerged again as an issue. Most rural school teachers, traditionally devoted to the direct (Spanish only) method, had not adopted the bilingual method—because of linguistic chauvinism, insufficient linguistic training, inadequate knowledge of an Indian language, or, often enough, sincere belief that literacy in an indigenous tongue would keep the Indians locked in isolation. Some Indians themselves resented being singled out for "special" methods. An evaluation of the method and its use was undertaken by Swadesh in 1956. He found some cultural promoters alienating people by preference for Spanish, others making no noticeable effort to encourage use of Spanish, to Indian objections. More often than not, Indians favoured bilingual materials because these facilitated learning Spanish. In effect, two rights had to be secured and balanced: to use language, and to learn Spanish.

There is yet a further lesson: respect for native intelligence and potential, for past cultural achievements, and provision for literacy, do not in themselves solve the problems of integration and improvement. Those who taught Spanish to Indians might succeed only in loosening them from one community to leave them marginal to another, still at the bottom of the national social scale, and, in human terms, worse off. After generations had focused upon language policy as the key to a general Indian policy, responsible officials and scholars began to understand the complexity and problematic nature of the relationships among language and other aspects of social life. In particular, linguistic integration was equivalent to socio-economic integration; certainly linguistic success was not sufficient for socio-economic

---

* Courtney Cazden, Vera John, and Dell Hymes (eds.). *The Functions of Language in the Classroom.* New York, Teachers College Press 1972.

success. And they realized that the relationships among language and other aspects of social life might be different in different sectors of the country. Just as national integration did not require linguistic uniformity, neither did it require uniformity of educational policy. The local cultural conditions which rerouted earlier language policy have been recognized, and the merits of decentralized policy-making admitted. Each of the states of Mexico can choose among three policies with regard to its particular purposes and circumstances (Chapter Eight).

There is much more of interest about the functions of language, especially, in Chapter One, with regard to Nahuatl; the spread before the Conquest of Nahuatl as an official lingua franca, and its cultivation as a literary standard in Texcoco; spread of Nahuatl after the Conquest by some friars and recognition of it for a time by the Spanish Crown as *the* Indian language; the loss of certain cultivated functions after the Conquest; yet eighteenth-century praise of Nahuatl as exceeding Latin in poetic expression and rendering of abstract concepts (Benaduci 1746, Chapter Two, note 30); and the nineteenth-century recommendation that Nahuatl, Tarascan, and Otomi be treated as 'classical' tongues, study of which would discipline the mind (Mora in Chapter Four, notes 25 and 26). Such views are found intermingled with expectable stereotypes and prejudices. The nineteenth-century liberal Mora, though he translated the Gospel of Luke into Nahuatl, elsewhere denied that there were any Mexicans ("those called Indians") who used such languages, or any who did not speak Spanish. A contemporary claimed that "we discover in the Indian languages obvious signs of their servility" (Pimentel 1864, Chapter Four, note 53). And in his charming and revealing Pastoral, translated in the first Appendix to this book, the eighteenth-century Bishop Lorenzana had noted that his colleague, the Lord Bishop of Oaxaca, reports a language "which is only fully intelligible in the day time, and after the sun goes down at night, certain things cannot be communicated because their meanings are conveyed with gestures" (note 17), as part of an argument for the necessity of Spanish.

The acceptance of the Indian contribution to Mexican national culture, beginning in the second half of the nineteenth century, should be of special poignancy for Americans, who have, perhaps, accepted much of the contribution to United States culture of Spanish-Americans and Afro-Americans. Here indeed lies a great significance of this book: it holds a mirror up to us. In Mexico one cannot but recognize that language policy in education is inseparable from the issue of national identity, as it has developed over the years. In the United States we seem to behave as if such issues were behind us, as if language policy in the schools was entirely a technical matter, of research into practical obstacles. The resurgence of racist thinking in 'high' places—an expectable resurgence, if the alternatives are blaming the system (including its procedures such as testing) or blaming the children—ought to suggest that the issue is deeper and even hidden. The issue has to do very much still with who is accepted as "American," who can accept themselves as "Americans." If a white Texan can become President without having to change his dialect, why such necessity for a black child to change his dialect to get an education or a job? How could it happen that a year or two ago Spanish-speaking children were assigned to classes for retarded children because they could not pass tests in English? Are we perhaps far behind Mexico in accepting the cultural diversity within our borders? And until we accept it, and the identities bound up with it, can we expect much success in education?

There is much else in the story told by Dr. Heath that speaks to general questions: the interplay of anthropological, social, and missionary concern in the efflorescence of indigenous education in Mexico; the motives for development of anthropology, first the Indian as cultural heritage, then the Indian as social problem; the problems of relevant social science, first in maintaining independence of government, then in operating with personal links to government, then in functioning within centralized, coordinating bureaucracy. Dr. Heath points out that the study of language in education in Mexico is far from finished, but it is already a full story with many lessons. I hope that her book will bring knowledge of the Mexican story to many, both for its intrinsic interest and for the sake of comparison and reflection as to analogous problems elsewhere.

Dell Hymes
University of Pennsylvania

Preface

To enter a field of study during its pioneer stage of development can be a uniquely exciting and intellectually stimulating experience. In the mid-1960's numerous students carrying out their advanced work felt the pull of sociolinguistics, an interdisciplinary field then gaining its first momentum. Frequently described as the "sociology of language," the field especially attracted proponents from the areas of political science, sociology, and—as in my case—anthropology and linguistics. Multiple areas of research opened up, as conferences on sociolinguistics suggested relationships between language and society and repeatedly emphasized the implications these might have for social change, language standardization, and national integration.[1]

Scholars particularly interested in the application of sociolinguistics to the solution of societal language problems pointed out one important area for future research—that of language planning in developing nations. Language planning, or the process of conscious decision-making resulting in language changes, characterizes many developing and developed nations alike.[2] However, within developed nations having a tradition of literacy among the majority of their citizens and an active literary elite, language planning has been virtually synonymous with language standardization. A central agency authorized to rule on spelling reforms, to influence educational and political interests in their selection of grammatical forms and lexical items, and to prepare dictionaries to guide writers and speakers to the official language norm, has prescribed internal changes in the language. For these nations, language planning has meant normative deliberations on the efficiency and adequacy of systems within the structure of language.

On the other hand, formerly colonial nations without a large literate population have typically expanded their concerns in language planning beyond the structure of language to its functions. The colonial experience left these nations with ethnically and linguistically fragmented populations, and their language planners have been forced to consider the communicative and identification value of language in varying political, social, and economic settings. Language planners have become policy-makers whose decisions are grounded in integrative plans for the social and economic transition of the indigenous population to modernity. Moreover, these decisions require local change agents' direct and active participation in the implementation of language policies. Thus, both the kinds of language problems and the kinds of decision-making are vastly more complex in developing nations than in more advanced countries, while the language-planning process is apt both to reflect and to effect greater sociocultural changes.

As a result, developing nations offer excellent opportunities for case studies of the language-planning process set in a sociocultural context. Such studies might give us clues as to why certain language policies succeed or fail, how certain procedures and methods of language teaching have operated in national education programs, and what differences have existed among the general decision systems which approved various language policies. The findings might also supply a body of information from which hypotheses could be drawn for testing in comparative studies.

The paucity of such case studies led me to direct my research efforts in that direction. My original survey of language-planning policies in independent Mexico soon gave way to a more extended study that included all three major eras of Mexican history—the period of the Aztec empire, the age of Spanish colonialism, and the period of nationalism—since the post-Independence policies could not realistically be separated from those of the earlier eras.

While innovative twentieth-century language policies are much in evidence, modern Mexico has merged with rather than submerged the older eras.

The choice of Mexico as a subject for the study of language planning was based on several considerations. The major factors were Mexico's long history of language-planning efforts and the ready availability of records through which those efforts could be studied in their broader cultural context. Major sources of data for the Aztec and colonial periods were Mexico's carefully preserved official government documents, letters directed from local elites to the Crown, and chronicles prepared by Church representatives. For the first century after Independence, evidence has been drawn primarily from federal documents and the writings of government officials. Personal interviews and official publications contribute most of the information for the years since 1920.

Anthropologists and linguists have consistently proposed Mexico as fertile ground for further research on the relationships between language and culture. Anthropologists have pointed to divergent attitudes toward the adoption of Spanish by Indian-speaking groups in Mexico as an example of the functional evolution of languages.[3] Anthropological studies have shown that inter-group relations between Indian groups and the Spanish authorities in Mexico affected the natives' reception of the Spanish language.[4] Linguists calling for a synchronic and diachronic description of language contact in Mexico have termed Mexico "close to an ideal laboratory" for such a study.[5] These scientists have contributed treatments of local contact situations in Mexico; others have included Mexico in broad and general surveys of types of bilingualism in Latin American.[6] However, no one has attempted overall coverage of the processes and policies concerning language as social behavior in colonial and national Mexico. This is the vacuum my work is intended to fill.

The purpose of the book is to provide a narrative description of cultural contexts in which the language-planning process has been operative in Mexico throughout that country's history, tracing particular actions in the fields of politics, religion, education, and inter-group relations that have had special relevance for the process. This case study of a nation held as a colony of Spain for nearly 300 years, transformed into a new developing nation in the nineteenth century, and jolted by a social revolution in the comparatively recent past portrays the historical background of the processes of selection, implementation, and execution of language policies in a particular cultural setting. It also provides the basis for formulating some tentative generalizations about the social and political contexts and consequences of language planning. This study has been inspired not by a desire to retell the familiar story of *indigenismo* across Mexico's history or to present the structural linguistic changes resulting from language contact in Mexico, but rather by the need to examine the views and policies resulting from social-change agents' appraisal of language as social behavior.

Political scientists have, for some time, debated the problem of the influence of various elite groups on decision-making within the more powerful political institutions. In this case study, elites at the input level have been local agents of social change—missionaries, Church officials, teachers, social scientists—who have mediated or attempted to influence policies made at the highest levels of political institutions. For the purposes of this study, policy-makers and decision-makers are assumed to be those members of the political institutions of the empire or nation who could enact legislation to incorporate the suggestions of local agents of change. These agents of change—intellectuals of the sciences and arts in the Aztec empire, clergymen and Crown officials in the colonial period, intellectuals, politicians, and social scientists in the modern era—reflect attitudes prevalent in their social spheres of activity. Their story reveals language as an instrument of empire and nation in Mexico's history.

An author who attempts to follow a single policy thread throughout the complex cloth of a nation's history risks certain obvious perils. Drawing a single concern, such as language planning, out of the broad range of social and political history in Mexico, the researcher faces the danger of either overstressing or ignoring historic influences not immediately or directly related to the selected topic. It is, of course, obvious that assumptions about language were not the only factors affecting the evolution of language policy, and it is easy to forget that within the processes of Christianization, national unification, and the Mexican

Revolution, policy decisions which affected language were not made as a direct response to existing language conditions. Therefore, I have tried to combat any tendency to attribute to all those who effected language policy a primary concern for that topic.

In the organization, I have chosen to separate historical narrative and theoretical analysis. In particular, the linguistic models and theories which have provided a frame of reference for research in this study have not been exploited in the historical-sociological presentation. Although attention has been paid to the technical linguistic models and theories of linguists who have dealt with language-planning processes, these matters are explicitly drawn into the study only in the final chapter where they may provide some comparative generalizations in applied sociolinguistics. To be sure, integration of abstract conclusions from this case study with the narrative of events would have made for some advantages. However, it has seemed to me that the resulting interruption of the narrative flow and the distraction of attention from the historical process would have raised more problems than the organization adopted. Moreover, the theory which may be found in the course of this history of language planning did not evolve in any planned sense from a series of metaphysical decisions, but instead came in bits and pieces in a colony and a nation where men made decisions in pursuit of values they deemed most crucial—self, *los indios*, God, or country.

A word about the title. It is both a pun and an attempt to sum up the central point of the book. A case history of language policy indicates how very telling—or revealing—language can be. In both the colonial and national settings, language, whether an Indian tongue or a variety of Spanish, has often been the primary key to group membership and class status. Tongues have told much about the cultural and psychological mold of individuals, who have been cast into greater or lesser stations according to their speech habits. Similarly, the central figures—both political elites and local change agents—have prescribed or taught the standard of their task or time. Rather than being a matter of free choice for the individual, language has been the object of much telling by various agents representing monolithic institutional interests of the Church, the Crown, or the Mexican nation.

Shirley Brice Heath

Contents

EDITOR'S NOTE
FOREWORD
PREFACE

I   LANGUAGE, INSTRUMENT OF EMPIRE   1
       Nahuatl in the Aztec Empire
       The Castilian Background
       Practice over Policy in Early New Spain

II   INDIAN TONGUES IN THE SPIRITUAL CONQUEST   15
       Missionary Techniques in the Field
       Nahuatl, Universal Language of the Indians
       Indian Literacy

III   A CODE FOR THE ELITE   37
       Spanish for the Indians
       The Struggle to Establish a Code

IV   THE NATION BETWEEN OLD AND NEW   57
       Heritage in Education
       Confirming a National Standard

V   SPANISH AND THE PLAN FOR CONFORMITY   81
       Incorporation through Education
       The Direct Method

VI   BILINGUALISM AND NATIONAL UNITY   99
       Emerging Integration
       Little Nationalities
       The Move toward Indigenism

VII	THE PROGRAM OF ACCEPTANCE Campaign for Literacy From the Community to the Region Retreat and Reevaluation	123
VIII	REALITY AND RESPONSIBILITY The New Departure A Measure of Reality	151
IX	OVERVIEW AND CONCLUSIONS The Historical Process Social Science Perspectives	171
ACKNOWLEDGEMENTS		205
APPENDIX I	Translation of *Pastoral*	207
APPENDIX II	Translation of *Edicto XV*	215
NOTES		221
BIBLIOGRAPHY		265
INDEX		289

CHAPTER ONE

Language, Instrument of Empire

Nahuatl in the Aztec Empire

The Conquistadors walked into a solution and made it a problem. In the century preceding the arrival of Spaniards on the coasts of New Spain, Aztecs had subjugated diverse linguistic groups in the course of their territorial expansion. Nahuatl, official language of the Aztecs, spread with the territory of the warriors, becoming a language of privilege and prestige throughout the conquered territory. One of the most notable feats of the Aztec domination over numerous tribes was this establishment of Nahuatl as the official language of the empire. The Aztecs trained members of their own tribes as Nahuatl scribes and interpreters in the administrative affairs of the tributary system. The conquering Spaniards, representing the Crown of Castile, did not adopt this solution to the problem of language in their new empire. Despite recognition by Isabella and later Spanish monarchs of the use of language as an instrument of empire, the Conquistadors failed to perpetuate Nahuatl as the standard tongue or to introduce Castilian in its place.

Before the arrival of Hernán Cortés in 1519, political facts and linguistic diversity in ancient Mexico called for a standard language. The warriors of the Mexica tribe, popularly called the Aztecs but technically the most powerful tribe of the Aztec alliance, extended their invasions and tributary system from the

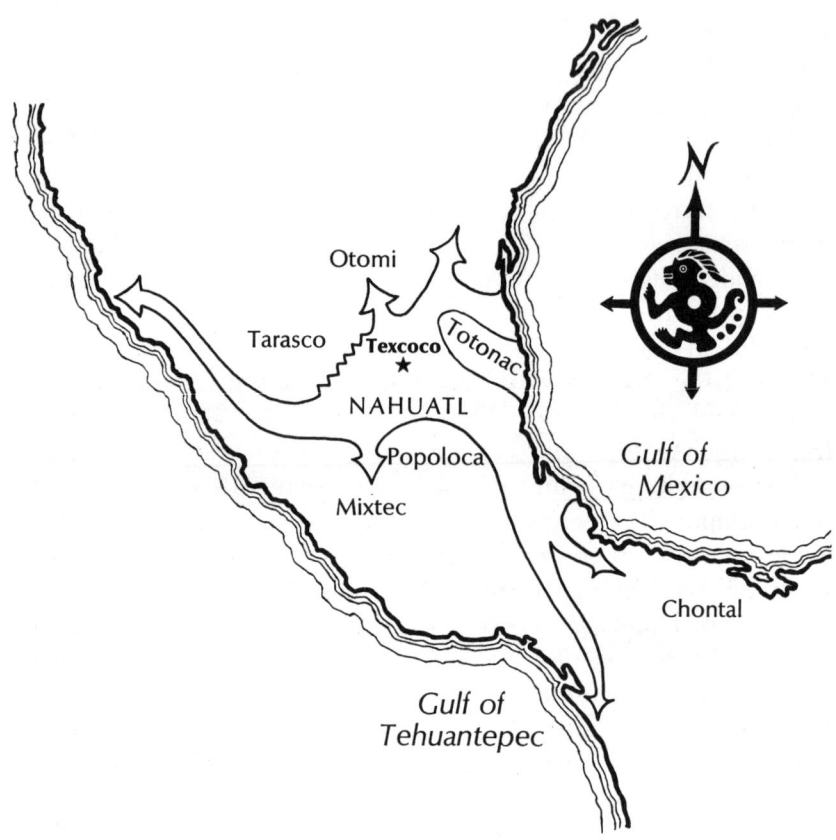

valley of Mexico southward into the Isthmus of Tehuantepec and northward toward territory held by the nomadic and barbaric Chichimecs. Nahuatl, the language of the Mexica warriors, became the tongue of common intercourse among the subjugated peoples of different language backgrounds. As the fierce warriors marched beyond the valley of Mexico, they incorporated groups speaking Nahua, an older dialect, and tribes using many diverse tongues. Conquests during the fifteenth and early sixteenth centuries brought Otomi, Totonac, Popoloca, Chontal, and Mixtec speakers into the tributary system of the Aztecs.[1]

The numerous native languages in the areas of conquest were barriers to trade, alliance systems, and political influence, and though the Mexica limited the territory which they themselves primarily occupied, their authority was extensive and powerful in the administration of certain internal affairs. The Mexica tribe, the apex of power in the Aztec empire, shared tribute and the administration of state affairs with four other tribes—the Acolhuaque, Tepaneca, Chalca, and Xochimilca—all Nahuatl-speaking. Within the military organization of the late Aztec empire, the central valley's six separate army units were made up exclusively of Nahuatl speakers.[2] Membership in the close and real Nahuatl language community gave tribes under the powerful Mexica a right to political distinction and social dignity. Those tribes for whom Nahuatl was not the native tongue suffered a loss of privilege and prestige. Not only could they not share in administrative decision-making within the empire, but also they could not escape the contempt of Nahuatl speakers. The derogatory labels given the tongues of neighboring tribes by the Nahuatl language community remain today as the official name for several tongues still spoken: Chontal (foreigner), Popoloca (unintelligible), and Totonac (rustic).[3]

The subjugation of communities located far from Tenochtitlan, the Aztec capital, and tribute collection in these distant areas encouraged the use of Nahuatl as the language of politics and finance. Within the tributary system of the Aztec empire at the time of the arrival of Cortés, more than eighty different languages and dialects were spoken.[4] The use of and acceptance of Nahuatl as the standard idiom of commerce, law, and economics permitted the Aztecs to maintain efficient communication among the wide-spread territories and diverse peoples. The chronicler Mendieta, writing over thirty years after the arrival of the first Spaniards, commended the Aztecs on their spread of Nahuatl and compared its use as a standard language to that of Latin in Europe:

> This Mexican language [Nahuatl] is the common tongue which runs through all the provinces of Spain, inasmuch as there are innumerable languages within each province, and even within sections of each village. Moreover, throughout all parts of New Spain there are interpreters who understand and speak Nahuatl, since this language is spread here just as Latin is through all the realms of Europe.[5]

Interpreters who understood and spoke Nahuatl worked in all the territories and cooperated with record-keepers to insure an accurate accounting of the empire's affairs.

Bernal Díaz spoke briefly of those records kept in Tenochtitlan: "I remember that at that time his [Montezuma's] steward was a great Cacique to whom we gave the name of Tápia, and he kept the accounts of all the revenue that was brought to Montezuma . . . and he had a great house full of these books."[6] Scribes especially trained for the task prepared codices written with characters which were both ideographic and syllabic. Concern with not only written records but also the oral word reached its height in Texcoco, the cultural capital of the Acolhuaque in the fifteenth century. The Acolhuaque, who of course spoke Nahuatl, ranked second in power and prestige to the Mexica, and Texcoco, their tribal capital, ranked first as an intellectual and cultural center among the Aztec tribes. Ixtlilxochitl, Texcoco's sixteenth-century historian and a descendant of the tribe's royalty, recounted the amazing activities of this city's council of arts and sciences during the fifteenth century.[7] Not only did the council judge the merit of scholarship in the territory, but it also encouraged poets and orators. Historical compositions, oratories, and poems were recited in what was known throughout the Aztec empire as the purest form of the Nahuatl language. Texcoco was the center of arts, where the leading gentlemen of the Aztec empire sent their sons to learn "the most polished form of the *Nahuatl* language, poetry, philosophy, [and] theology."[8] In the fifteenth century, Nahuatl in ancient Mexico compared with

Latin in Europe not only in its use as a *lingua franca*, but also in its acceptance as the standard language for science, art, and the education of the elite.

THE CASTILIAN BACKGROUND

The Castilian Crown's official language policy for New Spain derived not from any rational assessment of Nahuatl's existence as a standard language in this New World colony, but rather from politics and philosophy in the Old World. Language planning for New Spain was at once a continuation and an expansion of policies prevailing under Ferdinand and Isabella in Castile in the late fifteenth and early sixteenth centuries. The final attack (1482-92) on the "Moorish" state of Granada signified the end of the seven-hundred-year Spanish *reconquista,* the struggle of the Catholic kingdoms of the north to wrest the Iberian peninsula from the control of the Moors. To follow this military victory in the crusade against the infidels, the Catholic queen drew up plans for political and religious, as well as cultural, conquests. Isabella concentrated intensely on preserving her royal power, solidifying her sovereignty on a firm Catholic basis, and uniting her kingdom under Castile. All of these ambitions and the power exercised in their behalf were to determine the course of language planning for New Spain by future Spanish monarchs.

Isabella was intent on "Castilianizing" the kingdom under her rule; Castilian became the official language of those diverse regions brought under the standard of Castile during the reconquista. Isabella's reform program to raise the moral and intellectual standards of the clergy and the religious orders brought changes which profoundly touched the men who were to be the early missionaries in New Spain. Isabella's confessor, Archbishop Francisco Jiménez de Cisneros, strictly enforced a return among the Franciscans to the simplicity of the Rule of Saint Francis, and he saw to it that the young clergy were rigorously trained as men of God in monasteries and seminaries under his rule. Cisneros' demand for a strict observance of moral standards among the Franciscan friars spread to other orders as well.[9]

Playing out their role as Catholic Kings (a title conferred on them by Pope Alexander in 1494), Ferdinand and Isabella undertook to purify Spanish society and to bring Castilians together in a spirit of Christian unity. Resorting to the Inquisition to help purge the kingdom of Jewish and Arab influence, Isabella began a program of religious nationalization which later monarchs carried on toward identification of Catholicism with Castilianization. With the banishment or forced assimilation of Jews and Moslems, Ferdinand and Isabella turned their attention to the spiritual uneasiness in the Church. Austerity and discipline, coupled with a strong sense of evangelistic purpose, were the prevailing characteristics of reformed training among the friars of the mendicant orders.

Added to this sense of religious mission was the influence of humanistic scholarship, encouraged by Archbishop Cisneros and Isabella. Cisneros founded the University of Alcalá and there directed the editing of the Polyglott Bible in Latin, Greek, and Hebrew. Humanistic scholars, trained in this tradition, were later to carry their enthusiasm and skills for language study to the New World. Grammars, vocabularies, and Indian-language translations were to bear mark of the friars' thorough study of the classical tongues, especially Latin. The Queen brought foreign scholars to Castile, and her traveling court spread new influences and intellectual approaches throughout the literate portion of the kingdom's population. Isabella learned Latin, encouraged its use, as well as that of Castilian, and found in her royal historiographer, Elio Antonio de Nebrija, a humanist who combined his interests in the classical and the vernacular in his preparation of a Latin grammar, a Latin-Spanish dictionary, and the first modern Spanish grammar. Nebrija "nationalized" Castilian in his *Gramática sobre la lengua castellana;* he advocated teaching the "things of the nation" in the language of the nation.[10] In presenting Nebrija's grammar to Isabella in 1492, the Bishop of Avila crystallized the Castilian queen's approach and set forth a principle which succeeding Spanish monarchs were to try to adopt in their official language policies at home and in Spain's colonies: "Language is the perfect instrument of empire."[11] The impact of language emphases in fifteenth-century Spain was both to increase cultural chauvinism by redefining and reasserting Castilian as the Hispanic tongue and to impart to friars both the desirability and the tools for Indian language study.

The reciprocity of cause and effect between Castile's robust intellectual spirit and the successful domination of its language and culture over that of other parts of the Iberian peninsula cannot be denied. Castilian was the standard of politics, scholarship, and art. The enthusiasm of the Court for intellectual and cultural contacts outside the kingdom encouraged the literates of the society. The traveling court of Isabella entertained lyric poets, scholars, and translators presenting their works freshly printed in Castilian. The dramatic novel *La Celestina* reflected Castile's enthusiasm for life, exuberance of learning, and the stylistic varieties of the Castilian tongue. The language of *La Celestina* alternated between the cultured speech of nobles and the racy idiom of commoners. Appropriate standardization of Castilian was guaranteed by the printing press and the productivity of Castile's scholars and literary artists. Yet the national tongue remained flexible enough to fill the expressive and communicative needs of all members of the language community. Castilian was a vigorous tongue—the cultural and political instrument of a self-proclaiming society.

Practice over Policy in Early New Spain

Isabella's Castilianization campaign should have insured that her agents would bring their cultural and linguistic confidence to the New World. Legislation for the expanded empire tried to guarantee that social and cultural habits—not only of infidels at home, but also of Indians abroad—be shed in favor of Castilian-Christian practices. Perhaps most important, these laws stressed that emissaries of the Crown bore responsibility for the redemption and education of the natives of the New World. Legislation promulgated prior to the conquest of New Spain, which provided for the settlement of the natives in villages and their instruction in reading, writing, and matters of faith, had the avowed purpose not only of exposing the Indians to Christian influence but also of rendering them more fully subject to Spanish control. Official Crown policy made it clear that the extension of the Castilian language was an acknowledged concomitant of the expansion of the Spanish Catholic Empire.

Indian legislation contained in the Laws of Burgos issued in

1512 required all Spaniards owning more than fifty Indians to provide for "the salvation of their souls, as well as for the profit and utility of their persons and the conservation of their lives."¹² The preamble to the Laws and their specific legislation left no doubt that Castile's Crown intended for the Indians to be civilized and redeemed in their social customs and living habits as well as in their religious spirit. Recommendations for the natives' "improvement" included settlement of the Indians in houses near the Spaniards; provision of meat and fish for Indian households; donation of wearing apparel suitable for "reasonable men"; and strict enforcement of monogamy. The Crown entrusted the altering of the Indians' cultural habits—social, religious, and linguistic—to the *encomenderos*. These men were Spanish trustees who received rights to the personal services of Indians living in a given number of Indian villages. The encomenderos were to teach the Indians to cross themselves and recite in Latin the Ave Maria, the Pater Noster, and certain creeds of the Catholic faith; ritual and rote recitation were the order of the day. To ease the burden of teaching for the encomendero, he should train one native teacher who would in turn teach his new language and religion to other natives in the indigenous tongue.¹³

Serious dicta these, and all handed out in the spirit of religious and cultural purification and unification which permeated the self-proclaiming society of Castile. But the Castilianization-Christianization program at home rested on the mood of exuberance and idealism prevailing within Isabella's post-reconquista kingdom. This mood dissipated as conquistadors and the variety of persons and classes who came in the aftermath of conquest met the realities of the New World and found it impossible to carry policy into practice. Legal pronouncements telling Castilian emissaries how to Christianize and Castilianize the natives of the New World reached dimensions comical in the face of practicalities. Perhaps the epitome was reached in the manifesto drawn up by Ferdinand and his advisers and termed the *requerimiento*. This document, which was to be read to Indians by interpreters before the conquerors initiated hostilities, required that the Indians accept the Church and the Castilian Crown and that they submit to the teachings of the Faith; if the Indians refused this "requirement," the Spaniards were compelled to punish them.¹⁴ Perhaps most representative of the highly impractical, if not impossible, nature of this document was the prerequisite that translators be available to read to the Indians in their native tongue. Early adventurers saw no other way to fulfill this order than to defy the spirit of the requirement and seize Indians as captives in their skirmishes on the coasts of the New World. In the two-year period before the 1519 voyage of Hernán Cortés to New Spain, this practice by other captains contributed to a series of incidents which would help move the Spaniards of New Spain away from their responsibilities as sons of the Catholic Church and the Castilian Crown.

In the early months of 1517, Hernandez de Cordova and a group of restless Spanish soldiers left Cuba to explore new lands. In their first skirmish with the natives of the land the Spanish called "Yucatan," the soldiers took two prisoners. These Indians, baptized Julian and Melchior, traveled with the soldiers down the coast of the Yucatan peninsula to Campeche. There the soldiers heard the natives cry "Castilan" and believed that they were not the first Spaniards the Indians of this area had seen. In 1518, Juan de Grijalva returned to the Yucatan peninsula and continued up the coast of Mexico to what is today the state of Vera Cruz. Though he had with him as interpreters the Indians Julian and Melchior, Grijalva was forced to resort to sign language in his "conference" with a cacique under the rule of the Aztec emperor. The Indian translators from the Yucatan peninsula could not understand Nahuatl, the Mexican language. Grijalva followed Cordova's pattern and took one of the Indians of this area as a prisoner. The Spaniards baptized him Francisco, and he returned to Mexico in 1519 with Cortés' expedition.¹⁵ Thus Cortés carried with him Melchior who spoke Maya and Francisco who spoke Nahuatl, both of whom had been taught some Spanish in their short periods as captives.

When Cortés landed on the island of Cozumel, one of his primary concerns was to determine whether the cries of "Castilan" by natives of Campeche in 1517 had meant there were captive Spaniards in that area. Melchior learned from *caciques,* local Indian rulers, that Spaniards were held prisoner on the peninsula, and Cortés sent messengers and a ransom payment in an effort to have the Spaniards return to Cozumel and join his expedition.

After eight days, Cortés' messengers returned with no word of the Spaniards, and an angry and disappointed Cortés left Cozumel. But a leak in one of the ships forced him to return. This incident, termed by a contemporary chronicler, "a very great mystery and miracle of God,"[16] provided Cortés with his first trustworthy interpreter, for Jerónimo de Aguilar, a Spaniard dressed as an Indian of Yucatan, appeared in a canoe as Cortés waited at Cozumel for the ship to be repaired. Cortés learned that Aguilar had been educated for the church in Spain, a shipwreck had left him on the coast of Campeche eight years before, and he had learned the Mayan language working for a cacique during his captivity.

Aguilar joined Cortés and gave the soldiers of the expedition a welcome sense of security. He spoke Mayan dialects and was able to translate for Cortés until the group passed beyond the area of the Grijalva River. Moreover, he was loyal—an asset bitter experience quickly taught Cortés to value highly in interpreters. Soon after the Spaniards reached the region of Tabasco, Melchior, the Yucatan Indian, escaped, joined the Tabascans, and advised them to make war on Cortés. After the first skirmishes, Aguilar talked with Indian prisoners and learned of Melchior's role in the attack. Following a final and decisive battle with the Tabascans, Cortés, determined that Melchior not stir up any further treachery, demanded his return. The Conquistador was satisfied only when he learned that the battle's outcome had set Melchior's fate; the Tabascans had offered him as sacrifice in return for his foolish counsel.

Before leaving the Tabascans, Cortés inquired through Aguilar where the Indians obtained their gold and jewels. "Culua" and "Mexico" were their answers—terms meaningless to Aguilar. However, Francisco, the native of Mexico taken prisoner by Grijalva in 1518, interpreted the term "Culua" by making signs to show it was far ahead.[17]

As Cortés left the Tabascans and continued up the coast, he carried with him many gifts, including twenty Indian women. Landing at what is now the port of Vera Cruz, Cortés was met by the Indians of the area who remembered Grijalva's recent "conference" and were anxious to communicate with Cortés. The Conquistador, however, wanted to know more than sign language could tell him. But Aguilar, the only interpreter Cortés could trust in this important encounter, was of no use, for he did not know the language of the Mexica. Here again a chain of accidents provided the translator Cortés needed so desperately in his first contact with the subjects of Montezuma.

Cortés learned that among the women presented him in Tabasco was a woman born near Vera Cruz, but given in her youth to Indians from Xicalango, who had then passed her on to the people of Tabasco. Malinche, or Doña Marina, became Cortés' most famous interpreter, and through her knowledge of both the customs and the language of the Aztecs, she was able to help Cortés throughout the Conquest. Her major advantage to Cortés initially was that she knew Nahuatl as well as the language of Tabasco. Since Aguilar knew the Mayan dialects, the two could understand one another, and Aguilar could translate into Spanish for Cortés. Later, as Cortés penetrated the territory of the Mexica and realized the extent of use of Nahuatl in the tributary system of Montezuma, he encouraged Doña Marina to learn Spanish and she became the major channel of communication between the natives and Cortés. Bernal Díaz credits her joining the group as "the great beginning of our conquests." [18] Thus translators had served very well in the entry to Mexico, but their very success contributed to the Spanish settlers' failure to teach significant numbers of Indians the Spanish language.

As Cortés had set the pattern, so the encomenderos continued. Though within the first decade after the Spaniards' arrival, a few soldiers learned enough Nahuatl to serve as interpreters for civil officials, these were soon displaced in favor of Indian translators.[19] The custom of having interpreters active in the administrative affairs of the Aztec empire was well-known, and enterprising Indians, quick to see the Spaniards' need for translators, learned enough Castilian to qualify for service to the Spanish. However, Indians who learned Castilian did so not to teach others, but to interpret in the extension of the conquest beyond the valley of Mexico and in the administrative affairs of the expanding empire. Translators accompanied expeditions of discovery, sat in courts and civil offices, and directed native labor forces. Spanish adventurers used interpreters as informers in planning military tactics and finding caches of idols and wealth;

the Crown prescribed a loftier mission for the go-betweens. A 1526 ruling by Charles V reminded the Spaniards that each new group of natives the soldiers met must be told in their native tongues of the Crown's high purposes in New Spain. The Spaniards had come to teach the Indians good customs, to dissuade them from their vices, and to instruct them in the Catholic faith; technically, the natives were to be given the opportunity to accept the benevolence of the intruders before being subjected to hostilities.[20]

While some interpreters marched with soldiers to discover new wealth, others remained in the valley of Mexico with civil and religious officials. These *naguatlatos,* or Indian translators, learned not only the conqueror's tongue but also his deceits. Interpreters assigned to local courts did not truthfully translate Indians' statements before judicial officials. Judges demanded extra tribute and punished innocents for infractions which existed only in the words of the naguatlatos. Such additional payments often helped satisfy the appetite of naguatlatos for a share in spoils of the Spanish takeover. Salaries of interpreters were paid by local civil officials who found it to their advantage to place no curbs on Indian mediators who went about collecting their own salaries. Charles V consistently attempted to control thieving naguatlatos. They were to accept no bribes or gifts from Spaniards or Indians; they were to hear cases publicly; they were to be voted upon by members of the Indian community. To insure the interpreters' good behavior, the King ordered that civil officials require the presence of a "Christian friend" when an Indian presented his case through a naguatlato.[21]

The emergence of Indian translators who represented their own selfish interests and those of the greedy Spaniards, rather than the needs of the Indians, helped convince the encomenderos that not all Indians should be educated. The settlers could not chance teaching Castilian and reading and writing to numerous natives; those who had taken on the Castilian tongue had been too quick to speak out for their share of profit to be made at the expense of Indian masses. Moreover, the task, as laid out for the encomenderos in the Laws of Burgos, of converting and educating the Indians was time-consuming and foreign to the character of the robust adventurers. Thus, the settlers, originally charged with the religious education and language-literacy instruction of the Indians, ignored the Crown's charge. Bartolomé de las Casas, the friar who became the protector of the Indians of the New World, complained bitterly that the encomenderos refused to educate and care for the Indians; moreover, in the building of their own fortunes and feudal estates, they mercilessly exploited the natives. Las Casas repeatedly warned Charles V that the will of Isabella and the intent of the Laws of Burgos regarding the education of the Indians were not being carried out in the New World.[22] The New Laws of 1542, issued by Charles V partially in response to Las Casas' exhortations, were designed to reprimand the encomenderos for their failure to fulfill their obligations to the Crown and to conserve the Indian population.

Realizing the dangers inherent in the encomenderos' feudalistic system which gave them an immediate and powerful grip on the citizens of the New World, Charles V set out to reclaim the Indians for the Castilian Crown. He reasoned that if the Indians were educated, they would become subject to the Crown. Persuaded then by the need both to consolidate his own empire and to establish his sovereignty over the Indians, Charles V decreed that all Indians held in *encomienda* were transferred to the Crown and were to be taught the Catholic faith as free vassals of the Crown. The New Laws withdrew the encomenderos as agents responsible for the education of Indians; a substitute force would take over the civilization and redemption of the Indians.

Actually, Cortés had suggested a replacement as early as 1524 when he requested clergymen to handle the conversion and instruction of the natives. He had reminded the King that, after all, it was well known that most of the Spaniards who came to New Spain were crude, coarse, licentious, and given to all sorts of vices and sins. Alert to the evil influence these men could have on the Indians, Cortés and his officers had tried to restrict the soldiers' contact with the Indians. But the land was too large and the men too difficult to control; the Conqueror and his lieutenants could not halt the conversion of the Indians to the Spaniards' vices. No defensive task, this; what was needed here was an offensive force armed with sermons, moderate habits, and zeal for the conversion of the natives. In short, His Majesty should send friars to establish monasteries and to take charge of the Indians in the provinces.[23]

The dozen or so Franciscan friars already in Mexico at the time of Cortés' letter were shortly reinforced by Dominicans and Augustinians.[24] By 1535 Charles V had judged it time to hand over the education of the native elite to the friars. Encomenderos and Crown administrators were ordered to provide schools for the sons of Indian caciques, or local chieftains. In these schools, under the tutelage of friars, the young men would learn "Christianity, good customs, civility, and the Castilian tongue."[25] With the New Laws of 1542 and the transferral of all Indians held in encomienda to the Crown, Charles V removed educational responsibility for the Indians from the encomenderos. Now he had to convince the friars to accept the burden of responsibility for Castilianizing and Catholicizing not only the native elite, but also the masses of New Spain.

The very task given to the encomenderos in the Laws of Burgos—the training of natives to spread the Spanish language and the Christian faith—now became the charge to the religious men in New Spain. Early language-literacy instruction had been the responsibility of the encomenderos. When they and civil officials resolved their problems of communication with the natives by using naguatlatos, they overrode the Crown's policy of Castilianizing the inhabitants of the New World. Determined to gain the benefits of a Spanish-speaking native population in Spain's extended empire, Charles V asked friars to take over the linguistic education of the Indians. The encomenderos had refused to wield the Castilian language as the instrument of empire in New Spain; the friars were yet to be tested.

CHAPTER TWO

Indian Tongues in the Spiritual Conquest

Missionary Techniques in the Field

Conquerors and settlers ignored the Crown's policy of extending Castilian to New Spain's natives; early friars actively resisted it. Cisneros' reformed religious training had prepared the mendicant orders for their missionary work in New Spain, and the early representatives of the orders came to evangelize, not to Hispanicize. Strictly self-disciplined and imbued with a strong sense of evangelistic mission, these men had a no-nonsense approach to converting the pagans. Armed with their humanistic language training, they were prepared to learn to speak the Indian languages and to write grammars for them. To the friars the most efficient and effective method of getting through to the Indians was to learn to communicate in the natives' languages. Converting the Indians to good Catholics was their goal, and if any language other than the Indian tongue was of any use, it was Latin, not Spanish. They taught and preached in the indigenous languages; they used Latin for prayers, observances of the sacraments, and rote recitations.

Their use of the indigenous languages was not only a matter of conviction but one of necessity. The early friars had no translators to help spread the Christian faith. The Conqueror himself could not spare translators in the early years of settlement. By 1524, when the first sizable group of friars arrived in New Spain, there were probably at least 2000 Spaniards at work pursuing their own interests in central Mexico or marching off on secondary conquests.[1] The few interpreters who were available at this time, only five years after Cortés' entry, were needed by soldiers and civil authorities.[2] Forced, therefore, to become acquainted with the Indians without the aid of translators, early friars began studying the languages of their parishioners almost immediately. Furthermore, dedication to their evangelistic mission demanded that the friars do all within their power to guarantee that the conversion of the Indians be genuine and lasting. Knowledge of the Indian languages was thus a critical spiritual tool. The missionaries felt they had to communicate directly with the natives to be assured not only that the Indians had understood matters of the Faith but also that they were not planning mischief among themselves. Secret reversions to pagan practices, idolatries, and superstitions were common. The friars found it easier to introduce the basics of Christianity than to wipe out the native religions, for the Indian masses saw no reason why the Spaniards' deity could not coexist with their own gods. Painfully aware of the Indians' potential for committing heresies, the missionaries felt bound to learn the Indian tongues to keep in touch with all that was going on in their converts' lives.[3] For these early religious men, it was bewildering and irritating to think of the great contrast between the heroic task outlined for them by the Crown and the pitiful accomplishments possible with no knowledge of the Indians' tongues. They intended to fulfill the avowed Christian purpose of the Conquest of the New World—to establish the Catholic faith and to save the souls of the Indians. To do so, they had to prove to these pagans that Christianity had more to say than that which signs, symbols, and dramatized narratives of the scriptures could portray.

Fray Pedro de Gante, a lay brother of the Franciscan order, who arrived in 1523, was the first friar to learn the Nahuatl language. He saw almost immediately that the task of converting New Spain could not be realized until the missionaries learned the natives' languages. He went to Texcoco, the intellectual center of the Aztec empire, became a houseguest of Ixtlilxochitl, the Texcocan historian, and settled in as both witness and student of this strange and different society. The language presented great difficulties; to his astonishment, the Indians did not "write," for they had no letters or characters to represent the sounds of their speech.[4] He observed, listened, and wrote the Nahuatl words he could understand by transcribing them into the Roman alphabet. He used his observations of the Indians' methods of education to pattern his Escuela de San Francisco, a primary school set next to the *convento*. The Texcocan nobles had educated their sons in a "school" called the *calmecac* which was under the guidance of priests. The early Franciscans established their school at the side of the convento in Texcoco and enrolled the sons of the native elite. The students slept in the school and were taught reading, writing, singing, and such matters of the Faith as could be conveyed through signs.[5]

Twelve additional Franciscan friars arrived only one year after Fray Pedro de Gante and included such men as Fray Martín de Valencia, Fray Toribio de Benavente (Motolinía) and Fray Luis de Fuensalida, who later distinguished themselves as teachers of the Indians. These men were not satisfied with sign language in the Escuela de San Francisco. Initial efforts to teach the prayers and essential elements of the Faith in Latin were frustrating, and sign language certainly did not allow them to teach much more than the existence of only one God.[6] The friars looked to some other method, and the story of their resolution of the problem foreshadowed the field techniques of modern-day anthropologists and linguists. They used their pupils, the sons of the native leaders, as informants, and the friars became "children of the children."[7] They listened, remembered, and wrote what they heard. In the evening, after their charges were asleep in the adjoining dormitory, the Franciscans got together, compared field notes, and tried to resolve the mysteries of the language which did not say today what it had said yesterday.[8] Gradually, as the older students saw the earnest and serious struggles of the friars in learning Nahuatl, they became more cooperative as informants, asking questions and correcting the field notes.

A second help came to these early Franciscans in Texcoco from an interpreter. Cortés had not offered any, but the friars saw no reason why he should not grant them their own interpreter if they found the right person for the job. They learned that a Spanish widow had two children who had learned Nahuatl from their Indian playmates. Cortés approved their request of the woman for one of her children, and the child came to the convento at Texcoco to serve as a sixteenth-century "Samuel in the temple."[9] He was the first who could explain the mysteries of the Christian faith to the Indians in their own tongue, translate for the friars, and instruct them in Nahuatl. Working both in the monastery and in the countryside, this young boy was teacher to both Indians and friars.

This child (who later took orders and became Fray Alonso de Molina) was the first and probably the last lay Spanish interpreter the early missionaries had in the field; from this time on, the friars used Indian students as preachers or they themselves learned the Indian languages. Though some of the twelve friars could speak Nahuatl and understand it reasonably well after six months of linguistic study at Texcoco, many were afraid to preach in Nahuatl until they were sure of their knowledge of the language. Meanwhile, they asked the help of their recently recruited and cooperative informants; the young Indian students preached in practice sessions before the friars and then were allowed to go before other Indians throughout central Mexico.[10]

As the early Franciscans learned Nahuatl, they realized how valuable their knowledge could be to other religious men coming to New Spain. They wrote books which were purely utilitarian: grammars and vocabularies for studying the language, and catechisms and translations of the scriptures for preaching and teaching the Faith. In the forty-seven years between their arrival and 1570, the Franciscans produced more than eighty such works. Approximately one-fourth of these were written by Pedro de Gante, the twelve friars, and Fray Alonso de Molina.[11] The orders which followed the Franciscans to New Spain adopted their methods for converting the Indians. Duty as they conceived it was not to Hispanicize the Indians but to convert them to Christianity—and this they intended to do in the most efficient way possible.

Initial successes in mastering indigenous languages convinced the friars they should not follow the Crown's request that they teach Spanish to the Indians. By 1550, when it became clear that Charles V intended to push his plan that the friars include the Castilianization of the Indians in their Christian education program, some of the friars actively resisted and proposed that Nahuatl—not Castilian—be the official language of the Indians. In response to a royal directive urging the Franciscans to teach Spanish to the Indians, Fray Rodrigo de la Cruz marked off the task as hopeless, impossible, and, moreover, useless. In a letter written in May of 1550, the friar presented his case to the King.

Your Majesty has ordered that these Indians learn the language of Castile. Can you understand that some Indians will never learn it, while others will learn it badly? After all, we know that although the languages of Castile and Portugal are almost the same, a Portuguese gentleman may spend thirty years in Castile and never learn the language. Then how are these people whose language is so different from ours and who have such elaborate ways of speaking ever to learn Castilian? It seems to me that Your Majesty should command that all the Indians learn the Mexican language [Nahuatl], for in every village there are many Indians who know this language and learn it easily, and many confess in it.[12]

Such evidence from a spokesman for the Franciscan friars contributed to factors which prompted the King to issue an edict summarizing the Crown's evaluation of the linguistic situation in the New World. Apparently not certain how widespread this notion of promoting Nahuatl was among friars of other orders, Charles V made clear his opposition to the continuation or expansion of any indigenous-language policy in a 1550 order addressed to *all* friars.

Unlike the missionaries, who looked to immediate practicalities, the Crown considered the long-range implications of language policy-making. Charles V, after reviewing with his advisers the question of whether even "the most perfect language of the Indians" was suitable for use in explaining the scriptures, handed down his decision. He acknowledged that, to be sure, the friars had successfully taught the basics of the Catholic faith in Nahuatl, but he reminded them that they would face grave difficulties in interpreting the deeper mysteries of the Catholic faith in Nahuatl or any other Indian tongue. Therefore, for the sake of Christianity in the New World, a program to expand the teaching of Spanish was necessary immediately. The first step in his official language planning—establishing schools where friars taught Castilian and Christianity to the native elite—was not enough. Now schools and teachers must be available for all Indians who wished to learn the Castilian tongue. The young men who had learned a new tongue and a new faith from the friars should serve as sacristans, and as they had been taught, they in turn must teach others. Only by thus expanding the number of Castilian speakers could the Crown hope to reduce the barrier the diversity of languages represented to the religious instruction of the Indians.[13] Charles V had taken the field against the resistance of the friars; he chose also to go behind the lines to ask his opponents for surrender before the battle.

Perhaps thinking the Franciscans too entrenched in their position to be moved, the King turned his persuasion toward the Augustinians and the Dominicans. On June 7, 1550, he wrote letters to their provincials and carefully reviewed his reasons for asking the friars to take charge of this "very important and essential matter." He reminded them that he, like they, desired, above all, the conversion of the Indians to Christianity and that after careful consideration, he had concluded that the Indians had to learn Spanish in order to be secure in the Christian faith and to take on "our civility and good customs." The friars, by virtue of the love and affection the Indians held for them, were sure to succeed in any of the possible ways they might choose to teach the Castilian tongue. Charles suggested that certain members of the orders take language instruction as their singular task, training assistants and holding daily office hours in which the Indians could come to learn Castilian. He assured the friars he would enlist the viceroy to help in this program, and they could be certain he would cooperate.[14]

The same day, Charles wrote the viceroy, reporting his formal orders to the friars and asking that the missionaries be prodded to carry out this new program for the extension of Castilian in New Spain. The viceroy should pay salaries to any personnel recruited by the friars; in addition, he must set up schools in which the friars could instruct Indian tutors and very young natives.[15] If these children could learn Castilian and Christianity from an early age, they would be firmly entrenched in both their new tongue and their new religion. Convinced that this program, which would initiate the learning of Spanish by the youngest Indians, would not only insure the conversion of Indians but also prevent backsliding, the King never doubted his viceroy's support of the program.

But the King's long-range perspective and idealism counted for little against the realities of day-by-day operations in New Spain. There is no evidence that administrative officials saw any merit in the 1550 edicts on language planning. In 1558 Viceroy Luis de Velasco wrote Philip II, Charles V's successor, of his own plans to unify the Indians linguistically and socially. A college in Guadalajara should be the center for teaching Nahuatl to young Indians from various regions; these Indians would then go home and help spread the standard language within their own tribe.[16] These naguatlatos would serve also as scribes and interpreters, so desperately needed by both administrators and the secular clergy, who were not nearly so inclined to learn the native languages as the regulars were. The regulars were friars and members of a religious order; many of these came to New Spain fresh from the humanistic language training and reform program of Cisneros and Isabella. The seculars were priests and prelates who were not members of religious orders, but rather part of the traditional episcopal hierarchy. Having no taste for learning Indian tongues or living in remote Indian villages, they ministered to Spaniards in the large population centers of New Spain and left the conversion of the natives to the regulars.[17]

Hence, the regulars spread their missions across the numerous linguistic boundaries of New Spain, and the early friars set out to learn all the languages within the geographical limits of these missions. Attempting to particularize conversion techniques in their widespread and often different linguistic territories, these early missionaries set an impossible task for themselves. In the absence of a comprehensive survey that might have produced an accurate map of the distribution of Indian tribes and languages, the orders had divided New Spain into spheres of influence that often cut across linguistic and tribal unities. The early random geographic distribution of the friars meant that each and every order had need of friars trained in several languages. The Franciscans, because of their head start in learning Nahuatl and training members of their order in that language, early consolidated their efforts in Puebla and the region around Mexico City. However, as Franciscan missionaries spread out from these areas after 1540, they needed a similar knowledge of other languages. In the east they met Otomi speakers; in the west Matlalzinca and Tarascan speakers. These last belonged to the Tarascan empire which had remained independent of the Aztecs and did not speak Nahuatl.

To the south of Mexico City, the Dominican order established missions in what are today the states of Morelos and Puebla, and in the valley of Oaxaca and the Isthmus of Tehuantepec. This dispersal brought the Dominican friars into contact with speakers of Mixtec, Zapotec, and Chontal. The Augustinians pushed to the south between the Dominican missions of Morelos and Puebla, to the north into the present-day state of Hidalgo, and to the west into Michoacan. The Augustinians had arrived in New Spain in 1533, after the Franciscans and Dominicans had chosen those areas most desirable in location by either their proximity to Mexico City or their climate and agricultural promise. Therefore, the Augustinians distributed themselves in areas where they had to learn more languages and languages, moreover, which had the reputation of being even more difficult than those spoken in central Mexico. In addition to Otomi, Huastec, and Totonac in the eastern missions, and Tarascan and Matlalzinca in Michoacán, the Augustinians encountered speakers of Tlapanec and Ocuiltec as they pushed toward the eastern border of the present-day state of Guerrero.[18]

Especially notable are those individuals within each order who in their early zeal for spreading Christianity learned more than one Indian tongue. The uncertain duration of a friar's stay in a particular mission and the diversity of dialects within the territories of each order induced some conscientious friars to become polyglots. Some sixteenth-century chroniclers wrote of friars who preached in as many as ten languages.[19] Though this number is quite probably an exaggeration prompted by Mendieta's desire to impress the King and his advisers with the linguistic diversity of New Spain, several reliable sources confirm that a surprising number of early missionaries learned two or three indigenous languages.[20] Either by the extent of its territory or by the establishment of its missions in areas which had not been part of the Aztec empire, each order had a special need for polyglots. The Dominicans had under their charge the Mixtecs and Zapotecs, two large Indian groups who had remained largely independent of the Aztecs and therefore did not speak Nahuatl as an auxiliary language. The Augustinians' territory included Indian settlements too remote from the Aztec center to have been influenced by the empire's extension of the Mexican language. The Franciscans, more numerous than members of the other orders, not only covered widely distributed territories, but also established missions within the independent Tarascan empire and among the Otomi Indians. The latter had been part of the subjugated Aztec empire, but had remained resolutely independent of the linguistic tyranny of the Nahuatl speakers.[21]

However, in spite of good intentions and intensive language training, as they extended the reach of their missions, the friars realized the large number of Indian tongues scattered throughout New Spain represented a challenge even they could not meet. By 1574 the seculars, aided by naguatlatos trained by the regulars and left to serve as sacristans, began to take charge of established missions in central Mexico, and the regulars moved out to frontier regions. As the emphasis shifted from conversion of the Indians to maintenance of Spanish society in the populous center of the colony, the seculars could supplant the regulars.[22] Franciscans, Augustinians, and Dominicans left most of their former strongholds of influence and established new missions to the south and the north of the heart of the central valley. Each of these orders had members who had learned Nahuatl in the central areas of the colony. Therefore, as the friars extended their mission field, Nahuatl went with them. The friars found the Indians apt students who easily learned to speak, read, and write what the missionaries became determined to establish as the lingua franca of all the Indians of New Spain.

Nahuatl, Universal Language of the Indians

Faced with the plenitude of languages they met beyond the central valley of Mexico, the regulars insisted the number of languages in New Spain had to be reduced. They reasoned that if they continued the program begun by the Aztecs of spreading Nahuatl, use of other Indian tongues would decline. As early as 1550, Fray Rodrigo de la Cruz had written from the New

Galicia mission of Ahuacatlán, situated north of Mexico City, that there seemed no other solution to the problems posed by the numerous Indian languages than for the friars to spread Nahuatl. There was no doubt that the Indians learned Nahuatl much more readily than they would and could learn Castilian.[23] Other friars in New Galicia endorsed the teaching of Nahuatl to their diverse Indian groups, and by 1569 Franciscans from this area offered little excuse for this practice among their members.

> They have labored, because of the extreme diversity of languages in this area, to teach one language—the Mexican language which is the most widespread. They teach the Christian doctrine in this tongue, and generally, the Indians confess in it. . . .[24]

Nearly every New Galicia mission reported having members who preached and heard confessions in Nahuatl. Indian teachers assisted the regulars in their daily sessions to teach reading, writing, and the Christian doctrine in Latin and Nahuatl. The children learned to sing in Nahuatl and were very successful in attracting adults to the chapel's activities.[25] In religious plays adapted by the missionaries to incorporate certain features of native festivals, the Indians spoke their lines in Nahuatl.[26]

The commissary general of the Franciscans, Fray Alonso Ponce, visiting New Galicia in 1584, was astounded at the success of the friars' program to extend Nahuatl. In his official report, he described the extensive spread of the Mexican tongue as "a grand thing."

> This Mexican language runs through all of New Spain. Hence, anyone who knows Nahuatl can go from Zacatecas [a northern mission of New Galicia] . . . to the extreme border of Nicaragua, more than six hundred leagues in all, and through all of this area, he can be assured of finding someone who understands him. There is no small village, at least along the Royal Highway, where there is not a Mexican Indian or one who understands Nahuatl.[27]

The early missionaries in the frontier zones had built on the pattern of success begun by the Aztecs, and they had extended Nahuatl even beyond the limits of the former Aztec empire.

New Galicia was not the only section of the colony where ecclesiastics favored the expansion of Nahuatl at the expense of other Indian tongues. In the valley of Oaxaca, prelates faced with a diversity of languages among the Indians saw the teaching of Nahuatl to all the natives as a practical measure for saving both souls and sustenance. The small and extremely poor pueblos of Oaxaca could not support both a friar and native assistants trained in two or three languages. A "Doctor Muñon," speaking for religious leaders from the province of Oaxaca wrote the King in 1570 insisting the number of languages in this region be reduced in the only feasible way—by teaching Nahuatl to all the Indians of the area.[28]

In an effort to convince the Crown that their plan for spreading Nahuatl as the official auxiliary language of all the Indians was feasible, the friars continually appraised its potential as a standard language. They spoke of its authority, stylistic variety, and expressiveness. Both in the artistic community of Texcoco and in the scattered settlements of various provinces, Nahuatl was a language capable of precise statement of content as well as emotional poetic expression, the latter through elaborate metaphors.[29] Though the friars readily admitted that Nahuatl, and the other Indian languages as well, were curious when compared with the Latin and Castilian of Nebrija's grammar, they nevertheless judged the Mexican tongue quite acceptable as a means of expression. Nahuatl was no less elegant and pleasing than Latin, and the Indians had elaborate stylistic variations in their speech.[30] To be sure, by the last half of the sixteenth century, the Mexican language had probably fallen from the even more eloquent standard it must have achieved during the height of the Aztec empire. Mendieta speculated on the former state of the language:

I think the Mexican tongue was at one time more artful and refined in composition and derivation of words than it now is; this is certainly true of its metaphors, for the meaning and use of many of the most elaborate of these have been lost.[31]

The fall of the Aztec empire had brought an end to the political and religious forces which had inspired public orations and fired the spirits of Texcoco's poets and historians. However, after the loss of elites who had promoted the function and polished the form of its literary standard, Nahuatl remained functional in the area of everyday communication for the Indian masses.

To confound those who pointed to the lack of a conventional

writing system among the Aztecs, the friars never ceased to relate the astounding ability of the Indians to learn alphabetic writing. Mendieta wrote of their enthusiasm, as well as talent, in writing. The Indians learned very quickly to transcribe their language into Roman letters, which, to their fascination, represented actual speech rather than merely an idea, as did their own ideographs and pictographs.[32]

By 1570, the regulars had won their case. Philip II declared Nahuatl the official language of New Spain's Indians. Certainly the most persuasive of the themes running through his incoming correspondence on the linguistic situation of New Spain had been the refrain that the extension of the Mexican language was a necessary accessory for the establishment of the Christian faith among the Indians. Philip II, keenly sensitive to what he judged to be his duty to God, recognized the diversity of languages in New Spain as a threat to the missionary effort and the establishment of his sovereignty on a firm Catholic basis in the colony. In a royal *cédula* issued in July of 1570, the King explained to the viceroy and other civil officials in Mexico City his difficult decision to declare Nahuatl the official language of the Indians.[33] Only his iron sense of Christian mission led him to countermand not only his father's 1550 order that all the Indians learn Castilian, but also his own ruling of 1565 which had demanded that the missionaries learn the language of each group of Indians under their charge.[34] Now he was forced to admit the failure of both of these earlier rulings. The friars and local officials had convinced him that in spite of the valiant efforts of the friars who had learned several Indian tongues in order to minister directly to the natives, there could never be enough polyglot missionaries to insure the "spiritual conquest" of New Spain. The very fact that some small towns in the Oaxaca valley contained Indians of two or three different language groups was proof enough that his own 1565 ruling was not based on a realistic analysis of the extreme linguistic diversity of New Spain. Therefore, in the interest of the Indians' conversion, the King now felt compelled to order that lay and religious leaders take the necessary steps to reduce the number of languages in the colony. He decreed: "all Indians shall learn one language, and that shall be the Mexican tongue [Nahuatl], since it can most easily be established as the universal language of the Indians."[35]

Making sure that no one could doubt that a policy change had taken place, and, one might speculate, perhaps attempting to atone psychologically for altering his own and his father's policies, Philip quickly acted to buttress his 1570 order. One mandate after another covered the ramifications of the 1570 order and clearly demonstrated that the King intended to do all in his power to see that this ruling did not suffer from lack of royal support. He decreed that all seculars and regulars nominated for ecclesiastical offices should be Spanish sons, men of good example dedicated to the conversion of the Indians, *and* students of the Mexican language.[36] No clerics who did not know Nahuatl should be allowed to take charge of any missions or parishes.[37] Prelates in charge of each diocese had to test all clergymen's knowledge of Nahuatl before allowing them to go into the field.[38] To insure institutional support for the teaching of Nahuatl to New Spain's clerics, Philip II ordered the University of Mexico to establish a chair of Nahuatl. Determined that no University official should complain of a lack of financial support for this project, Philip suggested several ways of gathering revenue for the language courses, but he also announced that if these methods should fail, the necessary funds should be taken from the royal treasury.[39] A further decree resulted in forced enrollment in these courses. All clerics must not only present a certificate of dismissal from the University's Nahuatl course to their superiors before assignment to a mission or parish, but they must also carry this certificate with them at all times in order to avoid reexamination by traveling ecclesiastical officials.[40] In his numerous decrees issued between 1570 and 1592, Philip put a premium on Nahuatl as the instrument of conversion in New Spain.

Indian Literacy

Early friars had convinced the Crown of the practicality of teaching Christianity to the Indians in the indigenous languages. Royal power supported this technique for religious instruction in mandates issued throughout the last quarter of the sixteenth century. The missionaries, however, carried their enthusiasm for teaching in the indigenous languages into the schools, and they taught the Indian children to read and write their own languages in the Roman alphabet. As early as 1535, Charles V had given the religious men in New Spain the responsibility for teaching literacy to the Indians, but the Crown had not foreseen the implications of the friars' educational methods for language learning in New Spain. In its zeal to insure the rapid conversion of the Indians, the Crown had failed to consider the lasting effects on the youngest Indians of their becoming literate in their own tongues. The success of the Indian languages, especially Nahuatl, in the spiritual conquest shut out Castilian for the Indian masses, a result the Crown did not view favorably in its long-range language policy for New Spain.

Charles V had ordered the friars to teach the Indians to speak, read, and write Castilian. His son, Philip II, had first commanded the friars to learn the native tongues of all the Indians under their charge, but when this measure seemed highly impracticable, he ordered that all Indians and all ecclesiastics serving the Indians learn Nahuatl to establish it as the universal tongue of the Indians. None of his numerous orders supporting this mandate mentioned teaching the Indians to be literate in their native tongues. But the friars were in great need of literate assistants, and they therefore taught the best of their students to read and write not only Nahuatl, but also Latin. These students showed so much promise in Latin that ecclesiastical leaders soon called for secondary schools or *colegios,* in which a few young Indians might continue the study of Latin and other traditional subjects.

Fray Pedro de Gante founded such a colegio in Mexico City in 1529; the Augustinians followed with another in 1537.[41] Bishops supported the teaching of Latin and urged the Crown to supply financial support to provide more instructors able to teach Latin to the Indians in their own language.[42] The most productive of the colegios was Santa Cruz de Tlatelolco, opened in 1536, with the support of the first bishop of Mexico, Fray Juan de Zumárraga, and the first viceroy, Antonio de Mendoza. Initially, nearly eighty Indian boys from the major villages attended the colegio to study under distinguished Mexicanists, such as Sahagún who knew the culture and languages of the Aztecs well.[43] The friars taught the boys Latin in Nahuatl; their purpose was clear:

These Indians, knowing Latin and understanding the mysteries of the Sacred Scriptures, will be firmly rooted in the true faith and will confirm themselves

in the faith to others who do not know it so well. They will also help the
religious who do not know Nahuatl well, for they can translate to the Indians
in Nahuatl what the friars say in Latin.[44]

Ecclesiastical leaders reasoned that these young scholars who
knew Nahuatl and Latin could greatly increase the effectiveness
of the numerous friars in New Spain, who could neither teach nor
preach because they did not know Nahuatl. If the Indians were
taught to understand Latin grammar, then friars who did not
know Nahuatl could read to the students from Latin books,
especially the Bible and other religious works. Thus, once the
Indians knew Latin, they could go to the scriptures directly,
either by reading for themselves or by listening to the Bible
being read to them. They could also preach under the friars'
supervision, translate the scriptures into Nahuatl, and help the
friars translate the interpretations of the scriptures for their own
sermons delivered in Nahuatl. Hence, teaching Latin to a select
few helped the friars spread Nahuatl as the primary tongue of
the conversion campaign.

Therefore, those who learned Latin best worked as assistants
in the missionary field. Others who learned Castilian went into
service in the various levels of government of New Spain. In the
words of a contemporary Franciscan reporter, "they have been
useful in their service to judicial and governmental officials and
others in charge of the republic."[45] Though Spanish was certainly not central in the curricula of any of the colegios, many students picked up the Castilian tongue in the course of the daily
life of the schools and occasionally through formal instruction.
The Franciscans were especially eager for some young students
to learn Spanish so that they could translate Spanish works into
Nahuatl, and thus provide reading materials for the very young
children who were being taught to read Nahuatl in the village
schools set next to the conventos.[46] In 1544, Bishop Zumárraga
judged the literacy program of the primary schools so successful
that he issued a special call for books in Nahuatl to be made
available to those Indian students who had learned to read.[47]

The remarkable results achieved by the students, as recorded
by Sahagún and other colonial chroniclers, speak well of the
methods of teaching the friars employed in the colegios. Sahagún
reported that by working with the friars two or three years,
"the Indians come to understand all the materials of the grammar

of Latin, and to speak Latin, understanding and writing it, and even composing heroic verses."[48] According to Motolinía, they composed long and well-respected orations as well as verses written in exameter and pentameter. The Indian students were not without pride in their accomplishments as Motolinía related with approval.

A very good thing happened to a clergyman recently arrived from Castile, who could not believe that the Indians knew the Christian doctrine, the Pater Noster, or the Creed. When other Spaniards told him they did, he still remained incredulous. At this season, the students of the colegio had come, and the clergyman thinking they were just like any other Indians, asked one if he knew the Pater Noster. He replied that he did and the clergyman made him repeat it, and then he made him say the Creed, and he said it well. But the clergyman pointed out as incorrect a word the Indian had said correctly, and the Indian maintained that he had made no mistake; the clergyman maintained that he had. Therefore the student thought it necessary to test whether he had said it correctly, and he asked, speaking in Latin, *Reverende Pater, cujus casus est?* [Reverend Father, whose error is it?] Then, since the clergyman did not know Latin grammar, he was confused and embarrassed.[49]

Such confidence, which could easily be interpreted as lack of respect for the Spanish authorities, provoked strong objections to the colegios, especially that of Santa Cruz de Tlatelolco.

Members of the Dominican order objected to teaching Latin to the Indians and admitted that "the Indians who know Latin recognize by their saying of the masses and sacred rites which priests are idiots."[50] Furthermore, the Indians could and probably would spread heresies since they had been introduced to Christianity and civilization so very recently. Some noisy critics of the school and the policy of teaching Latin to the Indians questioned whether the Indians were even civilized now that they spoke Latin "as elegantly . . . as Tulio."[51] Jerónimo López, an adviser to the viceroy, reported to the King in 1545 that the Indians who had been educated in Latin refused to remain submissive.[52] A spokesman for the Franciscans, who never ceased supporting the principles of the school, struck down this objection as nonsense and reminded the school's critics that this characteristic was not reserved for Indian students in the New World.

And wouldn't it indeed be a marvel if the colegio students were not more shrewd than those that are brought up rudely in the rural villages? This same fact we have observed among the Spaniards and students of other nations: generally, the students who attend the universities of Salamanca and Alcalá are more aggressive than are those who remain at home with their parents. Furthermore, the former know and understand more and thus are of major benefit to all the republic.[53]

The Franciscan writer further argued that some Indians had learned not only Latin, but they had also acquired Castilian, politeness, cleanliness, and all the good habits and customs one could ask for even "in very staid old Christians." [54]

But the Crown was so influenced by the loud complaints of the school's opponents that it gradually withdrew its support. By 1595, the College of Santa Cruz de Tlatelolco was a primary school falling into ruins.[55] The crucial objection to the institution was its insistence on teaching Latin to the Indians. In the academic traditions the early settlers brought to New Spain, Latin was reserved for the elite: scholars, priests, and monks. The secular Spaniards and the members of the Dominican order who opposed Tlatelolco's colegio seemed to have had no objection to educating the Indians, so long as reading, writing, and skills were taught in their own languages. Bishop Vasco de Quiroga founded the College of San Nicolas Obispo in 1540, where he taught the students in their native tongue—"the only bridge by which he was able to reach the mind and heart of the Indians." [56] The Jesuits, called to New Spain in 1572 to provide a firm grounding in Latin and rhetoric for the sons of the Spaniards, founded the modest San Gregorio College for Indians in 1586, but they apparently trained so few Indians in Latin that no one bothered to protest.[57]

Moreover, the Jesuits saw more need for learning the Indian tongues than for teaching Latin to the natives. After the first few years of building schools for the education of the Spanish sons in the New World, the Jesuits found another job for some of the hardiest members of their society. The Indians of the northern area had a more nomadic way of life than their brothers in the south, and they, well aware of the cruelties of the Spanish settlers and soldiers, were becoming more successful at avoiding the conquerors. Therefore, the Crown handed over the care and control of the elusive Indians on the northern frontiers to the missionaries. The Franciscans had moved into Nueva Vizcaya and they were followed by the Jesuits in 1591.[58] In those distant frontiers with which the Aztecs had had little or no contact, it was difficult indeed to spread Nahuatl. The Franciscans were determined to try to extend the Mexican tongue, but the Jesuits, who had not had the long years of firm grounding in Nahuatl which had set the Franciscans' habits, held no such intentions. It was easier for each Jesuit brother to learn the Indian tongue predominant in his own particular mission. The Jesuits' plan was to establish missions, each of which was to become the nucleus of a Christian colony and a center of civilization.[59] Their purpose was not exclusively Christianization; it included also civilization. To prepare the Indians for the practical duties of community living, the Jesuits learned the Indians' languages, taught them technical skills involved in carpentry, spinning and weaving, building irrigation ditches, and planting and harvesting new crops, such as wheat. Native officials took part in the supervision of the established communities. In the elementary schools for boys, the Jesuits taught reading, writing, Spanish, and government, and gradually, both Spanish and the native language of the community were used in daily affairs. Preparation of the Jesuits in Indian languages was the responsibility of special seminaries established in Patzcuaro, Tepotzotlan, Oaxaca, Puebla, and the Chichimec territory. These seminaries provided instruction for young Indian boys, seemingly with the practical purpose that these boys would be useful as agents of change in each new mission in the northern area. From the boys, the Jesuits learned the Indian languages.[60]

In the southern frontier areas, the Yucatan peninsula, and the extreme southern highlands, Spaniards and Indians opposed the friars in their efforts to establish schools. As in the northern areas, the peninsula and other parts of the Mayan region offered resistance to Spanish civilization through the social organization of the native life of the area. Scattered widely in isolated villages, the Maya and their neighbors in the present state of Chiapas struggled against the Spaniards' attempts to "civilize" and convert them. The Spanish settlers faced the same problem rounding up the Indians for their labor forces as the friars did herding the natives to education and Christianity. Missionaries insisted that the Indians relocate in settlements away from their native villages; the Indians resisted this maneuver, as did the Spanish laymen. The latter bitterly opposed the friars' removal of the Indian children from their immediate jurisdiction and prevention of the children's conscription for field labor. Fray Diego de Landa, who first went to Yucatan in 1549, described the dual opponents who stood firm against the missionaries as: "the Spaniards who were the absolute masters of the country and wished everything done with an eye to their own gain and tributes," and "the Indians who were anxious to practice their idolatry." [61]

Not only did the Spaniards bitterly oppose the efforts of the friars to establish schools, but they also frowned on the study of the native tongues by the Crown's representatives on the Yucatan peninsula. Fray Landa and a few other missionaries learned the Mayan language, but the difficulty of this task coupled with the active resistance of both the Spaniards and the Indians soon led most religious men to rely on interpreters. Most notable among the few Franciscans who studied Maya was Luis de Villalpando who wrote a vocabulary and grammar for the Mayan tongue. Fray Jacobo de Testera, sent to establish a school in Valladolid, Yucatan, devised picture writing to instruct the natives, but he did not succeed in learning the Mayan language. His horror at the tactics used by Spaniards to recruit Indian labor forces and his disgust at the settlers' general opposition to the presence of the missionaries led Testera to abandon the project.[62] Almost thirty years after his arrival in Yucatan, Landa lamented that there were not enough translations of the scriptures, there were too few school teachers, and native schoolmasters were not a satisfactory substitute for trained friars who knew the native tongue.[63]

Thus by the end of the sixteenth century, primary schools under the direction of the religious regulars were a standard feature chiefly in the villages of central Mexico and in the frontier mission communities of northern Mexico. In these areas, the missionaries seemed to have an implicit agreement that conversational and literacy skills would be taught primarily in the native languages. Once again, the key question was practical: which language—Spanish, Latin, or an Indian tongue—would best serve the missionaries' purposes? Directed by their problems as they arose, friars chose what appeared to them to be the most workable solutions. First considerations had to be primarily numerical. All the Indians would have to be taught Spanish, if it were to be the language of conversion. Fewer Indians, to be sure, would have to learn Nahuatl, and the friars themselves could more easily learn Nahuatl or any of the Indian tongues than they could undertake the teaching of Spanish to all the Indians. Hence, early missionaries ruled out Spanish. They had neither the manpower nor the materials to teach Spanish to the Indians.[64] Moreover, their first task was conversion, and spreading the message of Christianity could not wait for a wide-ranging language program to go into effect throughout Mexico. Latin was merely a literacy tool which could be handled by Indian assistants who could read the scriptures directly and translate them into Nahuatl. But resistance to teaching Latin to the Indians had made that experiment short-lived. The Indian tongues remained as the practical and official medium of communication for all the Indians.

The immediate need had been to communicate with the Indians to convert them to Christianity; the expedient way to solve this problem was to learn the natives' tongues. When the Crown placed the responsibility for literacy in their hands, the friars had simply turned this task to their own purposes: transcription of the Indian tongues into the Roman alphabet. The scarcity of books—in any language—had been one of the problems the missionaries had met in this way. The students could prepare their own materials after they learned to write their language; furthermore, not only were these handwritten pieces useful for the Indian students, but newly arriving missionaries learning the Indian tongues could practice reading these religious materials.

Once the first stages of the conversion campaign were over in central Mexico and the friars were left either to maintain small parishes or to move out to the frontiers, the regulars continued the use of the indigenous languages not only for the benefit of the Indians, but also for the functional purpose it served them as members of the closed Indian villages. By 1551, the Crown had ordered that the Indians be congregated in villages and that no Spaniards, other than friars, remain in these villages.[65] The unity of a common tongue enabled these religious isolates to live in harmony with the natives and to exclude any outside Spaniards who might come into the villages for only a short time. Furthermore, some friars respected the group identification the Indians derived from their maintenance of tongue which signaled their membership in a particular tribal group.⁶⁶ Finding no purpose in altering the Indian customs and attachments so long as they were not religious, the friars ardently defended the indigenous language retention of their charges. As the first generation of religious leaders in New Spain died and were replaced by *criollos* (creoles) who had learned the Indian languages in their training, these Mexican-born sons of Spaniards continued the techniques and tasks of missions established in the sixteenth century. The use of the Indian tongues remained highly functional for these criollos, who used their linguistic knowledge to protect their positions and put the prelates from Spain at a distinct disadvantage among the Indians.

Philip II's intense support of Nahuatl had laid an official foundation for language policy in the central valley and adjacent regions. However, when missionaries moved into the far north pacifying roving Indian tribes and converting them to Christianity and a village way of life, a general policy of learning the particular language common to specific mission populations became necessary. Hence, immediate practicalities and then entrenched habits reestablished the early policy of favoring the use of indigenous languages in general, rather than the specific choice of Nahuatl. Thus Philip III found it necessary to revive his father's 1565 ruling that missionaries learn the language of the Indians under their charge. In 1599, he urged the viceroy to see that professional teachers in the Indian languages were available for training clergymen to go among the Indians.⁶⁷ In 1603, Philip III, perhaps thinking of the missionaries' comparatively recent move to the frontiers, twice ordered that no regular was to go into the field without knowing the Indian tongues. He especially cautioned that friars fresh from Spain must learn the language of the Indians to be under their charge before assignment to a mission. The decree strongly emphasized that religious leaders were expected to execute this mandate.⁶⁸ Apparently wishing to put some force into his 1618 reissue of his father's decree that no clerics who did not know the Indian tongues should be allowed to take charge of any missions or parishes, Philip III issued the next year an order that any cleric not knowing the indigenous language of his charges should be removed from positions in the field.[69] One of the last official orders supporting the Indian tongues came in 1627 when Philip IV reminded the University in Mexico City that there should be courses in the indigenous languages used most predominantly in the provinces.[70] These official and institutional chartings for the policy that clerics know the native tongue of the Indians under their care helped set all-too-firmly a course the Crown was later to attempt to reverse.

Throughout the sixteenth century and well into the seventeenth century, religious leaders had perpetuated the use of the Indian tongues. They had little intention of helping the Crown realize its ultimate goal of establishing Castilian as the standard language among the native subjects of New Spain. By 1599 when Philip III had reminded the viceroy of the Crown's ultimate desire that the Indians learn Castilian, the viceroy had answered: "I am obliged to say that this is not only a difficulty but almost an impossibility. . . ."[71] For an entire century, the divergence between the Crown's long-range assumption that Castilian would be the ultimate language of empire and its desire to promote a rapid conversion program for the Indians slowed the pace at which a definite linguistic policy could move. The Crown had alternated between proclaiming Spanish as the language of empire and promoting the indigenous tongues as the instrument of conversion. The Crown could not deny that perhaps the Indians could best be taught Christianity in their own tongues; the royal powers also considered it necessary that new Spanish subjects learn Castilian in order that the Crown might more directly control them. But immediate practicalities in the New World had overruled any long-term considerations the Crown held, and the indigenous tongues remained the major channel of communication between Spaniards and Indians.

CHAPTER THREE

A Code for the Elite

Spanish for the Indians

The maintenance of the Indian tongues and the promotion of literacy in these languages did not escape notice in Spain, and by the middle of the seventeenth century, the Crown was showing its willingness to reevaluate the long-standing contradictory language policies for indigenous New World citizens. Early in the century, Philip III had rated Spanish as the tongue of the cultured and the virtuous. In 1612, he requested the viceroy to see that "houses of correction for Indian maidens" begin operating in the major cities of New Spain. Authorities should shut the girls away from the vices of the world and find matrons "of good example" to train them as proper young ladies. The girls' instructors should devote considerable attention to teaching these Indian maidens the Spanish tongue, so they might learn the Christian doctrine and be able to read literary and religious works in Spanish. To help insure that the girls learned Spanish, the King ordered that they not be permitted to speak their native tongues.[1]

In 1634 Philip IV issued a decree which implied more clearly than previous orders a long-existent but seldom-specified question. Why should the Crown consider a Spanish-speaking population desirable in the New World colonies? Did the royal powers see Spanish as merely the vehicle for effective conversion and administrative control of the Indians? Or was it an instrument of empire to bring the Indians to an Hispanic way of life and a relative uniformity of customs and language? The decree of 1634 echoed the sentiments of Isabella as they had been expressed in the Laws of Burgos and the views of Charles V as he had stated them in his 1550 orders for the establishment of schools to teach Spanish to the Indians. The learning of Castilian should be coupled with the acquisition of "our cultured ways and good customs."[2] The Laws of Burgos had attempted to provide the Indians with models of the Christian and civilized man. The Indians were grouped near the encomenderos to learn by example, and they were to be provided with the hammocks, clothes, food, speech, and religion of the Spaniard. To Charles V the Castilian tongue was a key not only to Christianity but also to Hispanization in a much broader sense. His 1550 decrees had repeatedly urged that the Indian learn Spanish so that he might be introduced to the Catholic faith and the ways of a Spaniard of "good breeding."

Now in 1634, Philip IV not only endorsed the goals of his predecessors, but he also added his own expectation that teaching Spanish to the Indians would bring them more easily under the control of Spanish officials. Philip therefore commanded the priests in the Indian missions and parishes to use the "most delicate means" in compelling the Indians to learn Spanish. In teaching the Indians the Castilian tongue, the clergy could help guarantee the Indians' salvation and their comprehension of underlying tenets of the Christian faith. Moreover, Philip reasoned, if the Indians learned to speak and understand Spanish, administrative officials could control the natives with more ease and efficiency than they had in the past. As the spread of Castilian among the Indians facilitated direct communication between Spaniard and Indian, improvements in the natives' "control and way of living could be expected."[3] The King's intent in this decree was not only to render the Indians more subject to God and the Spanish Crown, but also to link Spanish with their customs and habits in daily life. A celebrated court lawyer of the seventeenth century agreed that language should be the instrument of Hispanization in the extension of the empire. Juan de Solórzana y Pereyra drew on historical precedents other nations had established in their imperialism to support his premise that commanders of subject nations had always made certain that the conquered took on the language and customs of the conqueror. Thus, the conquerors firmly established their authority and superiority in the eyes of the new subjects who, through the imposed cultural unity, became tractable and easy to govern as a unified body.[4] Conquerors had the inherent right to dictate linguistic and cultural conformity, not only because of their superior military positions, but also by reason of the obvious need to secure unity within the newly-governed provinces.

The colonies heard of the new policy and remained silent. By the end of the third quarter of the seventeenth century, Charles II had grown impatient with the failure of religious and lay officials to respond to Philip IV's 1634 order that the Indians learn Spanish. Apparently determined to understand the possible reasons for the puzzling silence from the colonies, Charles himself reviewed with his Council the entire history of Castile's language policies for the New World colonies. He concluded that in many parts of the empire, the Indians were continuing to use their own tongues just as though the conquerors had never arrived. In 1686, Charles presented in a lengthy summary decree the history of language planning for the colonies and the rationale for his own judgments on the matter. He sternly warned ecclesiastical and civil officials alike that the time for ignoring the laws of the *Recopilación* was past, and he intended to see that they established Spanish as the language of the colonial empire. They had turned aside Charles V's 1550 call for schools to teach Spanish to the Indians; they had ignored the order of Philip IV in 1634 that the priests take charge of Castilianizing the Indians. Charles II's cédula closed with a forceful charge to all Church and State officials that they put into immediate effect all laws promoting Spanish and that they furnish the King with accounts of the progress of this program of Indian education.[5]

Religious leadership in the New World took note of the sternness of the order, and quickly decided to break their silence and advise the King of the serious practical problems inherent in his program. The Archbishop of the church in Mexico City fired off a letter reminding the King that the very people he had suggested as teachers of Spanish—the sacristans—were the Indians who taught matters of faith in the natives' tongues. Furthermore, even if Spaniards were available to teach school, they would have to be paid. His list of such practical problems was lengthy: the Indians were too poor to pay a teacher for their children; they would have to be forced to send their children to school; the Indians were not "inclined" to speak Spanish, since they did not see that it was of any use to them; those who did know some Spanish would not speak it. The bishop of the church in Valladolid voiced his discontent more indirectly: "the execution of this order would be impossible without the admission of some difficulty." [6]

Charles II was not going to be dissuaded by mere practicalities. He responded that to know and teach the matters of the Christian faith, the sacristans should know both Spanish and an Indian tongue, and therefore, these people were charged with the duty of teaching their fellow Indians Spanish as well as reading and writing. The King reminded the bishops that he wanted the Indians to learn Spanish not only because it would improve their understanding of Christianity, but also for the "society and communication" it would foster between Indians and Spaniards.[7] He strongly urged that if the Church hierarchy had not formerly looked upon this task as part of their responsibilities, they begin to do so now for the service of God and the King.

The King's harshness apparently did prompt some direct action in New Spain. In a letter written to the King in 1688, the bishop of Oaxaca reported that he had obeyed the King's 1686 order and had initiated a program of Castilianization for the Indians of his diocese. Now, two years later, he was prepared to evaluate the program and offer suggestions for changes which might guarantee its success. The bishop had made a survey in his area and along the coast to the south. In the villages he had found a few Indian boys who, when examined, could repeat part of the Christian doctrine in Spanish, but it was evident that they did not understand what they were saying. However, he had found one successful Indian leader who spoke Mixtec and Spanish "with equal perfection," and the bishop was thus convinced that with the proper motivation, the Indians could and would learn Spanish. The motivation was to be found in office-holding, for the Indians held in high esteem the offices and positions of local leadership in the government of New Spain. Therefore, if the learning of Spanish were prerequisite to the holding of positions of responsibility, the Indians would see the need to learn the new language.[8] Two years after the bishop's suggestion, the King ordered that preference in the selection of mayors and councilmen for Indian villages be given to those who knew Spanish. Judging this method of inducement to be most "convenient and delicate," the monarch allowed the provinces four years to carry out the order and to give those Indians who did not know Spanish time to learn the language.[9]

Not content with earlier warnings and treatises he had issued on the seriousness of this matter, Charles II issued another summary decree in 1691. He reiterated the issues covered in his orders since 1686, and he made specific his plans for schools in the Indian villages. He requested that in the larger towns there be two schools—one for boys and another for girls; in the smaller villages he proposed that girls and boys attend school at different hours, and that girls over the age of ten not be allowed to go to school. The Indians themselves were to support the schools and the teachers; if an Indian village was too poor to support the school, the entire village should work one *milpa*, or cornfield, specifically designated to support the school. He reminded the ecclesiastics again that he expected the teachers to be intelligent young men who spoke Spanish well and were in general agreement with the fundamental purpose of the program—to confirm the Indians deeply in the Christian faith.[10]

The cumulative force of the four decrees in five years could have left little doubt in the minds of religious leaders that Charles II felt they had served neither God's cause nor the Crown's. They had complained and argued; quite probably, they would disobey. What the King needed was a watchdog force to insure his program's success, and he intended to recruit just such a force. In 1693, Charles II sent word to the viceroy and leading authorities of New Spain that hereafter civil officials should watch over the language program.[11] Even though civil leaders did not hold direct control over the churchmen, local political figures could perhaps indirectly maneuver the religious personnel into supporting the King's language program. If local civil authorities made certain that Indians sent their children to school to learn Spanish, the ecclesiastics would be forced to provide teachers. Ironically, the Archbishop of Michoacán had made this suggestion in a letter dated December 16, 1692, in which he advised the King that there had been a boost in attendance records in his area when judicial authorities had helped enforce the education orders.[12] The question remains open as to whether the Archbishop's call for help from lay officials was a ploy to avoid full responsibility for an impossible task. In general, neither religious nor lay leaders favored teaching Spanish to the Indians, but thus far the Church had borne the major weight of the King's charge. With the distribution of some responsibility to the laymen, the religious community might have expected a let-up in pressure from the Crown. New Spain's ecclesiastics knew top-level civil leaders did not share the King's enthusiasm for the language program; therefore, any royal plan to involve local political and judicial authorities in its execution would never reach the provincial officials.

Spanish laymen's opposition to the Indians' learning of Castilian derived naturally from long-standing segregation policies. Separation among the Indians, Spaniards, and *mestizos* (persons of mixed Indian and Spanish descent) had existed from the sixteenth century both in education and in housing. Separate educational opportunities recognized four distinctions among those to be educated: Indians, mestizos, criollos, and *peninsulares* (citizens born in Spain).[13] The Crown had ordered that the Indians be gathered from their scattered settlements into villages patterned on the Spanish model. In these *congregaciones*, the Indians could be evangelized and settled in a civilized life style.[14] The management of the village was given over to friars who became the single religious, political, and judicial authority in their own closed communities. Indians were not to travel from one village to another. Merchants with business in the villages were compelled to complete their affairs in three days and then move on; other Spaniards were allowed only one day.[15] The original aim of the separation of Indians from Spaniards had been the protection of the natives from the corruption and exploitation of the New World colonizers. Cortés had pointed out to Charles V the Spaniards' potential for converting the Indians to vices rather than virtues; Las Casas had urged reform in Indian legislation on the grounds that the Indian in his natural state was being debased and exploited by the vile and greedy Spaniards. Hence, the Crown provided laws to segregate the Indians from the Spaniards and thus insure the protection of the indigenous peoples; but in their "protected" state, the Indians' only contact with the "civilized" Spaniard tended to be either religious or illicit.

And in these illicit contacts "with vile and irresponsible people, such as mulattos, negros, mestizos, and Indian household maids," [16] the Indian learned Spanish. The seventeenth-century Spanish layman strenuously objected to the Indian's use of Spanish because, as a seventeenth-century reporter pointed out, in mingling with Spaniards, the Indians "learn the Spanish tongue and become ladinos, which is the first step toward their becoming impudent; . . . while they speak their own language, they are more humble." [17] The Spaniards viewed those Indians who learned Spanish as crafty rascals who wanted to work around the rules of the socially prescribed system; thus, the term *ladino*, meaning "cunning" and applied in Spain to Moors who learned Castilian, was the derogatory tag the colonists gave these Indians.

Many Spanish colonists and their descendants, especially the elites, thus realized the desirability of the policy of segregation, as they saw the effects of the all-too-frequent violations of the King's laws. Indians who learned Spanish threatened the social stratification system which assumed Spanish superiority and Indian inferiority. In 1692 officials became especially concerned over the contact between Spaniards and Indians in urban areas and ordered that the policy of separation of living areas be enforced in Mexico City. The need to keep the Indians from losing their "natural simplicity and humility" was the justification for asking religious and civil officials to see that the Indians stayed within their own *barrios*, or sections of the city. Spanish officials, wanting to be sure no Indian could claim ignorance of the new orders, posted notices outlining the confines and travel rules in Nahuatl.[18]

Attitudes formed by the elite Spanish colonists and their descendants struggling to maintain Indian-Spanish segregation determined their negative response to the Crown's plan that the Indians learn Spanish. Through their practices, civil and legal authorities contributed to the partially self-perpetuating momentum of separation. They saw no need for the Indian populace to learn Spanish, so long as there existed a sufficient supply of Indian scribes and interpreters to help handle the business affairs of the colony. In the courts and in the administration of labor and civil affairs, naguatlatos remained the major official channel of communication between Indians and lay Spaniards during the seventeenth century and well into the eighteenth.[19] The Indian masses had neither incentive nor opportunity to learn Spanish. The friars had refused Spanish as the general language of the Indians; instead they had trained only a select few in Spanish to serve as their assistants or in the civil affairs of the colony. In attempting to reverse this trend and to extend Spanish to all Indians, Charles II had commanded and cajoled both lay and religious officials. But all his efforts were to no avail. The cultural Hispanization of the Indians could not be legislated effectively, for this process depended on the gradual evolution of the attitudes and customs of peoples directly involved. A seventeenth-century Spanish writer put the thwarting of the Crown's power this way:

Particularly in provinces so distant and remote from their Kings . . . the royal mandates tend to be empty or they become diluted, and they are given wide interpretations by residents, or local authorities, who are inclined to regard as licit all their whims desire. The temerity of human beings easily leads them to despise that which is very remote. And just as doctors consider the cure of diseased lungs to be very difficult because medication must travel through the stomach, following a very long, narrow or obstructed route, so it is that the remoteness of the Supreme Power scarcely makes it reasonable that these distant provinces can hope for or obtain appropriate remedies with which they can halt or alleviate their troubles and ills.[20]

Later Bourbons, especially Charles III, were to face a long and difficult struggle in their determined efforts to provide an opportunity for the Indians to learn Spanish.

THE STRUGGLE TO ESTABLISH A CODE

Strangely enough, in the early part of the eighteenth century, the Crown found support for its linguistic policy of Spanish for the Indians in a most unlikely group. In 1728, descendants of Indian nobles forwarded a lengthy plea to the Archbishop of Mexico City asking that the College of Santa Cruz de Tlatelolco for Indians be reopened. Included in the document was an urgent appeal for an effective program to teach Spanish to the Indians. The group presented an extensive list of grievances against the Crown and its religious representatives who had failed to prepare Indian youth for social life in the new world.[21] In spite of laws and decrees to the contrary, the Indians were still unable to raise themselves to any position of power, social status, or even self-esteem. The abandonment of any means of preparation for the Indians' participation in the new society created by the Spaniards and the severe disruption of their own old society had left the natives suspended—unable to take part in the new and left without the security of the old.

The politics of the Indian leaders led them to direct their arguments toward the deficiencies in the religious life of the natives, but their plea contained numerous straightforward attempts to force the Archbishop to look at more than the sad state of the Indians' souls. They suggested that if the Spanish religious leaders were to go into the countryside, they would find Indians condemned to Hell through not only spiritual ignorance but also sins committed as a result of the direct influence of Spaniards. In spite of segregation policies, the Spaniards had taught the Indians to indulge in drunkenness and lewd and lascivious practices which disrupted the cultural patterns of Indian society. Traditional family obligations and community responsibilities weakened, and the entire social structure of Indian community life shifted uneasily. The remedy for the social maladies with which the Spaniards had infected the Indians was to be found in the prescriptions left by the sixteenth-century friars who had founded the College of Santa Cruz de Tlatelolco: train native ministers to go among their own people and carry both the spiritual message and means of social and cultural education, acceptance, and unification. If two or more individuals from each linguistic region (and the Indians obliged the Archbishop by naming those areas they felt most neglected) were trained at the College, they could go out to teach the youth of the most isolated and untouched territories.

The descendants of Indian nobles addressing their plea to the Archbishop in 1728 added a crucial requirement to the College's curriculum—the Spanish language. They admitted that the diversity of languages had impeded both the religious and social progress of the natives, and the future of the nation and their own social well-being dictated that the Indians learn Spanish. Ignorance of the Spanish language had left them "wrapped in a thousand errors and idolatries," cut off from God and the state.[22] Past regents had stipulated that Indians were eligible for religious, political, and military positions, if they possessed the necessary qualifications.[23] Knowledge of Spanish was a prime prerequisite for office-holding, and though schools were supposed to have been made available to teach the Indians Spanish, their scarcity and methods of teaching left little chance for the ranks of the Church or the state to be glutted with Indians. In those few instances when instruction was available outside the Church, it was offered in Spanish by teachers unable to understand or be understood by their charges.

The list of grievances and suggestions for a revived Indian education program in the eighteenth century had little immediate effect; the doors of the College of Tlatelolco remained closed. Any extensive plans for higher education for the Indians had to wait for more funds and the successful establishment of primary schools. Earlier stipulations for the establishment of a seminary in Mexico City had stated that one-fourth of the students be Indians.[24] For the time being, the Crown apparently judged this gesture, offered by Charles II in 1691, sufficient to take care of the higher education of the Indians and rested its hopes for the spread of Spanish on the execution of the numerous orders that the religious personnel teach Castilian to the Indians in rural primary schools. But numerous eighteenth-century ecclesiastics, especially those born in New Spain, shared their predecessors' negative attitude toward teaching Spanish to the Indians. Creole priests were much more likely to know an Indian language than clergymen born in Spain; thus the indigenous-language prerequisite for appointment to parish posts had virtually assured the numerical superiority of creole curates in rural areas. If they taught the Indians to speak Spanish, they threatened the perpetuation of the single qualification which most aided the selection of creoles over peninsular Spaniards for parish positions.

The growing competition between ecclesiastics who favored Castilian for the Indians and those who insisted on the Indian tongues, added to the regrettable isolation of the Indians, provoked the Archbishop of Mexico, Antonio Lorenzana y Buitron to protest to Charles III. Lorenzana wrote the King in June of 1768 of the need for schools to teach Spanish to the Indians so that they might be eligible for full cultural, political, and economic participation in the colony. Extending the century-old thesis of the Bishop of Oaxaca that the Indians should learn Spanish in order to hold offices, the Archbishop reasoned that Spanish would also help them in their daily lives as homemakers and as agriculturalists.

The children will advance themselves by learning to read and write, and in addition, they will learn to care for their homes, become officials of the Republic, and explain themselves before their Superiors. Thus they will raise the esteem of their nation and destroy widespread ignorance, not only of the mysteries of the Faith, but also of the most efficient and effective means of cultivating their lands, caring for their livestock, and trading their goods.[25]

By the next year, the Archbishop had extended his reasons for spreading Spanish; a successful language program was necessary to redeem the deplorable state of Christian education in the Indian villages. The appointment of clerics qualified not by their administrative ability or theological training, but rather by their knowledge of indigenous tongues threatened the spiritual well-being of the Church in New Spain. Clerics who knew the Indian tongues and little else were given curacies, while well-educated youths, grounded in the study of divinity and civil and canonical law, were denied appointment because they knew only Castilian.

In October of 1769, Lorenzana published a lengthy *pastoral* summarizing other major trends and problems centering around language policy since the Conquest. He left few aspects of the dilemma untouched in his thorough treatment of the history of the haphazard use of "language as the perfect instrument of empire." His major points catered to Spanish political and religious prejudices:

1) The dependence of Cortés and the early Spanish conquerors on interpreters had initiated a trend which had become an established pattern in all areas of colonial life.
2) The extension of influence into formerly untouched areas had necessi-

tated more translators, and the supply had not been able to keep up with the demand in such areas as Puebla and Oaxaca, where there were many more idioms and dialects than the original Spaniards had imagined.

3) In spite of decrees to spread the Spanish language, practice had not kept pace with principle and royal directives were even more ignored in the eighteenth century than they had been in the past.

4) No nation had ever attempted to establish colonies without simultaneously extending the language of the mother country; he cited the Greeks, Romans, and the Castilians themselves on the peninsula of Spain for support of this point.

5) Unity in tongue would bring unity in spirit within the nation and foster the congenial and productive participation of the natives in the social, political, and spiritual life of the country.

6) The elimination of the diverse languages was necessary for the proper and classical education of the Indians.

7) The Church and its representatives had grossly neglected the general education of the Indians and, most especially, their duty to teach Spanish to the Indians.

8) The use of interpreters and the maintenance of linguistic barriers between the Indians and the civil officials had perpetuated the exploitation of the Indians and undermined their confidence and self-respect.

9) The past practices of the Church had created discord and fomented the animosity of the Indians toward the Spaniards. Isolation of Indians of the same tongue in villages administered by the early missionaries had provided security which turned to fear and hatred when the early protectors who spoke their tongue died.

10) The use of force and fear of punishment to make the Indians send their children to school had negated any beneficial experience the young might have gained from their teachers.[26]

The Archbishop closed his list of grievances by calling for the combined efforts of secular and religious, Spaniard and Indian to extend the Castilian tongue.

Another powerful sponsor, the Marqués de Croix, Viceroy of New Spain, underscored Lorenzana's recommendation in a letter to the King the same year. Enthusiastic response came from Madrid almost immediately. Sufficiently jolted by the implications of Lorenzana's summary statement, Charles issued a decree giving royal sanction to the recommendation of the pastoral.[27] The decree summarized parts of the Archbishop's historical presentation, but the major emphasis of the lengthy argument was an examination of why indigenous languages had ever been promoted and retained in the colony. The King did not deny the need for the early friars to learn the Indian tongues, but he added that practical considerations should have led the missionaries to a wider concern for the complications which soon resulted from this method of spreading Christianity. Aside from the fact that numerous languages were revealed in the extension of the empire, the grouping of Indians in communities often brought several tongues together in the larger towns, making it impossible for the prelates to keep up with the number of languages they might encounter in their own village, as well as in the countryside. So intense was the dedication of the early regular clergy, in particular, to teaching Christianity in the native tongues, that they occasionally influenced the secular priests to do the same. Grammars, vocabularies, and catechisms added support to later missionaries and ministers preaching to the Indians, and the King concluded that by the end of the sixteenth century the precedent was so strongly established that future laws and monarchs could not alter the pattern. He lamented that the early conquerors did not put force and determination into an effort to teach Spanish to the Indians, for if they had, perhaps within fifty years, the program would have been successful. Charles III ordered all authorities, secular and religious, in Peru, New Spain, and New Granada to extend Spanish and to extinguish the other languages of the territories. The King's stated purposes were:

1) to end the need for interpreters;
2) to eliminate the needless competition between creole curates and peninsula-born priests;
3) to make it possible for priests to be understood in all the towns of their dioceses;
4) to reduce the chances for duping and cheating the Indians;
5) to allow more uniform educational opportunities;
6) to permit the King to govern all the possessions with more convenience.[28]

The ends seemed useful enough in terms of the Crown's need to gain efficient government for the entire empire. But the means for handling the numerous problems both Lorenzana and the King had so meticulously laid bare depended upon practical ends far removed from those of Charles III.

Carrying out the King's decree called for a change of heart in the majority of priests who had over the past century been urged to teach Spanish to the Indians. Creole curates and priests born in Spain were at cross purposes in the language controversy. The former supported instruction in the Indian tongues to secure their own position in the closed Indian communities; the latter endorsed teaching Spanish to the Indians in order to open the parishes to ecclesiastics who knew only Castilian. Clergymen who spoke an Indian tongue had not allowed their parishioners to learn Spanish. They looked upon the Indians' use of Spanish as a sign of disrespect and punished those who used the language in the priests' presence. For these curates, maintenance of the Indian tongues was the key to shutting out competition from clergymen who knew only Castilian and were frequently better trained and more thoroughly grounded in theology.[29] The self-protective stance of a large portion of the parish priests, added to that of the Spanish lay elite, left little chance of their cooperation in a program asking for a Spanish-speaking congregation in New Spain. Hence, the Archbishop and the King could not realistically hope for the implementation of a plan capable of upsetting a social stratification system which had perpetuated itself for two centuries.

The Marqués de Croix's successor, Antonio Maria Bucareli, saw the potential of the King's language policy for disturbing New Spain's status quo, and he set into motion administrative tactics designed to paralyze its execution. By his own admission, he well knew that the distant laws of Spain counted for little in the actual government of New Spain; he observed that "the disorder to which the nature of man is inherently inclined" made it impossible to carry out Crown rulings.[30] Bucareli's obstructionist tactics included publishing a proclamation directing the village mayors to initiate preliminary surveys he claimed necessary before any direct action on the King's 1770 order. On December 10, 1772, Bucareli ordered the mayors and town councilmen to inspect the records of community properties; to count the number of school-age children in each village; to calculate the salary of the teacher (based on a portion of community wealth); to establish a curriculum of Spanish, Christian doctrine, reading, and writing; and to tax each family in proportion to the number of children, if the community wealth could not provide an adequate salary for the teacher.³¹ But the viceroy issued the proclamation only once, and he made no efforts to follow up this single empty gesture toward compliance with the King's order to establish schools to teach Spanish.

Other decrees related to Charles III's language policy received even less attention from Bucareli. Twenty-four hours before signing the decree to spread Castilian through the Spanish possessions by establishing schools for the Indians, Charles had ordered the foundation in New Spain of a college for Indian nobles and commoners. This school was to train teachers for the Indians, a practical suggestion stemming from the requests made in 1728 by a group of descendants of Indian nobles and Lorenzana's insistence that the Indians be taught by trained teachers from their own group. Detailed plans for establishing such an institution had been made in New Spain by Bucareli's predecessor, the Marqués de Croix, and the Visitador José de Gálvez. In November of 1770 they had agreed to establish a new building for the school which was to be named San Carlos in honor of the reigning monarch. Charles III agreed to the plans for the colegio, and he issued a decree in September 1772 underlining his approval and urging the administration to put the proposal into action. Bucareli had taken office in 1771 and applied his usual delaying tactics to the plans for the colegio—a slow methodical approach to inform himself of all the matters concerned in the decision. New decrees issued by Charles III in 1774, 1776, and 1778 did not stir the viceroy.³² Finally, in July of 1778, the viceroy answered the King's pleas in a lengthy letter of explanation covering the history of efforts to open a school for the Indians. Sufficient funds to maintain the kind of preparatory school Charles III had requested were not available, and therefore, the viceroy had arranged for a few clergymen to teach Spanish in the formerly Jesuit College of San Gregorio.³³ Bucareli's letter was plaintive but forceful, making clear to the King that he would not put into effect any program fated to be ignored by local religious and political agents. Of what good was a colegio for the Indians if the primary schools in the countryside would never have their doors opened? And the King's plan for the maintenance of these schools from community levies and the Indians themselves doomed any hope for the success of the project. Bucareli never published a proclamation covering the King's 1778 order to establish schools in the villages.[34] Faced with rebellious Indians in the north and the stubborn resistance of creole clergymen in central Mexico, Bucareli was in no mood to be concerned with educating the Indians of central Mexico. These masses were quiet, and as long as he did not force the King's orders for Indian education on parish priests, the countryside offered him no trouble. He could turn a deaf ear to the King's orders easier than he could risk open dissensions in the central valley. Thus Bucareli listened to the creoles and heeded the lessons of expediency in government, knowing full well that governing the parish curates and their Indian charges best meant governing them least.

Those clergymen working in the Indian villages who did learn of the King's order that the Indians learn Spanish responded with bitter denunciations of the Crown's total Indian policy. Many condemned the Crown for removing the Indians from their land and historic identification with the milpa, or maize land, and for attempting to congregate them in villages where the clergy had to reconcile them to their new living conditions.[35] Isolated in this way, the Indians were naturally inclined to continue the use of their own language, customs, and superstitions and to resort to hiding, trickery, and duplicity to avoid Spaniards. A censor of the Inquisition wrote that people in Spain were much easier to manage than those in Mexico, because of the unity of language in Spain. The innumerable languages in Mexico allowed the Indians to slip away from their "shepherd's care" and to prevent their children from attending school.[36] But teaching Spanish was not the solution to the many problems created by the Crown's long-standing Indian policies.

Echoing the pleas of the sixteenth-century missionaries, the religious representatives in the villages urged the establishment of boarding schools for the Indian children and the opportunity to determine the dominant language in each area according to the judgment of local clergymen. With numerous difficulties occurring in each area of the field, the religious leaders had to be allowed to devise suitable methods for coping with their particular prevailing circumstances. General rules handed down by the King were to no avail.[37] In those missions where a few religious leaders were teaching and preaching Spanish, the Indians resisted. Though many Indians seemed to know some Spanish, they "abhorred" the idiom, and, according to some observers, revealed their hatred for the language by refusing to name their children with any names other than those of their own tongue.[38]

Reports of successes were extremely rare, though not unknown. One notice from Sonora in 1785 heaped praise on the Indians and their capacity for learning Spanish quickly. In six primary schools of the area, the Indians had learned in a very short time to speak Spanish so fluently that they could say of themselves: *"Finally we are all Spaniards."* [39] A colegio in the area was the home of fourteen Indian youths who were rapidly learning Spanish and adopting Spanish dress.[40]

Debate, effort, and a variety of solutions were not enough to lay to rest the question of language in colonial New Spain. Thus as Spain's rule over its colonies drew to a close, the issue of language was very much alive. The Bourbon Crown had promoted Spanish as the common tongue of its administration and as the proper tool to rebuild the uneven and unsatisfactory structure of Catholic Christianity left by the early missionaries. Many of the creole priests remained convinced that teaching in the indigenous languages was preferable to instruction in Spanish. Attempts to establish civil schools to supersede the ecclesiastical schools had failed because of the unsatisfactory provisions made for employing teachers in the Spanish language and for financing the schools' operations. Education and the total life style of the Spaniard separated him from the Indian, as did his language. Ironically, the recent language decrees of Charles III helped widen this gap.

In the midst of all the administrative slow motion, intellectuals and journalists of Mexico City were intent on reporting current educational ideas prevalent in Europe which might influence their own language instruction. These self-appointed guardians of European elite traditions in New Spain were interested neither in Indian languages nor in language for the Indian. José Antonio Alzate y Ramirez, a student of astronomy and natural science and the editor of *Gazeta de Literatura* published from 1788 to 1795, hoped to see those of pure European descent in New Spain schooled in the principles and practices of modern science. He lashed out against Scholasticism and its antiquated impractical methods of teaching, and language study received much attention in the letters and columns of his *Gazeta*.[41] One writer complained to the editor that he had had great difficulties learning French, because of the ancient mania of teaching a new language in the idiom to be learned. By this writer's suggestion, all the "inhuman teachers" using the method of memorization should be condemned to memorize fifteen lines of Nahuatl daily for one year.[42] His comment called attention to the general recognition that those who learned the difficult and different languages of Mexico did not do so by the methods recommended by the scholastics.

The recent decrees of the King on language learning intensified this reassessment of language teaching methods, and the grammar of Nebrija was passed over for the text of Juan de Iriarte recommended by Charles III in his 1768 decree.[43] Scholars writing to the *Gazeta* confirmed the practicality of the King's suggestion and affirmed that teaching Latin with the Iriarte text which gave the rules in Spanish enabled the students to learn much faster.[44] Concerned only with the education of the elite Spaniards, however, these writers never extended their suggestions to new methods for the teaching of Spanish to the Indians.

Through the pages of the *Diario de México*, a weekly pamphlet established in the early nineteenth century, ran commentaries and news items reflecting the concerns of those Spaniards anxious to fashion New Spain's elite culture on the best European models. The *Diario* reported that which concerned "the good of society"—causes *célèbre* which should be brought to the notice of all "good citizens."[45] The writers who urged uniformity in dress, customs, and education embraced as their norms the best traditions in Europe.[46] Jacobo Villaurrutia, co-founder of the *Diario*, proposed a college which should offer throughout its curriculum French, the "universal living language," and in the fifth year of study, Latin and Spanish. The former was necessary because of its continued use in public exercises, and both languages were useful for their "general notions" which might be found in all languages.[47]

Purity of Spanish in the colony based on a close imitation of the peninsular speech provoked this happy speculation by *el criollo mexicano*, an anonymous writer in the *Diario*:

> How glorious it would be for New Spain to raise its speech to the standard of the mother country! Then the pleasing sound of the true Castilian tongue could resound throughout the provinces, and even the American Spaniards would deliver Castilian with all of the excellence which it deserves. Within a few years, even those of the lowest birth who are just now being born would achieve this standard.[48]

He blamed the parents of creoles who had failed to teach their children the proper pronunciation of Spanish for the fact that "we criollos in general do not pronounce our Spanish tongue with perfection."[49]

For the peninsulares and wealthy creoles, the esthetic perfection of the Spanish language was a matter of the consensus drawn from the urban society in Spain. On the peninsula, grammars codifying the usage of "good society" supplemented dictionaries in the construction of the structured esthetic norm. The *Real Academia Española,* founded in 1713, was the codifying agency which began the publication of the six-volume *Diccionario de autoridades* in 1726.[50] In its first century of operation, this academy did not recognize contributions of Spanish in the New World, but rather concentrated its attention on the code of the elite in Spain. Therefore, those members of the Spanish colonies most anxious to identify with the traditions of the peninsula urged the preservation of this same code, "the true Castilian tongue," among the "good citizens" of New Spain. The colonial Spaniard's concerns, frequently drawing him to the ideas of the Enlightenment and the *philosophes* of Europe, as well as to the traditions of Spain, turned him and his language more toward Europe than to his miserable neighbors at home. Spanish, as the code of the elite, bridged the ocean more easily than it bridged the chasm between the classes in New Spain as the end of Spain's rule over her colonies drew near.

CHAPTER FOUR

The Nation between Old and New

Mexico was slipping out of the Spanish Crown's grip and into the hands of the elites who were to mold the new nation in the nineteenth century. National unification was the refrain of political decision-makers throughout the first century of Mexico's independence. During the first fifty years, political leaders spoke only in general terms of the need for a unity of spirit and political ideology. Elites made few specific provisions for reorienting the masses for participation in the new nation's democratic plans; instead they debated education purposes and socioecoonmic cleavages. Concern with language policy as such was therefore both infrequent and inconsistent, often deeply immersed in conflicting views of the indigenous populations held by local change agents attempting to influence the course of educational development.

If the republic were to be successful in devising a language policy which would unite Indians, criollos, and Spanish classical Europeans, a changed educational system was needed. First, however, the policy-makers had to decide whether education should attempt to transmit the prevailing culture of the elites who supported the continued imitation of Spanish traditional patterns and practices in the colony, or whether education should restructure the society for a new republic. For the fulfillment of either purpose, there could be no great divergence or inconsistency between the decision-makers who articulated the society and those who would coordinate the educational system. Until the majority of the nation's decision-makers came to view the Indian as a specific entity rather than as a unity within a general category of "the poor," there could be no realistic appraisal of the linguistic and cultural divisions between the masses and the elite.

Educational theories put forth by both liberals and conservatives demonstrated their particular overviews of society which suggested attitudes toward language as a possible instrument of unification. The liberals, who were largely anti-clerical, pro-republic, democratic, and anti-Spanish, reasoned that education should prepare all citizens—including the Indians—to "fit" in the new nation. The conservatives, strongly Catholic, Spanish, and landed, insisted on improving the traditional system of education, continuing the elitist curriculum for the upper class, and maintaining separate religious and remedial instruction for the Indians. For the liberals, it soon became clear that popular education meant secular education. For the conservatives, the Church had to remain the bastion of the values and traditions of Spanish society. But even before liberals and conservatives in the new nation lined up against each other on the issue of social and educational reform, winds of upheaval in Spain and the colony tossed about ideas which would help mold politics and pedagogy in the soon-to-be nation. Royalty and citizenry alike took a close look at the education inheritance in New Spain. In 1815 Charles IV reminded administrators of the need to survey the state of education and make necessary changes to see that institutions were fulfilling the purposes laid out in the decrees of his predecessors. He did not have to read every one of the officials' first reports before reaching the sorrowful conclusion that all the efforts of the Crown had not brought any real measure of success to education in New Spain.[1]

Citizens confirmed his conclusion by pointing to the particulars of a system filled with inept teachers who stuffed their students with trivia. In 1816 José Joaquín Fernández de Lizardi, a product of primary-school instruction in Tepotzotlan, published *El Periquillo Sarniento*, a devastating satire of education. *Periquillo* condemned the ineffectual system of primary education which excluded the poor and allowed both teachers and students to suffer through a process of little value to anyone except the parents who prized the rite for their young. Influential creoles and Spaniards approved traditional educational content which made precision in penmanship and Latin oratory supreme goals.[2] Lizardi condemned not only the ineffectual system of education for upper classes but also the almost total neglect of education in the villages. He called for free and compulsory education for all citizens, pointed out the need for more schools, and underscored firmly the care officials should take to insure the selection of competent teachers.[3] With stinging sarcasm, in his "Testament and Farewell of the Mexican *Pensador*," Lizardi particularly noted the indifference of Spanish officials and administrators toward the Indians:

> I leave the Indians in the same state of civilization, liberty, and happiness to which the Conquest reduced them, finding most sensible the indifference with which the legislatures have regarded them, as evidenced by the few and uninteresting sessions in which [the Indians] have received attention since the first congress.[4]

The pamphleteer especially blamed priests and officials of the villages for perpetuating the ignorance and isolation of the Indians, who knew little of God and less of themselves and their rights.

In the period of reassessment between the end of the eighteenth century and 1821, confusion promulgated denunciations, recommendations, and little reasoned discourse. However, both in New Spain and on the peninsula, the Indian and the provisions for his new role were common subjects of debate. Manuel Abad y Queipo, a Spanish priest who served in Michoacán, had written to the King in 1799 predicting dire results if the Crown did not take steps to include the Indians in the privileges available to other elements of colonial society. Isolated by linguistic barriers and locked in ignorance by the absence of an adequate educational system, the Indians had no opportunity for improving themselves, even though laws indicated the Crown's willingness for Indians to have equal opportunities in the colony.[5] Miguel Ramos Arizpe, a priest from the northeast of Mexico, argued before the *Cortes* (assembly) of Spain that schools in his area were staffed by poorly paid, inept teachers who could not possibly prepare citizens of the Crown's colony.[6]

At home, leaders of the insurrection of the colony against the Crown wielded arguments similar to those of spokesmen who had appealed to the remnants of Spanish authority on the peninsula. However, most leaders in the movement for independence after the "Cry of Hidalgo" in 1810 called for individual liberties and social and economic amelioration for landless peasants; few pointed out the special needs of Indians. Participants in the Congress of Chilpancingo in 1813 proposed that land be given not only to soldiers of the independence struggle but also to Indians, and some members suggested specific methods of improving the "miserable state" of the Indians' diet, life, and work.[7] For the majority of lawmakers, however, Indians as such were not to be singled out in the social and political theory of the new nation. The insurgents had struggled to gain Mexico's independence from Spain in order to provide sovereignty to the people and to improve the general social welfare of the depressed classes. José María Morelos, the parish priest who had taken over the movement for independence after Hidalgo's death, saw the need to take economic divisions into consideration, but he showed little concern for the cultural cleavage between the Indians and the rest of the population. His statement to the Congress of Chilpancingo confirmed his major goals for social reform:

Since good law is superior to all men, our congress ought to be guided by that which binds them to constancy and patriotism, [in order that] they might curb opulence and indulgence, and thus augment the daily sustenance of the poor, improve their customs, [and] disperse their ignorance. . . .[8]

The Plan of Iguala, published in 1821, added to such well-intentioned legislation and reiterated the idea of the sovereignty of the people. The Plan read: "All the inhabitants of New Spain, without distinction among Europeans, Africans, and Indians, are citizens of this monarchy [the Empire of Agustín de Iturbide] with the right to all privileges according to their merit and virtues."[9]

The early leaders of the Mexican nation were supremely interested in power politics and theoretical debates over the extent of the franchise and the question of federalism versus centralism. Though influenced by the ideas of constitutional liberals in France and the experience of the United States, the framers of the Constitution of 1824 actually patterned the document primarily after the Spanish Constitution of 1812.[10] Thus both the abstract emphasis of the writings of early political leaders and the institutional provisions found in the Constitution were drawn from sources remote from the realities of the Mexican countryside. There was little desire to create a government the principles of which would be derived from an inductive consideration of the social and economic needs of the culturally-divergent peoples of the Mexican nation.

A contemporary historian and politician, Lorenzo de Zavala, pointed out that three-fifths of the population were Indians who owned no property, and farmed marginal lands and fished in order to provide themselves the barest sustenance. The other two-fifths of the population flourished. Those Spaniards and upper-class creoles included in the upper portion of the population received the benefits of political position and higher education, while frequently not even primary instruction was available for the masses.[11] Other contemporary reporters noted that unfortunately even in those rare instances when Indians did reach schools in the cities, they were trained not in practical matters, but rather in ecclesiastical sciences.[12] Such exposure could hardly be called education, for the students' instruction was controlled either by friars and clerics more interested in theology than basic literary skills, or by "ignorant laymen who taught them to read and write badly." [13]

A few local leaders looked at these facts and demanded a new education system as the means by which the nation could transform the Indian segment of the population and unify all peoples within the Mexican nation. They lashed out at the separations built into the legal, administrative, and most particularly, the educational system inherited from Spanish colonialism. The separate educations of the Spaniards, mestizos, and Indians had been as different as that which they would have received had they been citizens of different nations. In order to unify these diversely prepared groups for participation in the republic, education must be popular and in close conformity with the principles of government. The search for national unity, the evolution of concern for social equality and democracy, and the development of a popular system of education had to provide a place for *los indios*. Continuation of policies of class separation and maintenance of a paternalistic Indian policy effectively shut out opportunities for Indian mobility and communication between Indians and other segments of the population. In the words of one contemporary observer:

> To keep the Indian, therefore, in tutelage, under the fiction of minority, in the shadow of laws that do not govern, is to close to him the constitutional road granted him for enlightenment, employment, and other public offices; it is to submerge him for a third time in a sea of ignorance and misery.[14]

Others argued that Mexico not only excluded the present Indian populations from citizenship, but also refused to consider their histories a part of the republic's heritage. Surveys of the customs and character of Indian civilizations could be valuable to those trying to establish means of unifying the nation.

Juan Rodríguez Puebla, a liberal member of both houses of Congress in the 1820's, dreamed of a system of education designed by and for the Indians, in which they might continue the use of their native tongues. Specifically, Rodríguez Puebla proposed to the Mexican Congress in 1824 that the Colegio of San Gregorio, the Jesuit school for Indians reduced in 1767 to housing only a few Indian tutors, be granted additional support and redeveloped as a secondary school for Indians. Rodríguez Puebla, who proudly proclaimed that he himself was Indian, desperately wanted the state to provide a separate curriculum for Indians in the central university system and to help San Gregorio revive its historic tradition of educating Indian youths.[15] Vincente Guerrero, an Indian who became Mexico's president briefly in 1829, raised the nativistic hopes of a group of citizens who called themselves "educated Indians" and caused them to advertise the specific needs of Mexico's indigenous populations. Leaflets citing the degradation of Indians excluded from full citizenship because of their color, poverty, and ignorance were circulated in the capital. The anonymous pamphleteers foresaw education as the necessary force to remove the cultural barriers—religious superstitions, diverse languages, and ancient government forms—which set Indians apart from the rest of Mexico's citizens.[16] But Guerrero's assumption of national power was short-lived, and it remained for a few local spokesmen for the Indians to continue to try to make the nation's decision-makers view the Indian as a special victim of the colonial regime and the present heritage in education. Only through an education which offered them a meaningful entry into national life and an opportunity to maintain an appreciation of their cultural heritage could the Indians take their place among the decision-makers of a unified society and the coordinators of its educational system. However, such spokesmen for the Indians were neither numerous nor powerful enough to alter the direction of policy-making in education in the first half century of independence. Moreover, the nascent nationalism implicit in the sense of national purpose and unified participation espoused by most of Mexico's decision-makers had to evolve considerably before they considered such specific elements of popular education as the teaching of the national language and the transmittal of a sense of Mexican history which realistically incorporated the Indians.

José María Luis Mora and Valentín Gómez Farías, liberals and the major figures managing the educational system in the 1830's, were convinced that if the nation were to move forward as one, the Indians could not be singled out for special treatment. They would have to learn the traditions inherited from the colonial society and built into the creole concept of nationality. Rodríquez Puebla's proposals for what other reformers interpreted as the exaltation of the "Aztec race" and the establishment of a separate Indian system triggered swift negative reactions. Gómez Farías' administration announced its firm intention to hasten the fusion of the Indians with the general masses. As perhaps the nation's first Indianist, Rodríquez Puebla introduced ideas which provoked stern denunciations. Indianists were to hear the same arguments again and again near the end of the century: any special provisions for the Indian suggested the strengthening of separate Indian societies and a weakening of the nation's unity.

Early opponents to Rodríguez Puebla's Indianist notions were determined, therefore, that educational reforms would recognize not cultural minorities, but rather economic differences among the nation's citizens. Mora himself explained:

Thus it is that the distinction between *Indians* and *non-Indians* is not recognized in the acts of the Government. Instead the terms *poor* and *rich* are substituted [indicating the goal] of extending to all the benefits of the society.[17]

Indians, and indeed all citizens, could, with the benefits of public instruction derived from common traditions, learn to participate fully in the economic benefits of the nation. Mora proposed that the first constitutional congress ban the term *el indio* from public usage, and insisted that the law declare: "Indians no longer exist."[18] Neither the term nor the reality disappeared, although those participating in the congressional debates resorted to the phrase "those called Indians" in an attempt to fulfill Mora's request.[19]

By shouting their proposals for public instruction, Mora and Gómez Farías drowned out the few cries of despair over the liberal leaders' refusal to look realistically at rural society. Though funds were not available to support popular education outside the Federal District, Gómez Farías influenced several states to initiate their own education systems. There was a general public spirit of support for the Lancasterian schools introduced as early as 1822 to Mexico. The Lancasterian method, which advocated a system of instruction by which each one of the older students would, under the supervision of the teacher, monitor the recitations of the younger students, was dominant in the primary school system in the Federal District from the early 1830's until 1890. The basic notion of each-one-teach-one was to be revived and to influence Indian education in the twentieth century. Mora believed that primary education in the republic should mold men of "pure customs" and "moral virtues."[20] The states responded to this idea and incorporated instruction in moral and civic obligations in their traditional curricula. Most states mandated that all lessons at the elementary level be given in Spanish.[21] Some few states argued that although the Lancasterian system had the merit of economy, the instructors were poorly trained and often unable to teach the rural populations.[22] The political leaders, nevertheless, did not propose a suitable alternative plan for the improvement of primary instruction; they preferred instead to center their energies on secondary and university education.

Restructuring the old system of higher education was necessary to destroy the monopoly the Church held in education and to extend schooling to the masses so that they might participate in a democratic state. Mora reasoned that ignorant people left without public instruction while a select class monopolized education soon fell prey to oligarchs; therefore, public education had to be made available for the Mexican people.[23] In 1833, the same law which authorized federal control over education in the District and territories allowed Gómez Farías, the vice-president, to appoint members of the *Comisión del plan de estudios*. The purposes of the group: to wipe out those methods prejudicial to good teaching; to determine the content, materials, and pedagogical practices necessary for the new social state; to disseminate among the masses the necessary means for learning.[24] With these ends to justify their means, the committee abolished the University of Mexico and the colegios of the Federal District. Mora proposed six specialized *establecimientos* to replace the former colegios. Mora's complaints against education offered by the clergy in the former colegios was that the schools duplicated each other, did not encourage "a spirit of investigation and doubt," and offered instruction of little practical use for citizens in daily life. Mora argued for such practical measures as introducing students to Spanish before Latin in the curriculum and providing subjects such as commerce, agriculture, constitutional law, and political economy. In the colegio, or establishment, for preparatory studies, students studied Latin, Nahuatl, Tarascan, and Otomi. Mora recommended the latter tongues as the most notable of those spoken in the "ancient Indian nations." He reasoned these languages would be useful to students "more through instruction than through actual use, since this is a country where the Castilian tongue is common to all the members of the society."[25] This rationale for the study of Indian languages seems also to have been the basis for Mora's insistence that prerequisites for entrance to the establishment of ecclesiastical science include one course in either Aztec, Tarascan, or Otomi, and that the school's program contain both Aztec and Otomi. The liberal political leader even denied that "those called Indians" used these languages, and he categorized them as secondary "classical" tongues, the study of which would discipline the mind.[26]

A corollary of this concern with the "classical" led to the proposal in 1835 for an Academy of Language. A group of political leaders published a circular outlining the basic assumptions of the group. Lamenting their loss of Spain as a cultural link between Mexico and all of Europe, intellectuals who endorsed the Academy saw Castilian suffering from a lack of contact with classical models. They also attributed the decadent state of Castilian in Mexico to the high rate of illiteracy, the circulation of bad translations, and the scarcity of classics. The solution to these problems assumed a delusive simplicity: the redemption of the nation's "corrupt Castilian" depended on a watchdog language academy. This institution would:

1) conserve the purity of Castilian;
2) promote the reprinting and distribution of classics;
3) provide a dictionary of "legitimate" Spanish-Americanisms;
4) provide grammars and dictionaries of the "different" languages spoken in Mexico;
5) determine the proper models for the study of Spanish rhetoric and poetry;
6) gather materials for an ethnographic and linguistic atlas of Mexico;
7) censor the style of all legislative, scientific, and literary works published in Mexico;
8) establish annual awards in rhetoric and poetry.

The nominee for director, a former member of Madrid's Royal Academy of Spanish, was requested to model the Mexican Academy on the Spanish institution.[27] But the new republic had neither a sufficient number of intellectuals who could devote themselves to the execution of this grandiose scheme nor the political and economic security which would allow the assignment of language standardization to a high place in the list of national priorities. Furthermore, the idealism of the founders who drew up the charter of the Academy of Language dwindled before realistic struggles with inadequate finances and the country's floundering education program.

Education reforms of the liberals were suspended when Antonio López de Santa Anna took control of the government in 1834, and conservative thought came to the fore. Curiously enough, on paper, Santa Anna went beyond his predecessors; in 1842 he decreed the establishment of a public system of primary instruction. Among his reasons for endorsing popular education he included the need for widespread teaching of the national tongue; he noted, "for him who is ignorant of his own national language, the worthy rights of citizenship are in fact suspended." [28] Santa Anna also signed a law in 1854 reviving the defunct Academy of Language.[29] Neither plan, however, moved much beyond these gestures, and the dual problems of language diversity and the need for Indian education were not debated during the era of centralized government from 1834 to 1855.[30] Creoles who favored the Castilian traditional educational system not only prevented any national consideration of language unification; they also influenced the rejection of attempts at the local level to prepare the way for literacy in the Indian languages. Agents of the British and Foreign Bible Society and the American Bible Society had entered Mexico in the 1820's to promote the use in the public schools of Bibles printed in Spanish. Mora had been so taken with the idea of circulating the Bible and providing an impetus to reading in the primary schools that he himself had translated the Book of Luke into Nahuatl.[31] By mid-century, however, the work of Protestants in spreading Bibles and New Testaments through primary schools was seen as a source of discord among the Mexican peoples. Opponents of Protestantism and religion in public education pointed to the divisive implications they found in the fact that agents of the Protestant societies studied Indian languages: the study of Indian languages and the provision of reading materials in these tongues worked against the unity of the nation.[32]

The revolution of 1855 turned Santa Anna and his conservatives out of power and initiated a chaotic period during which liberals and conservatives vied for power, the nation suffered foreign intervention, and Maximilian, Archduke of Hapsburg, established a short-lived empire. In 1867, Benito Juárez, an Indian from Oaxaca who placed his hopes for the Indian in public education, became president. The Constitution of 1857, enacted in an earlier decade, provided for free secular education and laid the legislative groundwork for future progress in the unification of Mexico's citizens. However, the turbulence of the years between 1855 and 1867 had prevented both national and local leaders from carrying into action a public education program and from considering specific problems such as language diversity. A single event occurred during the period of Maximilian's empire, which did, however, foreshadow two trends the positivists of the next decade would follow as they accorded the language problem major considerations and as they recognized Indian contributions to Mexico's history. During Maximilian's short reign in Mexico (1862-1867), Mariano Jacobo Rojas, a young man from Tepoztlan, Morelos, had an interview with the emperor in which he convincingly presented the case for bilingual education in the Indian villages. Both Spanish and the Indian language of the area would be included in the primary-school curriculum, and the use of native instructors and the Indians' own tongues would ease the Indian children's transition from the home to the public school.[33] Though the emperor, a devoted student of indigenous cultures in Mexico, did not initiate such a program in education, he did begin to issue his decrees in both Spanish and Nahuatl.[34]

Neither independence, the philosophical assumptions and arguments of the liberal and conservative intellectuals in the years after independence, nor the Lancasterian vogue and the short-lived program of Gómez Farías focused the nation's attention on the problem of a separate series of Indian cultures. Though legally considered citizens if they fitted themselves into the creole mold and abandoned their village, customs, and language, the majority of the Indians maintained their insular state to the satisfaction of Mora and others who insisted "the Mexican character" should be sought only in those of pure European descent. To be sure, the early national leaders' efforts to provide educational opportunities for "the poor" as well as "the rich," and the occasional recognition by less influential commentators of the multilingual and multicultural state of the nation may have helped pave the way for a more realistic consideration of problems in the future. Progress, however, in the selection and initiation of a program for the acceptance of a national language had to wait for the stimulus of positivism in education and the rise to influence of social scientists.

Confirming a National Standard

When the Constitution of 1857 declared that education would be free and secular, there were those who saw in this move an opportunity to confront directly the question of linguistic diversity in Mexico. Ignacio Ramírez, governor of the state of Mexico, a member of Benito Juárez's cabinet, and one of that group of thinkers generally known as "positivists," agreed with his liberal predecessors who assumed that among those traditions of Spain to be preserved in the new nation was the Castilian tongue. However, Ramírez argued strongly against denying the existence of *los indios* and their idioms in Mexico. He based his plan for bilingual education, which provided for instruction in both Indian tongues and Spanish in schools within the Indian areas, on a keen awareness of the economic and cultural differences within the nation. Liberal and conservative spokesmen before Ramírez had either ignored these differences or, if admitting them, had denied they were the result of "Indianness;" they had proposed that equality of educational opportunity and the resulting civilization of "those called Indians" would bring "the poor" to Mexican citizenship.

Ramírez proclaimed that such conclusions were neither practical for educational policy-making nor consistent with economic facts. Meaningful citizenship meant nothing less than the ability to participate effectively in the economic opportunities of the local area as well as to know and understand the politics of the nation. For this objective, workers, artisans, farmers, soldiers and domestic servants needed instruction in two languages—the national standard and the local Indian tongue. Maya was the choice for the Yucatan peninsula, Nahuatl for Puebla.[35] Ramírez decried the uselessness of any instruction which did not take into account the occupational choices open to students. Classical studies were useless in areas where children who entered school remained only a year or so. He pleaded for practical teaching during the students' abbreviated terms in school: reading, writing, simple mathematics, and living languages useful in the students' own world.[36] Ramírez firmly supported the psychological benefits promised by the use of Indian tongues for instruction: "the indigenous will never attain true civilization, unless their intelligence is cultivated through the natural tool of the idiom in which they think and live."[37] He urged the immediate publication in indigenous languages of materials for village schools.[38]

Ramírez centered his program for language instruction

around practical considerations which he judged necessary for a realistic program of national unification. Foreign languages, such as French and English, had no place in the curriculum of a nation which needed to know itself and to educate eight million people in the tongues they used in everyday affairs: "the teaching of foreign languages is an absurdity. What kind of instruction is it when we are not able to account for our own fundamental language and when we cannot communicate with our own fellow citizens?"[39] Spreading publications and instruction in both Spanish and the Indian languages would bring the peoples of the new nation together, aware of their history and proud of being able to cooperate and communicate. Ramírez insisted that Nahuatl and other Indian tongues such as Maya, Otomi, Tarascan, and Zapotec, if sanctioned by the government for use in literature and history, would raise the level of interest, culture, and participation by those segments of the nation's population which "preserve in silence their history and original idioms."[40]

Furthermore, Ramírez argued that democratic participation by the Indians could never be possible so long as they were locked in their Indian nationalities by the barrier of language. Using Spanish only in sterile formulae and expressions of courtesy and obedience in the market and the Spanish master's home, the Indian did not consider Spanish a way out of his drudgery but rather a sign of his exploitation. If the languages of the Indians were to be used as tools for fostering participation at the local level of politics, the federal government should make territorial divisions on the basis of languages. The Indians should be encouraged to administer their area affairs and work under the central government. Ramírez suggested the Mexican nation might never be able to claim the Indians as members of the national community without due consideration of the "little nations" within the country's boundaries. Speaking to his fellow legislators in 1856, Ramírez had reasoned:

You wish to form a stable territorial division of the elements this nation possesses? Elevate the Indians to the rank of citizens; give them a direct influence in public affairs; but begin separating them by languages. In no other way is it possible to distribute our sovereignty over two million free men and six million slaves.[41]

What was new in Ramírez's language policy was not its end result but rather its plan of action—separate in order to unify. States organized on the basis of linguistic and cultural unities could control their own educational systems and train confident leaders to act as mediators between their own culture and that of the nation. Knowing their state's felt needs and cultural ways, local leaders could relate these to national political leaders and, in turn, determine the most effective means of transmitting national influence to the local levels.

Though certainly no other positivist directed himself so consistently to the problem of language unity as did Ramírez, other positivists did emphasize the need to integrate the Mexican peoples—socially, morally, and intellectually—but their method depended not on separation by linguistic divisions but rather on social and intellectual union through science. Gabino Barreda, fresh from studies under Auguste Comte in Paris and chief of the Commission of Public Instruction in 1867, viewed the transformation of the mentality of Mexicans as the primary mission of national education. Educated Mexicans were to pry themselves from their chaotic past and to impose order on the new society through the development of order and logic in their intellectual pursuits. The utilitarianism and scientific approach of the positivists supported the founding of instruction on social needs and the observation of experience. Barreda established the National Preparatory School as the most important educational center in the nation; he reorganized its curriculum to provide a maximum exposure to science and language study.[42] Politicians and educators imbued with positivism under Barreda were to influence Mexican educational ideas well into the twentieth century. The gap between verbal support of positivism and the actions it prompted was, however, extreme. By 1882, positivism was strongly denounced for its dogmatic stance and failure to prompt any noticeable improvement in national primary education. During the 1880's, political and educational leaders tried to transform the abstract philosophical notions of Barreda into workable measures; they carefully oriented rural teachers to the national scheme of education and they brought into the open the question of the Indian's intellectual potential for education.

The Minister of Justice and Public Instruction, Joaquín

Baranda, devised three steps in his program to improve primary instruction throughout the nation: first, provide a national teacher-training school; second, make primary instruction compulsory in the Federal District and build an elementary school system to serve as an example for the states; third, involve the states in debates over national educational policy-making. Baranda succeeded in all three phases of his program. The Normal School began operating in 1887; the Law of Compulsory Instruction was passed in 1888; the First Congress of Instruction convened in 1889.[43] Baranda called together representatives from all the states and asked for a general endorsement of popular education as the basic force behind the development of a unified Mexico. Two corollaries to Baranda's banner cause rode in on the assembly's mood of serious dedication: the states' acceptance of the responsibility to promote free compulsory primary instruction, and the firm espousal of faith in the Indian's intellectual capabilities. The Congress members recognized initially that uniformity had to be an ideal; moreover, compulsory primary-school instruction was the key to raising the general cultural level of the nation's masses and, hence, to achieving meaningful national unification. Though federalism prevented the First Congress of Instruction and the 1888 Law of Compulsory Instruction from extending direct national control of education to the states, Baranda enthusiastically advertised educational activities in the capital as a source of influence for the states' establishment of "national Mexican schools." Baranda saw elementary-school instruction in the Federal District as a model for the states, and he promoted instruction in the capital for teachers from Indian areas so that they might receive special preparation for directing rural schools and teaching in the indigenous tongues. Traveling teachers would have to carry to the countryside the ideals of the nation—the national language, civic instruction, and moral practices. "National Mexican schools" were to nationalize the culture of the nation's masses.[44]

To an extraordinary degree, the work of the 1889 First Congress of Instruction laid the foundation for the expansion of education theories upon which twentieth-century education practices would build. Foremost was the rejection of the racial inferiority of the Indian. The assembly delegates affirmed their faith in the Indian's intellectual abilities and potential for educational success by approving the majority report of the committee on compulsory elementary education. The report firmly rejected the notion of the intellectual inferiority of the Indian. The committee maintained that when the Mexican nation integrated the Indian into a uniform educational system, the myth of his inferiority would disappear, as he proved himself capable of the same academic achievements as the white man and the mestizo. This endorsement of the Indian's equality was basic to the general trend to see the Mexican heritage as a fusion of the cultural contributions of both Spaniard and Indian. Language was the first aspect of culture to be viewed in this new light. The First Congress of Instruction expressed a firm conviction in the central position of language in Mexico's popular education system. Basic to the curriculum, language instruction was now to correlate materials for reading and writing with the natural spoken standard and to encourage children to direct their attention to the speech they heard around them. Mexico confirmed her national tongue:

> not pure Spanish, but Spanish molded through a unique national social and physical makeup, through the remaining portions of those civilizations now partially disappeared, and through the creative circumstances that in Mexico have produced the mutual interfusion of the races.[45]

The national language of Mexico was to be the more Mexican for contributions from Indian tongues.

The recognition of Mexico's indigenous heritage made Indian culture a fashionable topic, capable of drawing government support and serious scholarly attention. The curiosity which had led a few politicians in the nation's early history to become amateur archaeologists and to read the works of foreigners on Mexico's Indian civilizations now became an important popular and academic interest for Mexicans.[46] A monument to the Aztec emperor Cuauhtémoc on the Paseo de la Reforma in Mexico City embodied Mexico's new-found esteem for her Indian ancestors. Mitla, Teotihuacán, and other archaeological sites drew national attention, and historians of ancient Mexico received government aid and occupied special chairs at the National Museum of Archaeology, Ethnology, and History. The writings of these scholars, who lived in the midst of the capital's flurry of enthusiasm for scientific studies, began to gain considerable recognition. During the last half of the nineteenth century, at least 100 scholars produced writings on the Indian languages of Mexico.[47] The Mexican Academy, a sister institution of Madrid's Royal Academy of Spanish, was founded in 1875, and one of its most prominent leaders was Joaquín García Icazbalceta, whose contributions to the Academy's *Memoria* included a defense of regional differences in Mexican Spanish and a compilation of "Mexicanisms."[48] Whereas just a half century earlier *el criollo mexicano* had called for a strict imitation of the language of Spain, the sophisticated Mexican of the late nineteenth century proudly claimed an evolved national standard which was the special product of his unique history.

Faith in Indian equality, acceptance of the Mexican heritage as Spanish and Indian, endorsement of unification through language instruction in the new national standard, and recognition of the need for scientific studies of indigenous cultures—these were the basic assumptions of the decision-makers of the 1880's and 1890's. To be sure, a paradox pervades modern interpretations of positivism during this period. On the one hand, the racist theories of Francisco Bulnes have repeatedly been identified as the essence of Social Darwinism endorsed by Porfirio Díaz's *científicos*, a group of intellectuals who emphasized scientific rather than metaphysical approaches. Bulnes flatly stated that the Indian's steady diet of corn had "dulled" his mental capacities, and he could never participate effectively in the same educational scheme as white men.[49] Francisco G. Cosmes, an editor of the positivist daily newspaper *La Libertad* strongly resisted proposals to include Indians in any education, save perhaps some contact with new agricultural methods. As beasts of burden and servants of the ruling classes for centuries, the Indians were incapable of being civilized. Furthermore, their indigenous tongues locked them in mental isolation and sentenced to failure all attempts to educate them in a popular school system which had to use Spanish as the medium of instruction.[50] On the other hand, there is a considerable list of positivists who derided the notions of the strict Spencerians and set forth theories which have been designated a fundamental influence on reform programs of the early twentieth century. Most outspoken of this group of positivists was

Justo Sierra, a member of virtually every committee which had supported Baranda's education programs, and later Secretary of Public Instruction and Fine Arts. Again and again, he affirmed his faith in the power of compulsory primary instruction to transform the Indians. Science could make them rational beings who would learn to turn away from drunkenness and superstition. The barrier of their indigenous tongues would be overcome by scientific methods and orderly planning. The Normal School in the capital would instruct teachers in an indigenous tongue; these teachers would be assigned to an area where they might use the Indian language as a basis for teaching Spanish.[51]

Numerous scholars, however, saw no progress for the Indian in purely academic studies and verbal statements of praise for indigenous cultural contributions. Díaz, though occasionally showing a passing romantic appreciation for Mexico's Indian ancestry, did no more than politely applaud efforts to provide education for the Indians. He set aside any social changes which might threaten the civil peace vital to financial stability, material progress, and the continuance of his own power. While leaving the Law of Compulsory Instruction on the books, Díaz left the application of the law in the Federal District and the extension of its influence to the states to the discretion of local authorities and virtual immobilization by a limited budget.[52] Hence, social scientists not directly linked to the decision-making center of the government pressed Díaz's intellectuals to use their influence to force the government to turn theory into action. Sociologists urged these prominent citizens to direct their scholarly concern for the Indian languages and cultures toward the initiation of practical measures for the "redemption of the Indian." Rafael de Zayas Enríquez pointed an accusing finger at not only conquerors and Spanish colonists, but also creoles who had maintained a racist policy of exclusion for the Indians. He strongly denounced the irrationality of shutting the Indians out of political and social participation because some scholars thought they had found signs of the Indians' natural subservience and primitiveness in the structure of their languages. Zayas Enríquez recommended forming societies to protect the Indians, to educate them, to reward parents for sending their children to school, and to promote the general improvement of Indian groups in the nation. Sociologists strongly suggested that policy-makers needed to know more about the day-by-day existence of the Indian. Officials should be forced to attend state programs of education to learn about area Indians.[53] Abraham Castellanos extended the notion of enlightening leaders by advocating the teaching of anthropological topics in the normal schools. He firmly believed a knowledge of the personality, customs, and religion of the Indians necessary before educators could plan integral programs of "transformation" for the Indians of each region.[54] These sociologists emphasized the need for further statistical data on the Indians, so that educational policy-makers might construct their programs with the reality of figures before them.

Social scientists' growing interest in the Indian and their desire to influence policy-making led to the formation of societies for the study of the Indian. Bulletins disseminated information collected by members of the Mexican Society of Geography and Statistics and the Mexican Indianist Society. The latter society, founded in 1910 by Francisco Belmar, a linguist and author of numerous studies of Indian languages in the late nineteenth and early twentieth centuries, had as its objective "the study of our indigenous races in order to promote their evolution." [55] The publication in this Society's *Boletín* of linguistic analyses of indigenous tongues accentuated for education officials the variety of languages in the nation and the difficulties their vastly different structures presented to the Indian child trying to learn Spanish. The leaders of the Society were determined to emphasize that their goal was unity in language in the nation. But they also desperately wanted to convince political officials that this objective could be reached more efficiently and effectively if plans for the linguistic education of the Indian children rested on a sound understanding of some basic linguistic and psychological principles. Belmar originally included as two of the primary aims of the Society "the knowledge and study of the Indian tongues in a purely linguistic sense" and "the extension of the use of Castilian among the indigenous." [56]

Porfirio Díaz, terming the Society "a beautiful idea," brought his cabinet to the first Congress of the Indianist Society on October 30, 1910. This prestigious captive audience prompted Indianists to condemn severely past treatment of the Indian and to demand immediate radical reforms. Díaz refused their proposals for "political and economic reasons." Rebuffed by the government's refusal to activate the Society's suggestions, Belmar proposed that future sessions be closed to "enemies of the indigenous race." The Society also refused to ask financial aid from the Secretary of Public Instruction, for fear criticisms of official programs involving the Indian would be muzzled.[57] The second president of the Mexican Indianist Society, Dr. Jesús Díaz de León, chose also not to align the Society closely with any government agency and insisted on the practical scientific approach the group would take in its evaluation of government programs for the Indian. During his administration, the government's formerly quiet resistance to the social scientists' ideas grew more vocal.

In effect, Díaz de León invited outspoken opposition when he made it clear that the Indianist Society did not favor the destruction of the Indian tongues. He reasoned that, though certainly the Spanish tongue was the "vital nexus" of Mexican political unity, the Indians should not forget their tongues; instead, they should learn Spanish as a second language to function primarily in the sphere of their political relations with the national government. Linguists should continue to study the indigenous tongues in order to assist archaeologists in unlocking the secrets of the ancient civilizations. But, more important, linguists must prepare agricultural and industrial arts manuals in the indigenous languages, so that the Indians could turn to these sources to direct their own progress in these important work areas.[58] This statement and others like it, which suggested that the indigenous languages be preserved alongside the national standard, brought cries of outrage from politicians and formulators of educational policy. Positivist Justo Sierra, ever fearful the delicate balance between Hispanic and Indian would be tipped by the Indianists, firmly denounced the Society's philosophy. Sierra recoiled from any notion that denied the bond which conformity in language provided a nation. He threw aside the pleas of the Indianists for the retention of indigenous tongues and proclaimed:

The polyglot state of our country is an obstacle to the extension of our culture and the full formation of the conscience of our fatherland. Only by means of compulsory public education throughout our entire nation, will we be able to avert disaster. . . . we call Spanish the national language.

[We do so] not only because it is the tongue that the actual Mexican society has always spoken, and because it is the nation's inheritance, but also because, as the only scholastic language, it will cause the atrophy and destruction of local idioms. Thus it will bring about the unification of national speech, the essential force behind social unification.[59]

Sierra firmly opposed the maintenance of the Indian tongues for any functional purposes they might serve the speakers. These languages were to be viewed as "simple archaeological documents." [60]

How then could Sierra explain the use of the Indian tongues in preparatory schools which had as one of their basic objectives the teaching of the national idiom? His answer implied a basic understanding of the bilingual method and the intermediate use of indigenous tongues en route to the acceptance of the national standard:

to teach the indigenous idioms to the teachers of the Indians has for us the prime objective of destroying them, of teaching to all the Castilian language, and of thus overcoming this formidable barrier to the unification of the Mexican people.[61]

As Minister of Education, he had an unswaying faith in the ideal of the creation of a national consciousness through obligatory education in the Spanish tongue. During the last years of Díaz's regime, an official publication found it necessary to declare that in spite of the two million individuals who spoke an indigenous tongue belonging to one of thirteen different families, Spanish was the idiom of the "entire social, educational and political life of the Republic," and the Indian languages had no influence over "the destinies of the nation." [62] Díaz himself proudly pointed to accomplishments the Federal District had made in teaching Spanish to the Indians; in a speech given before Congress in 1900, he noted that 364 children in the district of Xochimilco had been taught Spanish since 1896.[63] He, like his Minister of Education, assumed stability and progress in the nation demanded a unity of tongue and the creation by obligatory education of what Sierra termed a "Mexican soul." The school was central to the accomplishment of these aims: "the school has to be the hearth where the national unity is forged . . .; there we have to confirm the unity and the persistence of our language, the consolidation of our character."[64] Within the Mexican soul, the Spanish tongue persisted as a unique instrument of "supreme unification." The national standard had been confirmed by politicians, educators, and social scientists. Spanish was the language of unity; on this point decision-makers and local change agents generally agreed. But how were they to deal with the indigenous tongues and initiate an effective program to foster the Indians' acceptance of the national language and admission to Mexico's national community?

In the context of an intensifying upheaval in the countryside over inequities in the social system, many intellectuals grew convinced that Díaz's price for stability and progress had been too high, and too few had profited at the expense of too many. In repudiating Díaz, the privileged classes, and despotism, Mexico's revolutionary intellectuals rejected both the scientific pretension and the passive posture of the científicos. Intellectuals of diverse social backgrounds joined together to challenge, broaden, and, most importantly, to activate the education theory positivism had provided since the 1880's. Widespread apathy toward the Indian was superseded by pressure for civic participation, neglect by the development of a public sense of responsibility, and self-preservation by the call for sacrifice. By 1910, intellectuals were warning politicians not to talk further of unification without social reforms. Ceremonial solutions of social problems congenial to political authoritarianism stood challenged by the mood of reform and revolution.

CHAPTER FIVE

Spanish and the Plan for Conformity

Incorporation through Education

The first shots of the Revolution of 1910 and the cry for more schools, coupled with the threat which politicians saw in the implications of periodic pronouncements on the deplorable state of the Indian, had to elevate unification through education to a level of highest priority. In 1909 Andrés Molina Enríquez, in his important book, *Los grandes problemas nacionales,* noted the diversity of customs, languages, opportunities, and social histories which divided Mexican classes. Though creoles had condemned the illiteracy which cut Indians off from participation in the national interests, the elites had made no provisions for educating the Indians and transferring their community loyalties to the nation as a whole. Special programs to develop the Indians' devotion to their fatherland had to serve as a fulcrum to move the total unification program of Mexico.[1] Before a committee planning the Independence Centennial celebration, one speaker reminded his audience that in spite of the nation's official declaration that Spanish was the national standard, there were millions who neither knew Spanish nor realized they were citizens of Mexico.[2] Empty rhetoric proclaiming the unification of the Mexican peoples had prompted very few practical efforts to place the national language at the center of a primary-school curriculum which would move the Indians from their closed communities to an open national society.

In a fit of nationalistic fervor, politicians looked to the diversity of tongues as a first consideration for a realistic education program. The platform of the Popular Evolutionary Party, published in June of 1911, included as one of its major goals: "the diffusion of rudimentary instruction throughout the Republic, and most especially among the indigenous, teaching them to speak, read, and write Castilian."[3] Under the influence of education leaders Gregorio Torres Quintero and Jorge Vera Estañol, the Law of Rudimentary Instruction was executed in 1911. This law authorized the federal government to establish pre-primary rural schools which would supposedly, in two years, teach the Indian-speaking population, males and females of all ages, to speak, read, and write Spanish and handle the fundamentals of arithmetic.[4]

Opponents of the law judged it absurd to think that the teaching of the alphabet and the national language would transform the Indian in any meaningful way. With limited funds and no real federal authority over state schools, the political leaders could not hope, by the mere passage of an utopian law, to wipe out Indian languages and thus to produce a countryside of literate citizens. Torres Quintero's plan could not do anything but fail in its essential purpose: "to teach *principally the individuals of the indigenous race* to speak, read, and write Castilian,"[5] for it had aimed at "redeeming" not only school children but also the adult Indian population. Indian parents had neither the desire nor the leisure time to leave their cornfields and attend school to learn a language which was of no use to them in the daily life of their communities. Alberto Pani, Undersecretary of Education, proposed that instead of the literacy schools provided for in the Law of Rudimentary Instruction, the federal government place industrial and agricultural schools in Indian areas and encourage the Indians to try to raise their standard of living in practical ways. When two-thirds of the population were Indians in need of being "civilized," the teaching of the fundamentals of literacy seemed totally insufficient.[6] The more pessimistic opponents of rudimentary instruction argued that because of the Conquest and the extreme division historically maintained between Hispanic and Indian, there could never be any unity in Mexico except perhaps territorial unity. A soldier of the Revolution wrote Pani asking: "The Indians who might fight off a foreign invasion—why would they fight? In order to defend their right to die from hunger and to remain landless? for tradition? for language? for religion?"[7] There were few bonds to link the Mexican peoples against even a common enemy.

By 1917, it was possible to distinguish two chief strains of feeling in those calling for national linguistic unity. The first, more tradition-bound than innovative, more positivistic than radical in its outlook, represented the roots of conservatism. Torres Quintero, this group's spokesman and author of the Law of Rudimentary Instruction, favored only a traditional curriculum for the Indians. He agreed they might need a headstart of one to two years pre-primary language instruction, but once they entered primary schools, they were to follow the standard program of instruction. He emphatically objected to teaching Spanish through the intermediate use of indigenous languages:

Teaching them in their language contributes to the conservation of the native tongue, an idea which might seem beautiful and desirable to linguists and antiquarians, but [these native tongues] are a persistent and serious obstacle to civilization and to the formation of the national soul. If we do not teach the Indian in his native tongue, he will find it necessary to learn Spanish . . . and forget his native language.[8]

Torres Quintero pointed to the success of the military in teaching Spanish to the Indians who served during the Revolution and to the pedagogical reasons for the success of teaching in the language to be learned. Politicians and educators who joined Torres Quintero in support of a policy which would not provide any special program or privileges in education for the Indian were extremely suspicious of linguists, anthropologists, and other social scientists who supported special consideration for the indigenous.

This group, representing the second interpretation of patriotic and linguistic sentiments, had spoken out through the Mexican Indianist Society for a special program of education—a program based on social-science principles and an understanding of diverse Indian cultures. They had argued against Torres Quintero and his supporters at the First Mexican Scientific Congress in 1912. Now they were growing more determined to pressure political leaders to hear them and to adopt their methods in integration plans for the Indians. The anthropologist Manuel Gamio published a work entitled *Forjando Patria (Pro Nacionalismo)* in 1916, which pointed out the differences between the Indianists and their opponents and summarized the debates which had helped determine language policy and pedagogy since Independence. The "sociological myopia" of Mora and the reformers before Ignacio Ramírez had kept them from acknowledging the Indian majority of the population. In the 1880's, nationalistic fervor and the flurry of scientific activities designed to reveal the Indians' contributions to the "true history" of the nation had raised the central question of whether the six million Indians could and should embrace the ideals and culture of the Hispanic-oriented population. Gamio pointed out that the regionalism evident in every aspect of culture in such areas as the Yucatan peninsula had to be both respected and recognized by the nation's leaders. The assumption that literacy would produce the miracle of transformation for the starving and illiterate rural population had to be replaced with a more realistic approach to public education. The heterogeneity of the population, the diversity of languages, and the wide divergence in the ideologies of the various Indian groups demanded a new orientation—nationalistic integral education. Justo Sierra and other educators of the late nineteenth century had also spoken of "integral education," but for them the term suggested classical studies to train the mind. Gamio's "nationalistic integral education" was to be founded on information gained from the anthropologist's investigation of the aggregate of sociocultural factors contributing to an individual's socialization within a particular environment. Political, economic, social, and linguistic factors formed the cultural web into which government policy-makers had to integrate formal education. Neither the fundamentals of literacy and mathematics nor the disciplines of a uniform traditional curriculum could transform the Indians. The cultural evolution of the Mexican nation required special methods, teachers, and materials, in a holistic education program.[9]

The disruption caused by the Revolution and the political and social devastation of its wake allowed little opportunity for the implementation of a new approach to linguistic and cultural integration programs. Nevertheless, the period after 1910 produced many ideas which the members of the Constitutional Convention of 1917 considered in drawing up plans for education under the new constitution. The future of a national language policy rested on the matter of whether the new constitution would provide for federal control over education in the states, so crucial to providing an opportunity for the methods and principles of social scientists to disseminate from the capital in government-sponsored programs of education. If schools were to be the major agent of unification, the responsibility for rural education could not remain in the hands of local authorities, those who most frequently feared they had much to lose if the Indians were educated and learned to speak Spanish. The rudimentary schools had fulfilled the dire predictions of their opponents: by 1914, the height of the extension of rudimentary instruction, the federal government had been able to provide only 300 schools for the eleven million illiterates of the nation.[10] Local bosses had grown accustomed to the silence of school houses, and they influenced President Venustiano Carranza to support the omission of primary schools from federal authority in the Constitution of 1917. Article 3 guaranteed free and secular primary education; Article 31 made attendance at either private or public schools compulsory for persons under fifteen years of age, but the responsibility for rural education rested with local leaders.[11]

Against the tide of opposition to federal control over education, however, friends of the Indian exerted considerable force. On the floor of the Constitutional Convention, Félix F. Palavicini, Carranza's Secretary of Public Instruction, had thrown out an unforgettable challenge to his fellow politicians: "The Indians ... are the outcry of our conscience; they represent our greatest sin. Through the streets and plazas, they carry not only the weight of three centuries of colonization, but also the burden of a century of creole domination." [12] Though the Constitution itself did not meet this challenge to rectify the errors of the past, Carranza was willing to sanction limited programs incorporating new methods and approaches. In 1917 Carranza established a Bureau of Anthropology and Regional Populations to initiate Gamio's proposed nationalistic integral education.[13] Ten zones were selected, the populations of which represented diverse cultural, racial, economic, and linguistic histories. Each year, one or two zones were to become the central project for the Bureau. The only project ever completed through all stages of Gamio's plan was that one located in the valley of Teotihuacán. This area was the first chosen because of its proximity to the capital, its growing popularity as a tourist area, and its potential for showing off the success of the integral method. Among the aims of the program was the linguistic unification of the Indians. The achievement of this goal depended on a school in which the teachers used a program of direct teaching of Spanish. The instructors taught in the language to be learned and provided the children with texts written in Spanish. Their new language was only one of the recommended cultural habits which would enable the Indians to function as national citizens. The program was designed to select and conserve those values most useful to the Indian in his role as a national citizen and to exterminate those prejudicial to his full incorporation in the larger society.[14] Gamio's project report, which revealed that a great many people in Teotihuacán had no broader concept of "fatherland" than the village in which they had been born, shocked government officials, and they allowed the Bureau of Anthropology to continue its activities until 1925, though the grandiose plans to extend Gamio's integral approach to the nine other regions originally selected never materialized.[15]

As President Alvaro Obregón took office in 1921, leaders came into power who were not satisfied with Gamio's regional approach and felt the nation was ready to grant schools and hence to fulfill one of the promises of the Revolution. These politicians also saw the cohesive potential in the spreading of national values through a public school system administered by the federal government. The Constitution of 1917 was amended in 1921 to give the central government the power to establish, organize, and maintain all kinds of schools and educational institutions throughout the republic and to legislate in all matters related to these institutions.[16] José Vasconcelos, rector of the National University and author of the constitutional changes which provided for federal administration of rural schools, was given complete authority to organize the new system of public education. Vasconcelos' recommendations to the Congress outlined the structure of the Ministry of Public Education, to be headed by a Secretary of

Public Education with control over departments of schools, libraries, and fine arts. Much to Vasconcelos' chagrin, Congress added to his proposals the departments of Indian Culture and the Campaign against Illiteracy.[17] Vasconcelos' philosophy and carefully conceived plans did not include any such authorities, and he bristled at the very idea of separate provisions for the education of the Indian. Vasconcelos opposed both the integral action of Manuel Gamio, which had broken the nation into ten Indian regions for special projects of education and improvement, and the assimilation techniques which the North Americans pursued in their special Indian schools. According to Vasconcelos' interpretation, anthropological and scientific study of the cultural quirks of diverse Indian groups in the regions designated by Gamio served only to accentuate the Indian's separateness. Moreover, anthropologists were doing nothing more than patterning after the North American system of reservations and substituting the term "region" for "reservation." As Secretary of Education, Vasconcelos proposed that Mexico adopt a policy of "incorporation" through a national school system. No separate scientific studies of Indian cultures and no unique pedagogical methods for the Indian were to be necessary for Mexico's program of redemption and incorporation: "the policy of educating the Indian . . . according to separate standards of any sort, is not only absurd among us, but it would be fatal." [18]

Unification through a national school system was the supreme goal of the Ministry of Public Education, and if money and personnel were not available, Vasconcelos reasoned that he could turn to the masses for help. As an anti-positivist, Vasconcelos chose not science but the moral authority of the classics as his source of inspiration. He believed Dante, Homer, Pérez Galdós, and Tolstoy could direct men to the highest standards of morality and hence to participation in the Mexican democracy. This faith in the teachings of the classics led him to distribute Spanish editions among the illiterate Indians of rural areas; but more importantly, it helped inspire him to imbue his cultural missionaries with a sense of moral purpose.[19] Vasconcelos sent these young recruits from the preparatory schools of Mexico City into the Indian villages to carry the "good news" of redemption through hard work, self-discipline, and responsibility in freedom. Dedication to these virtues could bring schools to even the poorest village, for, if through their own labor and sacrifices the villagers provided a school building, the federal government would send a teacher. In each cooperating village the "house of the people" (*casa del pueblo*), Vasconcelos' rural school, became a reality. To a large extent the aim of these schools was the same as that of rudimentary schools in the past decade: to bring Indians of all ages to a knowledge of Spanish and the rudiments of civilization necessary for participation in the national culture. However, the "houses of the people" carried their aims further and included practical instruction in handicrafts and agricultural techniques. Ideally, three types of "houses" were proposed: the rudimentary, which was to teach Spanish, and the elementary and the consolidated, which were to carry out the traditional curriculum. However, only the rudimentary was ever begun, and this type functioned primarily in areas where the population was already bilingual. Large areas inhabited by monolingual Indian populations were not touched.[20]

Realizing that traditional teacher-training methods found in Mexico City's colleges could not produce successful teachers for work in the remote villages, Vasconcelos organized experts and teachers into "cultural missions" and sent them out to help retrain teachers already in the field. The first consisted of Rafael Ramírez (who was later to serve as director of the Department of Cultural Missions and head of the Department of Rural Schools), a soapmaker, tanner, music teacher, and doctor. Later groups included agronomists, carpenters, and other professionals. The task of the cultural missions was to travel to state centers, offer a brief introduction to the highly varied and special skills necessary for rural teachers, rekindle the community's enthusiasm for the school as a cooperative project, and then move on to encourage and aid teachers in other regions.[21]

Language training was one aspect of the rural teachers' deficiencies Vasconcelos was not prepared to admit. Though his representatives in the field reported to him the need for teachers with a knowledge of the Indian languages, the Secretary of Education was too much the Hispanophile to admit the indigenous tongues as an instrument of education. Though Vasconcelos talked of the fusion of the European and the Indian to create the mestizo Mexican of the future, he made a special point of denouncing the linguistic aspect of Indian culture; indigenous tongues had to be exterminated and replaced with the Spanish language. Vasconcelos maintained the Indian had no civilized standard common to all members of his race; the Indian, therefore, had to be forced to recognize the victory of the Spanish spirit in language. Even in the midst of Emilio Zapata's popular movement which broadened the definition of the Indian, Vasconcelos believed the Spanish tongue had manifested itself over the indigenous idioms. The leader of Zapata's revolt had spoken Spanish, a fact Vasconcelos interpreted as showing that even representatives of the Indianist spirit in the Revolution recognized the Spanish language was superior and to be preferred over the Indian tongues. To Vasconcelos, there could be no doubt of this thesis, for the Spanish language belonged to "one of the most illustrious 'races' of the world." [22] Furthermore, Vasconcelos contended, there were actually very few members of the nation who did not know Spanish. The results of the 1920 census which reported 4,179,499 Indians out of a total population of 14,344,700 did not entirely convince Vasconcelos that any special provisions for Indian education were necessary, but he was forced to concede that some preparatory instruction might be provided "in those rare cases in which the Indian does not know the Spanish language." [23] Teachers were, however, always to bear in mind that they would teach the Indian children Spanish so that the children might then pass into elementary schools where Indians and other Mexicans would receive the same instruction.

Vasconcelos' original scheme of incorporation expanded under Moisés Sáenz, appointed as Undersecretary of Education in 1925 by President Plutarco Elías Calles. Sáenz believed in the improvement of needy collective classes—mestizo subsistence farmers, and poor workers of the large estates and cities, as well as the Indians; only through education could these groups extend their economic opportunities and prepare for a civilized life as members of the Mexican "race." [24] This notion of incorporation, which both admitted and denied the Indian, had been a favorite of some positivist educators, such as Sierra, who though admitting the Indian's ability to contribute to national life denied his "right" to continue his Indian culture. Pre-Revolutionary intellectuals of the early twentieth century had expanded this view, as they maintained that only the incorporated Indian, stripped of his native cultural habits and reclothed in those of the Mexican mestizo "race," could function as an effective member of the modified economic structure. Even Gamio's project at Teotihuacán placed a negative valuation on numerous Indian customs of language, clothing, community structure, and beliefs. Vasconcelos' "cosmic race" exhibited no Indian cultural habits. Distinctions between assimilation as practiced by North Americans and incorporation as embraced by Mexicans existed not in intent, but rather in different methodologies determined by both the size of the indigenous populations and the amount of federal resources available. Whereas the North Americans gathered the Indians on reservations and provided teachers and school buildings to bring about the fusion of separate Indian identities into a national image, the Mexicans sent missionaries and established missions among the Indians. There government representatives urged the Indians to support a venture which discriminated against their culture and propelled their separate tribal identities toward incorporation in a Mexican whole which had not yet resolved the contradictions of its own dualistic base. Creole, mestizo, and Indian were to merge; yet, those who prescribed the ideal Mexican included no aspect of the cultural characteristics from Indian personality. The post-Revolutionary incorporation movement, while professing to include the Indian, resolved to do away with the Indian identity. The ideals of the incorporated nation and the moral redemption of the Indian demanded that he be Hispanicized.

Hence, claiming a new order, the incorporators equated the chaos of languages with a communication vacuum; only a common tongue—Spanish, the idiom of the "people of reason"— could fill the void. Through the Department of Indian Incorporation, Sáenz sent out teachers who spoke the indigenous tongues. These representatives were not to establish formal schools, but rather to hold informal socialization sessions to gain the Indians' trust and to convince them of their need for education and a new tongue. Once the Indians understood the government's ideals, Sáenz reasoned that even hostile Indian tribes would send their children to the rural schools, which were continuing the major purposes and content of the "houses of the people." The rudimentary year of the "houses" was replaced with the rural school's preparatory grade, which had a single purpose: "to teach the Indian children Spanish, since a common idiom is a culture's most valuable tool and the strongest link by which we may join these children to the customs and goals of the Mexican family." [25] This preparatory year was to incorporate the young Indian into the "little society" of the school, a culture alien to his home life; his entire scholastic education was to incorporate him into the civilized life of the nation.

The federal rural schools, of which there were 3,594 in 1930, incorporated the children through a formal program of instruction, which included language learning as a key portion of the curriculum. The first half of the elementary school year was spent in learning the language through oral practice; the second half of the first year, the children wrote exercises, using phrases from daily activities; they continued practicing these skills through the second year. The third year brought writing projects, such as letters and original compositions in Spanish, and reading in easy readers prepared for the rural schools. These standardized texts were to help teachers "correct regional defects in the language," as well as cultivate a patriotic attitude toward the collective nationality.[26] Teaching the national language was basic to the program for the cultural incorporation of the Indian and maintenance of the national ideal of solidarity. To this end of achieving "a harmonious and homogeneous unity out of the various social groups," plays with national legends and traditions, as well as public readings and radio broadcasts, were used.[27] Both Sáenz and Rafael Ramírez (Chief of the Department of Cultural Missions in 1927) pushed the dual goals of teaching the national language and fostering a sense of Mexico's history in the rural schools, cultural missions, and the recently established Rural Regional Normal Schools.

In all these institutions, teachers depended on the direct method of teaching Spanish. Lessons and texts in rural schools were in Castilian; learning through participation in the missions depended on the Spanish tongue. In addition to some introduction to the three R's, Indian children learned new methods of cooking, sewing, and tanning. Students were to communicate directly in Spanish with teachers in varied activities which provided opportunities for conversation and a natural vocabulary increase. Rafael Ramírez, in his training programs for rural teachers, proscribed the use of Indian tongues. He warned his teachers that if they used the Indian languages in the rural schools, they were not furthering the Indians' incorporation, but they themselves were in danger of being "incorporated" by the Indians. Children must learn Spanish as they had learned their native tongues; translation of school information into the Indian languages was a circuitous route to teaching and had no place in schools of incorporation.[28] Similarly, the plan of studies in the rural normal schools emphasized *la lengua nacional,* and teachers were impressed again and again with the notion that their major purpose was to incorporate the Indians into the general progress of the nation by instilling the values of the nation in the inhabitants of the smallest and most isolated villages.

The Direct Method

The direct method of language instruction, so firmly entrenched in Torres Quintero's rudimentary schools and Vasconcelos' "houses of the people," and endorsed by Ramírez and Sáenz in their enthusiasm for the cultural incorporation of the Indian in Mexican society, had a long history and record of acceptance. Variously called the "imitative," "analytic," "natural," "intuitive," or the "non-translation" method, the system of teaching the language to be learned without using the native language of the student was most frequently termed simply "the direct method."[29] Greeks and Romans, as well as European pedagogues, had valued the method because it did not necessitate translation, but rather allowed the student to assimilate and repeat the new language without translation into his native tongue. Finding its best example in the natural method of verbal acquisition among all infants and young children who, after all, listened from infancy to a "strange" tongue and learned by mimicking, the proponents of the direct method argued that the ear had to be the major organ for the learning of a language. With the direct method, the child heard the term, associated it with a mental image, and upon repetition and practice, the process of the association of the word and the mental image coincided immediately, and in the case of second-language learning, without the intervention of the native tongue. In addition to patterned practice and exercises to prod the memory, auxiliary activities, such as cooking, walking, and viewing maps, were highly valued for their importance in providing the students with a natural increase in vocabulary.[30]

A corollary of the direct method was the proscription of the native tongue. In Mexico, from the time of the initiation of the Law of Rudimentary Instruction until the early 1930's, most politicians or decision-makers in educational policy endorsed the direct method and forbade the Indian the use of his native tongue. Luis Cabrera, philologist and a member of Carranza's cabinet, spoke for a decisive program aimed at the disappearance of the Indian languages: "The problem here is to make the Indian idioms and dialects disappear, and to extend Spanish as the only idiom. The only way to do this is to teach Spanish to the Indians and to proscribe the use of Indian languages." [31] The seriousness of the maintenance of the indigenous languages as barriers to political and social coordination in the nation called for an immediate and definite stand for Spanish for all peoples in Mexico and allowed for no toleration of any educational method which might encourage the Indians in the maintenance of their tongues.[32]

He and others of his thinking argued that the Indian would be so grateful for those educational favors made available to him after the Revolution, he would grab at a chance to forsake his language and habits for "the language of God and of law." [33] Educators caught up in the spirit of incorporation could say of the rural teachers: "The Indians will see in those young whites, coming to them, no longer with the whip of the slave in their hands, but with a heart full of sympathy, the uplifted hand of their white brothers who at last have remembered them." [34] Laboring under the all-too-common belief in the inferiority of the Indian in culture and intelligence, many saw the gift of European culture and ideals—made possible through the acquisition of the Spanish language—as the only hope for the "redemption of the masses" and the Indian's incorporation into the nation.

Education programs have, however, a way of generating criticism from within, and so it was in Mexico. Although some pedagogues were convinced that the Indian could learn, he had failed to do so in rudimentary instruction and in the preparatory year of Sáenz's federal rural schools. By the end of the 1920's, educators began to look for the answer to why the Indian had not been successful in these programs of incorporation. Was the Indian not equal in intelligence? Or was it simply that the right program of de-Indianization had not yet been discovered to force these people to drop their closed-community sentiments? The Secretary of Education under President Calles, José Manuel Puig Casauranc, initiated a project which was to provide conclusive evidence that the Indian could be Mexicanized. The "house of the Indian student" (*casa del estudiante indígena*) began operation in 1926 as the temporary home of 200 students brought from twenty-four different Indian tribes. Here the teachers were to attempt to incorporate the students into the cultural life of Mexico through both a traditional curriculum of studies and opportunities for participation in cultural events of the city. The students were adept at taking on the culture they saw around them, and officials expressed amazement at the capabilities the Indian demonstrated; their performance even surpassed that of other students when the same tests were administered to both the Indians and pupils in Mexico City schools.[35]

The officials who selected the students had tried especially to choose students who knew the Indian tongues, but a large percentage of those who attended the schools were bilingual and some spoke only Spanish. So that the students might more easily be able to leave the school and return to their own regions as teachers and administrators, they were encouraged to form language clubs, use their native tongues outside the classroom, and teach those students who knew only Spanish to speak the Indian tongues of their own region. Outsiders questioned the maintenance of indigenous tongues in the school, an institution supposedly designed to Mexicanize Indian youths. Administrators were forced to explain why they considered Indian languages a definite asset to their future plans for these students. Firmly believing that these Mexicanized Indians could serve as cultural brokers between the nation and their native communities, the school's directors realized the need for the students to communicate in both an Indian tongue and Spanish. Singled out as future directors of rural education in their own regions, students were to leave the school as bicultural, bilingual agents who could effectively serve as examples of the Mexicanized Indian and hence influence other Indians to participate in the nation's education programs.[36]

Within two years, those who had worked most directly with the school concluded that the "house of the Indian student" had proved the Indian could be "redeemed." Though some educators had earlier stated their faith in the Indian's intellectual abilities and potential for equal educational achievement with other citizens, the "house of the Indian student" was now a national showcase of the Indian's capabilities. The Indian students had been so converted to the way of life they found in the city that they chose to remain in Mexico City for further studies; they did not wish to return to the countryside to help their less fortunate fellows. When the expense of the project brought severe criticism, Rafael Ramírez justified the high cost of educating so few by pointing out that the school had served its purpose by "proving that the native stock is capable of redeeming itself through education."[37] Because of its drain on government finances and the disappointment of administrators when the students would not return to their own villages, within two years the school was converted into a rural teacher-training institution, which would require students upon the completion of their stay to return to the rural areas to teach. However, even this plan did not work, for after completing their studies, most of the students wished to continue their schooling in the city; thus they avoided having to return to their native villages. The project was abandoned in 1932.[38]

Though it had not explicitly advocated educating the Indian through any approach other than the direct method of language instruction, the experiment of the "house of the Indian student" did manifest a definite concern with the need for communication with the Indians, which the "natural method" had ignored. Encouraging the students to maintain their native tongues while they absorbed the civilization offered by the city and learned Spanish was a step in the direction of bilingual education. This step was extended in the Centers of Indigenous Education, begun in 1933 with the budget previously assigned to the "house of the

Indian student." Eleven centers, boarding schools for the Indians, functioned in the midst of Indian areas, and these became the focus of cultural incorporation, bringing new methods in all areas of life to the Indian students. These centers did not replace the regular rural schools; instead, they supplemented them by providing socialization in the students' total environment. The children built the schools, planted and plowed the fields, made their own furniture and clothes, and learned skills which they could proudly take back to their own villages. Government officials tried to make certain that teachers in the centers knew the language of their students and were supporters of the *new* integral approach to Indian education. This last was a working plan approximating Manuel Gamio's nationalistic integral education in every way except its omission of the scientific investigations Gamio had proposed as the foundation of regional education programs.

Narciso Bassols, Secretary of Public Education between 1931 and 1934, objected to the founding of rural schools on the premise that the Indian had to be brought to a purely Hispanic way of life. Bassols asserted that regions should be the focal center for a program of education which would provide stimulation for the natural talents and interests of the Indian, while gradually supplying him with some formal schooling. Following these assumptions, the Indian boarding schools were neither to ignore nor to attempt to wipe out Indian values and customs in order to incorporate the natives to Western civilization. The students were taught Spanish in the formal education of the classroom, and they were not forbidden to speak their own tongues in the boarding schools. Upon leaving the Indian centers, the students returned to their villages to introduce technological and public health innovations, or they went on to the rural normal schools to prepare to teach in their native areas. At the rural normal schools, they met students who were not Indians, but who were being trained to speak the local Indian languages.[39]

Educators were therefore moving in principle and practice to a modification of the direct method and to a realization that rural schools of the traditional mold could not incorporate the Indian and move him to adopt the Hispanic way of life. Experience had led policy-makers to realize that teachers in the Indian areas had to know the native tongues in order to communicate effectively with the youngsters and to convince the adults to send their children to school. A basic change in the attitude toward the prestige and functional value which the Indian languages held for the speakers themselves had not taken place in the politicians of the capital. But a realistic approach to the effectiveness of the indigenous language as a tool for the transmission of the national culture to the Indian had led educators to train rural teachers in the local tongues and to try to provide native teachers in regional Indian centers. These centers were a step forward in that they indicated a recognition by decision-makers that educating the rural populace was not synonymous with "incorporating" the Indian. The rural citizens who spoke Spanish, did not embrace Indian customs, and did not consider themselves members of Indian communities could be educated in the rural schools. But the Indian's long separation from the Spanish way of life and his linguistic and cultural isolation meant his had to be a separate socialization process, and for the time being, this process had to be directed from the capital to the "little nations" within the isolated pockets of Indian areas.

As an early effort by the nation to test theory in a practical experiment, the "house of the Indian student" had provided a turning point in the complex of ideas contributing to the Revolution's education movement. Drawing from the contradictions of the old and the new, the movement between 1910 and 1930 played back many old themes and controversies. Members of the Constitutional Convention of 1917 rehashed numerous aspects of the early post-Independence debate over federal versus state control of education. Grandiose schemes, such as those of the Law of Rudimentary Instruction, gave way to economic and political realities, as had the liberals' designs Santa Anna had cut short. Substance and method in education suffered abrupt shifts at the decision-making level. The Indian was variously written off as underprivileged and embraced as an ideal in the Mexican heritage. Vasconcelos' faith in the Hispanic as the universal tradition in America recalled the traditionalism of the Bourbons and early national creoles. While professing an anti-positivistic philosophy, Vasconcelos and fellow educators carried out the task begun by positivists Baranda and Sierra. Nevertheless, from among these contradictions came a firm determination to ground Mexico's designs for unification in the realities of her present. Old ideas were as acceptable as new ones, if they could bear up under practical experimental conditions. The Revolution's education movement was emerging as one aspect of a transitional stage in Mexican politics, in which the elite intellectual was beginning to promote not only habits of thought for the political leadership but also modes of action. The intellectual directing Mexican education had taken from social science a sense of critical examination and an interest in Indian personality and culture. He had not yet learned much about specific social science methods and their application or strategies of combination of theory and method. He was to enter the 1930's still affected by his philosophical nineteenth-century inheritance but with an uneasy awareness of the new and active character of his future.

CHAPTER SIX

Bilingualism and National Unity

Emerging Integration

Incorporation had been overwhelmingly a one-way process; the rural school teacher went out from the nation's center to teach the Indian. The ferment of the 1930's was to develop a two-way line of action; Indian and national would meet to learn from each other in regionally determined informal integration programs. Above all, integration, the evolving theory which would support development of new Indian education practices, differed from incorporation in its emphasis on Indian cultures as positive contributors to nationally-supported regional programs. When educators looked critically at rural schools, they saw the Indian role as passive; all of the emphasis had been placed on national teaching, none on Indian learning. Beyond the efforts of Vasconcelos' cultural missions to foster a spirit of cooperation within Indian villages, there had been no substantial attempt to make the Indian an active participant in national socialization programs. Rural teachers largely ignored the language, religion, social organization, economic patterns, and family-community socialization methods of the Indians. Such ignorance was not necessarily willful or malicious; as yet, the majority of Mexicans active in the post-Revolutionary rural education program had only a general and vaguely defined notion of Indian culture. The social science concept that all peoples—even the most "primitive"—have a culture composed of interrelated interdependent characteristics had not yet touched the attitudes of teachers who still equated the term *culture* with national standard. Pedagogy had not spelled out techniques to help teachers adapt content and methods to regional and community needs. Therefore, until both theory and technique could provide definitive methods to integrate aspects of diverse cultures into national socialization schemes, the Indians were cut off from active involvement, and unification of the Mexican peoples remained an unrealistic goal.

The first step toward initiating the process of integration was a recognition of the legitimacy of Indian tongues in the learning process. The valuation colonial missionaries had placed on the Indians' retention of their own tongues was well known, and twentieth-century educators found much merit in the commonsense approach of colonial mission teachers. Language-learning was central to formal education, yet children of Indian communities rejected both Spanish and the traditional curriculum, because they could carry neither outside the school. Spanish clearly had no functional purpose for Indian children, and therefore learning should take place in the native tongues. Formal content should be adjusted to local needs and be extended only as the social and economic outreach of Indian communities made traditional literacy skills and the national tongue meaningful tools. But written materials in local languages were scarce and highly inadequate for primary instruction; few teachers knew both the Indian tongues and Spanish well enough to move the Indians from their native language to Spanish as a second tongue; and as yet, no modern method of teaching literacy in the Indian languages was available. These technical and practical advances had to precede an integration program. Therefore, while Rafael Ramírez and his followers still kept their interest in rural schools and the direct method of language instruction, they began to find themselves in the company of a growing number of critics who had hitherto endorsed incorporation. Now uneasiness over a sense of futility and failure came from teachers within rural schools, and as educators took a second look at rural education, they realized the need to find new and different education programs to integrate regional diversities.

Gamio, as early as 1915, had pointed out the regionalism of

such areas as Yucatan, and had accented the need for special considerations in education called for by the isolation of inhabitants of these areas.[1] Now nearly fifteen years later, politicians were painfully being led to reach the same conclusions. On a tour of the federal schools in the sierra of Puebla in 1927, Moisés Sáenz was appalled at the failure of rural school teachers to understand their students or to teach them Spanish. In one school of fifty-six pupils, Sáenz found only eleven who knew how to read. The teacher had found it easier to teach gardening and dancing than the fundamentals of reading and writing. Sáenz was greeted by Indian children who performed ceremonies in his honor in their native tongue, and through an interpreter, parents protested a tax put on them by local authorities.[2] As Undersecretary of Education, Sáenz drafted a critical evaluation of the direct method of teaching Spanish in the rural schools. He concluded that, despite rhetoric claiming the necessity of a national language for national unity, politicians and educators alike had not made a concerted effort to teach Spanish to the Indians. They left them to learn Spanish incidentally. Decision-makers in national language policy had not only failed to resolve the problem of teaching the national language; they had not even attacked the problem with any degree of realism. Sáenz' tour convinced him that daily classroom conflict between teachers who felt compelled to try to teach Spanish and Indian children who were determined to speak their mother tongue brought only frustration and bitterness which endangered the future of a rural school system. Furthermore, Sáenz reasoned, what if students should learn some Spanish in the three or four years they spent in the classroom, of what benefit was it to them? They went home to parents who did not speak Spanish, and their friends in the village certainly did not encourage them to continue using Spanish.[3]

In 1931, while walking through the streets of Panajachel on a visit to Guatemala, Sáenz found a solution to the dilemma. He met William Cameron Townsend, a missionary from the United States who had been living among the Cakchiquel Indians since 1917 and who had turned linguist in order to translate parts of the Bible into the local language. Townsend took Sáenz on a tour of his school and told him of literacy campaigns he and his workers had held to teach the Indians to read the Bible in their own tongue. Townsend had devised an alphabet for the Cakchiquels, analyzed the highly complex verb system of the language, prepared a primer, and had begun to teach the children to speak, read, and write Spanish as well as their own language. On the spot, Sáenz invited Townsend to Mexico to do the same for his country's Indians. Sáenz promised backing from the government and, more importantly, he reminded Townsend that Mexico could provide his literacy program with the support of a social movement which had not taken place in Guatemala. In November of 1933, Townsend set out for Mexico, in spite of the severe restrictions of the Mexican government on immigration. Stopped at the border, he showed the officials a letter from Sáenz inviting him to develop a bilingual program of education for the Indians of Mexico. Border officials, suspicious of any foreigner wishing to study the Indian languages and extremely wary of religious personnel, checked with the capital for confirmation of Townsend's invitation. Sáenz was out of the country. Word came from Mexico City that Townsend might enter the country, but he would not be allowed to study the Indian languages nor would his companion, an ordained minister, be allowed to preach.[4]

Arrival in Mexico City brought Townsend no encouragement; Rafael Ramírez, head of the Department of Rural Education, was opposed to teaching the Indians in any way except through the direct method. Thus, the technicians who were to help provide Mexico's integration program with needed linguistic methods and materials were almost shut out before they were given a chance. Townsend was, however, patient and waited for an appropriate moment to request Ramírez's permission to work among the Indians. Meanwhile, several highly respected visitors in Mexico sponsored a luncheon in Townsend's honor in Mexico City. Among the guests who heard a summary and praise of Townsend's work among the Cakchiquels was Frank Tannenbaum, a North American professor who had published an enthusiastic account of the Mexican Revolution and who counted both Moisés Sáenz and Rafael Ramírez among his closest Mexican associates. After hearing of Townsend's literacy methods, Tannenbaum inscribed his enthusiasm on the inside cover of his book, *Peace by Revolution*, for Townsend. This inscription, according to Townsend, provided the key for unlocking the closed doors of the Department of Rural Schools. In Monterrey the next month, Townsend met Ramírez and requested permission to work among Mexico's Indians and to study their languages in order to translate the New Testament. Ramírez refused initially, saying the Indians had had too much religion already, but upon seeing Tannenbaum's inscription in the book Townsend carried, Ramírez relented. He agreed to let Townsend visit a few Indian areas in order to see what Mexico's rural education movement had accomplished. In only a few months, Townsend's experience among the Indians, primarily in the states of Yucatan and Chiapas, convinced him of the need for more linguists to analyze the numerous Indian languages. His report to Ramírez and Narciso Bassols, Secretary of Public Education, indicated this need but otherwise commended highly the Mexican rural education program and won him an invitation to return to work among the Indians. However, Townsend knew he alone could not even begin to meet the demand which Mexico's Indian integration program would soon be making for linguists. He conceived the notion of a linguistic institute which would train students to work among the Indian tribes of Mexico, and in the summer of 1934, at Sulphur Springs, Arkansas, he taught the first session of Camp Wycliffe, later to become the Summer Institute of Linguistics.[5]

After inviting Townsend to Mexico in 1931 to try his methods of Indian education, Moisés Sáenz had continued to look for other approaches. In 1932 Sáenz proposed to Bassols that the Ministry of Public Education establish a center of study and action in an Indian region with the purpose of examining the question of how the native groups might best be brought to an acceptance of national life. Bassols, who had already examined the "house of the Indian student" and the rural schools and found them falling far short of their expressed goals for the redemption of the Indian, approved a short experimental program, and, in June of 1932, Sáenz and his group of social scientists and educators established themselves in Carapan, a Tarascan-speaking center of eleven villages in Michoacán.[6] Even though this area had probably had more exposure than most Indian areas to rural education, Sáenz found that children ranging in age from eight to twelve did not know enough Spanish to distinguish *ojo* (eye) from *oreja* (ear), nor did they know words such as *cultivar* (to cultivate or farm). Their greatest success in vocabulary came in their ability to repeat words such as *lápiz* (pencil), *gis* (crayon), *cuadernos* (composition book), and *pizarra* (blackboard), the practicality of which did not extend outside the classroom. The Indian students' conception of the connotation of words was extremely limited, and their rote learning of words in the classroom had no transfer value for them out of the immediate situation in which the words had been introduced and memorized. Sáenz gave up on teaching the adult Indians to read and on making up for the children's lost months in the classroom. Yet he had to bring these Indians some knowledge of the nation in which they lived. He and other members of the group decided to capitalize on the Indians' habit of receiving information through listening; daily newspapers from Mexico City were made available for the teachers to read to their students and staff members to the adults. However, teachers sabotaged this plan by filing false reports of the number of students who had heard them read from the paper each day. Sáenz discovered that the rural teachers felt inadequate and insecure when reading aloud, and neither they nor the youngsters had any interest in reading about the faraway world of Mexico City.

Sáenz decided that reading was a habit which would ultimately have to be cultivated among these people, and meanwhile, he would have to teach a few and depend on their custom of the oral transmission of knowledge to spread an enthusiasm for learning and reading. For any reading program to be successful, rural teachers would have to be taught to read so the Tarascans could understand them: to substitute simpler vocabulary items for the harder ones found in the newspapers and to read with feeling and emphasis. Sáenz and his group, which included for a short time the linguist Pablo González Casanova and anthropologists Carlos Basauri and Miguel Othón de Mendizábal, decided that texts for students in Indian areas would have to be specially prepared. They did not suggest that the materials be bilingual, but rather that they be simple, stressing more news of events from the immediate area and gradually introducing information about the state and nation. The people of the capital spoke a language different from that of the natives of Carapan—different not only in sounds and grammatical structure but also in content and setting.[7]

Elsewhere in Mexico, others were reaching the same conclusion. Julio de la Fuente recalled years later the frustration he, as a rural school teacher in Jalapa, had felt in 1933. Attempting to write texts for rural schools, Fuente found three markedly different student populations—small-town mestizo primary pupils, Spanish-speaking *campesinos* or peasant farmers, and monolingual Indians. Fuente quickly saw the mistake the Department of Rural Schools made in assuming all rural schools should be alike. Travels to Oaxaca and other Indian-populated portions of the nation brought Fuente in touch with rural teachers who thought Indians had perhaps begun to acquire a "civilized" form of communication, but because of their intellectual inferiority or physiological differences (oversized tongues, small chins, and so forth), they could never learn to speak Spanish properly. Fuente realized the deficiencies rested not with the Indians but with the teachers. He saw himself as a case in point. Previously, he had tried to provide standardized Spanish texts of national subject matter and simple content; now he began to advocate a combined method in which teachers used materials published in the native languages and worked first with the local tongue before teaching Spanish. Advanced study in anthropology and linguistics, under Jules Henry and Mauricio Swadesh, convinced Fuente that an intermediate acceptance of the Indian's tongue was only the first step in a social science based program of Indian integration to replace incorporation.[8]

Sáenz, too, altered his view of Indian education after his six-month stint as a teacher at Carapan. Previously he had advocated incorporation. Now he urged socialization, a two-way communication process of mutual benefits and responsibilities. To socialize the Indian did not mean to attach him to the state through legal declarations of membership, to draft him into a regimented pattern of behavior, or to exterminate him and his culture. Sáenz's Carapan experience led him to declare: "in order to socialize the Indian, we shall fervently have to socialize ourselves; and this means that being good Mexicans we shall learn also to be better Indians."[9] He proposed a Department of Indian Affairs which would coordinate all programs of Indian socialization, a department whose major concern would be the Indian, not the entire rural population. Realizing the drastic departure his proposals made from past theories of education, Sáenz pointed out that too often the goal of the school in the little village had not been in step with the needs of the Indians. Adults who two decades ago had been taught some Spanish in school now neither spoke nor read the language, and many could not write their names. These Indians had been taught under rudimentary instruction and a philosophy of "incorporation," had tried and failed to learn a foreign language, and had not since been called upon to use their so-called national tongue. With no circulation of reading materials, new ideas, or motivations for literacy, Indians soon lost any signs of contact with the Spanish language their short exposure to schooling had given them. Surely a break with these errors of the past was needed. Other nations, such as Germany, Russia, and Italy, had successfully integrated minority groups into a national culture; maybe Mexico should look to the policies and programs of these nations for the answer to her own problem. Meanwhile, perhaps a new name for the process of Indian education and an amalgamated agency could provide a new start.[10]

In 1934 Lázaro Cárdenas became Mexico's president, and the shuffling and soul-searching among educators of the early 1930's evolved into firm action. Cárdenas accepted Sáenz' suggestion and organized a Department of Indian Affairs to handle all matters regarding the welfare of the Indian. In 1936 the former Department of Indian Education and the Department of Cultural Missions were placed under the new autonomous Department of Indian Affairs. This step greatly encouraged those who now saw the possibility of realizing Sáenz's proposals for social anthropology, the combination of scientific sociological and ethnological studies of the Indian with social action.[11] Cárdenas, himself part Tarascan Indian from the state of Michoacán, enthusiastically sought to help the Indians, and he firmly believed that a "rational and scientific"[12] approach to a program of education would bring the desired improvement in Indian communities. The Department of Indian Affairs was given authority over all aspects of Indian life—administrative, economic, social, and educational. Thus the department focused energies and personnel on the Indian portion of the population. Manuel Gamio's integral action was at last given bureaucratic sanction, for reorganization extended not only to administrative machinery but also to methodology. Cárdenas endorsed ethnological studies which could provide information to help the Department's personnel plan effectively for projects in Indian areas. Forerunning the day when social scientists and educators would be institutionally united in Mexico's integration program, Cárdenas relied heavily on the Institute of Anthropology and History (formed during his administration) in both the execution of studies and the evaluation of those completed.[13]

Intensive regional investigations reported the geographic distribution of the population, percentage of illiterates, number and types of schools, preparation and number of teachers available, and cost of education per student. When data in one study were coordinated with the results of the 1930 census, the national illiteracy rate was computed at 59.36 per cent. Low attendance, early drop-outs, and little retention of knowledge characterized public education in rural areas, because there existed little opportunity to put formal learning to use. Moreover, many studies showed the highest rates of illiteracy to be in the heavily Indian-populated southeast and in the northern states where tribes were isolated from Spanish-speaking Mexicans. These studies consistently closed with a plea that bilingual education replace the direct method of teaching Spanish. In Yucatan, where most primary-level teachers taught in Maya, their native tongue, the illiteracy rate was only slightly over fifty per cent, a much lower figure than that calculated for other heavily Indian-populated states.[14] Statistical facts seemed to underscore the contentions of a growing number of social scientists and educators that bilingual education merited serious consideration in Mexico's developing integration program.

LITTLE NATIONALITIES

A strange assortment of bedfellows proposed bilingual education for Mexican Indians. Advocating that the Indians be taught the national language only after having developed a formal language background and literacy in their native tongues were both American missionaries and Mexicans inspired by the example of Soviet Russia. As early in the twentieth century as 1924, evidence existed that a small group of Mexican radicals had embraced the idea of bilingual education. In a report to the national convention of the *Confederación Regional Obrera Mexicana* (CROM) made that year, Vicente Lombardo Toledano, chairman of the Committee on Education of the Mexican Federation of Labor, explained the basis for the workers' support of bilingual education. He emphasized that "the workmen of Mexico need their own school thoroughly Mexican, based on a study of the peculiar conditions under which labor is placed in the various sections of the country. . . ."[15] In other words, in order for workers and their children to gain their major goals of intelligently conducting factories and judging social policies of their political leaders, they had first to challenge and overcome any local blocks to an increase in their general educational level. Lombardo Toledano termed the "isolation due to the variety of languages, the economic and moral isolation of certain groups from the social class that always conducted the national politics" a handicap to the economic progress of the Republic.[16] Thus, CROM members raised penetrating criticisms of a federal system which ignored the linguistic isolation of the Indians; moreover, the workers suggested that the polyglot nature of the countryside contributed to the economic depression of the peasants.

Furthermore, the prevalent attitude that the Indian had no legitimate culture of his own perpetuated the isolation of a group of people who had to participate in the country's economic progress before Mexican unification could take place. Lombardo Toledano included in the CROM's education committee report this statement:

It is a gross error to believe that educating the Indian means to make a European out of an inferior human being whose soul has no trace of life, or heritage or history. Such false opinion implies the following conclusions equally erroneous: since the Indians live in a state of barbarism, one must logically denounce them as a handicap to the civilized Mexicans; consequently the native dialects must be made to disappear (without studying what human ambitions and notions are shaped therein nor what spiritual force produced them).[17]

Lombardo Toledano himself later took a direct stand in favor of the instruction of the Indians in their native tongues and the incorporation of the positive aspects of native cultures into the national pattern. In his book *Un Viaje al mundo del porvenir* (A

Journey to the World of the Future), published in 1936, he listed as the third of five proposals for a solution to Mexico's problem of native communities the construction of alphabets for Indian languages so that Mexico's ethnic groups might become literate in their respective languages. His own contribution to this task was his doctoral dissertation, a study of linguistic diversity in the sierra north of Puebla. The study developed out of a desire to refute the comment of a rural school teacher that Indians learned slowly because they were naturally stupid. Lombardo Toledano, who had gone on record in 1924 as opposing any opinion that the Indians were "inferior," developed a technique, similar to that used by Spanish missionaries of the sixteenth century, for teaching the Indians to read and write in their native tongues. The teaching of Spanish was undertaken only after they had become literate in their own tongues.[18]

Lombardo Toledano, early favoring the socialist orientation in education policy-making, found comrades and conviction in the Ministry of Education which carried out the educational reforms of Cárdenas' Six Year Plan and the revised Constitution of 1917. Article 3 of the Constitution now read: "The education imparted by the State will be Socialist. . . ."[19] The Revolutionary Socialistic School, outlined in Cárdenas' Six Year education program, endorsed coeducation, sex instruction, and bilingual teaching, in addition to teaching doctrines based on Marxian scientific materialism. The school was to be a social agent in the community life, reforming parents, informing workers of their rights, and stimulating both community and national pride.[20]

National groups mobilized for the promotion of socialism and bilingualism, natural companions to those who accepted the Russian distinction between the "national community" and the "political community" and the Soviet program to coordinate the great traditions of the former with the cultures of the latter. In 1913, in an attempt to define *nation* and relate this concept to a national language policy, Stalin had distinguished between the "national community" or the nation, and "political communities" or local culturally unified peoples existing plurally beneath the common political government of the nation.[21] Arguing against those who viewed the cultural and linguistic pluralism of these small political communities as a threat to the stability of the nation, Stalin countered that the minorities were not a destructive force but rather an integrative constructive contribution to the nation. To those who insisted the official government language should be forced on all of Russia's minority groups, Stalin retorted:

> A minority is discontented not because there is no national union but because it does not enjoy the right to use its native language. Permit it to use its native language and the discontent will pass of itself. A minority is discontented . . . because it does not possess its own schools. Give it its own schools and all grounds for discontent will disappear.[22]

Mexican educators and social scientists of the 1930's heeded Stalin's advice and proposed that they consider adopting the socialist policy of "little nationalities" in their education schemes.

But if the philosophy and the spirit were borrowed, the total technique and the national purpose were not. Mexicans, to be sure, had studied carefully the socialist position. Lombardo Toledano had visited Russia to see theory put into practice; Bassols had translated John Strachey's *Theory and Practice of Socialism;* many other social scientists in Mexico had familiarized themselves with the premises and programs of the Soviet Union.[23] But out of the anti-positivist tradition had grown Mexico's faith in developing her own point of view; hence, Mexicans considered no imported theory or model in isolation, but rather reinterpreted each in the light of Mexico's own particular history. Thus, some Mexican social scientists equated Stalin's theories with the principles which had guided Mexico's sixteenth-century missionaries. Both allowed minorities the use of their native tongues and the continuation of cultural habits which did not threaten, in the first case, the maintenance of the Russian political and economic system, and in the second case, the promotion of Christianity. Sahagún and other Mexicanists of the College of Tlatelolco were pointed out as forerunners of twentieth-century socialists and social scientists who attempted to understand indigenous cultures before imposing new cultural habits. Missionary principles compared with those of Stalin, who, in an effort to maintain the pride and self-respect of minority nations, urged that their economic, social, and cultural life be studied in order that their incorporation into the political and economic programs of the Soviet Union be brought about with as little disruption of local cultures as possible.[24] Though guilty, perhaps, of overdrawing the comparison, the Mexicans were, nevertheless, not swept away from their own present-day realities to an irrational and wholehearted acceptance of either tried and tested old methods or promising and "scientific" new practices.

The Mexicans were far too familiar with their own situation to take as their policy a carbon copy of that of either their sixteenth-century counterparts, or the Soviets, or, for that matter, their North American neighbors. The writings of Othón de Mendizábal, Carlos Basauri, Julio de la Fuente, Luis Alvarez Barret, and Luis Chávez Orozco, to name a few, reveal their careful study of Mexico's colonial history, the contemporary practices of the Soviet Union, and the theoretical teachings of several North American anthropologists. The latter, including Robert Redfield, Jules Henry, and Sol Tax, proposed methods of social change which held as a first consideration the respect of native cultures and the introduction of new habits only after community members had themselves expressed their felt needs and could take part in the plans for change. Serving only to underscore similar tenets held by Mexican anthropologists, such as Alfonso Caso, founder of the National Institute of Anthropology and History, these North Americans cooperated in various community projects and training programs during the 1930's and 1940's. Though Mexican educators and social scientists of the 1930's borrowed the term "little nationalities" from the Soviets, they chose not to advocate those non-linguistic aspects of the policy which encouraged regional loyalties and more autonomy in local administrative and economic affairs than most Mexicans considered realistic for their own situation. Linguistic aspects of the Russian policy merged with both the psychological-anthropological theoretical approach and the Mexican point of view to form a plan of action stressing bilingualism and a serious consideration of regional social and cultural conditions in education policy-making. In this program to "Mexicanize" the Indians, socialist, Protestant missionary, and impartial scholar were to work side-by-side, cooperating as scientists. Philologists and linguists in the Department of Anthropology of the National Polytechnic Institute issued an invitation to other social science organizations, including the Summer Institute of Linguistics, to join them in the linguistic investigations and community studies which would be necessary before the Secretary of Public Education could effectively carry out the bilingual program of the "little nationalities." [25]

As early as 1933, when Narciso Bassols had previewed these suggestions by injecting a philosophy of cultural relativism into Indian education, the Institute of Linguistic Studies had been established at the National University to conduct research in all fields of indigenous life and to support regional academies for the study of Nahua, Otomi, Tarascan, and Maya. This organization's founder, Mariano Silva y Aceves, an early proponent of bilingual instruction, was anxious to promote linguistic research in Indian areas, so that the Department of Indian Affairs might have the materials and trained personnel necessary for the success of bilingual education. At his instigation, William Cameron Townsend, whose return to Mexico in the late summer of 1935 coincided with the Seventh Inter-American Scientific Congress, received a warm welcome in Mexico City from government officials. The growing fame of Mexico's interest in scientific projects and the wide recognition this Congress received provided a climate in which Townsend could be accepted, not as a Protestant troublemaker, but as a scientist.

Townsend chose the Nahuatl-speaking village of Tetelcingo, sixty miles outside Mexico City, for his first post. By early 1936, Cárdenas had heard of the work of Townsend and his linguists, and the President paid an unexpected visit to the tiny village. Assured that the work of Townsend was for the improvement of the Indians, Cárdenas returned to the capital and sent agricultural materials and help in many forms to the village. That spring three other linguists who had been trained under Townsend were working in Mexico: Kenneth Pike on the Mixtec language in Oaxaca, and Maxwell and Elizabeth Lathrop among the Tarascan speakers in Michoacán. The next fall, there were representatives from Townsend's Summer Institute of Linguistics among the Maya, Mazatec, Mixe, Totonac, Otomi, and Tarahumara speakers. Cárdenas and Townsend became close friends, and the work of the linguists continued to enjoy government support, and particularly the cooperation of education officials. Throughout the rest of the 1930's, linguists of the Summer Institute of Linguistics joined with professionals from Mexican institutions to travel among Indian groups making studies of thirty indigenous idioms, formulating an alphabet based on phonetics and phonemics, constructing grammars, dictionaries, and vocabulary lists, and instructing teachers in the techniques of bilingual education. However, while breaking into new territories, the social scientists had also to struggle against old enemies. Opponents to bilingual education argued that only through Spanish could the Indians obtain civilization; primitive tongues of the indigenous groups locked them in primitive approximations of civilization. Exponents of bilingual teaching patiently and carefully took apart each such subjective argument and set it against the objective reasons of social science theories or psychological experiments.[26]

But if the power of the movement at home was to be built up, it was most important that Mexican techniques of Indian education be recognized outside the nation's boundaries. In September of 1937, those who had been spreading bilingual education in Mexico received just such a boost for their work from an inter-American education conference. Bringing together teachers from all Indian-populated countries of America, the Third Inter-American Conference of Education provided a platform from which Mexican social scientists and educators favoring bilingual education could explain and promote their program. The conference members proved to be a good audience; they approved the groundwork in bilingual education which had been laid in Mexico by passing this resolution: "Bilingual education for the Indian is recommended in the firm belief that it will increase the effectiveness and ease with which we educate the indigenous; we thus affirm the cultural value of the native tongues in the extension of the national idiom."[27] The Conference members were telling the countries of Indo-America, in effect, not that they were promoting the Indian languages, but that as pedagogues and scientists they were undertaking the responsibility for adopting the means proved most effective for bringing Indians to literacy and the national tongue. Teachers thus committed themselves to a philosophy which, if carried into practice, would radically alter their own training and teaching techniques.

In the course of the next few months, scholars drew together the major tenets of Indian education, including the bilingual method, laid out by the inter-American teacher conference.[28]

Cárdenas read the summary carefully. He appreciated and respected the logic and common-sense approach which affirmed the cultural and psychological values of maintaining native dialects while bringing the Indians to the national idiom. The treatise summarized practical suggestions such as training in linguistics and relevant regional dialects for rural teachers. The language of the Indians was to be a "thing of value" to the teachers, first and foremost as an expression of the Indians' intimate thoughts and emotions, and secondly, as a vehicle to the national language. The ultimate disappearance of the dialects seemed inevitable in view not only of the national demand for a common tongue, but also because new economic and social connections were made possible by a knowledge of Spanish and the functionalism of local tongues was consequently reduced. In integration theory, consideration of the Indian came first in any program to move him to the national way of life; the external forces of incorporation were supplanted by internal motivation and cultural relativism. But, in addition to appreciating the substance of the treatise, Cárdenas recognized an additional significance it carried. Mexican educators had created a climate of opinion among teachers, within their own national boundaries and beyond, which, over the long run, would help fend off at the grass-roots level the immobilizing effects of any future battles of ideological extremes among top-level policy-makers.[29]

For the last decade the Mexican Institute of Linguistic Studies had been striving toward a greater clarity and uniformity of scientific research and data collection, but movement had not been continuously in the same direction. Some researchers had collected material related to diet and social institutions; others, with more linguistic training, had worked with native informants to gather linguistic data to be used in the preparation of primers. These scientists, some of them novices from the National School of Anthropology and History, had the desire, and acting together had the skill to make a reality of the vision of laying bare a map of the nation's education needs. Education planners were to learn which languages were used by the largest number of natives, and reviews, books, and periodicals were to be published so that each language group could have reading materials in its native tongue. But the efforts had little coordination because of the lack of a central coordinating agency. Cárdenas had provided the spirit for Indian integration, but he had left to social scientists and educators the strenuous task of pulling together the forces needed for a broad frontal advance.

Cemented by their common frustration as well as dedication, men like Luis Alvarez Barret, assistant director of primary teaching, and Luis Chávez Orozco, head of the Department of Indian Affairs in 1939, directed the energy and encouraged the efforts of the various scientists collecting data which they knew could be used to help policy-makers ground their Indian programs on a social science base. These men had a grasp of essentials, an analytical sense of the situation, and a sharpness of judgment which held together the scattered efforts of scientists in Mexico's field. Their masterpiece was the mobilization of various groups to introduce and maintain the philosophy and skills of the movement among rural teachers. Recognizing the need for books in Indian languages and the inadequacy of the alphabets made by the early missionaries, these two men called for the preparation of new primers based on linguistic principles. In spite of the work done by traveling linguists of the Summer Institute of Linguistics and scattered groups from the capital, most teachers in rural Mexico had no technical linguistic knowledge, and they attempted to mold the sounds and grammars of Indian languages to the Spanish alphabet and grammar, thus actually hindering the learning of the Indians. Kenneth Pike, the director of the Summer Institute of Linguistics after Townsend, offered his services and those of his staff to the Ministry of Education in the preparation of materials based on phonemic transcriptions.[30] Though many were not professionally trained to handle the technical aspects of the preparation of texts in the indigenous tongues and, as yet, had a minimal introduction to the technical aspects of bilingual instruction, teachers throughout the nation generally offered to help in any way possible with the preparation of bilingual materials. The First Mexican Congress for Popular Education held in December of 1939 urged its members to redirect their emphasis in rural education from *el indio* in general to the Indians of particular indigenous communities. They recommended that teachers devote the initial stages of the primary-level curriculum to the history and culture of the local region;

subsequent levels should introduce state and federal materials. As the Indian children learned of their own immediate environment in their mother tongue, so they should gradually learn the national language as they moved to an understanding of state and federal governments.[31]

The active interest in linguistic research and well-intentioned, though certainly scattered, contributions to Indian education made by Townsend and the Summer Institute of Linguistics' personnel and the linguistically-trained members of the Department of Indian Affairs continued to attract the attention of Cárdenas, who remained slightly uneasy over the lack of coordination for the workers' efforts. Therefore, in 1939, he suggested to Luis Chávez Orozco, head of the Department of Indian Affairs, that he call together Mexican and American scholars to assess the language policy of Mexico in the First Assembly of Philologists and Linguists.[32] Reviewing the history of Indian education since the Revolution, the Assembly participants, who included both North American and Mexican linguists and anthropologists, agreed that the direct method of teaching the national language had failed to do more than give a few Indians a bilingual veneer. Spanish was not meaningful for them, since they did not have enough of a foundation in the language to think in it, and if used at all, the national standard was reduced to sterile phrases, greetings, or interchanges in the marketplace. Repeating conclusions Sáenz had drawn six years earlier, Assembly members pronounced "incorporation" a dead theory; it had failed in its primary goal of teaching the national language to the Indians. Therefore, since the premise of the philosophy of incorporation had been that once the Indian learned the Spanish language, he would be able to enter the culture of the Mexican nation, the entire program had been of little benefit. Since the Revolution, political and education officials had accepted as an underlying premise of their programs the notion that the characteristic which distinguished Indian from rural peasant was the inability of the former to speak the national tongue. Hence, by extension, these officials had concluded that the Spanish learned by the Indians, in either rudimentary or preparatory instruction or in limited and relatively short-lived contacts with boarding schools or cultural missions, would bring them to the Hispanic way of life "enjoyed" by other rural citizens. But such had not been the case. Many had not learned Spanish at all; others were bilingual only for particular settings, a situation not unlike that which had prevailed before the day of rudimentary instruction. During the Colonial period, the Indian who learned Spanish did so to acquire a tool needed for a particular task; his relations with monolingual Spanish speakers determined—in degree and kind—the Spanish he learned. The peon who worked on the hacienda needed certain Spanish words in order to understand his orders; the agriculturalist sometimes needed limited Spanish vocabulary and grammar for use in trading his produce in regional markets. What the Assembly wanted was something more: an expanded bilingualism which could bring improved health, sanitation, and agricultural techniques—those aspects of modernization the Indian needed to achieve opportunities equal to those of other Mexicans. The aim, then, was not to extinguish the Indian's native tongue, which he used with his family and the members of his closed community; the goal was to add to this in-group language Spanish for use in those areas of life which the Indian might choose as profitable for his own economic or social advancement. The integration plan was not one of deletion, but rather one of addition.[33]

The Assembly confirmed, if they did not create, a fresh mode of operation that grew out of the fieldwork of their linguists. Literacy in the indigenous languages was to become a well-advertised topic; radio, billboards, leaflets, and murals would proclaim the merits of reading in the native tongues. Accustomed to a life based on oral communication through primary contacts (the family and the community), Indians would have to learn the possibilities of receiving information through a written channel and secondary sources outside the Indian village. Several technical prescriptions enabled linguists to unify methods of preparing texts and teaching reading. The Assembly urged the use of only one typeface for primers and other publications for the Indians. Several varieties of primers were to introduce the basics of history, arithmetic, geography, and natural science; whenever possible, content was to include local materials. All readers were to be prepared in accordance with Townsend's method for teaching reading, by which simple syllables composed of letters of marked contrast were introduced prior to complex syllables containing letters of slight contrast. Assembly participants agreed to prepare recordings of Indian languages for use in teacher training. In order that the carefully devised methods of teaching reading in the Indian tongues be carried out over a period of sufficient duration to allow students to acquire firmly the habit and skill of reading, the Assembly suggested that Spanish instruction not be begun before the second or third grade in schools of Indian areas.[34] On the basis of this group's recommendations, the Office of Linguistics under the Department of Indian Affairs prepared alphabets for ten of the major Indian languages, dictionaries for five of these, and the suggested recordings for several Indian areas.[35]

The Assembly's most notable achievements were the formation of the Council of Indigenous Languages and the initiation of an intensive literacy campaign in Michoacán among the Tarascan Indians. A permanent body of technical experts, the Council provided an opportunity for Mexican linguists to pool information and to exert influence as a unified group. The Tarascan Project incorporated all of the Assembly's recommendations for a true test of "action linguistics." The project was under the direction of Mauricio Swadesh, an American linguist teaching at the National School of Anthropology and History, the Mexican Alfredo Barrera Vásquez, and Maxwell Lathrop of the Summer Institute of Linguistics who had been in the Tarascan area since 1936. Swadesh trained twenty youths all of whom were natives of the Tarascan area, spoke the language, and had had some previous instruction in the normal schools or indigenous centers.[36] He trained these teachers to transcribe spoken Tarascan into the alphabet formally accepted by the Assembly for use among the Indians, and the Indian teachers prepared texts and materials for use by the Tarascan children and adults. These instructors went into the Tarascan area to teach literacy in the indigenous tongue and to introduce Spanish only after the students had learned to read and write in their own language. The results of the project provided undeniable proof that the Indians could learn to read more rapidly in their own tongue than in Spanish. Within a minimum period of thirty days and a maximum of forty days, the Indians of the project learned to read and write.[37] Henceforth, no matter what opponents said or did, the success of the bilingual method stood confirmed in a community project.

Enthusiastic over the success of the Tarascan Project, the members of the Assembly and the Department of Indian Affairs were anxious to extend the program to other "little nationalities." But by early 1940 it became evident that two emphases of the exponents of bilingualism and the socialists had to be shifted: the emphasis on literacy as the key to "nationalizing" the Indians and the concern with "little nationalities." The linguists themselves had suggested that learning the national tongue would not bring the Indian everything he might need for full participation in the national culture, but the limitations of funds and personnel cut off any moves toward a more integral approach. They had been able to initiate Gamio's recommendations for a thorough linguistic investigation of each Indian area before planning an education program, but they had not been able to bring in other social scientists to investigate thoroughly all the areas of culture and social organization which Gamio suggested for a truly integral approach. Limited funds and the failure of the bureaucracies involved in Indian education to unite their energies and directions had left the socialists and linguists with scattered community projects, far too few in number to alter in any radical way the multilingualism of the nation.

The Move toward Indigenism

But Mexican social scientists knew a way out of their difficulties: they must have an amalgamated agency independent of the Ministry of Education. During the 1930's they had enjoyed the favor of political support, but they could foresee a time when the lack of such support could immobilize their programs. In order that invention and valuable established processes be given every opportunity for a substantial test of time and changing circumstances, this agency must have the power to administer and coordinate Indian integration programs apart from current presidential or party enthusiasm. The indirect path which politicians sometimes chose in education policy-making must not be allowed to divert or bypass Indian integration. Twists and turns in this line of action must be determined by objective analysis and the critical judgment of social scientists. Once again, Mexicans found an opportunity to gain what their own nation needed by consulting with other Indo-Americans. For several years, Mexican social scientists had been anxious to confer with other Latin Americans faced with the problem of large indigenous populations. At the Eighth International Americanist Conference held in Lima, Peru in 1938, the Mexican delegation offered to host such a congress. Pátzcuaro, Michoacán was chosen as the location for the First Inter-American Indigenist Congress which met in April of 1940. The central concern of the group was scientific indigenism: how to select and implement successful programs of socialization for the Indians based on the research and recommendations of social scientists.[38] In his inaugural address to the Congress, President Cárdenas proudly acknowledged the influence social science had had in activating Mexican projects grounded in a recognition of the Indian as a social being capable of maintaining his cultural integrity while becoming oriented to national ideals. Cárdenas emphasized that Mexico now looked to goals such as improvements in health and sanitation, participation in local community affairs, and the gradual shift to participation in the economic, social, and political life of the nation.[39]

Absent from the debates and recommendations of the Congress were such former watchwords as *redemption* and *incorporation; emancipation* and *scientific indigenism* took their place. Methodological discussions centered around ways to apply the results of research among the indigenous populations to the solution of practical problems. Included in the seventy-two recommendations of the group were concrete proposals for the initiation of integral investigations of Indian groups, the utilization of applied anthropology in the planning and administering of programs for the welfare of the Indian, the protection of Indian art, the integration of the indigenous community into the national community, and the establishment of a council of applied Indian linguistics.[40] Gamio's exhortation in 1916 to a nation just beginning to struggle with how to govern and unify its indigenous population had been: "It is axiomatic that anthropology in the broadest sense ought to provide the basic understanding for the functioning of good government, since it is through anthropology that those who govern may know the population which they rule and for which they govern."⁴¹ More than twenty years later, Mexico had made a start at incorporating the recommendations from applied anthropology into government-sponsored projects, and now an international congress suggested that other nations of the Americas follow Mexico's example.

The Mexicans were the first to admit that the ideals often guiding those concerned for the welfare of the Indian could not be met within one generation's time, nor could they be fulfilled without a central agency to disseminate information and to coordinate programs based on social science research and principles. The Congress therefore proposed that each country establish a special organization—a National Indigenist Institute—for the development of programs of research and promotion for the indigenous populations within each nation. These national institutes were to be affiliated loosely with the Inter-American Indigenist Institute, which was directed by Manuel Gamio and headquartered in Mexico. As a first step toward the dissemination of the research and progress made by social scientists in the Americas, this organization began publication of a journal entitled *América Indígena*.⁴²

The term "Indianist" was dropped; the Congress participants substituted "indigenist." There were those who were convinced that the Indianism of the late nineteenth and early twentieth centuries had stirred suspicions that anthropologists were proposing the re-creation of Indian nations. Early suggestions by Indianists such as Jésus Díaz de León that the Indian tongues be maintained had convinced some government officials that anyone who supported bilingualism had to be subversively attempting to wipe out Spanish and offer encouragement to the Indians' separation into their own little nations. During the term of Cárdenas, opponents of bilingual education had viewed the Ministry of Education as the headquarters of the "Comintern of Mexico" and had accused Indianists of supporting the separation of the Indian communities from national political control and culture. Luis Cabrera, an opponent in the 1920's of the maintenance of Indian tongues, and many government officials throughout the 1930's suspected that bilingual education might be a way of isolating the Indians from the government. Mexican anthropologists were aware of this impression and wanted to avoid any such accusation; therefore, they proposed the substitution of the term "indigenism" for "Indianism." They were also anxious to underscore their conviction that the "Indian problem" was not a racial problem. Isolation and underdevelopment were characteristic of many Mexican natives who were not *racially* Indians: the problem was one of *cultural* differences which separated the indigenous from the mainstream of the national culture.[43] Mexican anthropologists, in particular, were anxious to have the government endorse a policy of indigenism, which they defined as the protection and development of indigenous Mexicans. Politics and shifting ideologies held by the nation's highest officials should not be allowed to affect the theory and practice of indigenism. Programs designed for the welfare of the Indians should not be abandoned with changes in political leadership. Alfonso Caso, an anthropologist active in Mexico since the 1920's and influential in the establishment of the National Institute of Anthropology and History during Cárdenas' administration, chose throughout the next three decades to work for the removal of extraneous political considerations from the theory and practice of applied anthropology in indigenism.[44] The change of administration in 1940 and further struggles among diversely organized and managed programs aimed at bringing the Indian into the national fold signaled the beginning of Caso's undertaking.

CHAPTER SEVEN

The Program of Acceptance

Campaign for Literacy

Manuel Avila Camacho, the conservative elected to replace Cárdenas, vowed to alter politics and pedagogy behind federal education programs. The Constitution of 1917 was modified to meet the political climate's shift to the right; omitted were the socialist trappings, and it was prescribed that education be democratic and stress moderation and national unity. Article 3, which had formerly stated that education would be socialist, now stated that education should develop all human faculties "harmoniously" and foster a love of fatherland and an awareness of international solidarity.[1] The influence of socialism and its prescriptions for nationalism based on Stalin's notion of "little nationalities" had given much of the education program of the 1930's a militant tone. Fear of the Soviet pattern and its promotion of socialism and bilingualism influenced Avila Camacho's appointment of Octavio Véjar Vásquez as Minister of Education; determined to purge education of leftist influence and to reconcile the Church and the school, Véjar Vásquez proclaimed "the new school." If socialism was the ultimate enemy of the conservative Véjar Vásquez, his proximate enemy was the political machinery of the education system. By ridding the education structure of those who had talked of maintaining cultural diversity, he could redirect instruction toward the maintenance of uniformity in Hispanic traditions. "Authentically Mexican," the new school the Minister proposed was to be based on "the commonality of origin, spiritual and material interests, idiom, habits and customs" which could unify Mexico.²

An arch-enemy of the bilingual method of instruction, Octavio Véjar Vásquez abandoned the Tarascan Project and made clear his opposition to any further proposals to make the Indians literate in their native tongues. The Cultural Missions Department was reinstated in 1943 and given the responsibility for the literacy campaign, which Avila Camacho endorsed in his Six Year Plan for Public Education. This idea, first proposed by the Congress which had given bureaucratic sanction to the Ministry of Public Education under Vasconcelos in the early twentieth century, had languishd over the preceding twenty years, and Avila Camacho was determined to push the program vigorously. He called for help from all sectors of the nation— academic, business, and artistic.

Véjar Vásquez enlisted the help of Frank Laubach, the developer of the each-one-teach-one system of spreading literacy. Laubach visited Mexico City in March of 1943, and the Minister of Education asked for permission to use his system in the literacy campaign. Laubach knew the history of Mexico's dependence in the nineteenth century on the Lancasterian system and the Ministry of Education's announced intention in the 1920's to launch a literacy campaign. After visiting several Indian areas, he realized that neither long familiarity with a similar technique nor espousal of the same objective had brought Mexico to an approximation of what Laubach saw as a meaningful literacy program. The visiting educator was forced to tell the Minister that there had in reality been no "campaign" among the Indians, for the Mission teachers had attempted to teach them to read Spanish without first teaching them to read their native tongue. Laubach's stay in Mexico lasted less than one month.³

Because of Véjar Vásquez' bitter opposition to the bilingual method, the staff of the Missions included no linguists, and instruction offered in the Missions included no acknowledgement of the native tongues. The Minister and other conservatives of his point of view were fearful of the cultural pluralism implied in the recognition of indigenous tongues and the use of linguistic aspects of the "little nationalities" policy of the Soviet Union. Instead of bilingual instruction, Véjar Vásquez pleaded for national unity through education, and the essence of his plan echoed Sierra's cry for equal schooling for the children of all classes issued forty years earlier. In the thinking of Véjar Vásquez and his conservative associates, rural and urban distinctions in education had been reinforced by the philosophy and practices of schools adapted in content and methodology to local conditions. According to the Minister, special schools to serve the Indian populations had maintained the existence of a separate class and opposed the ideal of unity for Mexico. Social scientists who were standing in the wings of Avila Camacho's administration during the early 1940's heard Véjar Vásquez proclaim the necessity of understanding the object of education as the individual and, in the next breath, prescribe the moral man which the new school should create.[4]

But Véjar Vásquez thought in different terms, moved with greater velocity, and battled with more pitiless weapons in building his prescribed "school of love" than most of the political leaders who surrounded Avila Camacho. With a pistol on his hip and a batallion of reactionary supporters, the new Minister closed schools he viewed as too communist-oriented, shifted teaching personnel, returned some parcels of school property to to the Church, and refused to denounce the confrontation of unarmed Polytechnic Institute students by armed officers. His purge of what he viewed as leftist and modernist influences in the nation extended to cultural activities, as he maneuvered a return to conservative fare in theatre, music, painting, and literature. The inconsistencies between the pistol-toting Minister's pronouncements on the "school of love" and the repressive measures he directed toward education and even culture raised a cry of protest in Mexico City and led to his ouster in 1943.[5]

Avila Camacho chose as the new Minister Jaime Torres Bodet, known as a moderate keenly interested in a meaningful literacy campaign for Mexico since his apprentice days as personal secretary to Vasconcelos during the 1920's. Both President and populace agreed it was time for the moderation which Torres Bodet exemplified. The severe overhauling of the rhetoric of educational policy in both Article 3 of the Constitution and in the Second Six Year Plan had been an attempt to move Mexico's education program away from the extremes to which a few had taken it during the 1930's. Avila Camacho wanted to bring the content of education back in line with Mexico's own heritage and the aims of the Constitution of 1917. Hence, though personality had temporarily superseded platform under Véjar Vásquez, the administration of Avila Camacho provided in the specifics of the Second Six Year Plan the opportunity for most of the social science programs begun in the 1930's to continue. Avila Camacho stressed general prosperity as the major goal of his administration; poor health, illiteracy, blocked communications, hungry stomachs, and limited vistas held Mexico back from her goal of "constructive solidarity" and "economic justice."[6] The organization and development of scientific contributions which might further the elimination of these barriers was a major tenet of both the general education scheme and of specific programs. The rhetoric of Avila Camacho's education program and that of contemporary social scientists were not too different, a realization which apparently did not escape the new President. Both admitted the necessity of teaching Spanish to the indigenous groups and the need for knowledge regarding the cultural diversity of the Indian population to increase the efficiency and effectiveness of economic and health programs among the Indians. Hence, the President openly urged government agencies to operate in conformity with programs outlined by scientific agencies and institutes.[7] Several of these were manned by social scientists active in Indian education during the 1930's, men who had frequently contributed to publications defending socialist educational tenets.[8] A conscious nationalist urge for modernization, while seeking to define and retain a national self-image, led politicians and administrators to look to scientific investigations aiding education as the way in which the culture of the past could be preserved for the indigenous groups as a solid foundation for national political socialization and economic progress.

Showing the timid beginnings of an official recognition of bilingual education, the Second Six Year Plan in Public Education endorsed the use of indigenous tongues for supplementary instruction and admitted the cultural and psychological differences represented among the Indian groups. Specifics of the plan showed the strong influence of the resolutions of the Inter-American Indigenist Congress held in 1940.⁹ Article 13 endorsed the use of indigenous tongues in out-of-school educational activities; radio, theatre, and plastic arts were to be utilized for the diffusion of national culture to Indian areas. Perhaps most indicative of the influence of the postulates of Indian education policy adopted by the Inter-American Indigenist Congress were articles in the Six Year Plan which read:

The study of linguistic problems shall be systematically intensified, for the better adequacy of the school in relation with the various ethnical [sic] divisions in which it acts; the plans, programs, and methods of teaching shall be adapted to the social and economical conditions of each region [and] to the psycho-physical characteristics of the inhabitants.[10]

The note of acceptance sounded openly, advising social scientists of their admission to the fraternity of policy-makers.

Anthropologists and linguists in Mexico City had waited quietly for Véjar Vásquez's strong-man tactics to bring about his removal. However, almost as soon as his successor had moved into his new office, a phone call announced the social scientists' shift in tactics. Alfonso Caso, director of the National Institute of Anthropology and History, reminded the new Minister of the cancellation of the Tarascan Project after its brief but impressive run. He asked Torres Bodet to assess the Tarascan linguistics project objectively; Caso suggested that the Council of Indigenous Languages, formed after the First Assembly of Philologists and Linguists in 1939, be authorized to reappraise the bilingual method of instruction. Caso was virtually sure that if the project could stand on its own scientific merits rather than as a socialist scheme, the project could sell the new Minister on bilingual education.[11] The Council, after evaluating the intensive literacy campaign begun in Michoacán in 1939 and carried out as the Tarascan Project, recommended the initiation of the Institute for Literacy in the Indigenous Languages. The Council's suggestions were incorporated in the Law for the Elimination of Illiteracy, which launched the literacy campaign in August of 1944. Article 14 of the law establishing the campaign provided for bilingual teaching and texts, to be prepared by the Department of Indian Affairs.[12] The Council also encouraged local societies for indigenous language speakers and the publication of bilingual newspapers in Indian areas. Torres Bodet himself became a champion of bilingual education for Mexico in the 1940's and for other nations through his influence in UNESCO during the 1950's.

Avila Camacho and Torres Bodet declared war on ignorance, and they mobilized forces in education and business. All literate Mexicans of both sexes, aged eighteen to sixty years, were ordered to teach at least one illiterate between the ages of six and forty to read and write; all illiterates were required to register. A hard-sell campaign was launched in 1944; planes dropped leaflets in the most remote regions to explain the program. By early 1945 the campaign was underway, and an imaginative system of rewards virtually guaranteed public participation. If a Mexican taught fifty illiterates to read, he received a medal from the President and the opportunity to win land in a raffle; for teaching twenty-five illiterates, one received a free pass for a year to his favorite movie house or a pass for free rides on buses and street cars. University students who taught fifty illiterates to read were not required to pay tuition. The manual used for teaching contained three coupons to be filled out by the teacher with the completion of each part. When these coupons were turned in, each teacher received a special card indicating his participation in the campaign; without this card a citizen could be denied a driver's license, building permit, passport, or travel on certain bus lines in Mexico City.[13] A special task force set up a specialized institute to train fifty bilingual teachers and prepare texts in Tarascan of Michoacán, Maya of Yucatan, Otomi of Hidalgo, and two dialects of Nahua. Alphabets had to be devised for all of these except Tarascan.[14] In the first stage of the campaign, Maurice Swadesh, the director of the Tarascan Project, trained fifty teachers to use these alphabets in literacy instruction; helping Swadesh were teachers, linguists, and anthropologists, many of whom had cooperated in the project in Michoacán in 1939. Then each of the fifty teachers trained ten more rural teachers in the bilingual method, and finally these went into the Indian zones to teach literacy in the Indian tongues as a way to prepare the natives to learn Spanish. Only the renewed Tarascan Project carried out all stages of the literacy campaign plans, and its success was primarily due to the groundwork laid by Maxwell

Lathrop in the many years he had worked in the area. The Otomi and Maya programs did not meet with much success and the Nahua programs were never completed.[15]

Meanwhile, anthropologists and social scientists were not satisfied that literacy training would solve the problem of the Indian areas. No fewer than 100 projects—economic, social, or cultural—were begun by social scientists in the ten most Indian-populated states. These were carried out by social scientists who sometimes had government support through either cooperating personnel or financial backing. The government sponsored a social science commission to help coordinate these projects.[16]

In addition to legislating specific practical programs for the social integration of the Indians, Avila Camacho's administration turned the ear of the national polity to the voice of the people. On December 18, 1942, for the first time in the history of Mexico, the Chamber of Deputies celebrated a formal session of homage to the Indian population. Delegations of Indians from the states of Yucatan, Mexico, Sinaloa, Aguascalientes, Michoacán, Baja California, and Quintana Roo spoke on the urgency of a realistic approach to the social problems of the diverse Indian groups in the nation.[17] Numerous other forms of governmental recognition of regional diversity and cultural contributions were extended to particular interest groups among the Indians: sponsorship of handicraft centers and regional fairs for the exposition of Indian arts, the recording and collection of Indian music, and the promotion of regional pride in archaeology and the history of pre-Hispanic Mexico. Government administrators and anthropologists worked together in recruiting Indian teachers and assistants to help in the projects of the Inter-American Indigenist Institute and the Department of Indian Affairs—especially the Betterment Missions, Centers of Indigenous Efforts, and Centers of Technical Preparations, operating in various rural regions during the 1940's.[18]

Politicians and anthropologists alike pointed with pride to Mexico's indigenist renaissance represented in their efforts to bring the Indian into the national life on the basis of realistic knowledge contributed by social science research regarding the culture and values of each Indian group. Indian educators of the late 1930's had strongly asserted that national unity did not have to signify uniformity throughout the nation; the cultural development of the Indian groups should seek not to level the cultures of the various indigenous societies, but rather to bring the societies to an acceptance of skills and sanitation measures which might be classified as positive values in all civilizations.[19] Jaime Torres Bodet echoed the convictions of these educators in 1945:

> When we speak of Mexican unity, we do not intend to invoke a vehement desire for uniformity; that would be contrary to the reality of existent conditions, and undesirable, as an ideal, in its consequences. [What we do intend in our use of the term *Mexican unity* is] a design for harmony, equilibrium, and cohesion.[20]

The use of bilingual textbooks containing illustrative and textual material drawn from existing Indian cultures and recounting historical events of Indian groups exemplified Mexican educators' efforts to make reading materials relevant for the Indian children. Torres Bodet went so far as to claim that national unification was not possible without a definite recognition of Mexico's cultural pluralism and the equal right of each indigenous group to representation in education materials.

> What cohesion can the teacher of the Maya, Otomi, Zapotec or Yaqui child expect when, in order to establish in him the essential Mexicanness we propose, he wishes to teach him to read by using publications which do not touch the child's culture and are filled with examples taken from objects, people, and landscapes he has never seen?[21]

In addition to policy statements and general laws, the national system of education reflected the decision-makers' adoption of a certain degree of cultural relativism in the nation's socialization processes. Methods and materials for national integration through education depended on an integral knowledge of the needs and cultures of the diverse societies in the Mexican nation; this was now an expressed tenet of official policy. During Avila Camacho's administration, the Department of Indian Affairs had even made a bid for secretarial rank, which, though unsuccessful, suggested the prominence the indigenism movement had achieved.[22]

But quantity and quality were largely antithetical; there were not enough trained anthropologists and linguists to carry out the necessary in-depth investigations for all of Mexico's Indian groups.

Therefore, intensive programs, such as the Tarascan Project and a personality investigation program in Tepotzlan, were few in number, largely restricted to communities rather than regions, and often dependent on the amount of groundwork social scientists had provided in the 1930's.[23] Hence, valuable programs could not be initiated and carried out in quantity. Coordination in the training, placement, supervision, and evaluation of young social scientists was yet to come, as was the organization of a centralized institution to plan and execute Indian integration programs based on the research findings of field workers. During the early 1940's, however, the indigenism movement had reached the highest levels of the education bureaucracy and had established as a matter of policy, if not of fully integrated practice, a course of rational treatment for Mexico's Indian groups.

From the Community to the Region

Under the presidency of Avila Camacho's successor, there came a considerable reorganization of personnel and reemphasis of philosophies which had guided much that had been done for the Indian in the recent past. Miguel Alemán, who became President in 1946, saw as his first responsibility the acceleration of the surge of industrial and business growth Mexico had seen during the early 1940's. With a business-like eye for efficiency and productivity, he denounced Indianism for its role in making the Indian an object of state charity.[24] Thus, Alemán disbanded the Department of Indian Affairs, which had been established under Cárdenas in 1936 and had worked closely with the Ministry of Education from 1940 to 1946. The responsibilities of the Department were now put in the Office of Indian Affairs under the Ministry of Education. Any remnants of the welfare state for Indians left from the Cárdenas period were wiped out; the goal was now to help the Indian help himself. Through national reform programs engineered by a political system openly patterning its means and ends of operation after big business, the Indians, and indeed all citizens who would participate, were promised a share of the benefits Mexico would reap through economic progress.

The same impulse that accelerated national economic development rejected the community as the central focus for improvement programs. Manuel Gual Vidal, who succeeded Torres Bodet as Minister of Education, chose as his banner phrase "unified schools," and self-determination in the name of either the individual, the Indian, or the local community stood denounced.[25] The rural school and its partner, the community, upon which rural education had claimed a growing dependence since the days of Vasconcelos' "houses of the people," waned in importance before massive public works projects which brought extensive social changes. The Papaloapan Basin flood control project, begun in 1947, brought the focus of big business to the countrysides of Oaxaca, Puebla, and Veracruz, with plans for electrification, new industries, mechanized agriculture, and hospital and school construction. In short, change was sweeping in both territorial and cultural range. The days of primary focus on literacy and rural education as the key to societal improvement were past. Advocated now was wholesale "integral transformation," involving engineers, agriculturalists, and architects, as well as sociologists, anthropologists, and linguists—all coordinating their efforts in regional projects.[26] Gual Vidal, a former businessman, looked at his Ministry of Education with an eye to seeing how it might help such projects function as efficiently and effectively as possible. He found the lack of coordination during Avila Camacho's term among educators and social scientists active in scattered projects a severe handicap to a truly integral approach. He joined social scientists in concluding that, in reality, during the 1940-46 period, the promotion of the literacy campaign and bilingual education had held top-level national priority, and only these goals had had any noticeable coordination from central authorities.[27]

Therefore, when he surveyed his inheritance in the Ministry of Education, he reshuffled the organizational structure and urged centralization to bring about the efficiency he felt necessary. The Office of Indian Affairs, in its demoted position, drew no consistent leadership nor direction in this transition stage. Briefly headed by anthropologist Gonzalo Aguirre Beltrán who called in Julio de la Fuente to assist him, the Office seemed immobilized by the inertia in Indian-affairs policy-making.[28] The former Institute for Literacy in the Indigenous Languages, renamed the Institute of Literacy for Monolingual Indians, continued its preparation of bilingual primers and ethnological studies of earlier designated Indian groups. In addition, it was swept into participation in the Papaloapan Basin project, which would be faced with the task of relocating numerous Indians now living in the areas to be inundated after the construction of the Miguel Alemán Dam. The Institute gathered linguistic information as an initial index to the number of Indians in the Papaloapan Basin and found that over 200,000 speakers of eleven different Indian languages lived in the area to be transformed by the flood control project.[29] The Minister and others quickly cautioned that in order for the funds supporting this work to be well-spent, the cooperation of local authorities as well as the people themselves had to be obtained by social scientists who could help direct the general social-change plan of action. Gual Vidal stressed the contributions education could make to the success of such programs which promised industrial expansion and economic development; he also made clear that the nation's ultimate goal, through the coordination of wide-sweeping change programs, had to be uniformity. But with uniformity in a post-World War II age came bureaucratization and centralization, movements which, though born of a spirit somewhat alien to the tenets of indigenism, helped provide the amalgamated agency the social scientists had hoped for.

Gual Vidal was not the only voice calling for a change in the organizational structure of groups handling Indian affairs. Alfonso Caso, appointed to a secretariat position in Miguel Alemán's cabinet, had influenced the President early in his term to appoint an advisory study group to reconsider Mexico's establishment of a National Indigenist Institute, an idea to which Mexico had committed itself at the First Inter-American Indigenist Congress in 1940.[30] To an extraordinary degree, the evolution of the Institute's goal of integration came not only from the cumulative force of the laments of community field workers plagued with the lack of coordination among their projects since 1930's, but also from the present emphasis upon economic growth. What was new in integration in this era was neither its ideas nor its existence, but its reach in a new setting—its practical potential for application in regional programs and its capacity to further the success of big-business undertakings, such as the Papaloapan Basin project.

But Alfonso Caso also revived the theoretical impetus for

the integral approach to the Indian in a speech entitled "Definición del Indio y lo Indio," which he gave before the Second Inter-American Indigenist Congress in October of 1948. He pointed out that "the problem of defining the Indian is not a racial problem but a cultural one, not an individual problem but one of human society,—the community." [31] His criteria for membership in the Indian community included preponderance of non-European physical characteristics and cultural attributes, but more important than these two were linguistic and psychological criteria. Monolingual Indian-language speakers and bilinguals who spoke Spanish in addition to their indigenous tongue were Indians, and had been counted as such in census materials. But there were also Indians who spoke only Spanish, and their criterion for designation as Indians was their psychological identification as members of an Indian community. Only by becoming aware of all the cultural accoutrements of Indian membership could social-change agents hope to include the indigenous in the national destiny.[32] On the 10th of November of 1948, Alemán signed the law which established the National Indigenist Institute (INI) of Mexico.[33]

The purposes of the Institute were similar to those proposed eight years earlier at the First Inter-American Indigenist Congress: the investigation of problems relative to the indigenous population and the study of methods for the improvement of the living conditions of these groups. But the organization of the Institute produced a very special nexus between social scientists and administrators in Mexico. The Institute was to be a direct line for communication between local change agents and decision-makers around the President. Article 2 stated that the Institute could not only make recommendations for Indian programs; its members could also participate in programs and help coordinate and guide the efforts of other governmental agencies active in Indian areas. The director of the Institute was a Presidential appointee, and an executive council was to include representatives from relevant secretariats of the government, including those concerned with education, health, agriculture, public works, communication, transportation, and agrarian affairs. In addition, four cultural institutions—the National Institute of Anthropology and History, the National Antonomous University, the National Polytechnic Institute, and the Mexican Society of Anthropology—

were allowed permanent representation on the Council.[34] At last, the government had officially given a central agency the opportunity to research, formulate, and help execute an indigenist policy in Mexico. Social scientists were to proceed with the planned acculturation of the Indians through the implementation of national aims at the local level.

Where did this emphasis on coordination of efforts and amalgamation of directing personnel leave bilingual education? Never firmly or widely established in the rural schools, the bilingual method had been primarily an instrument of the Indian Centers intent on introducing Indians to vocational skills, the Indian Affairs personnel, especially those active in the literacy campaign, and the Summer Institute of Linguistics. Now bilingual education, or literacy instruction in the Indian tongues, was subsumed under the general program of INI which had, in its early years, to devote its major energies to the collection of data and the recruitment of personnel. Bilingual teaching and the use of Indian-language primers were continued in the work of the Institute of Literacy for Monolingual Indians among the Maya, Tarascans, and Otomi; more primers were being prepared for Nahua and Nahuatl; and the ethnological studies necessary for the preparation of primers were begun among the Totonacs.[35] But linguistic research and the preparation of grammars and readers were now only part of a larger program of investigation and materials preparation, and during the transition years of the late 1940's and early 1950's, debate over language policy and practices was nearly nonexistent. Indigenists no longer had to apologize for their concern for the natives of Mexico, nor did they have to base their arguments for cultural relativism on a defense of the success of the bilingual approach over the direct method, as they had done during the early 1940's. The leaders of the National Indigenist Institute were the spiritual sons of the bilingual education movement, but they were sons who now placed language policy deep in the ideology of the reborn integrated regional approach of Manuel Gamio. From this point on in Mexico's history, discussion of language policy for the Indians was impossible without placing the topic in the context of the indigenism movement.

With an opportunity to coordinate knowledge, energies, and

plans for the initiation of an integral program of improvement for the Indians, the members of INI broadened the primary emphasis on education which had marked nearly all of the government's previous attempts to integrate the Indian into the national culture. In addition, they rejected the community as the focal point of development programs. After a careful study of the economics of the Indian areas, the Institute chose to focus Indian rehabilitation programs on the region rather than the community. Indian economics depended on a market town, usually the nucleus of a region in which both Indians and mestizos depended in various ways on this central urban and nation-oriented community. Moreover, common historical and ecological links had bound the inhabitants of certain regions together to determine patterns of community structure, functions of speech, and habits of intersocietal relations peculiar to specific regions and demanding special considerations in development programs. Alfonso Caso had earlier pointed out that patterns of settlement and the history of contact since the Conquest had differed in various sections of Mexico. For example, in the southeast there existed a greater density of Indian population and a larger number of monolinguals in the Indian tongues than in the central region, where the Indians had had more opportunities for contact with the world outside their community. The percentage of monolingualism in Indian languages was less in the central area than in the southeast, and the high concentration of other Indian cultural characteristics found among the inhabitants of the southeast, such as going barefoot, wearing native dress, and eating no bread, did not appear as consistently in the central area. Hence, the division of the nation into regions the inhabitants of which exhibited like cultural characteristics demanded that anthropologists redirect indigenist action from the community to the region.[36] Not only the Indians of these regions, but also the mestizos existing on the margin of the national culture were the concern of social scientists favoring the regional approach. The mutual dependence of Indians and mestizos linked them inextricably to the ecology of the region. Perhaps the most important new emphasis in the concept of regional integration was the study of levels of acculturation. This stress demonstrated the anthropologists' concern for moving both those who were largely free from the national culture and those who were only partially involved into the full stream of Mexican national life.

As the territorial reach of INI projects expanded, the range of cultural habits to be changed broadened. Social scientists and other personnel in regional integration now set out not only to introduce the national language and literacy skills to the indigenous, but also to alter customs related to diet, health, agricultural techniques, and economic participation outside the community. However, coordination among these diverse activities which INI members hoped to carry out within each Indian group in Mexico was impossible from a single central office in Mexico City. A base of operation at the regional level was necessary. Furthermore, limited funds and personnel made it clear that not all Indian groups could receive INI's attention; hence, some criteria for choosing the Indians to be involved in development programs had to be determined. The Regional Coordinating Centers became INI's own agency to carry out integration programs in designated regions. The criteria for choosing the regions in which INI would establish Centers were the amount of preliminary contact anthropologists had had with the Indians of the region and the severity of economic and health needs among the indigenous. Three major emphases directed the work of the Regional Coordinating Centers: economics, education, and sanitation. Specialists from the Ministries of Agriculture, Health, and Public Works united with representatives from the literacy institute of the Office of Indian Affairs in a common venture. Directed by an anthropologist from INI, educators, linguists, agronomists, medical technicians, and representatives from several other professions cooperated in directing their energies toward regional development. Almost as soon as the Institute was organized, its members began cooperating with the diverse personnel already at work in the Papaloapan Basin. However, since the nature of the administrative and investigative work there had to be particularly directed toward determining how the Papaloapan Project would affect the lives of the Indians of the area, this region was not the choice for the establishment of the first Regional Coordinating Center. Instead, in September of 1950, INI established the first Center in the Tzeltal-Tzotzil region of Chiapas, an area chosen because of the extreme poverty of the region's inhabitants and the preliminary work accomplished since the 1940's by various anthropologists and linguists located in the area. A second Center followed two years later among the Tarahumaras of Chihuahua, a state which had a long history of indigenist concern.[37] During these early years, the Office of Indian Affairs, directed by Mariano Samayoa chose to initiate some programs not connected with INI, primarily because of the director's objection to the use of the bilingual method, implicit in INI's philosophy and plan of action.[38] However, by 1952, the end of Alemán's term, several major projects involving the Indians were taken over by the National Indigenist Institute. The major institution touching the lives of Indians throughout the nation which did not take on the philosophy and practices of INI was the rural school; during the 1950's and early 1960's, the rural school continued to use the direct method of teaching and to operate largely outside the spirit of the indigenist movement.[39]

As the Centers became established and began to increase under Alemán's successor, Adolfo Ruiz Cortines, the lessons learned from bilingual education projects helped determine the evolution of policy and practice in the Centers. Taking a chapter from the program recommended by the First Assembly of Philologists and Linguists and later the First Inter-American Indigenist Congress, INI endorsed a respect for the Indian personality, sensibility, dignity, and "his positive habits" in social organization and other cultural categories. Uppermost on the list of cultural features to be respected was the Indian's native tongue, which was to be used in all initial stages of education and vocational preparation. Remembering the lesson taught by the "house of the Indian student," which had removed the Indians from the community to educate them, the Institute sent its educators, termed *promotores culturales,* to the regional Centers. These cultural promoters were to be natives of the region in which they worked, and they were to speak both Spanish and the indigenous tongue of Indians of the area. The rationale for the use of these promoters, who had had perhaps only four to six years of education, was that they could in reality be members of the Indian group and could act as agents of change within the community.[40] These bilinguals were able to reach Indian children not as outsiders or as former members of the community who had returned to "redeem" their neighbors, but as stable members of the community who were attached to the Coordinating Center as cultural brokers between the nation and the region. Cooperating with the Council of Indigenous Languages and the Summer Institute of Linguistics, INI prepared simple readers in the native languages of the regional Centers. In these, the local environment and culture provided the basis of information, and the primers pictured the Indians of the particular region in which the materials were to be used in native costume and performing tasks acceptable to the local culture.[41] Sáenz' observations in Carapan had led him to conclude that the habit of reading would have to be cultivated; INI wanted to foster the habit of formal education within Indian communities. Just as reading had been foreign to the Tarascans of Carapan, so studying in school and learning information derived from outside sources was alien to the in-group informal socialization methods of most of Mexico's Indians. Hence, adjustment to the culture of a formal learning situation involved adults as well as children, for the former had to learn to value what education could bring their children so that they would support the local school and encourage their children's regular attendance in school and regional Centers. On the other hand, the Ministry of Education was continually encouraged by INI and the literacy institute personnel to orient the teaching in the formal schools of the rural areas toward the cultural realities of the region and to prepare students to become promoters for the Coordinating Centers.[42]

During the late 1940's and early 1950's, Mexican indigenists were inspired not only by their own estimation of the success and promise of the integral method, which had in large part sprung from the tenets of bilingual education, but also by recognition from outside Mexico. UNESCO, which had held its conference in Mexico City in 1947, had initiated a pilot project in the state of Nayarit. On the basis of the success of this experimental program, termed "fundamental education" and directed toward educational as well as economic and health improvements, the Regional Center of Fundamental Education for Latin America (CREFAL) was established in Mexico in 1951. Jaime Torres Bodet, who had become Director-General of UNESCO, had taken with him not only the ideas, but also some of the personnel of Mexico's bilingual education movement. Alfredo Barrera Vásquez, active in promoting bilingual education among the Mexican Indians since the 1930's, assisted Torres Bodet in expanding the aims and methods of bilingual education and community development for adoption by UNESCO. Established in Pátzcuaro, Michoacán in 1951, CREFAL was to be an international training center for representatives from Latin American nations, who would specialize in fundamental education. At the dedication ceremonies, the Indians reminded the prestigous international audience that the UNESCO project was only a rejuvenation of the methods of Fray Vasco de Quiroga, who had taught the Indians of Michoacán in their native tongue and encouraged their local economy in the sixteenth century. The bilingual method and its basic philosophy which demanded "a local approach to local problems" had expanded not only into an integral regional development movement in Mexico, but also as a guiding principle of development projects sponsored by UNESCO throughout the world.[43]

Retreat and Reevaluation

Throughout Alemán's term, INI had established the administrative structure to carry out an integral regional approach; Mexico had won international fame as the leader of Indo-America's *indigenismo* movement both in theory development and in the management of practical programs. However, during the administration of Adolfo Ruiz Cortines (1952-58) came the test of whether INI as an amalgamated agency could pull together the institutional cooperation needed to support the Institute's energetic programs. Prior to the establishment of a centralized authority to evaluate and direct regional integration programs, social scientists had, to a great extent, been free to remain independent of political imperatives in the resolution of social problems. Financial assistance was often dependent on direct personal contacts, and favor with a single segment of the political hierarchy was often enough to insure the maintenance of particular programs. Townsend's community workers and linguists had received fruit trees and printing presses directly from Cárdenas; Sáenz had personally appealed to Minister of Education Bassols for funds to support the Carapan Project. The Ministry of Education had favored the "little nationalities" policy of some social scientists during the late 1930's; Alfonso Caso had appealed directly to Minister of Education Torres Bodet to revive the Tarascan Project in the early 1940's. Individual social scientists exemplified the tenets of sixteenth-century missionaries and religious leaders of the late eighteenth century when they determined principles and practices on the basis of local cultural characteristics and needs.

Now, only a few years after its establishment as an amalgamated agency to coordinate social scientists' efforts, INI had to account for itself as a centralized authority, ideologically and politically dependent within the nation's political system. INI was directed by a Presidential appointee; its governing council was composed of representatives from the various secretariats as well as personnel representing academic and social science interests. The council's purpose was to advise governmental personnel and agencies active in Indian areas and to recommend programs and procedures to policy-makers. During his campaign in 1952, Ruiz Cortines wrote to INI soliciting the opinion of its members on ways to resolve the "Indian problem." The response from Alfonso Caso, director of the Institute, came in the form of a plan drawn up by Gonzalo Aguirre Beltrán and Manuel Germán Parra who incorporated many of the ideals and methods of INI in their proposal. Ruiz Cortines included their suggestions in the six year plan of his Presidential campaign. In accordance with the anthropologists' proposals, the new administration approved the establishment of two more Coordinating Centers: one in the Mazateca and Chinanteca region of the Papaloapan Basin and another among the Mixtecs of Oaxaca.[44]

However, more often than not INI recommendations failed to become accepted practice and programs; INI's council had advisory authority, not executive powers. INI had been charged to manage and coordinate the diverse activities of government agencies participating in rural development programs. In the interest of the specialization and diversification required of personnel and projects in these programs, INI's council provided a forum for the discussion of problems encountered by road-builders, agronomists, teachers, doctors, and others at work among the indigenous. A strict division of labor was not characteristic of many Indian cultures, and the specialized bureaucratic offices set up in marginal areas to direct diverse development programs often found little understanding among the indigenous. The establishment of Regional Coordinating Centers and the use of bilingual cultural promoters had represented INI's effort to provide multilateral action through a loose division of labor in the Indian regions. Bilingual promoters were to help the Indians understand the functionally specific government agencies and to mediate between the marginal populations and Regional Centers.[45] However, the dependency of INI on the government to approve establishment of Centers and to distribute funds often resulted in a struggle between political expediencies and financial realities on the one hand, and the ideals of applied anthropology on the other. Authorities independent of INI continued to execute their programs as they chose, and the seemingly slow and methodological approach of INI's applied anthropologists, who urged that directed social change be based on scientific investigations, did not fit the mood of economic expansion which propelled other governmental agencies. Hence, some ministries and departments planned and directed their own programs, and their philosophies and personnel often conflicted with those of INI. Begun in 1951, the *Patrimonio Indígena* (Indian Patrimony) among the Otomi of the Mezquital Valley was an intersecretarial effort. The Office of Indian Affairs continued to operate Indian boarding schools and Brigades of Indian Improvement. The Institute of Literacy for Monolingual Indians directed literacy centers largely independent of rural schools. What plagued workers within INI, as well as the scattered social scientists linked to other Indians programs, was the failure of government personnel to cooperate and compromise for the benefit of the Indians. The Institute of Literacy for Monolingual Indians, in its years in the Mezquital Valley, had had little cooperation from rural teachers, and the literacy project and the formal education program of rural schools moved on parallel paths, often duplicating efforts. Directors of the Indian Patrimony varied in their acceptance of the work of literacy personnel, often because they disapproved of teaching the Indians in their own tongue.[46] Personnel in various development projects, as well as teachers within the rural schools, having had little, if any, exposure to social science training, misunderstood the principles and practices of anthropologists and linguists attempting to guide INI programs and to influence other development projects.[47]

In the years following 1952, bilingual education emerged as a major rancorous issue, often pointed out as the major cause for the failure of cooperative efforts among various development personnel in the field. Most rural school teachers, traditionally devoted to the direct method, had failed to adopt the bilingual method for many reasons including linguistic chauvinism, insufficient training in linguistics, inadequate knowledge of an Indian tongue, and, in many cases, a sincere belief that literacy in the indigenous tongues kept the Indians locked in isolation. Within certain indigenous groups, the Indians themselves resented the idea that they should be taught in their own tongue before learning Spanish; for example, the Otomi in the Mezquital Valley often spurned the efforts of personnel of the Institute of Literacy for Monolingual Indians to teach their children to read Otomi. In other areas where Indian leaders were familiar with the direct method of rural schools, they resented the promoters' use of special methods for the Indians. Some of INI's cultural promoters were not accepted among the Indians, and many felt their obligation to the bilingual method was a central reason for their rejection. An original idea of INI had been periodic evaluation of the achievement of objectives and the need for a reorientation of guiding theories. Now, after the first few years of operation, there was a clear need for reassessment, and bilingual education, a primary tenet in the development of an integral regional approach, became the first issue for fresh appraisal. Temporarily set aside was the dilemma of INI's financial and administrative dependence on a national political system and its ideological responsibility to the tenets of applied anthropology and decentralized decision-making.

In 1956, Mauricio Swadesh, who had worked in the Tarascan Project in 1939 and trained bilingual teachers in the Campaign for Literacy, toured the Coordinating Centers to evaluate the bilingual method and its use as a tool in the hands of the promoters. Though he heartily endorsed the motives behind the use of promoters, Swadesh was forced to note that there was no formula for success in an acculturation program which included teachers who did not endorse the program's ideals. In other words, if the bilingual method was not successful in the Indian regions, it was not the fault of the method, but rather that of the teachers who had ambivalent attitudes about the method or were not adequately trained in the linguistic skills and anthropological assumptions necessary to support the method. He noted that in several Centers the promoters did not know the language of the region well, and that in those Centers where personnel from the immediate region had not been available and outsiders had been brought in, there were signs of a strained relationship between the promoters and the residents of the area. He also found that some cultural promoters showed a preference for the use of Spanish which alienated the children and especially the adults. Translations to the native tongue were sometimes mechanical and deficient. Some few promoters spent too much time using the native tongue and made no noticeable effort to encourage the Indians to use Spanish. Swadesh found that teachers and residents of the Indian villages objected to the teaching of reading and writing in the native tongues, when they felt they were getting an overdose of literacy in the indigenous language and would not have an opportunity to learn Spanish. Curiously enough, Swadesh found that, more often than not, Indians favored bilingual materials because their use facilitated the learning of Spanish. Moreover, once they had come to literacy in their own tongue, the Indians wanted to be sure of a chance to move on to a reading and writing knowledge of Spanish. Therefore Swadesh urged administrators and directors of the Centers to begin oral instruction in Spanish the first day of school and to move the students steadily and progressively to a speaking knowledge of Spanish and then to skills in reading and writing the national tongue. Texts should present content in both Spanish and the indigenous tongues. In these ways the alleged threat of keeping Spanish from the Indians, much talked about in earlier periods and lingering yet in the view of some Indians, would be obviously denied. At bottom, Swadesh's own fear was fear of sabotage from within INI's own ranks; the more frequent the instances of inconsistent handling of language policy by INI workers, the more numerous the cases of suspicion and distrust among the Indians. Therefore, Swadesh urged that INI carefully define and advertise its language policy: that the Indians ought to be allowed to learn Spanish without losing the right to use their own native tongue.[48]

Swadesh's report prompted a reevaluation of INI's devotion to the bilingual method. The ideological aspects of the struggle between the direct method and bilingual teaching had held the attention of those who had debated language policy since the 1930's. Respect for the Indian's intelligence and his potential for effective participation in the national socioeconomic system, recognition of Indian history and culture, and the assumption by the nation's elites of the responsibility to protect the indigenous had been the most repeated ideological arguments for the bilingual method. Only a few had debated the technical aspects of direct versus indirect Castilianization. Torres Quintero in the first decade of the twentieth century had maintained the direct method cut out translation and was thus more efficient than bilingual instruction. Personnel of the Summer Institute of Linguistics had demonstrated in small community programs that the Indians learned most effectively through a comparative approach contrasting the sound and grammatical systems of their own speech with those of Spanish. Swadesh's Tarascan Project had implicitly assumed that since learning to read was a process independent of learning a foreign language, literacy in the maternal tongue before literacy in the national tongue was a necessary developmental stage. Now, in 1956, as a result of Swadesh's mission of evaluation, there was held within INI a series of meetings in which the bilingual versus the direct method was debated from a psycholinguistic or technical point of view. Spokesmen for the direct method were Ricardo and Isabel Pozas, directors of the Papaloapan Regional Coordinating Center. Long-time workers among the Mazatec, the Pozas' had used the direct method with considerable success, and they argued for its efficiency in bringing the Indians to literacy in Spanish. Texts were written in Spanish, but content materials were oriented to local conditions, a procedure first suggested by Sáenz on the basis of his Carapan experience in the 1930's. The implicit assumption of Sáenz and the Pozas' was that the learning of a foreign language and the learning of literacy skills were two inextricably related psychological processes, and that the final objective of bringing the Indians to a a speaking and reading knowledge of Spanish could be more rapidly achieved by the direct method than by bilingual instruction. Earlier in the twentieth century, proponents of the direct method had argued that Indian languages had no grammar or alphabet; these false notions linguists had helped dispel by demonstrating that all languages had sound and grammatical systems, and all could be represented phonetically. Furthermore, linguists had worked hard to dispel the notion that some languages were more "primitive" than others; ethnographic and linguistic research had shown that every tongue had an intrinsic value for its native speakers and carried a socially cohesive and communicative purpose among these speakers. In addition, linguists had argued that the so-called "primitive" languages could take on the functions of speech in modern industrial societies if language planners paid attention to vocabulary development. Aware of these arguments, Ricardo and Isabel Pozas, in a position statement written in 1956, admitted the intrinsic value of the indigenous languages of Mexico, but they asserted that merely writing these languages and conveying in them new and different types of information did not raise the social status of the idioms. Marginal to the nation's economy and active in a goods and information exchange system in which indigenous tongues served as a crucial oral channel of communication for daily facts and ancient folklore, Indians had no use for a written form of their languages. In essence, neither the present economic situation nor historical considerations justified writing these languages and using them as a transition stage to the national tongue. The position of the indigenous tongues as socially inferior to Spanish remained unchanged; hence, since literacy and mass communication in oral Spanish were the ultimate goals of social, economic, and education programs for the Indians, the direct method was the most effective and efficient technique of language instruction.[49]

Bilingual method proponents had an influential champion for their cause—the UNESCO report on the use of vernacular languages in education. At a special UNESCO session held in Paris early in 1951, representatives from around the world debated the technical aspects of the direct method versus the bilingual technique and overwhelmingly decided in favor of bilingual teaching. Representing Mexico were Kenneth Pike of the Summer Institute of Linguistics and Mauricio Swadesh; Alfredo Barrera Vásquez, a member of the UNESCO Secretariat, presented Mexico's Tarascan Project as a case history of the use of the bilingual method.[50] Many of the final points of the conference echoed the tenets of the Inter-American Indigenist Institute and numerous other inter-American conferences on education. Mexican anthropologists and linguists within INI reiterated these points in their 1956 reevaluation of the bilingual method:

1) The mother tongue is an individual's natural means of self-expression, and no language is inadequate to meet the child's expressive needs at home or in the early school years.
2) Nothing in the structure of any language precludes it from becoming a communicative tool for modern civilization.
3) A *lingua franca* or national tongue should not be considered an adequate substitute for the mother tongue unless children know the *lingua franca* before coming to school.
4) The success of bilingual education depends in large part on a consideration of the socialization processes and expressed needs of the community into which a public formal education system is being introduced.
5) Literacy is functional only if there is a need for reading and writing skills among adults accepted as models within the community; an adequate supply of relevant reading materials is necessary to maintain literacy.
6) During the child's first or second year at school, the national language should be introduced orally; throughout formal instruction, the use of this idiom should be increased gradually until it becomes the medium of instruction.[51]

The end result of the debate within INI confirmed the continuation of the bilingual method somewhat timidly. Though most agreed on the ideological and psycho-pedagogical grounds for the bilingual method, the reassessment had stirred some uneasiness over INI's total program of acceptance. Ideally, INI could endorse bilingual education in preparatory grades in areas where monolingualism in the indigenous tongues was high. However, finances limited the number of such preparatory schools INI could provide and most rural schools used Spanish as the only medium of instruction; moreover, few areas provided education beyond the fourth grade. Hence, the reevaluation highlighted the question of whether students in this abbreviated hopscotch pattern of literacy instruction could learn enough Spanish to become functionally literate. Moreover, the 1950 census had indicated that states containing the greatest number of monolingual Indian speakers did not consistently produce the greatest number of economically inactive citizens.[52]

These figures provided an impetus to social scientists who

argued that a shift in language meant very little in terms of the day-to-day life of the village-dwelling population, which remained isolated through minimal ownership of land and primitive agricultural and sanitation practices. The disappearance of Indian cultural habits did not necessarily correlate with increased economic and social participation. Essentially INI's indigenism meant acculturation, a process by which the Hispanicized portion of the population and the Indian portion exchanged and reinterpreted cultural characteristics to produce a new culture—a mestizo culture.[53] But this culture recognized few integrative aspects—such as language and social organization—of the Indian cultures. From Independence until the early 1940's, policy-makers in Mexico had assumed that a shift to the national tongue would bring the indigenous population to a simultaneous adoption of all other cultural ideals held by the nation's elites. Therefore, decisions handed down from the central government had forced its selection of the national standard on the masses, and policy-makers had justified their programs to bring about the acceptance of this standard by insisting that sociopolitical unification and linguistic unification were synonymous. Now theory and practice were bringing some government leaders, as well as social scientists, to the conclusion that the socioeconomic unification of the nation was the crucial issue in the integration of the indigenous communities within the national community. But would INI as a centralized bureaucracy be able to accomplish socioeconomic unification without bringing about the disintegration of Indian cultures? As social scientists expanded and intensified their research within marginal regions, they recognized a greater complexity in the pattern of interdependence of cultural traits for various Indian groups than early proponents of the regional integral approach had imagined. Thus, facts and figures emphasized the need for a flexible philosophy at the central authority level, and also an increase in the executive powers of INI to determine the number and resources of regional programs which would make decisions on the basis of local needs and particular patterns of economic and social activity. The Secretary of Public Education, José Angel Ceniceros, praised the progress Mexico had made in educating its public to understand the cleavages between Indians and mestizos as the result of class divisions and not racial problems. What kept the Indian from participation in the total class structure was not racial discrimination but cultural habits and the socioeconomic limitations the national society placed on him in the class structure.[54] There were more important matters than language to be considered in the integration of the Indian: his health standards, diet, agricultural techniques, the maintenance of his self-confidence and dignity, and his chances of class mobility. His own idiom in his community was vitally functional to the Indian and provided a tool with which bilingual promoters could instruct him in new techniques and skills. For the time being, INI and government officials admitted this integrative function of the Indian tongues only in their acceptance of bilingualism as a realistic and necessary transition stage to the national tongue.

President Ruiz Cortines attempted to influence the Ministry of Education to adopt both the philosophy and practices which guided indigenist education. In 1957, he established the National Technical Council of Education which had as its primary duty the adaptation of educational action to national problems. The speeches delivered at the inauguration of the Council rang with pronouncements of cultural relativism; Ceniceros re-titled the major goal of public education. During the previous administration, the nation's leaders had talked of education for *mexicanidad;* Ceniceros spoke instead of *mexicanismo,* which included not only regionalism and Mexico's national traditions, but also appropriate traits from "international culture."[55] In spite of the need for national unity, the nation's decision-makers noted the need to recognize the relative merits of diverse cultures both within Mexico and outside the nation. Ceniceros argued that a just interpretation of Article 3 of the Constitution called for tolerance as a crucial consideration in the formulation of Mexico's educational ideals. The school should help break down the barriers of prejudice between the mestizo and the Indian. Ideally, Mexican education should adopt as its goal: "to educate for liberty and responsibility; to form men and women whose lives will be personally satisfying and socially useful."[56] He asserted that the regional approach to integration promised equal opportunities for improvement to all the regions of the country; those areas long isolated from such national benefits as schools and roads should be provided with these opportunities for contact with the world outside their own communities and regions. The goal of the newly formed Technical Council of Education and the Ministry of Education would be "unity within multiplicity." The Minister of Education affirmed his view of the lessons Mexico had learned from her evolving indigenism movement: "we ought to be indigenists in order to conserve and strengthen the positive values of the indigenous, but in order to alleviate their problems, we ought to treat them as Mexicans, as citizens." [57] Though most certainly unaware of it, Ceniceros had expressed the essence of the ambivalence of the indigenist movement which some critics would take as cause for a new departure in the next decades. So far as a growing number of indigenists was concerned, the central grievance against indigenism was not that it had brought to national attention some cultural characteristics and contributions of the Indians, but that this phase of the movement had overshadowed the fact that few Indians entered the nation's competitive arena of social and economic life as participating citizens.

CHAPTER EIGHT

Reality and Responsibility

THE NEW DEPARTURE

Adolfo López Mateos, elected President in 1958, appointed Jaime Torres Bodet his Minister of Education and continued to push indigenism along the same regional development path it had taken since the 1940's. The new President accented the contributions of the indigenous populations to the national culture and advocated an increase in economic opportunities in Indian regions. Venerating the role of Mexican institutions of higher learning in bringing about a public recognition of the potential of the Indians, López Mateos called particular attention to historical studies and to action projects centered in Indian areas. Both had publicized the resourcefulness of the villagers, and both local communities and the nation had benefited in terms of financial contributions and increased awareness of Indian potential.[1] Embedding acceptance for the national linguistic standard in a broad socioeconomic program to integrate indigenous populations, the new President played back old themes as he emphasized the importance of unifying the nation in language and culture. Regional distinctions expressed through Indian cultures would not be denied, but the ultimate evolution of the Mexican nationality would be mestizoization, the synthesis of Mexico's varied cultural heritages. Spanish, creole, mestizo, and Indian would merge in a unitary culture. López Mateos asserted: "While we may be regionally distinct and nationally uniform, we are able to determine justly the dimension of spiritual solidarity that the nation requires for us to feel united in a single concert of Mexican souls." [2] The regionalism and special contributions, including languages, of the indigenous cultures were officially recognized, but a singleness of culture and spirit was clearly the goal of the nation's political elite.

Mestizoization, watchword of the late fifties, stood for a dualistic program of social and economic remedies designed to minimize the extremes of *indianismo* and Hispanicism in the national culture. It is no coincidence that indigenism had increasingly become the ideology of the modern urban mestizo. Early in the century Molina Enríquez had placed the hope of Mexico's future on the mestizo; Gamio had urged "the fusion of the races, the convergence and fusion of cultural manifestations, linguistic unification, and economic equilibrium among the social classes." [3] After World War II, the rising awareness of her role in international affairs had led Mexico to analyze her stage of development in the arena of modern nations. Widespread particularistic norms, functionally diffuse relationships, and a comparatively low level of political participation among her heterogeneous populations marked those aspects of political development Mexico had to undergo to advance its modernization. The first targets for reshaping were the indigenous marginal populations, whose linguistic or cultural boundaries did not coincide with those of the nation. To integrate these groups, Mexico's political elite had to mobilize the masses through increased public education and mass communication and shift their loyalties from traditional local groups to the nation. Increased literacy, industrialization, urbanization, and exchange of consumer goods throughout the nation became the goals of the political elite who financed and executed indigenism programs.

But many of these goals were drawn from the modernization programs of nations whose indigenous were far different in number and cultural characteristics from Mexico's Indians. If Indian-mestizo integration meant common and equal membership in the nation's citizenry for the Indian, the process had to be two-way—acculturation for the Indian and acceptance by the mestizo. Furthermore, if acculturation—not assimilation—was the final goal of integration, some Indian cultural traits should remain in the mestizoicized national culture. Now, even though there was not yet open discussion of the need for Mexico to define its own modernization process and to shape mestizoization to the realities of the prevailing relationships between mestizo and Indian, the increased emphasis on integration seemed certain to bring about the challenge of a new departure. Meanwhile, insistence in practical programs continued to be on changing the Indians, not on eliminating the prejudice and discrimination held by the mestizo as self-protective devices to keep the Indian from moving out of his historically-entrenched lower-class status. Since the Conquest a numerical majority but a social and political minority, the Indian populations represented various levels of cohesion, cultural autonomy, and socioeconomic security in particular territorial regions.[4] Few Indian groups had anywhere near a full range of cultural traits distinctive from those of other marginal populations, but those cultural features which the Indians had retained were crucial to their group identities and their protective stances against exploitation by mestizos. Indigenism programs emphasizing integration of the Indian were designed to alter many of those cultural habits which had persisted since the Conquest: agricultural techniques and associated religious rituals, community organization, and socialization methods. Mestizoization through indigenism was a program of directed cultural change which attempted to insure Indian acculturation with as little disruption as possible of Indian traits the modern mestizo did not see as impeding the integration process. Therefore, transition stages admitting certain aspects of Indian culture could be useful in smoothing the course of integration.[5]

In line with accepting the regional as a transition step on the way to a national standard, the Ministry of Public Education endorsed bilingual education in 1963. Specifically, this agency advocated that bilingual teachers introduce literacy skills in the indigenous tongues before reading and writing instruction in the national tongue. In the next year, this Ministry revived the National Literacy Program in Indigenous Languages shut down during Ruiz Cortines' administration, and chose as its administrators anthropologists and linguists active in Indian education since the Tarascan Project. The National Service of Cultural Promotors and Bilingual Rural Teachers was created to extend teaching in the indigenous tongues to groups of Indians who had not previously had this instructional service.⁶ The number of Coordinating Centers increased, and cooperation between INI personnel and the Secretary of Public Education, as well as the Summer Institute of Linguistics, was more in evidence than in past years. Duplication of efforts was admittedly a problem which had not been overcome, and communication between agencies was infrequent. However, in large part, a rough division of labor existed. The Summer Institute of Linguistics prepared primers and other teaching materials and carried on linguistic research among the numerous dialects which had not yet been analyzed and recorded in alphabetic writing. INI, in addition to the diverse duties related to directing the Coordinating Centers, prepared primers, and some of its members engaged in linguistic research. The Secretary of Public Education managed the rural schools and some special Indian programs provided for in his administrative structure and bore a major responsibility for the printing of primers and educational materials used in Indian areas.⁷

The transfer of the Presidency from López Mateos to Gustavo Díaz Ordaz, who served from 1964 to 1970, represented no significant shift in Indian affairs but a new emphasis on the use of Indian cultures in the transition stages of acculturation. Díaz Ordaz spoke of "Mexicanization"—not as the superimposition of national cultural characteristics such as language on the indigenous members of the nation, but rather as the identification, transformation, and integration of Indian communities within the community of the nation as a whole. Most certainly, the Spanish idiom, having been enriched with regional tongues, would ultimately become the national language of all Mexicans, but immediately the acceptable stage was bilingualism in the population. Díaz Ordaz specifically gave his support to what he termed the basic requisites of indigenism in Mexico: "the bilingualism of the population, the shift toward a scientific view of the world, and the modification of tribal organization toward a more modern type." ⁸ These modifications could best be brought about through the gradual introduction of new economic opportunities and some accepted concomitants of modernization: electricity, roads, schools and vocational training centers for men and women, medical and sanitation improvements, and new jobs and self-help projects. Díaz Ordaz accented the active nature and ultimate goal of indigenism in Mexico; the Indian could not be indefinitely maintained as an Indian, nor should the government treat the Indian as a ward of the state; instead he should be given the opportunity to participate in programs which would enable him to enter into the nation's full-range of social and economic activities.⁹

Such statements, which might have been welcomed by indigenists in an earlier decade of the twentieth century, only accentuated a growing sense of uneasiness among Mexican anthropologists, some of whom were not certain they wished to be part of the present phase of the indigenism movement. Anthropology students who did their field work among the Indians and saw the effects of an increased emphasis on economic expansion in rural areas became discouraged. Hydroelectric projects, new highways, and intensive tourist promotions admitted the Indians into these new economic activities at the same low level of the social scale they had always occupied. Furthermore, Indians altered the craftsmanship of their native wares to produce objects which appealed to tourists; some became hucksters selling their handicrafts to tourists. Meanwhile, families still traded their few agricultural products in regional markets, and others hired themselves out as cheap labor for regional economic projects. During the 1960's, the main force of the indigenist movement was called into question by students and professionals alike; the "science of development" Mexico had adopted in her modernization program was open for review. In 1963 Pablo González Casanova, professor in the National School of Political and Social Sciences, wrote *La democracia en México* in which he examined development and democracy in Mexico. The political sociologist pointed out that the Mexican political elites' idea of political action assumed a popular democracy with widespread participation and eager civic interest in national affairs. Political development had, therefore, to depend on the build-up of mass participation and the reduction of cultural and economic heterogeneity in the countryside. Summarizing the statistical evidence of marginality in the population, González Casanova was, however, forced to conclude that in spite of integration and development programs, Mexico retained a marginal population victimized by internal colonialism. As Mexico's internal colonies, the Indian communities still held the characteristics of a colonized society: regional "ruling centers" controlling Indian commerce and credit, mestizos discriminating against Indians in salaries, job opportunities, and judicial and political affairs.[10] But González Casanova blamed the maintenance of internal colonialism on not only mestizos and politicians, but also anthropologists who had failed to see Indian integration as a political problem. He challenged Mexican anthropologists "to study systematically the problem of exploitation and politics."[11]

The student movement and open confrontation between the military and students in 1968 helped fan the critical attitude already sparked in the ranks of anthropologists. Mexican university students, like those of many other nations during this period, turned to the writings of Mao Tse-tung, Karl Marx, and other critics of capitalist governments. Professional anthropologists reacted not only to the readings and thoughts of their students, but also to the contradictions they themselves witnessed in the rural areas. Initially the indigenism movement had had as its goal the protection of indigenous Mexicans and the integration of the Indians into the mainstream of national life. However, as these trends had developed since the 1940's, the indigenous had been neither protected nor integrated.[12]

Since Independence, the Indian had been locked in a caste-like system, which defined his position at the bottom of the nation's socioeconomic hierarchy. Throughout the nineteenth century and in the early years of the twentieth century, shifting land-holding policies had alternately denied him communal ownership of land and reinstated modified indigenous communal land-holding practices. Some groups had, through these crises, maintained closed community systems, or had, at least, held the community as the haven of significant cultural values which helped the Indian define primary membership roles. Therefore, community sentiments were, in many cases, strong; in other areas, membership in a particular tribal group, such as the Zapotecs or Otomi, bound identification and determined acceptable roles and behavior for group members. But indigenism-integration policies and practices had sometimes disoriented community and group loyalties and behavioral values. Many Indians had, through one or more indigenist programs, been introduced to just enough trappings of the national culture to become restless in the Indian community. Primary schools had taught of the outside world, but few areas could provide the secondary training necessary for participation at anything other than the unskilled level of the national economy. Therefore, Indians who migrated to regional and urban centers often became employees of mestizos, frequently and historically the main exploiters of the Indian. Hence, the integration movement had, in many instances, worked to free the Indians from their formerly isolated closed community status, which had, in itself, been a form of protection. Indeed, some critics argued that integration efforts had, in effect, turned the Indian out of his own community and into the exploitive grasp of mestizos eager to capitalize on the Indian's inability to participate in any but the lowest level of the national labor market. Those who had moved to the cities were not equipped for well-paying jobs, and they were becoming part of the growing urban marginal population. Professionals and students alike pointed to the centralization of INI and education programs, as well as public works projects, and began to argue that neither integration nor centralization could, by their very nature, respect the Indian groups and their need for self-determination.[13] Once again, as in the late nineteenth century, Mexico's dualistic cultural base and her quest for national unity were facing each other in opposing stances. If integration had to come through centralized agencies, which, through their very guidelines for efficiency, had to generalize their modes of operation and, to a certain extent, their goals, then the peculiarities of Indian groups could not be respected. Furthermore, as developers made inroads into formerly isolated areas, they paved the way for exploiters and cultural intermediaries whose actions were not assuaged by the humanistic spirit within indigenism. Did national unity have to mean the political, social, and economic integration of the Indians? Did the community structure, economic patterns, and language of each Indian group have to be molded to a centralized pattern? Did the maintenance of the separate cultures of the indigenous groups threaten national political unity?

In late 1969, a group of anthropologists in Oaxaca gained the permission of the state's governor, Victor Bravo Ahuja, to establish an Institute of Investigation and Social Integration in an attempt to answer some of these questions. Characterizing the relations between the valley's indigenous groups and the outside society as "colonial," the Institute set out to determine external and internal societal structures of the valley and to define their interrelationships. A basic premise of the group was to allow the Indians self-determination in the use of their own languages, arts, and forms of social organization. On the surface, the Institute may have seemed little different from others established through the indigenism movement. But the idea of colonized-colonizer, implying that the nation was the colonizer intent on using indigenous groups as colonies, was a phrase the older indigenists were hearing frequently from the critics of former indigenist policies.[14] Before the Oaxaca project had time to get firmly established, its director, Gloria Ruíz de Bravo Ahuja, and several of its personnel were moved to Mexico City for new duties. The new President Luis Echeverría Alvarez, elected in 1970, appointed Victor Bravo Ahuja, the director's husband, as Minister of Education. As Oaxaca's governor, Bravo Ahuja had distinguished himself as a firm supporter of improved education opportunities for the Indian and a state leader capable of initiating practices and programs independent of national sponsorship. These two characteristics of Bravo Ahuja's performance as governor carried over into the major trademarks of his reform program as Minister of Education.

The new President and Bravo Ahuja were determined, in short, to build education reform into a bridge that would connect two innovative aspects of the administration's total program: decentralization of funds and responsibilities and redefinition of political, economic, and social development. Echeverría promised state leaders a greater share of federal funds and executive powers than they had held in the past. The proliferation of bureaucratic offices and the resultant maze of communication among government offices had, in past administrations, decreased the capability of political elites to carry out public policies. For Mexico's heterogeneous populations, the usual programs for development—centralization of political powers, increased economic growth rate, urbanization, and mass mobilization to a single communicative standard—had been tried and found unsatisfactory. Echeverría proposed instead decentralization, a slowed economic growth rate, a shift of development emphasis from urban industrialization to agriculture and related industry, and regional mobilization through direct primary-level communication. Six months into his term, the new President was asked the purpose of his extensive travels and the multilateral nature of his activities. Echeverría replied that Mexico could not be governed from "behind a desk" nor could the legitimacy of Mexico's democracy be established through mass communication. He added: "There coexists within our vast territory populations which live at distinctly different levels of material and cultural evolution. All these groups have social and economic needs which demand attention; all these people need to express directly—and in their own language—their problems and cooperative projects." [15] Direct contact with the populace, a decrease in structural differentiation and functional specificity within the bureaucracy, and an open-ended socioeconomic program dependent on dialogue between governing and governed were Echeverría's goals.

Implicit in the new philosophy of government was a challenge to government departments to communicate and cooperate. Hereafter, the location of new roads should be determined by the possibilities of not only increased efficiency in the transportation of goods, but also increased access to schools and new salary opportunities for rural workers helping build national highways through their region.[16] Land distribution methods should be localized and particular attention given to Indian regions.[17] Bravo Ahuja reflected this emphasis in his announcement of an education reform program which placed a premium on creative plans of action which complemented the integration efforts of other ministries. The new Ministry included four sub-secretariats: Primary and Normal Education; Middle, Technical and Higher Education; Popular Culture and Extra-Scholastic Education; and Planning and Educational Coordination. Most relevant for Indian affairs was his appointment of Ramón Bonfil, long an exponent of bilingual education, as Sub-Secretary of Primary and Normal Education and Gonzalo Aguirre Beltrán, former director of the Inter-American Indigenist Institute, as Sub-Secretary of Popular Culture and Extra-Scholastic Education.[18] Alfonso Caso, who had directed the National Indigenist Institute since its inauguration, had died earlier in the year, and Aguirre Beltrán had relinquished his post at the Inter-American Institute to become the director of INI. Now, communication and the coordination of efforts between the Ministry of Education and INI was embodied in Aguirre Beltrán, officially established in both institutions. Appointed as technical sub-director of Aguirre Beltrán's agency in the Ministry of Education was Evangelina Arana de Swadesh, widow of Mauricio Swadesh and a linguist who had centered her professional work in the Oaxaca valley. Active in both the evolution of methodology and the recruitment of personnel throughout INI's history, she was prepared to help Indian areas provide their own specially tailored fundamental education programs and development plans.

Shortly after Echeverría's inauguration, a delegation representing Indians of the Sierra Occidental called on the President to present their suggested program of development for the Tepehuanos, Coras, and Hiuchols. The President listened to their plans and abruptly suggested he and his staff members directly concerned with Indian affairs visit the area the next week. The astonished delegates were asked to prepare maps of the area; Echeverría's staff members prepared accounts of the previous work of their particular agencies in the area. Met by a delegation which included Fernando Benítez, a novelist and outspoken defender of the Indians, Echeverría fielded an array of questions which helped him pinpoint a shift in indigenist policy under his administration. When asked of development plans for the area, the President asserted the need for roads, irrigation, electricity, and industry, but he stated firmly his desire to hear what the Indians themselves felt they needed. A delegation of Indians complied with his request: schools, land, fertilizer, and technical training centers were their felt needs. When spokesmen for the Indians warned that roads and industries could bring exploiters and intermediaries who did not promote the Indians' interest, Echeverría pointed to his sub-secretary of coordination, Secretary of Public Education, and director of INI as personnel representing his administration's special emphasis on the coordination of regional development plans to prevent the Indians' exploitation.[19]

On a more theoretical level, the debates of anthropologists themselves had set the stage for the formulation of new guidelines in the relationship between anthropologists, political decision-makers, and the Indian populations. Issues of *América Indígena*, throughout the election year of 1970, reported a defense of one or another position and served as a forum for differing opinions. Aguirre Beltrán and others defending the historical evolution of Mexican indigenism argued that the movement had to have as its goal national integration through democratic development. Indigenists wanted to enable Indians to escape their ethnic caste-like status and seek representation in the economic stratification system open to all citizens. Aguirre Beltrán spoke of the indigenist as one who centered his interest in the nation as an overall unity and not in the Indian as an individual.[20] Spokesmen for the new departure argued that the ethnic and cultural identity of the Indian should be maintained; the Indian should not be integrated through a paternalistic approach maintaining the status quo in class relations. Referring to the arguments of Stalin, Lenin, and Marx, these anthropologists asserted that the Indian's loyalties to his own culture—social organization, language, and religious habits—were not necessarily inconsistent with national allegiance. Therefore, sub-national loyalties and cultural divisions need not threaten political integration, unless the nation's decision-makers fostered resentment and forced rebellion by denying cultural and ethnic autonomy to sub-national groups.[21]

Indicative of the influence of the questioning attitude among anthropologists in political decision-making positions within Echeverría's administration has been the specific review of language policy. The time-worn issue of direct method vs. bilingual education has reared its head again, but this time for the purpose of redefining the direction of language policy in Mexico. Previously, bilingual education proponents endorsed the use of the indigenous tongues as a transition stage to the adoption of the national language. Gradually, anthropologists influenced policy-makers to de-emphasize a shift to the Spanish tongue as a significant index of integration; thereafter, political decision-makers favored economic development programs over language instruction and basic education in integration plans for Indian regions. The present administration's initial position has been to balance the role of economic and education programs and to coordinate efforts among the various agencies directing each phase. Prior to Echeverría's policy of decentralization, various patterns of language loyalty at work among the Indian cultures blocked, deflected, or redirected the route of national language policy; some groups refused the national tongue; others asked for special methods; still others helped social scientists turn literacy programs into vocational training. Increased social science research has now enabled administrators to understand the complex interdependent culture patterns which rerouted earlier language policy, and to admit the merits of decentralized policy-making. Mexico's increasingly secure sense of national identity has enabled her to determine a process of modernization suitable to her populations' special needs. Political elites can now distribute funds and responsibilities at the state level and suggest that a collective national sentiment need not depend on the destruction of multiple linguistic and cultural loyalties functional at the sub-national level.

Governors in cooperation with regional representatives have been asked to determine the language policy of local education programs. No national model exists, and national officials can praise state programs for their intense consideration of "not only the different idioms and dialects, but also the idiosyncrasies of the diverse communities."[22] Three choices are available for adoption by state policy-makers for their particular purposes and cultural settings. The first proposes that Indian languages be used throughout the primary school years and only bilingual teachers instruct the Indian children. Implicitly, such a program can be followed only with relatively large groups speaking a language which has been thoroughly analyzed and in which written materials covering a broad range of topics can be prepared. The range of functions for these languages can be extended as its speakers engage in new tasks, and new vocabulary items and concepts can be introduced as linguists standardize these Indian tongues for new functions. The second policy maintains that the indigenous languages should be used for school instruction, but Spanish should be introduced as soon as possible. Implicit in this view is the assumption that Indians may keep their native tongue for in-group associations and identification, but they will adopt Spanish as the language of special functions—political and economic—in order to increase their potential for participating in the nation's range of socioeconomic activities. The third view holds that only through Castilianization by the direct method can the Indian adopt the Spanish language and adjust his behavior and role identification to bring him into the national community as a participating citizen.[23]

Mexican language policy and the debates it has engendered represent no final resolutions. As advocates of both the new departure and the traditional indigenist evolution in Mexico admit, the central spirit of action linguistics and applied anthropology in Mexico has been bold, persistent experimentation; there is no reason to believe that the dialectic of new and old will end or that the direction of language planning and indigenism will cease being determined within this on-going process of evaluation. Nevertheless, what is clear from both the history of language policy in Mexico and, within the past thirty years, its immersion in the indigenism movement, is that language policy will not be consistent throughout the nation. With no centralized agency to plan, coordinate, and enforce a national language policy, language maintenance mechanisms within various cultures will determine local language policies. Some Indian groups will continue to retain their native tongue for a broad range of functions; others will take on Spanish as a second tongue for use in a different set of functions and temporary roles; still others will take Spanish as their first language, adopt other mestizo cultural characteristics, and move out of the Indian community to enter the national socioeconomic hierarchy as mestizos. Hence, the extent to which Indian languages will be maintained and integrative behavior will be adopted depends, among other things, on the nature of the general decision systems molding policy at the local level and providing technical and advisory assistance from the national level.

A Measure of Reality

Any assessment of the historical process of policy-making brings the obvious question—what have the quantitatively-measured results of policy changes been? Social scientists have always been reluctant to turn to census data as a reliable index of change, but linked with an historical narrative of policy changes, these data may serve as a corollary tool of analysis. The statistical data examined here rely on figures from the Mexican national census of 1940, 1950, 1960, and 1970.[24] The primary questions asked are: What linguistic shifts have occurred in certain Mexican states during these periods? Do these changes parallel the shift in national language policy from instruction by the direct method and the promotion of a single standard, to the acceptance of bilingual education and bilingualism among portions of the population?

The tables make use of census data for the top ten states ranked according to the number of monolingual and bilingual Indian speakers. Table I indicates that the percentage of Spanish

TABLE I

PERCENTAGES OF POPULATION FIVE YEARS OF AGE AND OVER, SPEAKING INDIAN LANGUAGES AND SPANISH, INDIAN LANGUAGES EXCLUSIVELY, AND SPANISH EXCLUSIVELY, AND PER CENT CHANGE, 1940-50, 1950-60, 1960-70

State	Per Cents of State Totals				Per Cent Change		
	1940	1950	1960	1970	1940-50	1950-60	1960-70
Chiapas							
Bilingual	11.7	12.4	22.5	10.8	+ 6.0	+81.5	−52.0
Monolingual*	21.3	13.8	15.5	11.4	−35.2	+12.3	−26.5
Spanish	67.1	73.7	61.9	77.8	+ 9.8	−16.0	+25.7
Guerrero							
Bilingual	6.2	8.4	10.1	5.7	+35.5	+20.2	−43.6
Monolingual	14.0	7.6	10.0	6.5	−45.7	+31.6	−35.0
Spanish	79.8	83.9	79.8	87.8	+ 5.1	− 4.9	+10.0
Hidalgo							
Bilingual	14.9	16.7	15.8	12.5	+12.1	− 5.4	−20.9
Monolingual	18.6	8.5	12.2	7.9	−54.3	+43.5	−35.2
Spanish	66.6	74.7	71.8	79.6	+12.2	− 3.9	+10.9
Mexico							
Bilingual	13.9	12.2	8.6	5.8	−12.2	−29.5	−32.6
Monolingual	7.0	3.3	2.3	.7	−52.9	−30.3	−69.6
Spanish	79.1	84.4	89.0	93.5	+ 6.7	+ 5.5	+ 5.1
Michoacán							
Bilingual	3.8	3.3	3.0	2.6	−13.2	− 9.1	−13.3
Monolingual	2.3	1.0	.8	.6	−56.5	−20.0	−25.0
Spanish	93.8	95.6	96.1	96.7	+ 1.9	+ .5	+ .6

TABLE I—Continued

	Per Cents of State Totals				Per Cent Change		
State	1940	1950	1960	1970	1940-50	1950-60	1960-70
Oaxaca							
Bilingual	23.1	30.6	26.5	27.7	+32.5	−13.4	+ 4.5
Monolingual	31.7	17.5	20.4	12.1	−44.8	+16.6	−40.7
Spanish	45.2	51.8	53.1	60.2	+14.6	+ 2.5	+13.4
Puebla							
Bilingual	14.4	13.0	9.7	12.0	− 9.7	−25.4	+23.7
Monolingual	14.8	8.7	8.0	4.5	−41.2	− 8.0	−43.8
Spanish	70.8	78.2	82.2	83.6	+10.5	+ 5.1	+ 1.7
San Luis Potosí							
Bilingual	5.4	8.4	8.8	8.3	+55.6	+ 4.8	− 5.7
Monolingual	8.8	4.0	4.7	2.5	−54.5	+17.5	−46.8
Spanish	85.7	87.5	86.3	89.2	+ 2.1	− 1.4	+ 3.4
Veracruz							
Bilingual	8.9	9.6	8.6	8.5	+ 7.9	−10.4	− 1.2
Monolingual	9.1	5.1	5.1	2.8	−44.0	0	−45.1
Spanish	82.0	85.2	86.2	88.6	+ 3.9	+ 1.2	+ 2.8
Yucatan							
Bilingual	46.6	53.9	43.7	46.7	+15.7	−18.9	+ 6.9
Monolingual	27.4	10.0	12.6	8.8	−63.5	+26.0	−30.2
Spanish	26.1	35.9	43.6	44.5	+37.5	+21.4	+ 2.1
Total 10 states							
Bilingual	14.9	16.9	15.7	14.1	+13.4	− 7.1	−10.2
Monolingual	15.5	8.0	9.2	5.8	−48.4	+15.0	−37.0
Spanish	69.6	75.1	75.0	80.1	+ 7.9	− .1	+ 6.8
Total Mexico							
Bilingual	7.5	7.6	6.6	5.7	− 1.3	−13.2	−13.6
Monolingual	7.4	3.7	3.8	2.2	−50.0	+ 2.7	−42.1
Spanish	85.1	88.3	89.1	92.1	+ 3.8	+ .9	+ 3.4

* Monolingual is the percentage representing monolingual speakers of indigenous languages.

speakers grew in every state from 1940 to 1950 and 1960 to 1970; in the intermediate decade (1950-1960), this percentage increased in only six of the ten states. The percentage of bilinguals increased in seven states in the first period, three in the second and third periods. The percentage of Indian monolinguals decreased in every state from 1940 to 1950, and 1960 to 1970, but this percentage increased in six states and remained the same in a seventh from 1950 to 1960.

Absolute figures in Table II show that in all three decades, Spanish speakers increased in every state. Bilinguals increased in every state in 1940-1950, and in seven states in 1950-1960 and 1960-1970. Indian language monolinguals decreased in every state between 1940-1950 and 1960-1970, and increased in eight states between 1950-1960.[25] Since it might be argued that the increase in the number of bilinguals represents nothing more than an increase in the Indian population, it should be noted that in the decade of 1940-1950, seven states showed a greater increase in bilinguals than in the total population; in the last two decades three states showed a greater increase in bilinguals than in the total population. The bilingual increase exceeded the increase in the number of Spanish speakers in five states in the first decade, four states in the second, and two states in the third. Within the nation as a whole the percentage of the monolingual and bilingual indigenous populations aged five and over was 14.9 in 1940, 11.3 in 1950, 10.4 in 1960, and 7.9 in 1970. In absolute figures, there were 2,490,909 persons speaking Indian languages in 1940; 2,447,607 in 1950; 3,030,254 in 1960; 3,156,616 in 1970.

Interpretive conclusions drawn from these data must be very tentative, until microsociolinguistic studies are done in Indian regions to verify these suggestions. However, several provisional reactions may be offered to explain the pattern of linguistic shifts shown in Figure 1. Between 1940 and 1950, the first decade of active bilingual education, there was a sharp absolute and relative decline in monolingualism. During the next decade, there was a moderate increase in both relative and absolute figures representing monolingualism. However, during the most recent decade, these figures have swung back again to show a decrease. In the first decade when monolinguals decreased in number and proportion, bilinguals and Spanish speakers increased; when monolinguals peaked during the middle decade, both bilinguals and Spanish speakers showed a relative decrease. However, during this period, the increase in the number of bilinguals was greater than that representing Spanish speakers. In the decade of the

TABLE II

NUMBER OF PERSONS FIVE YEARS OF AGE AND OVER, THEIR LINGUISTIC STATUS, AND PER CENT CHANGE, 1940-50, 1950-60, 1960-70

State	Raw Figures				Per Cent Change		
	1940	1950	1960	1970	1940-50	1950-60	1960-70
Chiapas							
Population	568147	756559	1005439	1301140	+33.16	+32.87	+29.41
Bilingual	66404	93843	225913	140116	+41.32	+140.70	−37.98
Monolingual*	120735	104244	155844	147720	−13.66	+49.50	− 5.21
Spanish	381008	557660	622379	1013304	+46.36	+11.61	+62.81
Guerrero							
Population	622231	776978	992810	1322091	+24.87	+27.78	+33.17
Bilingual	38363	65452	100378	75091	+70.61	+53.36	−25.19
Monolingual	87173	59241	98999	85091	−32.04	+67.11	−14.04
Spanish	496695	651624	792488	1161909	+31.19	+21.62	+46.62
Hidalgo							
Population	652792	712434	831254	991009	+ 9.14	+16.69	+19.22
Bilingual	96940	119228	131588	123500	+22.99	+10.37	− 6.15
Monolingual	121372	60401	101751	77868	−50.24	+68.46	−23.47
Spanish	434480	532199	596894	789641	+22.49	+12.16	+32.29

Table II—Continued

State	Raw Figures				Per Cent Change		
	1940	1950	1960	1970	1940-50	1950-60	1960-70
Mexico							
Population	976047	1175026	1575334	3127510	+20.39	+34.07	+98.53
Bilingual	135931	143844	134685	180046	+ 5.82	− 6.37	+33.75
Monolingual	67852	39207	35662	20683	−42.21	− 9.04	−42.00
Spanish	772264	991232	1402549	2926781	+28.35	+41.50	+108.68
Michoacán							
Population	1008026	1199648	1544017	1919728	+19.01	+28.71	+24.33
Bilingual	38580	39167	45867	50525	+ 1.52	+17.11	+10.16
Monolingual	23561	12106	12432	12325	−48.61	+ 2.69	− .86
Spanish	945885	1147324	1483989	1856878	+21.30	+ 2.93	+25.13
Oaxaca							
Population	1016386	1212258	1459762	1816959	+19.27	+20.42	+24.47
Bilingual	234480	371333	386099	502533	+58.36	+ 3.98	+30.16
Monolingual	322077	212520	297319	220015	−34.01	+39.90	−26.00
Spanish	459829	627549	775427	1094411	+36.47	+23.56	+41.14
Puebla							
Population	1104877	1376306	1653336	2093224	+24.57	+20.13	+26.61
Bilingual	159473	178519	160736	251946	+11.94	− 9.96	+56.75
Monolingual	163616	118971	132621	94194	−27.29	+11.47	−28.98
Spanish	781788	1076306	1358302	1747084	+37.67	+20.76	+28.62

San Luis Potosí							
Population	572518	720242	868302	1058668	+25.80	+20.56	+21.92
Bilingual	31185	60124	76750	87945	+92.76	+27.65	+14.59
Monolingual	50586	28972	41087	25953	−42.72	+41.81	−36.83
Spanish	490747	630224	748861	944770	+28.42	+18.82	+26.16
Veracruz							
Population	1374343	1718041	2286745	3171851	+25.01	+33.10	+38.71
Bilingual	121673	165421	196264	270686	+35.96	+18.65	+37.92
Monolingual	125375	87318	115940	89623	−30.35	+32.77	−22.70
Spanish	1127295	1462955	1971850	2811542	+29.78	+34.79	+42.58
Yucatan							
Population	359726	437493	525464	643432	+21.62	+2.01	+22.45
Bilingual	167538	235857	229477	300700	+40.78	−2.71	+31.04
Monolingual	98447	43523	66403	56570	−55.79	+52.56	−14.81
Spanish	93741	156845	228924	286162	+67.32	+45.96	+25.00

* Monolingual is the figure representing monolingual speakers of indigenous languages. In some years the sum of Spanish monolinguals, Indian monolinguals, and bilinguals will not total the entire population five years of age and over; speakers of foreign languages account for this difference.

sixties, the pattern of linguistic shifts leveled to show a moderate absolute and relative decrease of monolinguals, a relative decrease and absolute increase of bilinguals, and both an absolute and relative increase of Spanish speakers. Within each decade since 1940, there has been an absolute increase in both bilinguals and Spanish speakers.

The pattern of these linguistic shifts may be interpreted to show a peaking of enthusiasm for the national language in the first decade, a reaction in the next decade, and the beginning of a leveling period in the 1960-1970 period. The Mexican Revolution provoked a movement toward national culture which peaked during the early forties as a result of Cárdenas' strong push for Indian integration and the active literacy campaign of Avila Camacho's term. Thereafter particularistic reactions between 1950 and 1960 in certain regions of the nation may have offset this shift to the national. However, in the last decade, the expanded activities of INI, the national endorsement of bilingualism in indigenism, and the increase of technical knowledge and trained personnel have helped increase the number of Indians learning Spanish. Karl Deutsch, in an effort to delineate the laws underlying the processes of assimilation, noted that the linguistic assimilation of minority groups to the national language correlated with the intense feelings of nationalism arising first during a period of intensive modernization.[26] After this initial rise, linguistic assimilation may level off while the national economy and culture absorb those persons newly entered into the national society. Immediately following the Mexican Revolution and for the first twenty years thereafter, presumably the liberal members of the Indian communities learned Spanish to improve their economic opportunities to take advantage of the atmosphere of mobility inspired by the Revolution and the Cárdenas regime and the increased industrialization and urbanization of the postwar era. Today the traditional Indians of that period and their descendants are not being assimilated into the national language or occupations other than agriculture, forestry, or fishing; that is, they are not being assimilated into economic activities which would necessitate the learning of the national language.

In states where the number of bilinguals has increased, Regional Coordinating Centers have been most active since 1950.[27]

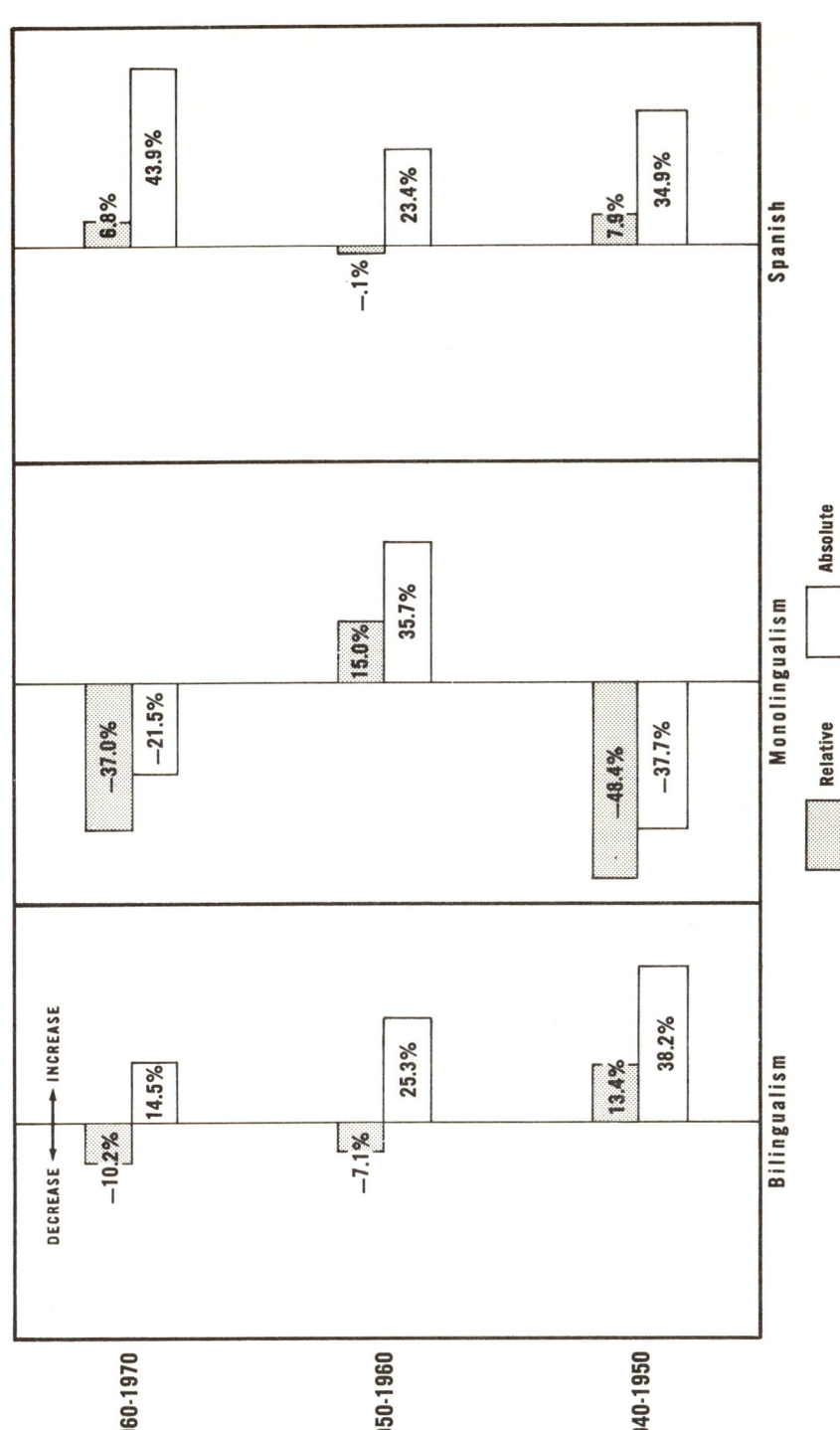

Figure 1: Linguistic Shifts, 1940-1970: Per Cent Changes — Ten Indian States

The acceptance of bilingual education by the Indians and the increase in the number of bilingual cultural brokers working in cooperation with government organizations attempting to integrate the Indians has led to an increase in the numbers of those maintaining their mother tongue while learning Spanish. The hierarchy of functions of these languages has increased as bilingual promoters have taught agricultural techniques and various technical skills in the Indian tongues and provided adult monolingual Indian speakers with the opportunity to pass on this information to other monolingual Indian speakers.

In 1958, Oscar Lewis, interpreting figures from the census returns of 1940 and 1950, predicted that monolingualism in the Indian languages would decrease at an annual rate of 3.5 per cent and disappear around the year 2007.[28] He judged linguistic shifts in Mexico before what appears to have been the beginning of the leveling stage in linguistic assimilation. This stage appears to be a pragmatic approach to the maintenance of the rural populations in efficient and effective production in their own cultural environments. Certainly, the present leveling stage of linguistic assimilation corresponds with Echeverría's emphasis on rural development. The maintenance of the Indian tongues in an expanding hierarchy of functions and the increase in a differentiation of functions for Spanish and the Indian tongues would seem to suggest that the leveling stage will continue much longer than Lewis' predictions assumed, and the Indian languages will not disappear as rapidly as he suggested. In the 1930's, Mauricio Swadesh predicted that if the rate of extinction of Indian languages during the past 400 years of educational neglect continued, it would take 200 additional years for all the indigenous tongues of Mexico to disappear; that if the forced direct Castilianization program of the national period prior to the 1930's were continued, the linguistic resistance of the Indians could hold out another 600 years. However, under a policy of indigenism which would eliminate the exploitation of Indians by mestizos and provide realistic opportunities for Indians to improve their social and economic conditions, the Indian tongues might well disappear within a century.[29] Under such a policy, many Indians would learn Spanish while retaining their own tongue and would subsequently alter other habits for the improvement of their health or living conditions.

Swadesh's predictions for the modernization of Indians through bilingual education seem to be supported by the data in Table III. Implicit in programs of directed change during the 1940's, 1950's, and 1960's was the assumption that bilingualism in Spanish and an indigenous language was a transitional stage in the process of changing a monolingual aboriginal speaker to a monolingual Spanish speaker. A corollary of this assumption was that bilingualism was the mark of a former Indian in transition from his indigenous customs to the acquisition of living habits customarily associated with non-Indians. Culture change in Mexico and movement from one social status to a higher status in the national classificatory scheme have been very much bound up with learning the national language. The relationship between change or stability in habitual language use, on the one hand, and on-going social and cultural processes, on the other, has been assumed to be a close one.

The data in Table III attempt to answer the question of whether the linguistic status of the Indian population in Mexico can be seen as the base with which other typically coexistent characteristics of Indianism correlate.[30] The composite Indianism percentage was higher than the language percentage in all states, except Yucatan, in both 1950 and 1960. Therefore, one may tentatively suggest that Indians have learned the Spanish language earlier than they have abandoned their Indian cultural patterns and habits. Only the state of Yucatan showed in both 1950 and 1960 a higher percentage for the retention of Indian languages than for the retention of Indian customs. Since the state of Yucatan is not highly industrialized, does not have a diversity of native languages, and has a number of local market economies which are carried out in the native language, one could suggest that the means of production are not so totally derived from a monolingual Spanish speech community as are the means of production throughout the rest of Mexico. Elsewhere, INI integration programs have been more numerous and, presumably, the members of the economically active population, either through industry or national (and often regional) market commerce for agricultural products, find it economically necessary to learn the national language for particular functions.[31] Furthermore in most Indian states in Mexico, it seems apparent

TABLE III

INDIGENOUS LANGUAGE RETENTION
AND COMPOSITE OF INDIANISM

	Indigenous Language Retention**		Rank Order		Indianism Composite*		Rank Order	
	1950	1960	1950	1960	1950	1960	1950	1960
Chiapas	26.18	37.97	3	3	70.31	53.48	3	4
Guerrero	16.04	20.08	6	5	72.91	60.57	2	1
Hidalgo	25.22	28.07	4	4	67.06	53.95	4	3
Mexico	15.58	10.82	7	9	63.18	40.67	6	8
Michoacán	4.27	3.78	10	10	51.26	40.97	8	7
Oaxaca	48.16	46.82	2	2	73.03	56.92	1	2
Puebla	21.62	17.74	5	6	65.06	53.39	5	5
San Luis Potosí	12.37	13.57	9	8	61.30	49.46	7	6
Veracruz	14.71	13.65	8	7	46.26	31.94	9	9
Yucatan	63.86	56.31	1	1	21.95	23.56	10	10

* This Indianism composite was determined by averaging the percentages for that portion of the population either going barefoot or wearing sandals, and the percentage of the population not eating bread.
** This figure includes both monolingual Indian speakers and bilingual speakers, since during the 1950's and 1960's it was generally assumed that the latter were in a state of transition and were often more fluent in the Indian language than in Spanish.

that members of the economically active population find it desirable to accept not only the national tongue, but also some modern cultural characteristics in habits of food and dress.

These conclusions, resting on the use of statistical analysis as a corollary tool with the historical process of language planning in Mexico and the implications of linguistic and anthropological theories, suggest the need for more research at the community and regional level. Studies carried out in individual communities in Mexico could indicate who says what to whom when and how, as well as much about the social and economic life of the community and its functional relationships with broker institutions or individuals linked to the national society. Systematic and comparative studies of the language component in the social and economic integration of Indian communities and regions could be especially helpful when linked with national case studies of linguistic and national integration through national language planning.

CHAPTER NINE

Overview and Conclusions

The Historical Process

History has shown that the Conquistadors did, indeed, walk into a solution and make it a problem. The solution Cortés and his men found in the Aztec empire's territory was the expansion of Nahuatl as the official language of the empire by bilinguals from *both* the Aztec community and subjugated and neighboring tribes. Nahuatl spread as the instrument of political and economic intercourse between the Aztec interpreters and record-keepers and members of the tribes in the Aztec tributary system. The Aztecs designated certain members of their group to learn the language of subjugated tribes and to serve as interpreters. The tribes from whom the Aztecs collected tribute and their neighbors, in turn, learned Nahuatl for use in their trade with one another; Nahuatl provided the bridge of communication among diverse linguistic groups. The use and acceptance of Nahuatl as the standard idiom of commerce, law, and economics permitted all groups except those, such as the Tarascans, who held themselves linguistically apart in autonomous nations, to have a lingua franca.

But Nahuatl was not only a highly effective supranational linguistic standard within the multilingual tributary system of the Aztec empire and among other groups in pre-Hispanic Mexico; it was also a standard language with a full range of functions for native speakers within the Aztec empire. It was the medium of communication in the daily activities of workers as well as in the poetry of artists and the discourse of scientists. The council of arts and sciences in Texcoco, the cultural capital, judged both poetry and scientific treatises, guarding the intellectual achievements of the empire and the maintenance of the purity of Nahuatl. This council served the function of a modern-day language academy, codifying the aesthetic norms of both the standard language and the poetic idiom. After the Conquest, Mendieta, Sahagún, and other Spaniards judged Nahuatl capable as a language of scientific discourse and literary expression, effective and pleasing in its formulation and rendering of precision and abstraction. In total impact, Nahuatl had a hierarchy of functions comparable to that suggested in modern theoretical discussions of the functional differentiation of a standard language. Linguists of the Prague School have particularly regarded the functions of language and stylistic variations of language as differentiated according to various functions. Their schematic survey of the functional differentiation of a standard language includes conversational, workaday technical, theoretical (scientific) technical, and aesthetic communication, each with its own stylistic variations according to setting. Conversational language depends on the connotative and denotative values made automatic and intelligible through the shared cultural background of the speakers. Matter-of-fact or workaday technical assumes a high degree of information transmission on the basis of a unified vocabulary with referents made definite by convention.[1] Presumably, as suggested by the materials available from the periods immediately before and just after the Conquest, interpreters and scribes determined the conventional language exchanged between representatives of the Aztec empire and bilingual members of subjugated tribes. The council of arts and sciences watched over the aesthetic and scientific functions of Nahuatl, insuring that the lexical units of the latter were accurate and precise. In judging poetic language, the council considered it necessary that relation of vocabulary to referents be both clear in meaning and capable of calling attention to the devices of language for a full appreciation of both content and expression. Nahuatl was a language with a rich literary heritage, both written and oral. The

Spaniards found that Nahuatl's hierarchy of functions compared both similarly and favorably with that of Latin; that is, both tongues served in workaday technical inter-group and intra-group communication in politics, economics, and law, and Nahuatl functioned, as Latin had in the past, for conversational, scientific, and poetic expression within its own native-speaking groups.[2] The only deficiency the Spaniards found in Nahuatl as a standard language was its lack of a conventional writing system, and early teachers soon found that ideographic writing could be translated to alphabetic form, and spoken speech could be transcribed in the Roman alphabet.

But the Conquistadors failed to adopt the standard language of the Aztecs as a coordinate idiom to be used with Castilian in the administrative affairs of the colony; thus, they rejected the solution the Aztecs had devised for the problem of linguistic diversity within their empire. The Conquistadors and early settlers brought to Mexico the cultural and linguistic confidence of a nation fresh from the Reconquest and an intense "Castilianization" program. The vigorous and flexible speech of the court of Castile was the model for those who manned the vice-regal court in Mexico. Determined to link Castilian culture with a program of religious nationalization at home, Isabella and her sixteenth-century successors also insisted that within the colonies Catholicism be identified with Castilianization, so that the barbarians of the New World would be made subject to God and the Crown. Nebrija, Isabella's court historiographer, insisted on an active role for language in the building of the empire and prescribed that the religion and ideology of Castile be taught in the Castilian tongue.

But expediency and a short-range satisfaction of the need to communicate with the natives directed lay Spaniards to a false sense of security in their use of translators pulled from the indigenous societies and taught Spanish in order that they might serve as go-betweens in the administrative affairs of the colony. Unlike the Aztecs, the lay Spaniards trained only members of the subjugated peoples as translators and interpreters; they did not train members of their own group as secretaries and translators. Naguatlatos worked as interpreters in the secondary stages of the Conquest and later they kept local records in Nahuatl. Religious regulars trained the naguatlatos as legal secretaries, record-keepers, court translators, and, occasionally, lower-level government officials. Cortés and the early settlers set a precedent which continued during the next 200 years.

As for the religious Spaniards, they felt their cause too precious to trust entirely to native translators, and they quickly delegated members of their own group to learn the indigenous tongues. Wanting a real, rather than an apparent transformation in the Indian's soul, the religious regulars, fresh from Cisneros' moralistic revamping and humanistic language training, learned to speak to the Indian in his native tongue and attempted to understand his culture through his medium of communication. Through their own experiences which convinced them of the bond between language and cultural habits, the dedicated linguists among the regulars attempted to persuade both the religious seculars and the lay officials that the only sure way to bring the Indian to a Christian way of life was to teach the native with an understanding of his culture and through his own tongue.

Meanwhile, though quite admittedly their purpose was not the political incorporation of the natives into the Spanish colony, the religious regulars advised local administrators that the promotion of Nahuatl as the universal language of the Indians was not only the most effective technique for Christianization, but it was also a sure method for reducing the number of diverse tongues spread throughout the colony. A decrease in linguistic diversity would surely facilitate the Indians' political and cultural socialization, making it possible to govern the Indians as "reasonable men" living in communities under the Spanish pattern of social organization. As the regulars, especially the Franciscans, trained scribes and translators as well as sacristans and clerical assistants in the schools they provided for the Indians, they encouraged the retention of Nahuatl as the language of the Indians. The natives pled their cases in court through naguatlatos; the regulars mediated between them and the Spaniards and God. In the village churches, they confessed in Nahuatl, and either the friars or native assistants preached in Nahuatl.

Had the Crown encouraged its lay representatives to learn Nahuatl in order to carry out the business affairs of the colony, the religious policy of perpetuating and spreading Nahuatl would not have left the Indians isolated from the social and political ways of the Spaniards and dependent on the all-too-frequent duplicities of native translators turned henchmen for the Spaniards. Language did not become the perfect instrument of empire for Castile, because of the wide divergence between the Crown's avowed policy to link Catholicism with Castilianization and the actual practices carried out by local Crown representatives in New Spain. Philip II encouraged the regulars to teach Christianity in Nahuatl, admitting the merit of instructing the natives in their own tongue, but he and other monarchs before him made few and feeble attempts at including an intensive program for Castilianization in the instruction the religious offered the Indians. And after the initial refusal by the conquerors and encomenderos to teach the ways of living of "reasonable men" to the natives, the Crown did not turn again to lay representatives in the New World to serve as cultural brokers. The Indians were grouped in villages patterned on Spanish models, but they were left to the charge of the Crown's religious representatives who spoke the native tongue, and Spaniards were prohibited from mingling with the Indians in these protected communities. Politics and Hispanic society—literature, fine dress, and social ideals—were largely confined to Mexico City. The simple Spanish used by native foremen to give work orders, and the servile phrases required of domestics by Spanish ladies who wished to accentuate the subservience of the Indians' position comprised the primary remedial elements of bilingualism for workaday communication in the world outside the conventos.

The first serious renewal of efforts by the Crown to link Castilian with any cultural element other than religion came over 100 years after the Conquest, when Charles II ordered that religious and secular leaders see that the Indians learn Spanish and other "good habits of reasonable men" for the benefits these would bring in their dealings with Spaniards. However, the instructors in the schools the King suggested as the basic institution for dissemination of the Spanish language were still the friars who, for their purposes, had no desire to teach all Indians Spanish. Moreover, the friars were disposed to change neither the cultural habits nor the language of the Indians, so long as the natives became Christians. The religious were in the New

World to perform their duties to God, the Pope, and the King as the royal representative of the Church; they were, in their own view, not emissaries of the King as the chief official of the Castilian state. Hence, they did not judge it their duty to see that the Indians became good citizens in the King's empire. Providing instruction for the natives in schools taught by lay teachers was a preposterous notion, and both the religious regulars and the King's political administrators knew the Crown had enough problems providing education opportunities for the Spanish subjects of the New World. Therefore, Charles II and future Spanish monarchs found it necessary to entrust language instruction to religious representatives and to hope that a barrage of decrees and official pleas would induce the regulars to include the teaching of Spanish in their responsibilities toward the Indians.

But neither a considerable amount of badgering by Charles II and Charles III nor the intense efforts of Archbishop Lorenzana changed the practices of the priests, and at the time of Independence, Spanish was strictly the code of the elite, that is, of peninsular Spaniards, creoles, and a few descendants of Indian nobility. During the first years after Independence, the new nation's political leaders closed their eyes to the masses in the countryside, declared there were no Indians in Mexico, and centered their energies and interests in education on the debate between Church and state. For over sixty years, education was largely immobilized, even for the upper classes, and little attention was given the Indians. With the political stability of Porfirio Díaz's regime, a few political and educational leaders turned their attention to the indigenous populations, and they debated the contributions of these to the nation's history and the state's responsibilities to the Indians. In 1875 Mexican intellectuals organized the Mexican branch of the *Real Academia Española,* and the nation's educational leaders announced the choice of the standard language for Mexico—the Castilian not of the Iberian Peninsula, but the Spanish forged from the unique Mexican cultural heritage. And this heritage included not only the predictable Hispanic bestowals, but also the contributions of Cuauhtémoc's descendants. A flurry of efforts to concentrate the attention of the populace on the Indians and their cultural contributions to the nation's past coincided with efforts to codify the national standard. Intellectuals debated the inclusion of Mexicanisms, words or phrases which had crept into the Spanish of Mexico, in the official Academy dictionary. To standardize the lexicon, pronunciation, grammar, and orthography "in a struggle for the maintenance of the language"[3] was the duty of the Mexican Academy members.

Educators filled the pages of their professional journals with discussions of the need to codify the national standard. They not only listened carefully to the proceedings of their own national codifying agency, but they also drew heavily on methodologies endorsed by language academicians in nations such as Germany, France, and Russia. Before Mexican educators accepted spelling reform according to the principles of *fonetismo*, which would alter the spelling of words for better agreement with pronunciation, they carefully studied the recommendations of famous grammarians and examined the success of phonetism in orthographic reform adopted by other Latin American nations.[4] Teachers' reading materials and texts continually quoted a wide array of authorities who insisted Mexico needed a norm codified through grammars and primers used in schools. Government leaders in education prepared readers and spellers which incorporated the endorsed orthographic reforms. Both educators and Academy members watched over the development of vocabulary to handle the growing number of scientific concepts, which positivists had so enthusiastically introduced in the schools' curricula.

Contributions from the Indian tongues were the concern of linguists and anthropologists active in the newly formed Indianist Society. They traced the evolution of place names and certain phonetic influences of the Indian tongues on Spanish. They also attempted to map the distribution of languages in pre-Hispanic Mexico and studied the structures of numerous Indian tongues. Some Indianists even advocated the maintenance of the Indian languages for the clues they might provide to Mexico's indigenous past.

Even before the turn of the century, Justo Sierra and fellow statesmen spoke out for the acceptance by all Mexican citizens of a standard language to unify the nation. To the nationalistic statesmen and educators, the Indian tongues were doubly accursed—appeal though they might to the Indianists—because they both isolated their speakers from the mainstream of the Mexican culture and threatened the nation's unity against outsiders. To statesmen like Sierra, multilingualism was further questionable because it represented the maintenance of "little nations" and little nationalities more concerned to preserve their own identities than to foster the national identity. Sierra's plea for national unity through a common tongue and a program designed to eliminate the Indian languages was superseded by the campaign of the Hispanophile, José Vasconcelos, to bring not only the Hispanic tongue but also the moral instruction of literary classics to the indigenous population. The perfect picture of national unity included not only a common tongue, but also sweeping strokes of Hispanic culture and ideals. Spanish-speaking teachers were to wipe out regional "defects" through a concentrated program of teaching in Spanish using texts written in Spanish. Once the Indians learned Spanish by the direct method, they would be incorporated directly into the nation. The Spanish language was the primary path to Hispanic cultural ideals. National solidarity must stand on the same language, religion, juridical and political norms, and social habits for all Mexican citizens.

Yet, the government made no consistent directed attempt to teach Spanish to the Indians. Now that the nation's leaders had selected the national standard, they needed a plan to implement the spread of Spanish among those citizens who did not speak Spanish as their primary tongue.[5] Moreover, education leaders worked to dispel the notion of the intellectual inferiority of the Indian, and many policy-makers pleaded for a national educational system which would allow Indians to prove themselves capable in the classroom. But the only agent for the implementation of a national language policy through education was the schoolteacher in the rural school, and the government had no direct control over education in the states. The capital was primarily an information dissemination center, and through national education conferences and the personal influence of government officials in outlying normal schools, pedagogical techniques were left to spread at random. Therefore, before the nation's decision-makers could do more than select the national standard and preach its merits for national unity, the federal government had to take over the responsibility for education in all the states. The Law of Rudimentary Instruction, passed in 1911, elected as its major task the teaching of Spanish to the indigenous populations, but, again, the random influence of federal education policies plus limited personnel and funds restricted both the breadth of the program in the countryside and its intensity in the Federal District.

The archaeological discoveries of Alfonso Caso and other anthropologists in Mexico brought international fame and prodded politicians to realize that Mexico held not only archaeological remnants of past civilizations, but also living cultures descendant from Mexican antiquity. Decision-makers lamented that Mexico had so long neglected the living remnants of past civilizations, and 400 years of culture contact had brought Mexico a unity neither of interests, ideals, nor language. The 1910 Revolution helped redefine the Indian and set the stage for a political reconsideration of the role of the Indian in the on-going Mexican Revolution. Numerous distinct historical traditions within Mexico's borders blocked a unity of ideas; the diversity of religious and social customs stood in the way of unified ideals and customs. But decision-makers saw language diversity as the primary impediment blocking the integration of Mexico's assorted Indian cultures into the national union. In the early 1930's, a prominent Mexican intellectual termed language a vigorous and vital bond of nationality and "the embodiment of the spirit of a culture." [6]

If national unity in Mexico depended on a common tongue, then by definition the linguistic question was basic to the national socialization process. After the revision of the Constitution of 1917 to allow the federal government to control education in all the states, a common tongue was promoted through direct teaching in the federal rural schools and through scattered programs especially designed to incorporate the Indians of the countryside. The frustrations of teachers and educators who found that the teaching of Spanish did not transform the Indian into a productive member of society sparked a flash of "action schools," in which the Indians learned, in addition to Spanish, agricultural techniques, health measures, and other customs designed to improve their standard of living. The "house of the Indian student" was an experiment designed in part to prove the Indian could be educated in Spanish while preserving his native tongue. The success of the program and the ability of the boys to teach one another their native tongues convinced the officials that the preservation of the indigenous tongues was an efficient and effective route to real communication with the Indians. But the boys did not want to return to their villages to serve as agents of change, and though bilingualism as a technique in Indian education was recognized for its practicality, the decision-makers did not yet link bilingualism with other phases of an integration program. Even Gamio's Teotihuacán project did not set a strong precedent for including bilingual education in a nationalistic integral education program, since Gamio had not found many monolingual Indian speakers among the residents of the zone located so close to Mexico City.

In his write-up of his experiences at Carapan, Moisés Sáenz noted the Soviet pattern of national socialization. After him, educators and policy-makers in the Ministry of Education and the newly formed Department of Indian Affairs chose the most applicable aspects of the "little nationalities" policy of the Soviet Union to adapt and adopt in Mexico's national language program. The indigenous tongues were to be preserved as a route to the spirit and understanding of the Indian children, and the Indians were to have their own schools in which they would learn first of their own culture, then of that of the region and the nation. Social scientists endorsed the Soviet program more out of practical considerations than out of any wholehearted ideological endorsement of socialism. Anthropologists had come to suspect the promotion of the Hispanic culture from an intellectual perspective as essentially an ideology, or system of ideas. The normative view of culture and identification of culture with a given tradition of ideas, espoused by Sierra and Vasconcelos, as well as lesser officials, denied the existence of units of culture as aesthetic patterns or institutions. Anthropologists and education officials supported the promotion of bilingualism in the Soviet pattern, because of its apparent utility and the soundness of the psychological and sociological principles on which it stood. Socialization grounded itself in authenticity—the concentration of reading material and conversational topics in the children's native idiom in local history and culture and a gradual and natural proceeding to national symbols and heroes. This policy of re-sowing and fertilizing an identity with the local group before moving on to produce an identity with the nation as a symbolic whole built self-confidence and pride in the Indians. Aspects of the method were similar to practices of colonial missionaries: the polity's cultural brokers learned the indigenous tongues, studied Indian cultures, and attempted to strain the instruction of national values through the Indians' linguistic and cultural grid.

Language planning as it has developed since the 1930's is a case study of the coordination and cooperation of social scientists and public administrators in a program of directed cultural change. In 1948, the President of Mexico signed a bill which provided the National Indigenist Institute (INI), an amalgamated institution which included on its board of directors politicians, administrators, and educators as well as anthropologists and linguists. The Institute was to provide a direct line of communication from researchers and field workers to the capital's decision-makers. The shift from a community emphasis in Indian integration programs had been marked by the inauguration of the National Literacy Campaign in the early 1940's, but the investigations of social scientists and their reports had convinced the officials of the Ministry of Education that something more than a national approach was needed to achieve literacy among the indigenous populations. The Institute of Literacy for Monolingual Indians was formed to work in Indian regions and to prepare ethnographic materials suitable for readers used by the children and adults of these regions.

The National Indigenist Institute soon adopted the regional approach and dropped the community-centered programs of the 1930's. Anthropologists wanted to avoid any techniques which contributed to the boundary maintenance of communities; they preferred instead to emphasize the unity of regions linked through ecological factors, the market system, and community fiestas enjoyed by members outside, as well as inside, particular communities. As the Institute of Literacy for Monolingual Indians had prepared special materials for the literacy campaign in certain Indian regions, so the INI staff prepared particular materials for a full-rounded integration program in the Indian regions. INI trained bilingual cultural promoters to serve as cultural brokers between native groups and the national culture. The promoters were trained in agricultural techniques, sanitation measures, elementary literacy skills, and they brought the national culture to the villagers in a way which provided authenticity for the new cultural exposures of the Indians.

Very soon, the achievement of Spanish as a single common tongue was de-emphasized in favor of the development of bilingualism. During the early 1940's eminent anthropologists had warned of the dangers implicit in the government's emphasis on incorporation. All too frequently, the Indian who learned the Spanish language and changed his native dress and eating habits to become a mestizo had been forced to leave his community, for it was his sense of being a member of his Indian community which reinforced his former Indian habits. Indians passing as mestizos migrated to Mexico City and other growing urban centers, where they floated between two cultures, unable to return to the old and incapable through a lack of technological training and urban know-how to fit into a new culture. Anthropologists saw a much more efficient economic future for the country if the Indians and only partially acculturated mestizos remained in their villages than if they migrated to urban centers. Within their own communities, the Indians could learn effective agricultural techniques, cooperate with irrigation-project personnel, and increase the agricultural productivity of the countryside. INI and other governmental agencies would take the necessary skills and resources to the village. In providing bilingual cultural promoters in the villages and by cooperating with other branches of the government active in agrarian reform and irrigation projects, the members of INI established Regional Coordinating Centers to help the Indians adopt the technical skills and improvements provided for them through Mexico's economic and education socialization program.

Cultural homogeneity in Mexico was being replaced by the ideal of unity within diversity. Both social scientists and public administrators endorsed bilingualism as a transition stage for the shift from a regional language to the national standard. As a nation with a primary center of dissemination of both policy and practice, Mexico kept its planners close to its political administrators. Communication among planners in the social sciences, especially anthropology, was the result of the veneration of first archaeology, and later cultural anthropology, within Mexico's borders. During the 1960's and the early 1970's, indigenists who helped mold the bilingual education approach began to carry on a tolerant and mutually profitable dialogue with social scientists arguing for a new departure in Mexico's integration policies. The long chain of influence from Mariano Rojas, who had first proposed bilingual education during Maximilian's reign, to Alfonso Caso, Rojas' student at the National Museum of Archaeology, Ethnology, and History, was broken with Caso's death in 1970. Caso's successor, in national stature as both a political influence and an anthropologist, was Gonzalo Aguirre Beltrán, who had immersed himself in the history of Mexico's intersocietal relations as well as the ideological tenets of minority-majority relations in the Western and non-Western words. In this age of broad social speculation, Aguirre Beltrán and his associates at INI and within the Ministry of Public Education have heard arguments maintaining several grievances against centralized, official indigenist policy. Suggesting the Indians' cultural and linguistic authenticity must be preserved while introducing modern technological advances, other anthropologists have argued for a focus not on the community, but on the cultural and societal relations between the nation and the Indian groups. Specifically, they have proposed the coexistence of old and new, Indian and national in a bilingual-bicultural nation, accepting Indians as workers participating in various stages of the socioeconomic class hierarchy.[7]

Programs and policies of Echeverría's administration bear the mark of a reform of education and a redefinition of development for Mexico. Decentralization of finances and responsibilities to state-level officials promises to clear the way for new departures in indigenism. Presumably, those who know local Indian regions best—governors, educators, and representatives of INI who have centered their energies among certain Indian groups—will determine the policies and practices they themselves must implement. Putting a premium on inter-departmental cooperation and direct communication with the populace, administrators and anthropologists alike have recognized that bilingualism may well be a semi-permanent state, functionally efficient and effective in Mexico's newly revamped particularistic plans for the social and economic transition of her indigenous populations to modernity. Access to scientific knowledge and the discovery of modern techniques necessary for equal chances in the competition for socioeconomic gains now stand as the prime reasons for the Indian's addition of Spanish to his linguistic repertoire.[8] Always, in the past, language planning has been in the forefront of social movements for the indigenous. If the history of Mexico's language planning allows any predictions, bilingualism—the acquisition of Spanish for special functions and the maintenance of Indian tongues for in-group identification—will be the policy of the future in many Indian regions.

Social Science Perspectives

The problems of language diversity and language standardization in a variety of countries have stimulated linguists and sociolinguists to issue some tentative theories and to construct models of language planning. Their general schemes provide an opportunity for social scientists to compare the concerns of language planning in developed and developing nations and to determine the organizations and techniques of policy-makers at local and national levels. In the past, when social scientists have examined language policy within individual nations, they have viewed language either as it functioned in the historical evolution of a *developed* nation which maintained two or more tongues both associated with viable traditions, or as it progressed in acceptance from a rural vernacular to a generalized norm rivaling the official state language. The new *developing* nations, faced with nationhood after a long colonial history, inherited the language and cultural standards associated with the Christian faith of the metropolitan country; the indigenous peoples offered no major language linked with a great religion which had dictated the economic, cultural, and political lives of its adherents. In an effort to achieve national integration, the new developing nations have had to consider a multicultural approach in order to balance the need for modernity with a respect for the indigenous past.[9] Linguists or anthropologists who have looked at language planning in these nations have viewed it primarily as it operated at the local level in nations which have in the comparatively recent past gained their independence from a colonial power.[10] Within these nations, elites of the colonial domination did not comprise the numerical majority of the citizens of the newly independent nations. Therefore, the choice for a national standard language has, in various nations, been among former standard languages, none of which is indigenous to the nation's population; among indigenous idioms fighting for designation as the language of national unity; or between indigenous tongues and the metropolitan standard. In most new developing nations the political decision-makers have selected the colonial linguistic standard because of its ties to technological and political modernization.

Perhaps it is only in Latin America that social scientists have had an opportunity to view the history of language policy in nations whch have evolved through several hundred years of domination by colonial powers, relatively recent independence, and nationalistic struggles for identities all their own, trying to set themselves apart from European and North American influence. For those linguistically fragmented Latin American nations with large indigenous populations, language planning has had a special urgency. The acceptance of a national standard by Indians within these nations has often been equated in policy-making with a transition from local group identification to nationalistic loyalties and from tradition to modernity. Mexico, as a nation which, after a century and a half of independence has reached political stability and a new awareness of its indigenous population, offers an opportunity to view language policy as it has evolved since colonization by Spain in the sixteenth century. In view of Mexico's long history of colonial domination, a likely choice for the new nation's standard was Spanish, the idiom of the metropolitan country. Mexico's process of selecting a standard code had extended over the entire colonial period, and no educational system to enforce the masses' acceptance of the official language existed. The new leaders of independent Mexico passively assumed Spanish would be the nation's standard. The political and social dominance of criollos, in cultural bondage to the traditions of Europe and most particularly Spain, assured the elites' unquestioning acceptance of Spanish as the common tongue of Mexico's citizens. Until the late nineteenth century, the new nation's leaders did not examine the background of their official language legacy or initiate the active selection and determination of a national norm. Mexican Spanish became legitimate only in the last years of the nineteenth century.

Einar Haugen, a linguist and student of national language planning in Norway, has suggested that any movement for an alteration in the linguistic repertoire of a society's speakers might include four processes.[11] These alternate between initiation and implementation, between form and function. The first, the initiation of the form, is the selection of the standard norm. In Mexico's case, this selection process was extended through the colonial period and developed out of the social situation which maintained the political, social, and economic dominance of the Hispanic society over the indigenous groups. During the colonial period, Spanish, the language of the recognized elite, prevailed in international affairs, official transactions, and the culture of the dominant society. This situation continued after Independence, until political stability, a flourish of nationalistic interest in Mexico's history, and the investigations of social scientists which called attention to the Indians of the past and the present, led decision-makers to announce in the 1880's an official choice of Mexican Spanish as the national code.

The second process, which Haugen calls codification of form, assumes a literate society using the norm in written form and speech, according to certain rules of spelling, pronunciation, grammar, and vocabulary choice. In Mexico codification was the concern of the Mexican Academy of Spanish and the education leaders of the late nineteenth century. These intellectuals listened to the dictates of the Royal Academy in Madrid, and, moreover, they tried to incorporate appropriate Mexicanisms into Mexico's standard code. The Mexican Academy turned especially inward in 1951 and 1956 at the First and Second Congresses of the Academies of the Spanish Language. At both sessions, there was considerable debate among participants over the loosening of ties between the Hispanic-American academies and the mother institution in Madrid.[12] Supporters of increased autonomy in the decision-making processes of the Academies argued that strong dependence on the Madrid institution restricted their freedom to deliberate and rule on problems unique to their own national standards. Mexican spokesmen led the debate, as they insisted the rules and regulations of Madrid's institution were no longer highly significant for the idioms of the Spanish-speaking Latin American nations.

The debate provided a platform from which some members pled for an appreciation and realistic consideration of the uniqueness of the Spanish of each Latin American country, which had forged of the Castilian linguistic inheritance a norm particular to the society and culture of only that one nation. Opponents of the nationalistic rumblings expressed their long-standing devotion to the Hispanic ideals which had marked literary and linguistic evaluation by Mexican intellectuals since the forming of the Academy. José Vasconcelos urged fellow Congress participants to unify under the Hispanic sentiment: "Here we are called to fortify the bastion of the language, to add turrets and cupolas to the cathedral of its grandness, not to dissipate it in the chapels of divided nationalisms." [13] His opponents retorted that he and others of his thinking had reduced *hispanidad* to Spanish with the narrowest of meanings and the most traditional and conservative of models. Historical facts and the nationalistic struggles of Spanish-speaking Latin American nations denied the truth of other statements issued by various Academy members to call their wandering nationals back of the fold of the mother institution. The Hispanicists claimed: "the Spanish man loves the unity that is born of confidence," "the Spanish man rejects sectarianism because his mind is universal," "the Spanish man is not a reformist because he possesses the truth." [14] Mexican nationalists denied the existence of such a narrow-minded and arbitrary *hombre español;* instead they pointed to the joint heritage upon which Latin American nations had built their own particular languages, as well as political individualities. The unity of Spanish speech as the common tongue of all the Hispanic nations was a unity in diversity; "the *hispanidad* of Mexico is *mexicanidad;* that of Cuba, *cubanidad;* that of Colombia, *colombianidad;* that of Peru, *peruanidad,* etc.," forged from the special vitality and spirit of the people of each of these nations.[15]

More often than not in the ensuing years, the language academies found the "spirit of the people" in the literary productions of the elite and the culture of the urban speech community. The academies lauded writers for their defense of the idiom; poets cheered the codifying agencies for their role as watchdogs of the Spanish tongue. However, very recently, members of the Mexican Academy have turned their attention to practical discussions of their functions as codifiers of the national tongue beyond the urban centers. At a celebration of "the day of the Spanish language" held in April 1971, the president of the Academy urged his associates to join him in influencing the mass media to spread acceptable pronunciation and usage of the national standard. Unlike the citizens of Spain who took excessive freedoms with their language, the president suggested that Mexicans spoke Spanish well because they spoke it as a foreign language. The Academy had determined that sixty per cent of Mexico's population spoke the national code, while forty per cent mixed Spanish with their indigenous tongues. For this latter portion of the population, radio, movies, television, and the press had the special responsibility of strengthening the learning of Spanish; furthermore, those newly come to literacy skills needed increased opportunities to put these skills to use.[16] For the first time since its rejuvenation in 1951, a recognition of the rural speech communities caught up in Mexico's modernization program seemed implicit in the concerns of the Mexican Academy.

Other language planners and codifiers have not been content to restrict their interests in language to their own nation; they have wanted rather to determine the existence of a Latin American Spanish code. In 1964, linguists from North, Central, and South America agreed to cooperate in a coordinated project to codify the urban cultural linguistic norms of the major Hispanic American cities. The coordinator of the project to determine the phonetic, syntactical, and lexical characteristics of the norm spoken by the cultured groups of Latin American cities is a Mexican linguist, Juan M. Lope Blanch. Committee members have devised questionnaires and other recording techniques to solicit from the informants in each city the information necessary for linguists to analyze and determine the norm of the urban culture. Having done this, the linguists will help educators implement changes in their teaching of the standard norm so that students will learn the modified form.[17]

Haugen's third process, elaboration of function, is the initiation of efforts to expand the vocabulary to cover technical terms of specialized fields. For Spanish, this task was primarily the duty of the Academy in Madrid in the late nineteenth and early twentieth centuries. Mexican intellectuals had as their special task the adaptation of vocabulary items from Indian languages to cover common terms necessary in the daily lexicon of numerous Spanish speakers. Because of the heightened Indian integration program in Mexico since the 1920's, linguists and technical experts in these programs have found it necessary to compile suitable lists of agricultural and cultural items with which Spanish speakers should be familiar.[18] However, the adaptation of Indian vocabulary items has been largely a regional phenomenon and has varied according to the local density of communication between Spanish speakers and Indian monolinguals. Regions have also varied in the amount of phonetic influence Spanish has felt from the indigenous tongues; for example, Nahuatl has had a particularly strong influence on the Spanish spoken in those regions of Mexico where there is a high percentage of Spanish-Nahuatl bilingualism. In general, as might be expected from its pre-Hispanic prominence and subsequent maintenance in many areas throughout the colonial period, Nahuatl has had the strongest lexical and phonetic influence on Spanish speech of any of the indigenous tongues. However, the Spanish of speakers in Mexico City exhibits very little influence from Nahuatl.[19] In contrast, historians have noted that in the Oaxaca valley, "the few residents of Spanish origin speak fifty Nahuatl words for every fifty Spanish words," particularly for verbs and adverbal expressions.[20] The diverse functions of language in the urban centers and in the rural areas, as well as the higher density of communication between Indians and mestizos in the rural areas, help account for the different patterns of influence on Spanish speech.

This very regional variety, not only in Mexico, but also throughout Latin American nations, has led planners in the Hispanic American language academies to become more and more concerned with the elaboration of the function of Latin American Spanish.[21] In 1969, Academy members joined in the first Hispano-American Congress of Lexicography with the primary aim of standardizing the rising diversity of scientific and technical terms proposed by their nations' speakers. Linguists agreed to prepare a "Dictionary of Americanisms" to serve as an international guide, listing hemispheric Spanish words and defining their use in each country. The need to make as close to universal as possible scientific and technical terms was expressed by one delegate: "If each region continues to invent new words that remain local, after a century or two we won't be able to understand each other." [22] Presumably the goal of the newly created Institute of Hispano-American Lexicography will be to prepare a dictionary which will codify not only nationalisms reflecting the vitality and spirit of each Latin American state, but also to elaborate the functions of the Spanish lexicon to include scientific and technical terms, which would become standard throughout all the Latin American nations for an increased efficiency of communication.

Haugen's final process, the implementation of a program of acceptance for the standard language, began in Mexico with the policy statements of Justo Sierra and with governmental officials calling for a common tongue to promote unity in the nation. In line with this policy, the Law of Rudimentary Instruction had as its primary task the teaching of Spanish to the indigenous population. However, a practical program of acceptance began only after the federal government accepted the responsibility for education in all the states, and decision-makers and educators realized that the direct method of teaching had not successfully incorporated the Indians into the national community. In the words of a contemporary observer of the initiation of bilingual education: "Incorporation means the destruction and disappearance of the indigenous tongue, and complete Castilianization." [23] The negative tone of the policy of incorporation was superseded by a positive program of Castilianization and interculturation. Through an integral bilingual and bicultural program, the Indian was to develop self-respect, to see himself as a worthwhile citizen of his own community and region; gradually, he was to meet national heroes in his bilingual readers and appreciate the uniqueness of Mexico's history.

In Indian integration programs of the 1960's, the promotion of the national code as a single standard was replaced by an acceptance of bilingualism. The work of the Regional Coordinating

Centers and a realistic study of Indian regions brought the recognition that bilingualism is a semi-permanent linguistic state in Mexico. Governmental rationale for this situation is that bilingualism allows the execution of an effective and expedient program of economic and social change. The nation can absorb those who have learned to speak Spanish, have taken on the national culture and technical skills, and have moved away from the village to participate in industry within the cities. Meanwhile, the exodus from the rural areas to the cities should decelerate, while bilingual cultural promoters train the rural population to participate more effectively in their traditional economies—agriculture and fishing. The program of acceptance for the Spanish language is now based on the assumption that when the Indian is secure in his own tongue and in his evolving socioeconomic community, he will learn Spanish for its value as a code to bring him in touch with increasingly attractive aspects of national life.

If governmental personnel defend Mexico's semi-permanent bilingual state with economic and social-change justifications, what contributions can linguists make to explain why bilingualism may be reasonable for parts of the indigenous population? Linguists in the Prague School have been particularly concerned with language as a functional system. From the point of view of function, language is a system of means of expression appropriate to a need, and one cannot realistically judge any fact of language without referring to the social system in which it appears.[24] Spanish represents a distinctive hierarchy of functions for its monolingual speakers in Mexico City and other urban centers of Mexico; for these speakers the elaborateness of the code for the transmission of workaday technical or scientific information necessitates complex syntactic relations and a large specialized lexicon. Among those who acquire Spanish as a second language, the hierarchy of functions may initially be very simple, consisting only of interchanges in the marketplace and polite formulae. Until the Regional Coordinating Centers initiated the use of bilingual cultural promoters, the number of functions required of Spanish learned by speakers whose primary tongue was Nahuatl, Otomi, Maya, or another language was greater than it now is; Spanish was the only code through which Indians could acquire information from the nation's political center or learn of new agricultural techniques and economic improvements. However, now that many Indians of the rural areas are being given this information in their native tongue, they may expand the functions of their individual repertoires to teach others new technical information in the Indian language.

Joshua Fishman, a student of language maintenance in the United States has added to the concept of function by suggesting that there are also various domains of language behavior.[25] A bilingual may use one or the other of his languages not merely for different functions (expressive, poetic, referential, contextual, etc.[26]), but he may also use one or the other idioms in larger institutional-role contexts. For example, an Indian speaker may use his native tongue in his home, among close acquaintances, and on the street, but he will use Spanish in official dealings with townspeople and in the marketplace. Bilinguals will vary with respect to the number of domains and the overlap of institutions and roles which call forth one or the other language. Obviously, the attitude of the speaker and the reaction he predicts from his audience determine where and when a bilingual will use a particular idiom.[27] For example, the high valuation placed on Spanish by residents of certain villages in Chiapas is revealed by the fact that when bilingual males drink together they use Spanish; when they meet each other casually, they speak in their native tongues. Drinking together is special, making Spanish, a special language, appropriate.[28] Among the Chontal speakers of Oaxaca, children learn Spanish as their first language in the home, but during adolescence they receive instruction from their parents in the idiom of their ancestors. Parents instill a sense of group pride in their children so that the transmission of cultural traditions will be insured.[29] Such instances excite the linguist's curiosity and point out the need for more research on the functions and domains of bilingual usage.

One in-depth study of a Mexican Indian community with some bilingual members is A. Richard Diebold Jr.'s report of a Huave community.[30] Though the community was eighty-one per cent monolingual in the Indian tongue, Diebold found that a few bilingual males were internally recruited as intermediaries between the village and the Spanish-speaking community at large. Those who learned Spanish did so for inter-group situations, primarily economic in purpose, as they represented the interests of Huave-speaking farmers, fishermen, and artisans. Spanish was rarely used in the home and played no part in conversational or workaday technical intra-group communication.[31] Those who became bilingual were bilingual with diglossia; that is, the use of Spanish as a separate code within the social community was restricted to certain roles and situations.[32] Bilinguals were middlemen between their small, rural insulated community and the outside world; bilinguals served a particular purpose and role for their family or their community.

In the village studied by Diebold and in other communities or regions where it is evident that indigenous speakers are making a concerted effort to maintain the Indian tongue as their primary language, linguists and language planners in particular have asked why some speech communities place a high valuation on the retention of the mother tongue, and others do not. In 1967, Uriel Weinreich, a linguist calling for social science research on the analysis of the association of language with group integrity, proposed the term "language loyalty" to designate "the state of mind in which the language (like the nationality) as an intact entity, and in contrast to other languages, assumes a high position in a scale of values, a position in need of being 'defended'." [33] Assuming then that language is integral to a group's sense of identity and unity, linguists have proposed that languages may serve either separatist, prestige, or unifying functions.[34] Mexican students of particular language groups have suggested that both separatist and prestige functions serve to maintain the native tongues of certain Indians in Mexico. Ethel Wallis, a long-time student of the Otomi, has suggested that though there is no prestige associated with the speaking of Otomi, the tribe has resisted a linguistic shift and has used language as a "weapon to ward off the threatening invasion of a larger society with far more prestige." [35] On the other hand, the Zapotecs of the Isthmus of Tehuantepec retain their language for the prestige function it serves, as they foster among their members a sense of pride in not only their language but also their "national identity." [36]

The problem of the unifying function of language is particularly relevant for social scientists concerned with nationalism and nation-building. It is commonly accepted that a self-respecting political body needs a common language; moreover, it is frequently asserted that linguistic unity is a prerequisite for the effective mobilization of the citizenry behind the building of a nation.[37] The history of language planning in Mexico reveals the ups and downs of this notion among decision-makers. Certainly, most political leaders during the colonial period and since nationhood have accepted the need for a common tongue in Mexico; however, their motives for promoting a unified tongue have varied considerably. They have invoked a common tongue in their promotion of various symbols of unity: religion, socio-cultural union, historical uniqueness, and a national mission. At times they have been willing to accept the existence of more than one tongue; on other occasions, they have not.

Colonial religious regulars saw a common tongue as an effective bond of communication to expedite the conversion of the Indians. The Crown, maintaining the viewpoint that Christianization meant Castilianization, counted on religion as the national symbol behind which the citizens of the New World would rally. When, over a century after colonization, Charles II found it necessary to attempt to unify citizens of New Spain behind shared cultural values other than religion, he boosted the Spanish language to the position of highest priority in a program of Hispanization and the promotion of an increasing amount of social and cultural contact between Spaniards and Indians.

After Independence, fifty years of political instability and Church-state conflicts immobilized effective efforts toward unity beneath any common symbol. When politicians after 1857 embraced the idea of a new society in Mexico, based on the freedom of the individual according to the Mexican point of view, these leaders projected that a nation was not a nation without an active historical sense which unified dissimilar peoples and provided unity to the nation as a whole. Mexican Spanish, as forged through Mexico's peculiar history, was a primary symbol of unity for decision-makers; the national language was the more Mexican for its contributions from the indigenous tongues. The crisis of the Revolution stimulated similar pronouncements, except the orators injected their messages with a stronger dose of indigenism. The unity of Revolutionary Mexico depended on taking the best of the Indian past and incorporating it in the Mexican soul, but political leaders found it hard to identify worthy elements of indigenous cultures. Political leaders who feared the tension between the nationalistic and the particularistic in Mexico's culture pointed to the maintenance of the Indian tongues as a special threat to the nation's unity. The Indianists and the nationalists held polar positions, according to both educators and politicians who favored the direct teaching of Spanish to insure the incorporation of the indigenous populations into the national culture. Mexico could not reach the fullest measure of nationhood without a common tongue.

However, the quickened pace of social change and the enthusiastic initiation of limited projects of bilingual education under President Cárdenas gave anthropologists, with the combined status of intellectual and politician, the opportunity to initiate a national mission of the protection of the indigenous and the provision of socioeconomic opportunities for all Mexican citizens. Social scientists implemented and preserved concrete programs, which served both to further social change in the countryside and to provide literate consumers and factory workers in the cities. Confidence in the uniqueness of Mexico and an evolved indigenism combined with political stability to convince decision-makers that the major prerequisite for nationalism was similar socioeconomic backgrounds and opportunities. The new emphasis is not unity behind a common tongue, but the transition of monolingual Indian-language speakers to a bilingual status, in order that their transition from conservative isolation to modernity might be brought about with a minimum of cultural disruption. Mexican unity stands behind a policy of indigenism which, in large part, has evolved from a promotion of bilingualism as a transition stage to the national standard to an acceptance of bilingualism as a semi-permanent state among some Indian populations.

With the endorsement of an evolved policy of indigenism as a national mission has come the need for anthropologists to remain as stable members of the decision-making elites of the nation.[38] Since 1940, in spite of avowed shifts in educational policy and opinions by political leaders on how to integrate the Indians, anthropologists have remained remarkably stable in their influence of and direct access to government officials.[39] Through the autonomous National Indigenist Institute, anthropologists have been able to initiate and maintain programs which have endured. As a national political authority which could initiate participative reactions within the indigenous regions, INI has served as the center of a web of special "group relationships which connect localities and national-level institutions."[40] Bilingual cultural promoters have become economic and political brokers of nation-region relations. Acceptance by the government of the relationships between language and culture has underscored the fact that anthropologists' goals and those of the nation correlate, and anthropologists, because of their specialized training, techniques, and knowledge, have become modern elites necessary for the success of governmental aims. The linking of aims in a nationalistic purpose has helped social scientists master the art of politics in language planning as well as the science of language planning.[41] Throughout the twentieth century, anthropologists and linguists have demonstrated their skill in influencing political elites; more often than not, the suggestions of the social science research of one decade became the national policy of the next decade.[42]

Language in Mexico's history from colony to nation has been a significant nexus between the goals of decision-makers and social and cultural development. The extent to which language planners have taken into consideration language as an indicator of social interaction, cultural values, and group identification has determined the success of language policies throughout Mexican history. Decision-makers' insistence on the assimilation of all groups to Spanish as the single Mexican linguistic standard was blocked because the linguistic loyalties of some Indian groups were too firmly set to be uprooted. The promotion of bilingualism as a transition state in the movement of the indigenous population to modernity marked an intermediate period in which policy-makers recognized the interdependence of cultural traits which met in the acculturation of Indian and national. A secure sense of national identity and a newly defined process of modernization have, in the very recent past, prompted the political elites' endorsement of bilingualism as a stable linguistic status among particular indigenous groups. This evolution in the twentieth century has depended in large part on social science guided approaches which politically potent anthropologists have implemented and carried out in bilingual and bicultural integration programs.

Certainly, neither the historical process of language planning nor the present linguistic situations of other Latin American nations is identical to that of Mexico.[43] However, other Hispanic nations have felt pressures of colonial language policies very similar to those imposed on Mexico and have also inherited with nationhood large indigenous populations. Today nations such as Peru, Bolivia, Ecuador, and Guatemala face problems closely analogous to those Mexican anthropologists and political administrators confronted forty years ago. Among the Latin American nations with a high degree of linguistic diversity, Mexico is the nation to provide a case study of language planning which may offer valuable suggestions for a systematic social theory guided approach to other national language programs in Latin America.

ACKNOWLEDGEMENTS

This book could not have been written except in response to the influence of many associates, though I am, as are all scholars, solely responsible for any errors of fact or judgment. I wish to give initial recognition to those Latin American historians who admitted a case study of language policy as a legitimate method of gaining a new perspective on colonial and national relations in Mexico. Charles Griffin encouraged my first efforts to set down my ideas on language planning in Mexico; Herbert Klein helped me bring together the historians' and the anthropologists' notions of social change; Miriam Williford aided me through her knowledge of the bibliography of Latin American History. Thanks are due above all to my husband, Frederick M. Heath, who has provided his conceptual insights into the history of Mexico during many hours of exploring the argument of this book with me. His advice has been indispensable. He has in this, as in all my work, been my constant mentor, patient editor, and crucial supporter.

Many anthropologists and linguists have shared with me information drawn from their field experiences in Mexico. Charles Wagley, Pedro Carrasco, Munro S. Edmonson, Joseph Grimes, Nancy Modiano, and William K. Wonderly provided many observations on the practical aspects of implementing language policy. Elaine and William Cameron Townsend have kindly interpreted the process of language policy-making for the period they were active in Mexico, as they have given this story of language planning their informed, imaginative, and affectionate attention. The scholarly concerns of Harvey Pitkin, Dell H. Hymes, and William Labov are evident throughout this book. They have to my benefit, and that of our common interests, been a provocative influence. I am honored that Dell Hymes has provided the foreword. Discussions with a number of colleagues have proved stimulating and profitable. Conrad Arensberg, Philip Phenix, and Lambros Comitas have read and commented on parts of the present volume in the course of preparation.

I wish to give special recognition to those Mexican scholars who tolerated my probings and provided a variety of opinions and research leads which helped me obtain a synthesis. Gonzalo Aguirre Beltrán, Fernando Cámara, the late Alfonso Caso, Andrés Iduarte, Juan M. Lope Blanch, Rodolfo Stavenhagen, Evangelina Arana Swadesh, and Alfonso Villa Rojas facilitated my research by granting me access to out-of-print materials and by submitting to long interviews or repeated correspondence.

There are others of whom special mention should be made, for they have assisted in the preparation of this study over many years of friendship. I wish to thank Peggy Haskel for her patient assistance on questions of style, Virginia Kays Creesy for the translation of the appendix and repeated editorial assistance, T. Norman Tomazic for his excellent map, and also Martha A. Tomazic for the cover design. Florence Blakely of Duke University Library has facilitated my research by offering her skill and knowledge. Connie McCormick, my typist, has through her unending patience and concern for accuracy, been of immeasurable assistance. My colleagues of the Sociology Department at Winthrop College have offered encouragement and help in many ways.

Long before any of those already mentioned knew of this book, John B. Carroll helped me in a very memorable way; he kindly and generously set me to the study of linguistics.

My children, Brice and Shannon, deserve special mention for helping insure that I always kept this book in proper perspective. Finally, the book is dedicated to my mother and father who perhaps without being aware of it have been an inspiration through their indefatigable energy and enthusiasm.

Shirley Brice Heath

APPENDIX I

Pastoral V
In order that the Indians learn Castilian.*

Two and a half centuries after the Conquest of this kingdom,[1] we are still weeping and lamenting, because we need interpreters of the natives' languages and idioms as badly as if we were the illustrious Conquistador Hernan Cortés himself, and we now need even greater numbers of interpreters than were needed at the beginning of the Conquest. For the Conquistador understood through Geronimo de Aguilar and Doña Marina[2] the speech in many provinces from Yucatan to Mexico and from there to Guatemala,[3] while now the number of languages has so multiplied within even a single diocese that we can affirm that sometimes neither an ecclesiastical minister nor an interpreter has been found just to confess some criminal in the jails. In the dioceses of Puebla and Oaxaca there are many idioms quite different from those of the diocese of Mexico.[4] And whereas the decree that the Indians should learn Castilian, the language of our sovereign, has been urged on the two dominions and has been one of the most saintedly and justly repeated decrees in the laws of these kingdoms, its execution, instead of being moved forward, every day seems more impossible.

There has been no civilized nation in the world which, when it extended its conquests, did not endeavor to do the same with its language. The Greeks regarded other nations that did not know its language as barbarians. After they conquered the Greeks, the Romans so strictly compelled them to accept their Latin language—the language of Latium, the area around Rome—

---

* Lorenzana, D. Francisco, y Buitron, *Cartas pastorales y edictos* (México: Imprenta del Superior Gobierno del Br. D. Joseph Antonio de Hogal, 1770), pp. 91-100.

[1] Counting from the date of Hernan Cortés' arrival at Vera Cruz, exactly two-and-a-half centuries have passed. See the volume of the first two Councils and the one on the history of the Conquest.

[2] Doña Marina de Escobar: with these two interpreters, Cortés conducted operations throughout the entire Yucatan peninsula and in New Spain, according to eyewitness statements by Torquemada, Solís, Herrada, and others.

[3] Pedro de Alvarado went to Guatemala for his Conquest.

[4] The reason being that Mazahua emerged from corrupted Othomí, and others arose in a similar fashion out of the barbarism of the Indians who fled to mountain retreats.

that they permitted no one who spoke a foreign language to enter into any of the Senate's affairs.

As soon as the Romans made themselves lords of our country, Spain, they ordered everyone to speak and write in the Roman or Latin language, which was corrupted after the invasion of the Goths, leaving the Romance language, or corrupted Latin.[5] In Tuscany and France they likewise introduced Latin, and even after so many centuries one can rightly call Tuscan and French Latin dialects.[6] Having attained such a degree of eminence throughout the Romans' vast dominions, Latin has become the language common to all nations and that used in all books written for international audiences so that Latin is now the mother tongue of all scholars much as—and to even a greater degree than—Greek was formerly. For this reason it used to be that anything that came up in the ecclesiastical courts in some dioceses in Aragon and Catalonia still was acted upon in Latin, but our sovereign has corrected that situation.

The Roman idiom put down such strong roots in Spain that during the Goths' rule and later the Arabs', the people did not adopt these invaders' languages [7] but kept to their Romance language, or adulterated and corrupted Latin, as one can see in the *Leyes del Fuero Juzgo* and those of the *Partida;* and even the public instruments and grants were done in Latin until the time of King Alonso el Sabio [8] who ordered that henceforth everything be written in Castilian.

In writing of the confusion of tongues, Filon [Philo of Alexandria, 1st cent. B.C.] stated the very serious injuries that resulted in all periods and nations from permitting different languages among peoples under the dominion of the same ruler, noting that many have died through unforeseen treachery, or been taken unawares, because of their ignorance of the local language. There are examples of this in the Holy Writ, when some died because they couldn't pronounce the word "Scibboleth," [9] and in profane history, when some have perished because they couldn't speak other words.

[5] For the word *Romance,* as well as information on the Spanish colonies and towns that were granted civic liberties similar to Rome's and the right to stamp money with Latin inscriptions, see D. Antonio Covarrubias. See D. Antonio Agustin and Rmo. P. Flores on rare Spanish coins.

[6] Valencian is corrupted *langue d'oc,* the language of Limogne in France. Catalan is corrupted French.

[7] The Christians who lived in Toledo, Cordoba, and other towns where they were allowed to mix with the Arabs were called *Mixtárabes* in Latin (*Muzárabes* in corrupted Latin), but they always held fast to their own mother tongue and true culture.

[8] Greek never crossed the borders of Greece, but Latin is understood and spoken today throughout the world. D. Alonso el Sabio introduced and extended the use of the Romance language, and his grants (called *rodados* for the wheel used in his mark and seal) were framed in Castilian: for example, he wrote the *Siete Partidas* in Castilian. The languages of the common people in Asturias, Galician, and even Portuguese are almost identical to this early Castilian.

[9] *Judges* 12. 6. *Dic ergo Scibboleth (quod interpretatur spica) qui respondebas Sibboleth: : statimque apprehensum jugulabant.* Something like the *Efrateos,* the Arabs cannot pronounce *Scin,* which means *espiga* (ear of corn), but say *sin*

APPENDIX I   209

Tumults, insurrections, civil seditions grow much larger when they are hatched among subject people speaking a foreign language. Indeed, this very difference in customs itself inflames them with a recollection of their former lords and with that mischievous notion to which human nature is prone that their own languages, dress, liberties, heathenism, and other vices are superior to others'.[10]

A nation's speaking a single language, that of its sovereign and only monarch, engenders true love and good will among individuals, an ease of intercourse not found among those who do not understand each other, and a fellowship, brotherhood, civility, and politeness that is very favorable to spiritual government, domestic dealings, commerce and politics. Moreover, it is very conducive to a conquered people's gradually forgetting their enmities, their divisions, their partialities, and their aversion to those who rule.[11]

World events and tales have confirmed this to such an extent that (according to Plato in *Timaeus*) a full union, stable peace, constant amity, and perfect subordination to the sovereign have never been arrived at without a common understanding of the same language. For, according to the Holy Writ, God divided the nations in the Tower of Babel as a punishment for their presumption, saying: "Come, let us confuse their language, that no-one may understand nor hear the voice of his neighbor." [12]

Turning now to a consideration of the various idioms of the Indies: who will seriously refuse to admit that, just as their society was barbaric, so was—and is—their language? Who would compare Mexican with Hebrew which, for all its being a dead language, nonetheless is the language, as some say, which God taught our first father Adam to speak? [13] Who will compare it with Greek which was such an elegant and fertile language, even though it is dead now or almost dead? [14] For all that there is no longer a nation where the populace speaks pure Latin, who would put Mexican ahead of Latin, in which tongue we have as exquisite a translation of all the sacred books of the sainted Greek fathers as has ever been written in the world? If shifts of power and changes of circumstance brought the Chaldeans and Syrians to destroy the purity of the Hebrew language and

instead. The same thing happened in Sicily in the time of Charles of Anjou, and many nations like the French and the Italian cannot pronounce these words as forcefully as Spaniards do: *cebolla, garbanzos, calabaza*.

[10] The diversity of languages is the greatest cause of religious warfare, national discords, and civil seditions. Solórzano, *loco sup., cit Ind. Gub*.

[11] Read about what happened in Lorraine where, in order to put an end to discords, the transfer of whole populations had to be resorted to.

[12] Ch. 11, *Genesis*.

[13] See Calmet's dissertation on this point, although he is not favorably disposed to nor does he affirm this opinion.

[14] The Greek language is the most fruitful, the most fertile in tenses, and the most elegant of all languages. The eloquence of Chrysostom, the acuteness of St. Basil and that of St. Peter Chrisólogo can be best appreciated in it.

nearly extinguish that tongue,[15] if they caused the Greeks to extirpate the Chaldean and Syrian languages and the Romans to do the same with Greek, and if all nations have done this even with the most learned languages, then why must we maintain the Indians' languages?

The Castilians who learned the inherently limited and barbaric Mexican language enriched it by inventing various synthetic words to adorn it:[16] the Indians had no terms in their language for the Church's holy sacraments nor for the mysteries of our sainted faith, and today there are still no appropriate terms for explaining these things which convey their full significance. Nonetheless, the Spaniards who learned the Indian language and the mestizos have set forth the entire Christian doctrine in Mexican. Who is not aware of the very grave, troublesome consequences that can result from a doctrinal misunderstanding? Who does not see that the blame for the Indians not learning Castilian must fall upon the prelates, the parish priests, and the ecclesiastical ministers? For the *alcalde mayor* is not the one who preaches to them, confesses them, or teaches them Christian doctrine; nor does he spend all day talking with them as does the parish priest whom they look to as their father, teacher, and spiritual director. And who can be blind to the fact that if the evangelical ministers determinedly undertook the teaching of Castilian, they would accomplish it within perhaps a few years at most?

If a prelate ordered a parish priest who had no training in the classics to make an extemporaneous explanation of the mysteries of the faith in Latin, how many solecisms and how many heresies would he utter? Indeed, even with space for reflection, this is a very difficult task for a highly educated person. Then how are some vicar-clerics, ordained simply because they know the native tongue—whose education consists of a little grammar and an acquaintance with Larraga's compendium in Spanish—to explain these mysteries in Mexican, in Othomi, Huateco, Totonaco, Mazahua, Tepehua, Zapateca, Tarasco and innumerable other tongues?[17] How are they to do this when the catechism, which is taken from the quintessence and substance of the Church councils and Church fathers, is the most difficult of all works to understand and very eminent individuals have had to labor to do so? How are idolatry and superstition going to be extirpated if the parish priest or vicars happen not to understand the peculiar words in which the Indians express themselves with deliberate cunning so that not even ministers who

---

[15] After the captivity of the Hebrew people, their language became mixed with Chaldean and Syrian, and, as a result, one must know these last in order to understand fully some sacred books of the Old Testament.

[16] Castilian missionaries and parish priests invented almost all the words naming the sacraments and explaining the mysteries and other holy things. See the confessional written in Mexican by Father Juan Bautista.

[17] In his Pastoral, the illustrious Lord Bishop of Oaxaca says that there is a language in his diocese which is only fully intelligible in the daytime, and after the sun goes down at night, certain things cannot be communicated because their meanings are conveyed with gestures.

know the native languages may understand them?[18] How are they going to explicate the sins confessed to them when the Indians turn into dumb, inanimate objects, waiting to be questioned, and there is no way to draw a single word out of them? When, according to what I have heard from zealous ministers who know their language, not even they can understand the nature of the sins the Indians have committed?

It is our desire, therefore, that the sheep understand the voice and ordinary speech of the pastors,[19] not that the latter adapt themselves to the varied bleatings of their sheep. The bishop is the foremost parish priest and chief among all his parish priests, and he does not nor can he understand the many different idioms in his diocese;[20] but if Castilian is extended, he will successfully understand what is spoken in all the villages he visits on his official rounds. And he will attend more promptly to the need for providing more curates and vicars than he can now while the natives' willful linguistic isolation makes it necessary for him to consider the ministers' linguistic ability rather than simply their personal suitability when disposing offices.

Regarding the political realm: lord viceroys and the members of the Royal Audiencia are now precluded from being able either to hear or understand the complaints of the Indians because these pretend to be mute. Rather, they use interpreters as a result of which a claim can take on a different character or what is confidential can be made public. Honors are taken away all at once from parish priests, *alcaldes mayores,* and all the *justicias* to the accompaniment of horrendous calumnies; petitions are written by suspicious characters, based on only the clownish statements of the natives; writing on his knee in the portals of low cafes, a scribe concocts a petition that later stirs a great fire in the courts: all these harmful things are born from the Indians not speaking Castilian and growing daily more ignorant because of the distrust with which they treat their betters.

This is an immutable truth: maintaining the Indians' language is a caprice of men[21] whose fortune and knowledge reduces them to speaking that child-

---

[18] Parish priests of irreproachable conduct have assured me of this and also of the fact that, in attempting to elucidate for some Indian penitents their sins against the sixth Commandment, they have had great difficulty understanding the Indians.

[19] *Cognosco Oves meas, & cognoscunt me mea : : : Oves mea vocem meam audiuns.* Joan. 10. v. 14. & 27.

[20] Sr. Montenegro (Book 1, tr. 1, Sec. 9) gives priority to the curates knowing the native idioms, but he ignores the fact that this procedure leads to a continual increase in the number of Indian languages and the decay of the Castilian language and that the bishop on his visitations needs to hear the Indians' complaints against their curate and to be informed secretly, without an interpreter, of many hidden impediments to the dispensing of justice before the tribunal of conscience which the Indians do not want to reveal to any other party; and finally, despite the Gospel's doctrine that the pastor must understand his sheep, the illustrious Sr. Montenegro himself knew full well that he did not know all the idioms in the diocese of Quito.

[21] In order to further the orders' interests, the friars alleged that the secular clerics did not know the language of the Indies; now that the clerics have learned it they are very tenacious in keeping it alive because they believe that in this way they secure offices for themselves with less learning and education.

like language. It is a contagious disease that removes the Indians from social intercourse with Spaniards. It is a plague that perverts the dogmas of our Holy Faith.[22] It is a harmful expedient for separating the natives of some villages from others through the diversity of tongues.[23] It swells the expenses of the parish priests who must have ministers of different idioms in their one district.[24] It renders impossible government by the bishops, the distribution of curacies, and the reward of decent, honorable, well-educated and worthy Spaniards and Indians. It places an *alcalde mayor* among people who do not understand him—nor does he understand them any better than if he were in Greece or Barbary. It obscures the natives' errors so that their betters may not correct them. It causes the natives to fail to form an idea of the divine majesty of God or of that of His Son and to fail to properly value the precepts of their *justicias mayores* and the preachings and reprimands of their parish priests. For if the Indians send their sons to school, it is from fear of punishment rather than a desire for their instruction and proper education; there they memorize more than they retain later; and as experience shows, given a less than zealous minister who is lenient on them, they soon revert to their crude natural state. So ultimately this practice is equivalent to harboring a burning coal in one's breast: a fomentor of discord and constant scandal, it results in the vassals of the same sovereign taking an aversion to one another.

At the beginning of the Conquest it was imperative for the evangelical ministers to study the native idiom if they were to succeed in converting the Indians, but today this is no longer at all necessary. The Liman and Mexican Councils originally recommended the practice, but since the latter met in 1585, the natives easily have acquired or have been able to acquire instruction in Spanish. It may be added, the laws of this kingdom expressly order this, in the following words: [25]

May teachers apply themselves to teaching the Indians the Castilian language, since after a thorough study it has been realized that the mysteries of our sainted Catholic faith cannot be properly and well explained in even their most perfect language without great incongruities and flaws resulting. And the archbishops and bishops are entreated and charged with ordering and making provision in their dioceses for curates and others to teach the Indians Christian doctrine by the most gentle means possible, with arranging and seeing to it that all Indians are taught the Spanish language and taught Christian doctrine in that language in order that they become better versed in those mysteries, come closer to salvation, and otherwise profit by it in their government and way of life.

[22] For example, calling the consecrated host a tortilla, which is what the Indians eat.

[23] And it causes them to not want to recognize the authority of the *cabezeras*, or principal parish priests.

[24] Only the short distance of three leagues from Mexico City is Tanepantla and a little further on, Quantitlan, where Castilian, Mexican, and Othomite ministers are required.

[25] Law 18, Tit. 1, Book 6 of the *Recopil. de Indias.*

When clerics are qualified by their administrative ability rather than their knowledge of the native idiom,[26] the prelate can ordain them with greater confidence and satisfaction. And therefore—remembering that, if they are Spaniards, they must propagate their language in order to do just honor to the glory of their descent, and if they are Indians, they are obliged to celebrate the extension of the Catholic faith in these realms—all are to reject, refuse, and put aside any other preoccupation, give thanks to God that He illuminates them with evangelical light, exile all that acts as an impediment to greater illumination, Christianity, and civilizing the natives, and wholeheartedly make every effort to procure the greatest spiritual and temporal well-being of the Indians, which undoubtedly consists in large part in their all speaking the same language and communicating with Spaniards and all of us being united by the tie of charity.

So we command and order all the parish priests, vicars, and clerics of the archbishopric, in virtue of the rule of Sainted Obedience and under the gravest penalties, that they be our beloved Benjamins, using Castilian both for the explication of Christian doctrine and in common dealings with the Indians so that the latter may learn the language and grow fluent in speaking it even in those commercial matters, economic dealings and plaza activities that they call *Tianguistlatolli;* and we command them to do so in the knowledge that their scrupulous compliance with this order will be a merit in our eyes of the highest possible recommendation and a most relevant proof that they look for the true well-being of the Indians. And we ask, beg, and charge all secular judges, hacienda owners, and other persons that they likewise contribute to such an important end, so that, intimately united with our Sovereign's will and our own in doing and completing this work of charity for the nation which is so much in the service of God, they may merit, each and every one, the greatest blessings from His all-powerful hand and the blessing that we now bestow in His sainted name: From our archiepiscopal palace of Mexico, on the 6th of October, 1769.

[26] This refers to appointing a vicar for a town.

APPENDIX II

Edicto XV
In which is published the *Real Cédula* on the extension of the Castilian tongue.*

He who reverently approaches the throne of his Majesty ought always to trust that clemency and justice are located there. If his plea is denied, he must trust that this results because the sovereign, from his very elevated observation point, has weighed with the correct balance the specific advantages and disadvantages with the general ones, and the far-reaching consequences to the community. And if the Sovereign condescends to favor his plea, the overwhelmed heart of the vassal seals the royal mercy with proper gratitude and submission.

We owe this gratitude for the publication of the Pastoral Letter setting forth royal consent to the decree that parish priests must take pains to ensure that the Indians learn Spanish and the Christian Doctrine be taught to them in that language, for reasons which the Royal will has taken into account. These reasons are so powerful that, in addition to rendering our due obedience, we intend to execute this measure promptly and immediately with the greatest possible vigilance, for the sake of the benefit that will result for all.

Some sainted fathers tell of the division of the (primal) language into 72 tongues after the separation of men in the Tower of Babel, others of its division into 105 tongues. And Acosta, speaking only of the Kingdom of Peru, affirms that it had more than 700 idioms. Withal, work has been done for the spread of Castilian and has succeeded almost everywhere, as a result of which we cannot lack confidence that it will succeed in New Spain.

The most learned and intelligent authors who deal with the customs of the Indies and royal decisions defend with very solid arguments not only the idea that the Indians ought to be taught to learn Castilian but also that they can be obliged to do so. They substantiate this judgment with the example of the Hebrew people, who in the space of the seventy years of their Babylonian Captivity lost their native language and learned the

---

* Lorenzana, D. Francisco, y Buitron, *Cartas pastorales y edictos* (México: Imprenta del Superior Gobierno del Br. D. Joseph Antonio de Hogal, 1770), pp. 143-152.

Chaldean tongue of the Egyptians, with the result that, in order to understand the original texts of the sacred books of the Old Testament, a knowledge of Hebrew was needed for the books written before the Captivity, of Chaldean and Syrian for the writings during or after the Captivity, and of Greek for some of the New Testament and for the Septuagint version of the Old Testament.

The Sainted Patriarch Joseph of the ancient law almost forgot his native language while in Egypt and became so familiar with that of the Egyptians that he needed an interpreter afterwards in order to speak with his brothers.

An understanding of Castilian is still desirable for spreading and propagating the Evangelical Law, since the most learned and fervent missionaries (then) will not have any obstacle to traveling to the remotest provinces to preach the Gospel, and a widespread understanding of Castilian will open fields to the secular and regular clergy for the exercise of their sacred ministry. With these ends in mind, our Catholic Monarch, with his superior understanding—desiring the greatest possible spiritual and temporal enrichment of the Indians—has written and sent his royal proclamation with the following import:

"THE KING—In a letter of June 25th of the past year, the Very Reverend Archbishop of Mexico has represented to me that, in order that the Catholic faith be propagated in the vast dominions of America, all my concern and that of the lord kings, my glorious predecessors, and of my Council of the Indies has been to publish laws and direct royal proclamations to the viceroys and diocesan prelates to the end that the Indians be instructed in the dogmas of our religion in Castilian and be taught to read and write in this idiom which ought to be understood throughout those dominions and which ought to become the one and universal idiom there by virtue of its belonging to the monarchs and conquerors. This universal knowledge is necessary in order to facilitate the governing and the spiritual guidance of the Indians; in order that the latter might be understood by their superiors, conceive a love for the conquering nation, banish idolatry, and be civilized for purposes of business and commerce; and in order that men might not be confounded with a great diversity of languages as in the Tower of Babel. To achieve this, all ranks of churchmen have been ordered many times to establish schools in the Castilian language in all the villages and the bishops and parish priests ordered to supervise their execution. (The Archbishop has informed me) that these sainted, just and repeated royal orders and decrees have not succeeded in securing any effect and it seems that each day men's souls are more indisposed to comply with them. One may point out with regard to this that after two-and-one-half centuries, many different idioms are maintained in (even) the best-known and civilized places, as is the case in Mexico and Puebla—idioms in which the Indians are isolated, refusing to learn Castilian and to send their children to school. Even in the neighborhood of the capital of Mexico, in the short space of two leagues, in a single curacy there are Mexican-speaking and Othomite-speaking villages. This same situation can be witnessed elsewhere—not because the natives do not

APPENDIX II

understand Spanish, but because they do not wish to speak it. It happens that one sees poor Indians who understand Castilian, Othomi and Mexican, yet never speak to the curate and his vicars in Spanish; the same happens with the *alcaldes mayores* and *justicias*, who make use of interpreters. The root of this damage lies in the fact that the conferring of curacies on individuals who speak native languages has been scrupulously carried out. And since their parish priests and ministers, whom the natives constantly deal with and see, speak to them in their own language and preach and explain Christian doctrine to them in it, the situation has improved little or not at all; nor will it improve unless some remedy is applied. The result is that the parish priests and ministers rapidly become every day more fluent in the native idioms from frequent communication with the natives and there is no one who promotes the Castilian language in the villages. On the contrary, one hears that the clergy give them the impression that it shows a lack of respect to speak in Castilian or that they will be punished if they do so. Two reprehensible ideas give rise to this impression: the one comes from the creole clergy having persuaded themselves that the native idioms are the means of securing the filling of the curacies for themselves and of excluding all Europeans; and the other is that, with the Europeans excluded, it will be possible to take away their right to be ordained. Moreover, the inclination to retain their own language is a propensity of the natives which impedes their will to learn another and foreign language—an inclination accentuated by the somewhat malicious desire to hide their actions from the Spaniards and not answer them directly, when they believe they can be evasive. In order to lessen such evils and prevent them from growing greater each day, the sure remedy has been to fill the curacies with the most worthy individuals—even though there may be some persons in the villages who may not know Castilian—and charge them with maintaining a vicar fluent in the native tongue for urgent cases of administration of the sacraments.

"It is certain that the pastor ought to understand the voice of his sheep, and, because of this principle, some have believed that the most compelling obligation of the parish priest was to know the language of each village in America. But this reasoning is in no way convincing, because the bishops are the foremost pastors, who have to visit all the villages and cure the illnesses of their sheep—all of whose different idioms they neither understand nor can understand. And neither my predecessors nor I have ever thought to give preference to those who do know them, because nothing useful, and perhaps many injuries, would result from such preference. If only Mexican were spoken in a diocese, the obligation to provide parish priests fluent in this idiom might be natural and more urgent; but as there exists in the same archbishopric, besides Mexican, other very distinct idioms such as Othomi, Huasteco, Mazahua, Tepehua, and Totonaco; and in each diocese other very different idioms—so that in Puebla, in addition to those referred to above, there are Chocho, Misteco, Tlapaneco, Olmeco, two kinds of Totonaco, and in Oaxaca there are Tarasco and Zapoteco—a disorder results that can be appreciated only by experiencing it, for villages that are very close neighbors each maintain their own idiom as if they were many leagues apart. Even in Tlachco in the diocese of Puebla, it can be seen that of its two districts, one is Othomi-speaking and the other Tepehua-speaking. When Hernan Cortés was engaged in the Conquest, only Mexican—or the Culhua language, which is the same thing—was spoken from Yucatan to Mexico; and Doña Marina and Geronimo de Aguilar understood it perfectly although the Spaniards traveled across all of what is today the diocese of Yucatan, the province of Tabasco, the diocese of Tlaxcala, which is the Puebla de los Angeles, and the archbishopric of Mexico. And while it cannot be denied that the Conquistador knew only the Mexican and Othomi languages (the latter being used only near Michoacán), at present in all that territory there are other different languages, compounded from Othomi, with other diverse terms and pronunciation for which rules have been composed and methods of learning them. The fact is that the curate who is Castilian and knows no other idiom tries hard to extend his own language, charges and requires his parishioners to speak with him in it, promotes schools in Castilian; while, on the other hand, the curate who knows a native idiom always speaks in it and looks with little favor on the Castilian tongue, teaches the Doctrine in the idiom—not infrequently slipping into errors because it is very difficult or almost impossible to explain well in another idiom the dogmas of our holy Catholic faith, about which the Sainted Fathers and theologians have written so much—especially regarding the mysteries of the Incarnation and the Eucharist—in order to standardize and purify the forms (of expressing these things). So, because no effort is made to get rid of the native idioms, it happens that a clergyman of less merit, of low birth, and perhaps of worse personal habits, by virtue of knowing a native tongue, succeeds to a curacy that ought to be the reward of a more worthy individual. In the *colegios* of Mexico, Puebla, and other capitals are educated youths of the most distinguished lineage and ability; and, after exhausting themselves in the study of divinity, civil and canonical law, it is hard for them to see curacies given to clerics knowing the native language who, at best, have studied a moral compendium, for it costs Spaniards a great deal of effort and zeal to learn another language when they have not grown up with the natives. Wherefore, the Archbishop's judgment was not—nor could it be—that the villages should be left for the present without ministers knowing the native language, but rather that the principal concern should be that parish priests not be denied the benefices they want simply because they know only Castilian. Indeed, if at the beginning of the Conquest, all diligence had been directed towards teaching the Indians Castilian, this effort might have succeeded in less than half a century. The present poor knowledge of Castilian is accounted for by the fact that at first the regular clergy firmly secured the curacies to themselves, maintaining the native tongues, and after the secular clergy learned them, this harmful prejudice in favor of the native idioms triumphed; thus the process was contrary to the practice of conquerors such as the Romans who introduced their language in conquered nations. In order that this evil may be remedied, it also appeared to the Archbishop

APPENDIX II 219

that, if it met with my Royal pleasure, the bishops should be charged to consider only the most worthy candidates in the nominations they make for curacies, even if these may not know the native idiom—with the stipulation of having whatever vicars (that) may be necessary. On this score, (he said) he could cite cases of curacies in villages where only the native language was known being conferred on clerics with no knowledge of that idiom—as happened in Xumiltepec, which is in that archbishopric, in Huaquechula, San Felipe and Totomehuacan in the bishopric of Puebla—and it succeeded to the extent that in a few years the Indians might confess and learn the Christian doctrine in Castilian. The clerics born in those countries were not injured by this. Rather, the greatest possible benefit to the diocese would come from having as parish priests individuals trained in seminaries with better deportment, better education, and more disinterest than mercenary clerics. The latter cannot lose their right to be ordained, but an administrative office of the sort found in some dioceses of New Spain is more suitable to this kind of cleric. The suspicion that (only) Europeans were going to be parish priests was unfounded, because my Royal mercy would never let those born in that country go unrewarded; nor was it possible that the latter would oppose themselves to someone steeped in science and virtue being more than an ecclesiastical servant and not refused (higher office) just because he was a European. Finally, given the aforesaid, within a few years the Royal ministers could be understood by everybody without the need for interpreters, who can easily distort things for the Indians; the bishops would be equally well understood in all the villages of their diocese; the Indians would not remain so exposed to trickery in their business dealings, commerce, or law suits; the parish priests would be more uniformly qualified; the *colegio* students in so many loyal, law-abiding communities in those dominions would reap a reward for their efforts, and good would come from the rivalry for offices; and all the land could be governed with more ease. And the said letter with its information on the background of this matter having been examined in my Council of the Indies, as well as that information which the Marquis of Croix, my present viceroy in the said provinces of New Spain, has simultaneously set forth in a separate letter of the 27th of said month and year, my ministerial officers submitted it for judgment. Having been consulted on it the 17th of February of this year, I have decided to approve the measures that the said Archbishop of Mexico proposes and to order Royal decrees circulated, to the end that they may be uniformly practiced and observed in all my American dominions, with the admonition that in places where these measures may be found inconvenient in practice, they inform me of it. Therefore, for now, I order and command my Viceroys of Peru, New Spain, and the New Kingdom of Granada, the *Presidentes, Audiencias,* Governors, and other ministers, judges, and justices of the said districts and of the Philippine Islands and other adjacent areas, and I entreat and charge the Very Reverend Archbishops, Reverend Bishops, the Councils of the churches in vacant bishoprics, the *Provisores* and Vicar-Generals, the local prelates of the religious orders,

and any other ecclesiastical judges of those my dominions, that each one on his part, as it falls to his individual lot, should keep, comply with, and execute and cause to be kept, complied with, and promptly and effectively executed my declared royal resolution commanding that there be immediately put into practice and observed the aforementioned measures that the said Very Reverend Archbishop of Mexico has proposed—with the object that one day it come to pass that the different idioms used in those same doninions may be extinguished and only Castilian be spoken—as has been ordered by repeated laws, Royal decrees, and orders issued in this matter—and with the proviso that in those places where these measures are found inconvenient in practice they will inform me of it, forwarding all pertinent documents so that in light of these it may be decided what might be my Royal pleasure in the matter, my resolution being what it is."
Dated in Madrid, the 16th of April, 1770—I THE KING—By order of the King, our Lord—D. Tomás del Mello—Sealed with three rubrics.

Notes

Preface

¹ For a discussion of language planning in one of the earliest conferences which considered this problem, see Charles A. Ferguson, "Directions in Sociolinguistics; Report on an Interdisciplinary Seminar," *SSRC Items*, XIX (March 1965), 1-4. A summary of some specific problems in the study of language standardization is given by Einar Haugen, a participant in the 1965 Conference on Sociolinguistics, sponsored by the UCLA Center for Research in Language and Linguistics; Einar Haugen, "Linguistics and Language Planning," *Sociolinguistics,* ed. William Bright (The Hague, 1966), pp. 50-67. A conference held in 1966 emphasized the language problems of developing nations; these papers are brought together by Joshua A. Fishman, Charles A. Ferguson, and Jyotirindra Das Gupta (eds.), *Language Problems of Developing Nations* (New York, 1968). In his introduction to this collection ("Sociolinguistics and the Language Problems of the Developing Countries"), Fishman makes a special note of the scarcity of complete case studies of the processes of language planning and the societal developments in which they occurred. Fishman suggests that only two have been published; Shepard B. Clough, *A History of the Flemish Movement in Belgium* (New York, 1930) and Einar Haugen, *Language Conflict and Language Planning: The Case of Modern Norwegian* (Cambridge, Mass., 1966).

² Language planning as defined here is broader in scope than is the term as used by some linguists. Einar Haugen, in his writings on language planning in Norway, emphasizes what might be termed primarily "linguistic" aspects of language planning—the preparation of a normative orthography, grammar, and dictionary for the guidance of writers and speakers in a national speech community. This definition is implicit in his use of the term throughout his case study of language planning in Norway, *Language Conflict and Language Planning*. Other linguists see language planning as necessitating a normative science practiced to regulate and improve existing languages. See, for example, Valter Tauli, *Introduction to a Theory of Language Planning* (Uppsala, 1968) and Punya Sloka Ray, *Language Standardization: Studies in Prescriptive Linguistics* (The Hague, 1963).

³ Dell H. Hymes, "Functions of Speech: An Evolutionary Approach," *Anthropology and Education*, ed. Frederick Gruber (Philadelphia, 1961), pp. 55-83.

⁴ Edward P. Dozier, "Two Examples of Linguistic Acculturation: The Yaqui of Sonora and Arizona and the Tewa of New Mexico," *Language in Culture and Society*, ed. Dell H. Hymes (New York, 1964), pp. 511-20.

⁵ Richard Diebold, Jr., "A Laboratory for Language Contact," *Anthropological Linguistics*, IV (January 1962), 41-51.

⁶ Robert J. Di Pietro, "Bilingualism," *Ibero American and Caribbean Linguistics*, Vol. IV of *Current Trends in Linguistics*, ed. Thomas Sebeok (10 vols.; The Hague, 1968), pp. 399-410. A brief review of Mexico's situation in a cross-national perspective is provided by Oscar Uribe Villegas, "La Situación sociolingüística de México como marco de la condición indígena," *Revista Mexicana de Sociología*, XXXI (octubre-diciembre 1969), 1019-1026.

Chapter One

¹ Because many native languages expired after the Conquest and because the chroniclers' comments on languages and their territorial limits are brief and often untrustworthy, linguists have had difficulties in mapping language areas existing at the time of the Conquest. Comparing the maps offered in the following sources with the narratives of chroniclers—both secular and religious—provides some indication of the language distribution pattern at the time of the Conquest: J. Alden Mason, "The Native Languages of Middle America," *The Maya and Their Neighbors* (New York, 1940), pp. 52-87; Frederick Johnson, "The Linguistic Map of Mexico and Central America," *Maya and Neighbors*, pp. 88-114; Jorge A. Vivó, *Razas y lenguas indígenas de México: su distribución geográfica* (México, 1941); Norman A. McQuown, *History of Studies in Middle American Linguistics*, Vol. V of *Handbook of Middle American Indians*, ed. Robert Wauchope (9 vols.; Austin, 1967).

² Charles Gibson, *The Aztecs Under Spanish Rule: A History of the Indians of the Valley of Mexico 1519-1810* (Stanford, 1964), p. 22.

³ Eric Wolf, *Sons of the Shaking Earth: The People of Mexico and Guatemala—Their Land, History, and Culture*, Phoenix Books (Chicago, 1959), p. 41.

⁴ Mariano Cuevas, *Historia de la Iglesia en México* (5 vols.; Tlalpam, D. F., 1921-26), I, 35, 37. Cuevas emphasized the importance of the autonomous nations which were independent of the Aztec empire in 1521. An estimate of the number of languages and dialects spoken in these areas added to those spoken within the Aztec empire brings the total of indigenous languages encountered by the Spaniards in the sixteenth century to approximately 124. Of these, seventy-three are lost and fifty-one are known today, according to Cuevas, who relied heavily on a map and exposition published

by Manuel Orozco y Berra in 1864; *Geografía de las Lenguas y Carta Etnográfica de México* (México, 1864). There are several other estimates of the distribution of pre-Hispanic languages in Mexico, the most thoroughly researched of which is probably that of Wigberto Jiménez Moreno and Miguel Othón de Mendizábal, originally published in 1939. These linguists reported 125 pre-Cortesian languages, of which only thirty-two have disappeared. Wigberto Jiménez Moreno and Miguel Othón de Mendizábal, "Lenguas Indígenas de México," *Razas y lenguas indígenas*, pp. 24-57. This work includes a map entitled "Distribución Prehispánica de las Lenguas Indígenas de México," prepared by Jiménez Moreno and Mendizábal in 1939.

[5] Jerónimo de Mendieta, *Historia Eclesiástica Indiana*, Vol. III of *Nueva colección de documentos para la historia de México*, ed. Joaquín García Icazbalceta (5 vols.; México, 1870), p. 552. Other chroniclers echoed Mendieta's evaluation of the use of Nahuatl as the standard of the Aztec empire. See, for example, Francisco Cervantes de Salazar, who wrote that the nobility and leading gentlemen of New Spain looked upon Nahuatl as the "universal" tongue which they learned in order to be able to communicate with Indians of "diverse regions." *Crónica de la nueva españa* (Madrid, 1914; originally published 1597), p. 33.

[6] Bernal Díaz del Castillo, *The Discovery and Conquest of Mexico 1517-1521*, trans. A. P. Maudslay (New York, 1956), p. 211.

[7] William H. Prescott, *History of the Conquest of Mexico and History of the Conquest of Peru* (New York, n.d.), pp. 93, 99; Juan Bautista Pomar, *Relación de Texcoco* in *Relaciones de Texcoco y de la Nueva España*, ed. Joaquín García Icazbalceta (México, n.d.), pp. 8, 40-41.

[8] Lorenzo Boturini Benaduci, *Idea de una nueva historia general de la America Septentrional* (Madrid, 1746), p. 142.

[9] Cisneros' reforms and their influence on future missionaries of Spanish America are summarized by Charles Gibson, *Spain in America* (The New American Nation series; New York, 1966), pp. 68-70. Cultural achievements of Isabella's Castilianization program are reviewed by J. H. Elliott, *Imperial Spain 1469-1716* (New York, 1963), pp. 116-19.

[10] Antonio de Lebrija, *Gramática Castellana* (Reproducción phototypique de l'édition princeps, 1492; Halle, A. S., 1909). Nebrija traced the relationship between language and nationality from Abraham's day through his own day in Spain, demonstrating how superior powers established themselves over subjugated peoples by linking political supremacy and a policy of unity through a common tongue.

[11] Quoted in Lewis Hanke, *Aristotle and the American Indians: A Study in Race Prejudice in the Modern World* (London, 1959), p. 8.

[12] Lesley Byrd Simpson (ed. and trans.), *The Laws of Burgos* (San Francisco, 1960), p. 14.

[13] *Ibid.*, pp. 11-30 *et passim*. The specific law relating to the education of all Indians read: "Also, we order and command that whoever has fifty Indians or more in encomienda shall be obliged to have a boy (the one he considers most able) taught to read and write, and the things of our Faith, so that he may later teach the said Indians, because the Indians will more readily accept what he says than what the Spaniards and settlers tell them . . . ." p. 21. The Crown had to assume that literacy would be in the Castilian language, for at the time of this order, the practice of writing the Indian languages in the Roman alphabet had not been established by missionaries in Spain's New World colonies.

[14] An English translation of this document is given in Arthur Helps, *The Spanish Conquest in America and its Relation to the History of Slavery and to the Government of the Colonies* (4 vols.; New York, 1966), I, 264-67. The comedy of errors which this document sponsored in the New World is best summarized by Lewis Hanke, "The Requerimiento and its Interpreters," *Revista de historia de América*, I (Mexico, 1938), no. 1, pp. 25-34.

[15] Díaz, pp. 8-9, 18-25.

[16] "Carta de Vera Cruz, M.S.," cited in Prescott, p. 150, n. 6.

[17] Bernal Díaz, a member of Cortés' expedition, provides the most exhaustive account of the Conquistador's trials with interpreters; pp. 42-68 *et passim*. See also Francisco López de Gómara, *Cortés: The Life of the Conqueror by His Secretary*, trans. Lesley Byrd Simpson (Berkeley, 1964), pp. 56-57.

[18] Díaz, p. 68.

[19] The existence of Spanish translators is proved by a 1529 edict, in which Charles V warned Spaniards serving as interpreters not to take jewels, wearing apparel, women, or any form of payment from the Indians; Vasco de Puga, *Provisiones, cédulas, instrucciones para el gobierno de la Nueva España* (2 vols.; México, 1878-79), I, 140-41.

[20] *Recopilación de leyes de los reynos de las Indias* (3 vols.; Madrid, 1943), I, 1-2 (Lib. I, tít. I, ley 2). This order and others similar in content were updated versions of the *requerimiento*. Perhaps the edict which represents the most significant shift from the spirit of the requirement is one issued in the *Ordenanza del Patronazgo* (1574) by Philip II. He decreed that Indian interpreters accompany all expeditions of discovery and converse with the Indians in order to learn about their ways of living, especially their daily habits, religious customs, and manner of educating their young; *Recopilación de leyes*, II, 3 (Lib. IV, tít. I, ley 15).

[21] Sixteenth and early seventeenth-century Crown edicts which attempted to control interpreters are found in *Recopilación de leyes*, I, 477-80 (Lib. II, tít. XXIX, leyes 1-14).

[22] Bartolomé de las Casas, *Historia de las Indias* (3 vols.; Mexico, 1951), II, 89, 249, 460. The prelude to the issuance of the New Laws in 1542 and

the Crown's political and humanitarian concern for the Indians' treatment at the hands of the encomenderos is well told by Lesley Byrd Simpson, *The Encomienda in New Spain: The Beginning of Spanish Mexico* (Berkeley, 1950), pp. 123-44; Gibson, *Spain*, pp. 55-63; Lewis Hanke, *The Spanish Struggle for Justice in the Conquest of America* (Philadelphia, 1949).

[23] "Carta de 15 de octubre de 1524," *Cartas y relaciones de Hernán Cortés al emperador Carlos V* (Paris, 1866), p. 326-27.

[24] Robert Ricard, *The Spiritual Conquest of Mexico: An Essay on the Apostolate and the Evangelizing Methods of the Mendicant Orders in New Spain: 1523-1572*, trans. Lesley Byrd Simpson (Berkeley, 1966), pp. 22-23.

[25] *Recopilación de leyes*, I, 211-12 (Lib. I, tít. XXIII, ley 11). This order, originally published in 1535, was reissued by Charles V in 1540 and by Philip II in 1579. During the seventeenth century, Philip III published the order twice, once in March of 1619 and again one year later.

CHAPTER TWO

[1] Cuevas, *Historia*, I, 183.

[2] There is no evidence that Cortés considered the friars' need for translators. In his correspondence with Charles V, he made no mention of providing interpreters, but rather he offered laymen to handle financial matters, such as the collecting and distributing of tithes. "Cuarta relación, 15 de octubre de 1524," Cortés, p. 170.

[3] Mendieta, p. 219. For an account of the struggle of the Church against heresies among the Indians, see Robert C. Padden, *The Hummingbird and the Hawk: Conquest and Sovereignty in the Valley of Mexico 1503-1541* (New York, 1967), chapter 13.

[4] "Carta de Fr. Pedro de Gante al Rey D. Felipe II, 1558," *Códice Franciscano*, Vol. II of *Nueva colección de documentos para la historia de México*, ed. Joaquín García Icazbalceta (5 vols.; México, 1941), p. 204.

[5] For the best account of Fray Pedro de Gante's work in Mexico, and especially his concern with language in the conversion of the natives, see Tomás Zepeda Rincón, *La instrucción pública en la Nueva España en el siglo XVI* (México, 1933), pp. 10 ff; Ignacio Márquez Rodiles, "Nota bibliografica," *Cartilla para enseñar a leer*, de Fray Pedro de Gante (Facsimile reproduction of Huntington Library's copy printed by Pedro Ocharte, Mexico City, 1569; México, 1959), pp. 9-14.

[6] Mendieta, p. 218.

[7] *Ibid.*, p. 219.

[8] *Ibid.*, p. 220.

[9] *Idem.*

[10] *Ibid.*, pp. 223-26.

[11] These compilations were made from García Icazbalceta's celebrated bibliography and from Ricard's appendix which lists all of the *vocabularios, doctrinas,* and *confesionarios* written by religious men in the field between 1524 and 1572. Joaquín García Icazbalceta, *Bibliografía mexicana del siglo XVI. Catálogo razonado de libros impresos en Mexico de 1539 a 1600, con biografías de autores y otras ilustraciones,* ed. Agustín Millares Carlo (México, 1954); Ricard, "Native-Language Works," pp. 406-14.

[12] P. Mariano Cuevas, *Documentos inéditos del siglo XVI para la historia de México* (México, 1914), p. 159.

[13] *Recopilación de leyes,* II, 193 (Lib. VI, tít. I, ley 18), issued June 7 and July 17, 1550.

[14] The letter to the Augustinians is contained in Puga, II, 87-88; the Dominican letter in *Documentos inéditos o muy raros para la historia de México,* ed. by Génaro García and Carlos Pereyra (36 vols.; México, 1905-11), XV, 106-08.

[15] Diego de Encinas, *Cedulario indiano* (4 vols.; Madrid, 1946), IV, 339.

[16] Archivo General de Indias (Seville), *Audiencia de México* 58-3-8, cited by Ricard, p. 50, n. 50.

[17] For a further discussion of the distinctions between the regulars and the seculars, see Gibson, *Spain,* pp. 77-81; Ricard, pp. 243-63. Cortés offered a contemporary evaluation of the suitability of the two religious groups for service in the New World. In his fourth dispatch to Charles V in 1524, Cortés strongly favored the regulars, the group he felt more fit for the rigors of religious example. Bishops and other secular clergy would waste the tithes in vices and unnecessary pomp, set bad examples for the natives, and do more toward turning them away from Christianity than converting them. Cortés noted that Indian priests had been required to live honest chaste lives, and any violation brought immediate death. If the Indian masses were to see the behavior of the secular clergy, the natives would surely have nothing but contempt for the Christian faith. Cortés, pp. 170-71.

[18] This summary of the linguistic and geographic spread of sixteenth-century missionaries of the three orders is based on a comparison between Ricard's "Sketch Map of the Mendicant Establishments about 1570" and the map of the pre-Hispanic distribution of Indian languages in Mexico prepared by Miguel Othón de Mendizábal and Wigberto Jiménez Moreno. Ricard, pp. 62-63; Mendizábal and Jiménez Moreno in Vivó, *Razas y lenguas.*

[19] Mendieta, p. 249.

[20] Joaquín García Icazbalceta, *Códice Mendieta,* Vol. IV of *Nueva colección de documentos para la historia de México* (5 vols.; México, 1892), pp. 72-73; García Icazbalceta, *Bibliografía.* A survey of writings listed in this bibliography bears out the conclusion that several friars knew two or three indigenous languages well enough to write grammars, vocabularies, or sermons in these tongues. A discussion of some of these friars is found in

Agustín Dávila Padilla, *Historia de la fŭndacion y discŭrso de la provincia, de Santiago de Mexico, de la orden de Predicadores por las vidas de sus varones insignes y casos notables de Nueva España* (Brusselas, 1625; originally published 1596), pp. 649-54.

[21] For a brief discussion of the persistence of the Otomi language, see Ethel E. Wallis, "Sociolinguistics in Relation to Mezquital Transition Education," *Estudios antropológicos publicados en homenaje al doctor Manuel Gamio* (México, 1956), pp. 527-28.

[22] The Crown, displeased over internal bickerings among the mendicant orders and their establishment of local power centers controlling numerous natives, openly began to favor the secular clergy to maintain settled Christian society after 1574. The viceroy and the audiencia also favored the establishment of permanent missions among the "barbarous" tribes interfering with mining operations in the north. For discussions of the transition of conversion activities from central Mexico to the frontiers, see Gibson, *Spain*, pp. 77-81.

[23] Cuevas, *Documentos*, p. 159.

[24] "Relación que los Franciscanos de Guadalajara dieron de los conventos que tenía su orden, *Códice Franciscano*, p. 153.

[25] *Ibid.*, pp. 152-53. A typical entry in the report reads: "Izaulán, convento; there is a confessor priest for the Spaniards, and a confessor and preacher for the Indians; he has in his charge 1500 Indians, more or less.;" p. 152.

[26] Joaquín García Icazbalceta, "Representaciones religiosas de México en el siglo XVI," in *Opúsculos varios* (2 vols.; México, 1986), II, 311-12.

[27] Report of Commissary General Fray Alonso Ponce, cited by Cuevas, *Historia*, I, 36.

[28] The recommendation of "Doctor Muñon" is summarized in a decree, issued July 26, 1570, by Philip II; *Cédulas Reales*. Tomo 47. Archivo General de la Nación, México.

[29] Dávila Padilla, p. 31; Boturini Benaduci, p. 96.

[30] Cuevas, *Historia*, I, 46; "Carta de Fray Rodrigo de la Cruz al Emperador Carlos V," in Cuevas, *Documentos*, p. 159. An eighteenth-century scholar who extensively studied ancient Nahuatl codices felt he had evidence to support his declaration that Nahuatl "exceeded" Latin in poetic expression and rendering of abstract concepts. Lorenzo Boturini Benaduci, *Catalogo del Museo historico Indiano* (Madrid, 1746), p. 95.

[31] Mendieta, p. 552.

[32] *Ibid.*, p. 411; Toribio de Benavente Motolinía, *Historia de los Indios de la Nueva España*, Vol. I of *Colección de documentos para la historia de México*, ed. Joaquín García Icazbalceta (México, 1858), pp. 209-10. Fray Bernardino de Sahagún, the best known sixteenth-century ethnographer of the Indians, wrote this description of their method of recording history: "These people have neither letters nor characters, nor do they know how

to read or write. They make their records with images and pictures, and all their ancient records and books are painted with such figures and images that they know and remember the deeds their ancestors performed and recorded in their annals for *more than a thousand years* before the Spaniards came to this land.;" *Historia general de las cosas de Nueva España*, ed. Carlos María de Bustamante (3 vols.; México, 1830; originally published 1566-69), III, 80-81.

[33] *Cédulas Reales.* Tomo 47. Archivo General de la Nación, México.

[34] The 1550 order is found in *Recopilación de leyes*, II, 193 (Lib. VI, tít. I, ley 18). Philip II's 1565 order is in García and Pereyra, XV, 163-65.

[35] *Cédulas Reales.* Tomo 47. Archivo General de la Nación, México.

[36] Cédula of 1574, *Recopilación de leyes*, I, 44-45 (Lib. I, tít. VI, ley 29).

[37] Cédula of 1578, *ibid.*, I, 45 (Lib. I, tít. VI, ley 30).

[38] Cédula of 1580, *ibid.*, I, 132 (Lib. I, tít. XV, ley 6).

[39] Cédula of 1580, *ibid.*, I, 204 (Lib. I, tít. XXII, ley 46).

[40] Cédula of 1580, *ibid.*, I, 206 (Lib. I, tít. XXII, ley 56).

[41] Zepeda Rincon, pp. 15-18; Cuevas, *Documentos*, pp. 86-88.

[42] For an excerpt of a letter from the Bishop of Santo Domingo, Sebastian Ramírez de Fuenleal, to Charles V in 1533, see Cuevas, *Historia*, I, 386. Fray Juan de Zumárraga wrote Charles V in 1536 of his strong desire to establish a colegio for young Indians to learn Latin; Joaquín García Icazbalceta, *Biografía de D. Fr. Juan de Zumárraga, Primer Obispo y Arzobispo de Méjico*, ed. M. Aguilar (Madrid, 1929), pp. 260-62.

[43] Zepeda Rincon, pp. 31-33; *Códice Franciscano*, p. 62; Sahagún, III, 75; Mendieta, p. 415.

[44] *Códice Franciscano*, p. 62.

[45] *Idem.*

[46] Ricard notes that "although all collegians seem to have known Spanish, that language was banished from the curriculum." p. 224. There seems to be no evidence that the absence of Spanish from the curriculum was as deliberate as Ricard's statement suggests. The Franciscan accounts make it clear that Spanish was fostered in some of their programs, and as late as 1584 when Fray Alonso Ponce visited Tlatelolco, the students of the colegio delivered speeches in Latin and in Castilian. Mendieta, p. 411; *Códice Franciscano*, p. 63, and apendice II, p. 256.

[47] García Icazbalceta, *La instrucción pública en la ciudad de México durante el siglo XVI*, (México, 1893), p. 13.

[48] Sahagún, III, 33.

[49] Motolinía, *Historia*, I, 211.

[50] *Códice Franciscano*, p. 63; Cuevas, *Historia*, I, 389-90.

[51] Zepeda Rincon, p. 36, citing "Carta al Emperador."

⁵² Cuevas, *Historia,* II, 252.

⁵³ *Códice Franciscano,* p. 63.

⁵⁴ *Ibid.,* pp. 63-64.

⁵⁵ Mendieta, p. 418.

⁵⁶ "Fragmentos," cited by Romulo Velasco Ceballos, ed., *La Alfabetización en la Nueva España: Leyes, Cedulas Reales, Ordenanzas, Bandos, Pastoral y Otros Documentos* (México, 1945), p. xxxi.

⁵⁷ Gerard Decorme, *La Obra de los Jesuitas Mexicanos durante la época colonial 1572-1767* (2 vols.; México, 1941), I, 148-49. Jerome Vicent Jacobsen, *Educational Foundations of the Jesuits in 16th Century New Spain* (Berkeley, 1938), p. 117.

⁵⁸ Peter Masten Dunne, *Pioneer Jesuits in Northern Mexico* (Berkeley, 1944), pp. 10, 18-19; Herbert E. Bolton, *The Spanish Borderlands* ("Chronicles of America;" New Haven, 1921), pp. 189-91.

⁵⁹ Herbert Eugene Bolton, "The Mission as a Frontier Institution in the Spanish-American Colonies," *American Historical Review,* XXIII (October 1917), 43. This plan is evident in all accounts of the work of Jesuits among Indians in northern Mexico. See especially Dunne, *Pioneer Jesuits* and Herbert Eugene Bolton, *Rim of Christendom: A Biography of Eusebio Francisco Kino, Pacific Coast Pioneer* (New York, 1936).

⁶⁰ Actas de la Congregación Provencial, 25 octubre 1603, cited by Decorme, I, 55; Jacobsen, p. 222; Cuevas, *Historia,* II, 349; Antonio Astrain, *Historia de la Compañía de Jesús en la Asistencia de España,* IV, 410, cited by Decorme, I, 55.

⁶¹ *Landa's Relación de las Cosas de Yucatan,* trans, and ed. Alfred M. Tozzer (Papers of the Peabody Museum of American Archaeology and Ethnology, Vol. XVIII; Cambridge, Mass., 1941), pp. 70, 72, n. 319, p. 73, n. 326, p. 75.

⁶² *Ibid.,* pp. 44-46, n. 219, pp. 68-70, n. 311, n. 313, p. 80. For Landa's account of Testera's short-lived educational efforts, see p. 67.

⁶³ *Ibid.,* pp. 69, 80. Though Landa himself preached in Maya, he used translators in the Inquisition. Two natives, Gaspar Antonio Chi and Jorge Xia, knew Castilian and sided with the friars against their own people; the former wrote sermons and provided instruction in Maya for other friars. *Ibid.,* pp. 44-46, n. 219. The scarcity of schools in the region and the difficulties the friars encountered in learning Maya are reiterated by Francisco Cantón Rosado, *Historia de la instrucción pública en Yucatan desde el siglo XVI hasta fines del siglo XIX* (México, 1943), pp. 8-9.

⁶⁴ There were no books available for teaching Spanish until the publication in 1569 of Pedro de Gante's *Cartilla para enseñar a leer*. This was printed in Latin, Castilian, and Nahuatl, as were other readers printed after this date. But it is important to note that the religious regulars also continued to prepare *cartillas* written only in the various Indian languages, indicating

that even after readers in Spanish were available for teaching the Indians, the friars continued to teach literacy skills in the indigenous tongues. García Icazbalceta, *Bibliografía mexicana*, p. 57. This bibliography indicates that cartillas printed only in the Indian languages were being made available throughout the sixteenth century. See, for example, *Cartilla y doctrina en Chuchona*, published in 1580, entry 100, p. 310.

[65] *Recopilación de leyes*, II, 207-12 (Lib. VI, tít. III, leyes 1, 23, 24).

[66] Dávila Padilla, a sixteenth-century Dominican chronicler, commented on the identification of the Mixes with their language as they sought to maintain their fierceness in the face of the overwhelming numerical superiority of their enemies, the Zapotecs; p. 548.

[67] This is proved by a letter from Viceroy Conde de Monterrey to Phillip III, written June 11, 1599, in which the Viceroy responded to the King's earlier expression of concern over the linguistic situation in New Spain, Cuevas, *Documentos*, pp. 473-74.

[68] *Recopilación de leyes*, I, 132 (Lib. I, tít. XV, leyes 5, 8).

[69] *Ibid.*, I, 132 (Lib. I, tít. XV, ley 6); I, 95-96 (Lib. I, tít. XIII, ley 4).

[70] *Ibid.*, I, 204-05 (Lib. I, tít. XXII, ley 49).

[71] Cuevas, *Documentos*, p. 473.

Chapter Three

[1] *Recopilación de leyes*, I, 22 (Lib. I, tít. III, ley 19), issued in 1612 by Phillip III and reissued in 1624 by Phillip IV.

[2] Cédula of 1550, Encinas, IV, 339.

[3] *Recopilación de leyes,* I, 96 (Lib. I, tít. XIII, ley 5).

[4] Juan de Solórzana y Pereyra, *Política Indiana* (5 vols.; Madrid, 1930), I, 397-99.

[5] *Cedulario americano del siglo XVIII*, ed. Antonio Muro Orejón (Consejo Superior de Investigaciones Cientificas, XCIX. Sevilla, 1956), document 169, pp. 262-65.

[6] The Archbishop's letter is excerpted and the bishop's comment noted in Charles II's follow-up decree issued in 1688; *Cedulario Americano*, document 197, pp. 319-21.

[7] *Ibid.*, p. 322.

[8] The bishop's letter is excerpted in the King's 1690 decree issued in response to the Oaxacan's suggestion. Cédula of 1690, *Cédulas Reales*. Tomo 30. Archivo General de la Nación, México.

[9] *Idem.* This provision of the decree echoed orders given in Spain in 1567, which required that the Moors learn Castilian within three years. The mandate, originally issued as the Edict of 1526, was revived in 1566 by Diego de Espinosa, president of the Council of Castile, and reissued

January 1, 1567. The edict forbade the use of Arabic, and ordered the Moriscos to learn Castilian within three years. Roger Bigelow Merriman, *Philip the Prudent*, Vol. IV: *The Rise of the Spanish Empire in the Old World and in the New* (New York, 1934), pp. 85-88.

[10] Cédula of 1691, *Cedulario Americano*, document 279, pp. 444-46.

[11] Cédula of 1693, *ibid.*, document 325, pp. 511-12.

[12] The archbishop's letter is excerpted in the 1693 decree; *ibid.*

[13] For a discussion of education opportunities available for these groups, see Zepeda Rincon, pp. 39-43, 46-74 *et passim;* Velasco Ceballos, *Alfabetización*, pp. xxxv-xxxvii.

[14] *Recopilación de leyes*, II, 207-08 (Lib. VI, tít. III, ley 1).

[15] *Ibid.*, II, 211-12 (Lib. VI, tít. III, leyes 18, 23, 24).

[16] "Sobre los inconveniences de vivir los indios en el centro de la Ciudad," *Boletín del Archivo general de la nación*, IX (enero, febrero, marzo, 1938), 12, citing "Informe del Pe. ministro de San Pablo, acerca de la jurisdicción y distrito de su doctrina" by Fr. Bernabé Núñez de Páez.

[17] *Idem.*

[18] *Ibid.*, 1, 9.

[19] See the records of official transactions in the colony during this period; for example, Clero regular y secular. Tomo 103. Archivo General de la Nación. As late as 1770, Mexico's Archbishop decried the continuing need for interpreters in the courts and local civil offices. D. Francisco, Antonio Lorenzana y Buitron, Pastoral V, *Cartas pastorales, y edictos* (México, 1770), p. 97.

[20] Solórzano y Pereyra, I, 125.

[21] "Indios descendientes de nobles, elevan memorial al Rey Felipe V, para que el imperial Colegio de Santa Cruz de Tlaltelolco y de San Pablo, ambos para indios, sean reabiertos," cited in Velasco Ceballos, *Alfabetización*, pp. 57-71.

[22] *Ibid.*, p. 62.

[23] Such edicts were made by both Phillip V and Ferdinand VI; *ibid.*, pp. 60-61. Charles III issued a similar order in 1766; "Indios-que sean admitidos en las religiosos, y según sus méritos y capacidad, promovidos a dignidades y oficios públicos." *Cédulas Reales.* Tomo 89. Archivo General de la Nación.

[24] Silvio Zavala y José Miranda, "Instituciones indígenas en la colonia," *Métodos y Resultados de la Política Indigenista en México*, ed. Alfonso Caso et al. (Memorias del Instituto Nacional Indigenista, Vol. VI; México, 1954), pp. 102-03.

[25] "Reglas, Para que los Naturales de estos Reynos sean felices en lo espiritual, y temporal," Lorenzana y Buitron, p. 47. For the suggestion made by the Bishop of Oaxaca in a letter written to Charles II in 1688, see Cédula of 1690, *Cédulas Reales.* Tomo 30. Archivo General de la Nación.

²⁶ "Pastoral V. Para que los Indios aprendan el Castellano," Lorenzana y Buitron, pp. 91-100.

²⁷ "Edicto XV. En que se publica la Real Cédula sobre la extensión del Idioma Castellano," Lorenzana y Buitron, pp. 143-52. Both the Pastoral and the Edict are translated in Appendix I. These documents are not easily available to scholars, and there are scant references to them in secondary sources. They are valuable in their entirety as an appraisal of colonial language policy, and, in addition, they provide some provocative insights into the religious history of the period.

²⁸ *Ibid.*, pp. 149-150.

²⁹ For a convincing argument that splits over language and training qualifications were ultimately related to the vying for position between criollos and peninsulares, see John Tate Lanning, *The Eighteenth-Century Enlightenment in the University of San Carlos de Guatemala* (Ithaca, 1956), pp. 11-13.

³⁰ Romulo Velasco Ceballos, "Instrucción pública," *La Administración de d. frey Antonio María de Bucareli y Ursúa* (Publicaciones de Archivo General de la Nación, XXIX, XXX; 2 vols.; México, 1936), II, lxxii.

³¹ "Bando: Escuelas para indios en todo el virreinato, con la mira de desterrar los idiomas indígenas," *ibid.*, II, 287-88, 177-78.

³² Velasco Ceballos, *Alfabetización*, pp. lxxxviii-lxxxix; Velasco Ceballos, "Instrucción pública," *Bucareli*, II, lxxii-lxxx.

³³ Bucareli to Charles III, July 27, 1778, reprinted, *ibid.*, II, 183-93. After the expulsion of the Jesuits in 1767, the question of the future of the College of San Gregorio, established in the sixteenth century primarily for the secondary education of Indians, became central to the controversy surrounding a new colegio for Indians in New Spain. Who could claim the property and support funds for the colegio? Did these now belong to the Indians, in whose behalf the secondary school had been founded and supported through the years, or could it be taken over by lay Spaniards for their use? The controversy is summarized in this letter of Bucareli in which he mentions eight decrees and numerous legal documents circulated in New Spain on behalf of the College of San Gregorio's future.

³⁴ Velasco Ceballos, *Alfabetización*, p. xci.

³⁵ Joseph Joaquín Granados y Gálvez, *Tardes americanas: gobierno gentil y católico: breve y particular noticia de toda la historia indiana: sucesos, casos notables, y cosas ignorados, desde la entrada de la Gran Nación Tulteca a esta tierra de Anáhuac, hasta los presentes tiempos. Trabajadas por un Indio, y un Español* (México, 1778), pp. 124-26 *et passim*.

³⁶ Joseph María Carranza, *Discurso sobre el establecimiento de una escuela pública gratuita de primeras letras, y christiana educación de los niños pobres* (México, 1778), pp. 33, 36.

³⁷ Joaquín Granados y Gálvez, pp. 124-26, p. 528.

³⁸ *Informe general prevenido por Real Orden de 31 de enero de 1784, sobre las Misiones de aquellos dominios, comparando el actual estado de ellas con el que tenían las que entregaron los Ex Jesuitas al tiempo de su expatriación* (México, 1793), cited by Irma Wilson, *Mexico, A Century of Educational Thought* (New York, 1941), pp. 51-52.

³⁹ *Gazeta de México*, July 5, 1785, p. 331. A Cédula Real published in 1790 reminded the owners of slaves of their duty to educate them in the principles of Catholicism; *Gazeta*, June 22, 1790, pp. 122-24. However, no mention was made in the *Gazeta* of the laws covering Indian education in Spanish, and little news from the Indian areas was, in fact, published in *Gazeta de México, compendio de noticias de Nueva España.* Transfers of priests and their deaths comprised the greatest amount of news reported from the Indian areas in the years between 1785 and 1791 in the *Gazeta*.

⁴⁰ *Gazeta de México*, July 5, 1785, p. 331.

⁴¹ Articles showing concern with the method of teaching languages appeared in June and July of 1790; "Gramática latina: no debe enseñar en la misma lengua Latína," *Gazeta de Literatura*, June 22, 1790, pp. 153-56; "Nebrixa: censura de su Arte," *Gazeta de Literatura*, June 22, 1790, pp. 157-64; "Iriate (D. Juan de) elogio de este Literato," *Gazeta de Literatura*, July 6, 1790; "Breve idea del método que sigue," *Gazeta de Literatura*, July 6, 1790, pp. 169-72. Follow-up arguments continued into the next year; "Al Autor de la Gazeta de Literatura," *Gazeta de Literatura*, December 19, 1791, pp. 256-58.

⁴² "Gramática latina: no debe enseñar en la misma lengua Latína," *Gazeta de Literatura*, June 22, 1790, p. 154.

⁴³ "Breve idea del método que sigue," *Gazeta de Literatura*, July 6, 1790, pp. 169-72.

⁴⁴ "Al Autor de la Gazeta de Literatura," *Gazeta de Literatura*, December 19, 1791, pp. 256-58.

⁴⁵ *Diario de México* (México, 1805), I, frontispiece.

⁴⁶ "Proyectista," *Diario de México*, October 6, 1805, pp. 23-24.

⁴⁷ "Nuevo sistema de instrucción pública," *Diario de México*, March 26-31, 1807, nos. 542-47.

⁴⁸ "Señor Diarista," *Diario de México*, November 9, 1805, p. 166.

⁴⁹ *Idem.*

⁵⁰ Madaline W. Nichols (ed.), *A Bibliographical Guide to Materials on American Spanish* (Cambridge, Mass., 1941), p. 1. The role of academies in constructing the codified norm of a nation is an important consideration for linguists, especially those of the Prague School, concerned with language standardization. For a brief discussion of the activities of a language academy as a codifying agent, see Paul L. Garvin and Madeleine Mathiot, "Urbanization of the Guaraní Language," in *Readings in the Sociology of Language*, ed. Joshua A. Fishman (The Hague, 1968), pp. 365-74.

Chapter Four

[1] Hospitales. Tomo 25. Archivo General de la Nación, Mexico.

[2] José Joaquín Fernández de Lizardi, *El Pensador Mexicano* (Biblioteca del Estudiante Universitario No. 15; México, 1940), p. 23. See also *El Periquillo Sarniento* (2 vols.; México, 1942), I, chapters 2 and 3. For a discussion of the importance of caligraphy and its place in the traditionalism of colonial education, see José Torre Revello, "Algunos libros de caligrafía usados en México en el siglo XVII," *Historia Mexicana*, V (octubre-diciembre 1955), 220-27. The personal experiences which provoked Lizardi to satirize education are given by Luis González Obregón, *Don José Joaquín Fernández de Lizardi, El Pensador Mexicano: apuntes biográficos y bibliográficos* (Mexico, 1888).

[3] González Obregón, pp. 24-25.

[4] Fernández de Lizardi, *El Pensador Mexicano*, p. 46.

[5] Manuel Abad y Queipo, "Estado moral y político en que se hallaba la población del virreinato de Nueva España en 1779," *Obras sueltas*, ed. José María Luis Mora (2d ed.; México, 1963), pp. 205-06.

[6] Miguel Ramos Arizpe, *Discursos, Memorias e Informes* (Biblioteca del Estudiante Universitario, No. 36; México, 1942), pp. 43-44.

[7] José María Morelos, *La Abispa de Chilpancingo Escrita para perpetuar la memoria del Primer Congreso instalado alli el día 12 de septiembre de 1813* (México, 1821), pp. 256-58.

[8] "Sentimientos de la nación o 23 puntos dados por Morelos para la constitución," cited by Ubaldo Vargas Martínez, *Morelos: Siervo de la Nación* (2d ed.; Mexico, 1966), p. 109.

[9] *Informes y Manifiestos de los poderes ejecutivo y legislativo 1821-1904*, I, 496, cited by Moisés González Navarro, "Instituciones Indígenas en México Independiente," *Métodos y Resultados*, p. 115.

[10] J. Lloyd Mecham, "The Origins of Federalism in Mexico," *Hispanic American Historical Review*, XVIII (May 1938), 164-82. For the role of José María Luis Mora in this period, see Charles A. Hale, "José María Luis Mora and the Structure of Mexican Liberalism," *Hispanic American Historical Review*, XLV (May 1965), 200-02.

[11] Lorenzo de Zavala, *Ensayo histórico de las revoluciones de Mégico, desde 1808 hasta 1830* (2 vols.; Nueva York, 1832), I, 33, 35; II, 229.

[12] Lucas Alamán, *Historia de Méjico desde los primeros movimientos que prepararon su independencia en el año de 1808 hasta la época presente* (5 vols.; México, 1849-52), I, 23-27, *et passim*.

[13] Lorenzo de Zavala, I, 35.

[14] *La Abeja poblana*, num. 3, suplemento, 18 de diciembre, 1820, cited by Wilson, pp. 92-93.

[15] For Rodríguez Puebla's proposal made to the Mexican Congress on October 8, 1824, see Juan A. Mateos, *Historia parlamentaria de los congresos mexicanos de 1821 a 1857* (9 vols.; México, 1877-86), II, 966. The dissension between this early Indianist and other reformers is clearly indicated by José María Luis Mora in his "Revista Política," *Obras sueltas*, pp. 152-53.

[16] E. A. D., *Los Indios quieren ser libres y lo serán con justicia* (México, 1829).

[17] Mora, "Revista Política," *Obras sueltas*, p. 110.

[18] *Actas*, I, 52 (Mar. 13, 1824) and *Actas*, III, 9 (Nov. 3, 1824), cited by Charles A. Hale, *Mexican Liberalism in the Age of Mora, 1821-1853* (New Haven, 1968), p. 218. Hale offers a thorough discussion of the creole orientation toward social reform for the Indian in the chapter entitled "Liberalism and the Indian," pp. 215-47.

[19] *Ibid.*, p. 218. For a discussion of the continuing nineteenth-century folly of trying to eliminate the term *los indios* from congressional debates, see Moisés González Navarro, "El mestizaje mexicano en el periodo nacional," *Revista Mexicana de Sociología*, XXX, (enero-marzo 1968), 35-42.

[20] José María Luis Mora, *Ensayos, Ideas y Retratos* (Biblioteca del Estudiante Universitario, No. 25; México, 1941), pp. 91-92.

[21] *La instrucción pública* (Bound collection, Duke University Library; n.p., n.d.). This bound collection of materials on state rulings covering public elementary education in the first half of the nineteenth century offers numerous examples of state adoptions of Mora's recommendations for public education. Some states did, however, make some provisions for the education of Indians and their training in the Lancasterian method; see González Navarro, "Instituciones Indígenas en México Independiente," *Métodos y Resultados*, p. 135.

[22] The governor of Guanajuato reported to the Constituent Congress in 1826 that the Lancasterian system had not been effective in his area. The Otomi had not learned to speak Spanish, thus limiting the effectiveness of priests and teachers. The governor proposed that school attendance be made compulsory, "so that over a period of twenty or thirty years the Spanish language may be generalized." *Memoria que el gobernador del estado de Guanajuato formó para dar complimiento a la parte 8 del artículo 161 de la constitución federal, ampliándola en otros ramos para conocimiento del congreso del mismo estado, todo por lo respectivo al año de 1826*, cited by Wilson, pp. 141-43.

[23] Mora, "Revista Política," *Obras sueltas*, p. 110.

[24] *Ibid.*, pp. 115-20.

[25] Secretaría de Educación Pública, México, *Gómez Farías y la Reforma Educativa de 1833* (México, 1933), p. 32; Mora, "Revista Política," *Obras sueltas*, p. 124.

[26] Wilson, pp. 164-65. It is significant that the liberal reformers' myopia

led them not only to deny the existence of the Indian majority in the nation, but also to publish laws requiring all foreigners settling in Mexico to learn "the national tongue and Mexican customs." During Gómez Farías' administration, colonization and the integration of immigrants in the nation were issues more debated than the status of the indigenous population; Mora, "Revista Política," *Obras sueltas*, pp. 148-52. This is not to say that political leaders were indifferent to the Indian rebellions which occurred in the first half century. Liberals and conservatives alike debated ways to "civilize" the barbarians, but their plans were never put into legislative form, and some later historians have judged their response to Indian uprisings mild in contrast to their intense concern with colonization; see, for example, Hale, *Mexican Liberalism*, pp. 237-44.

[27] March 22, 1835, Circular de la Secretaria de Relaciones, número 1535, *Legislación mexicana: colección completa de las disposiciones legislativas expedidas desde la independencia de la republica*, ed. by Manuel Dublan y José María Lozano (19 vols.; México, 1876), III, 35-36. Among the signers of the circular were Carlos María Bustamante, Juan Rodríguez Puebla, and the conservative Lúcas Alamán. Rodríguez Puebla was, no doubt, responsible for prodding the group to include items four and six in their charter. It is puzzling that Mora did not sign this circular, though he did endorse a similar document circulated the next day in support of a National Academy of History; see *ibid.*, número 1536, III, 36-37.

[28] October 26, 1842, Decreto del gobierno, número 2451, *Legislación mexicana*, IV, 310-12.

[29] January 24, 1854, Decreto del gobierno, número 4179, *ibid.*, VII, 17-18.

[30] In 1843, there were only 1310 schools with a total of 60,000 students enrolled. The government set aside very little money to support public instruction; thus private aid supported most schools. Of the total, only twenty-one schools, with an enrollment of 2012 pupils, were financed by the Church. Ricardo García Granados, *La Constitución de 1857 y las leyes de Reforma en México* (México, 1906), p. 113. The national budget of 1846 indicated national priorities: 29,613 pesos were marked for education; twenty-two million for defense. Justin H. Smith, *The War with Mexico* (2 vols.; New York, 1919), I, 14.

[31] Mora, "Sociedad de la Biblia," *Obras sueltas*, pp. 615-16; Pedro Gringoire, "El 'Protestantismo' del Dr. Mora," *Historia Mexicana*, III (1953), 328-66. The inconsistency between Mora's firm statements denying the Indians' existence and the use of Indian tongues in Mexico and his own act of translating the Book of Luke must be placed in the broad context of Mora's view of education. The Bible taught moral virtues and "pure customs" and was certainly "classical" literature; thus the spread of the Bible helped fulfill what were for Mora two important aspects of education. As though to explain any contradictions or questions concerning his connection with the Bible Society, Mora noted: "no man that loves letters

and the progress of the human species is able to stand in the way of the success of the Bible Society;" "Sociedad de la Biblia," *Obras sueltas*, p. 615.

[32] *La Verdad*, num. 1, p. 1, num. 4, p. 77, 1854, cited by Wilson, p. 186. Centralists looked to Catholicism as the unifier of diverse peoples within the nation and reinstated the colonial missions, which had been secularized in 1834; *ibid.*, num. 1, p. 3; Hale, *Mexican Liberalism*, pp. 132, 221-22. But the number of ecclesiastics, especially the regulars, had sharply decreased in the 1830's, and the missions disappeared by 1859; Lorenzo de Zavala, II, 227; Hale, *Mexican Liberalism*, p. 222; González Navarro, "Instituciones Indígenas," *Métodos y Resultados*, pp. 139-42.

[33] Oscar Lewis, *Life in a Mexican Village: Tepoztlan Restudied* (Urbana, 1951), p. xxv. Mariano Jacobo Rojas became secretary of the Department of Public Education of the state of Morelos, published a Spanish-Nahuatl newspaper in Tepoztlan, and later became professor of Nahuatl at the National Museum of Archaeology, Ethnology, and History; *idem*.

[34] Maximilian, an amateur linguist, had great interest in the Nahuatl tongue. Had he followed his own inclinations, he might well have made Nahuatl "the official language of the court," or have put it on an equal basis with Spanish in the empire. Jack Autrey Dabbs, *The French Army in Mexico 1861-1867: A Study in Military Government* (The Hague, 1963), p. 285.

[35] Ignacio Ramírez, "Instrucción primeria," *Obras de Ignacio Ramírez* (2 vols.; México, 1889), II, 176-77.

[36] *Ibid.*, pp. 175-76; Ramírez, "Obras en idiomas extranjeros," *Obras*, II, 191.

[37] Ramírez, "Instrucción primeria," *Obras*, II, 177.

[38] Ramírez, "La lengua mexicana," *Obras*, II, 207; Ramírez, "Obras en idiomas extranjeros," *Obras*, II, 191.

[39] Ramírez, "Obras en idiomas extranjeros, *Obras*, II, 191.

[40] Ramírez, "La lengua mexicana," *Obras*, II, 207-08.

[41] Ignacio Ramírez, "Discurso sobre la discusión de la Constitución en lo general, en la sesión celebrada en el Palacio legislativo, el 7 de julio de 1856," *Galería de oradores de México en el siglo XIX*, ed. Emilio del Castillo Negrete (3 vols.; México, 1877-80), II, 264; Ramírez, "Lecturas de historia política de Mexico," *Obras*, I, 217.

[42] Basic documents and educational ideas of this period may be found in Martín Luis Guzmán, ed., *Escuelas laicas* (México, 1948). An overview of positivists active in education is available in Albert J. Delmez, "The Positivist Philosophy in Mexican Education, 1867-1873," *The Americas*, VI (July 1949), 32-44.

[43] Leopoldo Zea, "Hacia un nuevo liberalismo en la educación," *Historia Mexicana*, V (abril-junio 1956), 528-48. The most comprehensive

coverage of education events in the last two decades of the nineteenth century is found in Francisco Larroyo, *Historia comparada de la educación en México* (México, 1947), pp. 250-73.

[44] Isidro Castillo, *Mexico y Su Revolución Educativa* (México, 1965), p. 117.

[45] *Ibid.*, pp. 112-13, 109.

[46] Mora, Zavala, and Alamán had no great interest in Mexican antiquities; Hale, pp. 219-20. Zavala's scanty references to Indians testify to his passing concern for the natives; see, for example, *Ensayo*, I, 12-15, 33-35. For a general summary of the flurry of enthusiasm for the Indian in this period, see a speech by Francisco Belmar presented April 17, 1911, cited by Juan Comas, *Ensayos sobre Indigenismo* (México, 1953), pp. 80-81.

[47] These compilations were made on the basis of information provided in *Bibliografía indigenista de México y Centroamérica 1850-1950*), ed. Manuel Germán Parra y Wigberto Jiménez Moreno (Memorias del Instituto Nacional Indigenista, Vol. IV; México, 1954), pp. 63-107.

[48] Nichols, *Bibliographical Guide to Materials on American Spanish*, pp. 8, 81.

[49] See, for example, Frank Tannenbaum, "Some Reflections on the Mexican Revolution," in Stanley R. Ross (ed.), *Is the Mexican Revolution Dead?* (New York, 1966), pp. 202-04; and Frank Brandenburg, *The Making of Modern Mexico* (Englewood Cliffs, N.J., 1964), p. 41. For a discussion of the científicos and their attitude toward race, see Martin S. Stabb, "Indigenism and Racism in Mexican Thought: 1857-1911," *Journal of Inter-American Studies*, I (October 1959), 405-25. The same author treats the racism of the científicos and the development of modern indigenismo in Chapters II and IV of *In Quest of Identity: Patterns in the Spanish American Essay of Ideas, 1890-1960* (Chapel Hill, 1967), pp. 12-34, 58-101.

[50] Cosmes' objections to educating the Indian appear in *La Libertad*, February 16, 1883 and March 1, 1883. For a summary of his minority report to the First Congress of Instruction, see Leopoldo Zea, *Del liberalismo a la revolución en la educación mexicana* (México, 1956), pp. 151-53.

[51] For an appraisal of Sierra's contributions to the philosophical debates which set the stage for the rise of indigenismo, see Stabb, *In Quest of Identity*, pp. 45-46. The similar role of other intellectuals close to Porfirio Díaz is discussed by T. G. Powell, "Mexican Intellectuals and the Indian Question, 1876-1911" *Hispanic American Historical Review*, XLVIII (February 1968), 19-36. Specific responses of Sierra and Ignacio Altamirano to Cosmes are found in *La Libertad*, February 27, 28, 1883 and March 3, 6, 1883.

[52] Carl Lumholtz, an anthropologist traveling in Mexico between 1890 and 1898 reported that Díaz spoke of the Indians as "good people" and sponsored yearly feasts in memory of "aboriginal heroes" who sacrificed their lives in defense of Mexico; *Unknown Mexico* (2 vols.; New York, 1902),

I, 480. Some of the overwhelming evidence to support the fact that Díaz did little to alter the ruinous state of education during this period may be found in two collections of political and legislative materials from the period; Carlos Alvear Acevedo, *La Educación y la Ley: La Legislación en Materia Educativa en el México Independiente* (México, 1963), J. M. Puig Casauranc, *La Educación Pública en México a tráves de los mensajes presidenciales desde la consumación de la independencia hasta nuestros dias* (México, 1926).

[53] Rafael de Zayas Enríquez, *La rendición de una raza: estudio sociológico* (Veracruz, 1887), pp. 36, 126-27, 152. Zayas Enríquez was no doubt referring to such statements as that made by Francisco Pimentel: "we discover in the Indian languages obvious signs of their servility;" *Memoria sobre las causas que han originado la situación actual de la raza indígena de México y medios de remediarla* (México, 1864), pp. 82-83.

[54] Abraham Castellanos, "La Educación de la raza indígena," *Boletín de la Sociedad Mexicana de Geografía y Estadística*, III (1908), 78-85. For a view of Castellanos as a link between early twentieth-century educational theorists and practitioners, see Wilson, pp. 288-90.

[55] A letter from Belmar to President Porfirio Díaz, March 28, 1910, cited by Comas, *Ensayos*, p. 70.

[56] Numbers three and nine of the fifteen *Bases* for the founding of the *Sociedad Indianista Mexicana*, ibid., pp. 73-74.

[57] A letter from Díaz to Belmar, *ibid.*, p. 71; "Las ideas rectoras de la SIM," *ibid.*, p. 78.

[58] Jesús Díaz de León, "Concepto del Indianismo en México," a speech given before the Scientific and Artistic Assembly of the Centennial, *ibid.*, pp. 79-80.

[59] Justo Sierra, "Discurso pronunciado el dia 13 de septiembre del año de 1902, con motivo de la inauguración del Consejo Superior de Educación Pública," *Discursos* (México, 1919), p. 191.

[60] Agustín Yanez (ed.), *Obras Completas del Maestro Justo Sierra*, Vol. VIII; *La Educación Nacional: Artículos, Actuaciones y Documentos* (México, 1949), p. 113.

[61] *Ibid.*; see also Ezequiel A. Chávez, "Reseña de la alocución pronunciada por el Subsecretario de Instrucción Pública y Bellas Artes [Justo Sierra] en la Sesión de clausura del Congreso de Educación Pública," *Antecedentes, Actas, Debates y Resoluciones del Congreso Nacional de Educación Primaria reunido en la capital de la república en el mes del centenario* (México, 1910), I, 138.

[62] *The Mexican Year Book 1909-10* (Mexico, 1911), p. 9.

[63] González Navarro, "Instituciones Indígenas en México Independiente," *Métodos y Resultados*, p. 137.

[64] Justo Sierra, cited by Luis Chávez Orozco, *La escuela mexicana y*

la sociedad mexicana (México, 1940), p. 61; Justo Sierra, cited by Ermilo Abreu Gomez (ed.), *Justo Sierra, Educación e Historia* (Washington, n.d.), p. 31.

Chapter Five

[1] Andrés Molina Enríquez, *Los grandes problemas nacionales* (México, 1909), see esp. pp. 71, 293-95. A general appraisal of other intellectuals who agitated for a realignment of social forces before the 1910 Revolution is given by James D. Cockcroft, *Intellectual Precursors of the Mexican Revolution 1910-1913* (Latin American Monographs, No. 14; Austin, 1968).

[2] José Miguel Rodriguez y Cos, *Iniciativas presentadas por . . . ante la Comisión Nacional del Centenario de la Independencia, a fin de consolidar, por medio de la educación pública, el espíritu de la nacionalidad mexicana, é incorporar á esta á la raza indígena, y celebrar dignamente el 80° ániversario del nacimiento de C. General Porfirio Díaz* (México, 1907), pp. 3-4.

[3] "Base 5 del Programa del Partido Popular Evolucionista, publicado en 5 de junio de 1911 por el Lic. Jorge Vera Estañol," cited by Comas, p. 80.

[4] Gregorio Torres Quintero, *La instrucción rudimentaria en la república* (México, 1913), pp. 3-4.

[5] *Ibid.*, p. 3. Felix F. Palavicini, *Problemas de Educación* (Valencia, 1910), p. 46.

[6] Alberto J. Pani, *La Higiene en México* (México, 1916), pp. 159-67; Palavicini, *Problemas*, pp. 41-51. A detailed rebuttal to Pani's objections is found in Torres Quintero, pp. 6-20.

[7] Letter from "D. Carlos Prieto," August 30, 1912, cited by Pani, p. 177.

[8] Torres Quintero, p. 8.

[9] Manuel Gamio, *Forjando Patria (Pro Nacionalismo)* (México, 1916), pp. 12-19, 285-88.

[10] Manuel Germán Parra, "Las grandes tendencias de la evolución histórica de la política indigenista moderna en México," *Bibliografía Indigenista*, p. xxxv; Torres Quintero, pp. 20-21.

[11] *The Mexican Constitution of 1917 Compared with the Constitution of 1857*, trans. H. N. Branch, supplement to *The Annals of the American Academy of Political and Social Science*, May 1917, pp. 2, 28-29. See Felix F. Palavicini, *Historia de la constitución de 1917* (2 vols.; México, 1938), I, 225-26 for a summary of politicians' debates on the extension of federal power over education in the states. The revival of the issue in 1921 when the Constitution was amended to give the central government control of schools in the states is reviewed in *El Movimiento Educativo en México* (México, 1922), pp. 273-315.

¹² *Diario de los Debates del Congreso Constituyente*, ed. Fernando Romero García (México, 1922), I, 483.

¹³ Gamio, *Forjando Patria*, pp. 24-28 contain his proposal, originally made in 1915 to the Second Pan-American Scientific Congress, for a Bureau of Anthropology and the role this organization should play in formulating national education policy.

¹⁴ Gonzalo Aguirre Beltrán, *Teoría y práctica de la educación indígena* (México, 1953), pp. 55-59. Aguirre Beltrán points out that the lack of cultural relativism in Gamio's philosophy was misinterpreted and mishandled by teachers trained under the integral approach. The entirely negative valuation of the Indians' indigenous tongue and clothing led inspectors and teachers who had altered these customs to point to these superficial changes as indications of the integration of the natives; *ibid.*, pp. 58-59.

¹⁵ Manuel Gamio, *Introduction, Synthesis and Conclusions of the Work, The Population of the Valley of Teotihuacán* (México, 1922), pp. lvi-lvii, xci. Parra, "Las grandes tendencias," *Bibliografía Indigenista*, p. xxxiv.

¹⁶ *Movimiento Educativo*, pp. 480-81.

¹⁷ Parra, "Las grandes tendencias," *Bibliografía Indigenista*, p. xxxvi.

¹⁸ José Vasconcelos, in José Vasconcelos and Manual Gamio, *Aspects of Mexican Civilization* (Chicago, 1926), p. 97; José Vasconcelos, *De Robinson a Odiseo* (Madrid, 1935).

¹⁹ *Movimiento Educativo*, p. 37; Verna Carleton Millan, *Mexico Reborn* (Boston, 1939), pp. 44-45.

²⁰ Frank Tannenbaum, *Peace by Revolution* (New York, 1933), pp. 275-77; Aguirre Beltrán, *Teoría y práctica*, pp. 23-26. Katherine M. Cook, *The House of the People: An Account of Mexico's New Schools of Action* (Washington, 1932) gives a full account of these schools and their adaptation of elements of John Dewey's education philosophy.

²¹ Ramón Eduardo Ruiz, *Mexico: The Challenge of Poverty and Illiteracy* (San Marino, Calif., 1963), pp. 91-97; Louise Schoenhals, "Mexican Experiments in Rural and Primary Education; 1921-1930," *Hispanic American Historical Review*, XLIV (February 1964), p. 31. The development of the Missions is given by Guillermo Bonilla y Segura, *Report on the Cultural Missions of Mexico* (Washington, 1945). The teachers' enthusiasm for the missions is summarized by George I. Sánchez, *Mexico: A Revolution by Education* (New York, 1936), pp. 78-81.

²² According to an official of the Mexican federal education department: "Neither the National University nor normal schools produce ideal teachers with knowledge of native tongues;" cited by Cook, p. 21. Vasconcelos' work *La raza cósmica: Misión de la raza iberoamericana, Argentina y Brazil* (México, 1948) sets forth his views, which stirred considerable controversy in Mexico at the time of their original publication; Vasconcelos,

in Vasconcelos and Gamio, *Aspects*, pp. 89-90; Vasconcelos, cited by A. Mendez Bravo, *La escuela rural Mejicana: lo que Mejico espera de sus maestros* (Santiago de Chile, 1929), p. 82; see also Parra, "Las grandes tendencias," *Bibliografía Indigenista*, pp. xxxvi-xxxvii.

²³ Vasconcelos, *De Robinson a Odiseo*. Though it is generally agreed that population figures of the Revolutionary period are even more unreliable than the usual census figures which tabulated population according to race or language, numerous sources after the Revolution agreed that the rural population contained a large number of speakers of the indigenous tongues. One contemporary educator estimated that in 1910, 45% of the population was mestizo, 35% Indian, and in 1915, "out of the sixteen millions of souls in Mexico, at least eight millions are Indians." Manuel Barranco, *Mexico: Its Educational Problems* (New York, 1915), pp. 9, 12. See also Tannenbaum, *Peace by Revolution*, p. 21.

²⁴ Calles, cited by Mendez Bravo, pp. 87-88.

²⁵ Moisés Sáenz, cited by Parra, "Las grandes tendencias," *Bibliografía Indigenista*, p. xxxviii. An account of the rural schools and Sáenz' philosophy of incorporation during this period of his influence on Mexican education is given in *Reseña de la Educación Pública en Mexico en 1927* (México, 1928). See also Mendez Bravo, pp. 113-14 and Aguirre Beltrán, *Teoría y práctica*, pp. 27-33. A report from the 1929 National Congress of Teachers affirmed that the Indians belonged to a dead culture, one which had spent itself before the Spaniards' arrival and depended upon the infusion of ideas from other cultures for its very existence; Jorge Casahonde, *Cómo debe la escuela fomentar el espíritu de maestros* (México, 1929), pp. 3-5.

²⁶ Secretaría de Educación Pública, *Asamblea Nacional de Educación, reunida en México del 11 al 22 de agosto, inclusive, problemas que se sometieron a su estudio y conclusiones aprobadas* (México, 1930), p. 36. An evaluation of the program by José Manuel Puig Casauranc, Secretary of Education under Calles, is given by Cameron Duncan Ebaugh, *The National System of Education in Mexico* (Johns Hopkins University Studies in Education, No. 16; Baltimore, 1931), pp. 26-27.

²⁷ Ebaugh, pp. 20, 28-29.

²⁸ Rafael Ramírez, cited by Velasco Ceballos, *Alfabetización*, p. lxxviii.

²⁹ Gastón Bénédict, *La enseñanza viva de las lenguas vivas por el método directo progresivo*, trans. Juvencio López Vásquez (México, 1953), pp. 15-30 *et passim*.

³⁰ *Ibid.*, pp. 31-37 *et passim*. As early as 1913, Torres Quintero had summarized the bases of the direct method in his defense of the rudimentary schools' language instruction techniques; Torres Quintero, p. 8.

³¹ Luis Cabrera, "The Key to the Mexican Chaos," *Renascent Mexico*, eds. Hubert Herring and Herbert Weinstock (New York, 1935), p. 19. Cabrera charged those who would preserve indigenous languages with "academic snobbism" and with contributing to the maintenance of the Indians in

their primitive isolated state. His own justification for eradicating the Indian languages seems to be the judgment that of these languages, only Aztec had influenced Spanish and added vocabulary items, called "Mexicanisms;" *ibid.*, pp. 19-20. Today linguists and anthropologists generally do not accept this viewpoint as either relevant to the issue of teaching the national language or faithful to the linguistic situation in Mexico; see Juan M. Lope Blanch, *El Lexico Indígena en el Español de México* (Jornadas 63; México, 1969).

[32] Cabrera, *Renascent Mexico*, p. 19.

[33] Moisés Sáenz, "The Genius of Mexican Life," *The Genius of Mexico*, eds. Hubert Herring and Katherine Terrill (New York, 1931), p. 9.

[34] Barranco, p. 26.

[35] Secretaría de Educación Pública, *La Casa del Estudiante Indígena: 16 meses de labor en un experimento psicológico colectivo con indios, feb. de 1926-junio de 1927* (México, 1927) relates in detail the rationale of the school's development and program. See also Ebaugh, p. 45.

[36] *La Casa del Estudiante Indígena*, pp. 36-38. The final tally of students enrolled in the school showed 19 monolingual Indian students, 148 bilinguals, and 31 students who spoke only Spanish; *ibid.*, pp. 46-48.

[37] Rafael Ramírez, cited by Ebaugh, p. 46. For an evaluation of the program by its directors and the Mexico City press, see *La Casa del Estudiante Indígena*, pp. 74, 164.

[38] Sánchez, p. 156; Parra, "Las grandes tendencias," *Bibliografía Indigenista*, p. xliii, Aguirre Beltrán, *Teoría y práctica*, p. 45.

[39] Sánchez, pp. 157-60; Parra, "Las grandes tendencias," *Bibliografía Indigenista*, pp. xli-xliii.

Chapter Six

[1] Gamio, *Forjando Patria*, pp. 16-20; in 1926 Gamio reasserted these ideas in Vasconcelos and Gamio, *Aspects*, pp. 130-38.

[2] Moisés Sáenz, *Escuelas Federales en la Sierra de Puebla: Informe sobre la visita a las escuelas federales en la Sierra de Puebla* (Publicaciones de la Secretaría de Educación Pública, Tomo XV, num. 5; México, 1927), pp. 16, 28-29.

[3] *Ibid.*, pp. 93-94.

[4] Ethel E. Wallis and Mary A. Bennett, *Two Thousand Tongues to Go: True-Life Adventures of the Wycliffe Bible Translators Throughout the World Today* (New York, 1964), pp. 39-41.

[5] Personal interview, September 1970.

[6] The development of the project and Sáenz' evaluation of its comparative importance in the history of Indian education in Mexico is told in Moisés Sáenz, *Carapan, bosquejo de una experiencia* (Lima, Peru, 1936).

[7] *Ibid.*, pp. 190, 225-37.

[8] Julio de la Fuente, "Ocho Años de Experiencia en el Medio Rural," *Revista Mexicana de Educación*, I (agosto 1940), 57-67. An overview of Fuente's introductory years in rural education is provided by Gonzalo Aguirre Beltrán, "Introducción," Julio de la Fuente, *Educación, antropologiá y desarrollo de la comunidad* (México, 1964), pp. 2-6.

[9] Sáenz, *Carapan*, pp. 308-09.

[10] *Ibid.*, pp. 311-31 *et passim;* Sáenz' specific delineation of the responsibilities and structure of the Department of Indian Affairs is found at the conclusion of the Carapan report; *ibid.*, pp. 346-52. An expansion of Sáenz' views on integration is found in his *Mexico integro* (Lima, 1939).

[11] The decree of President Cárdenas, issued 1 January 1936, is cited in full in Comas, *Ensayos*, pp. 102-06. To be sure, Sáenz' social anthropology was highly normative in that its end was the Mexicanization of the Indian. However, future policy-makers in Indian education also tended to reject the scientific study of Indians by scientists not interested in helping Indians improve their health and economic standards and to endorse scientific research as a basis for action anthropology. For a discussion of Sáenz' social anthropology, see Aguirre Beltrán in Fuente, *Educación, antropología y desarrollo*, pp. 7-10 and Juan Comas, *La Antropología Social Aplicada en México* (México, 1964), pp. 27-32.

[12] Emilio Portes Gil, *The Mexican School and the Peasantry* (Mexico, 1936), p. 2.

[13] *La Educación Pública en México, desde el 1 de diciembre de 1934 hasta el 30 del noviembre de 1940* (3 vols.; México, 1941), I, 31.

[14] "Liquidación de analfabetismo en México," *Revista de Educación*, II (enero 1938), 3. This particular report states that Oaxaca had an illiteracy rate of 77.96%, Chiapas, 77.89%, but Yucatan had only 50.04%. No comment is directed to these figures, but the anonymous author strongly advocated the need for publications in the Indians' own languages. Others also pointed to the Yucatan area, especially Merida, as an area where the direct method had not been effective and bilingual teaching was preferred. Guadencio Peraza, "La Educación del Indio," *Revista de Educación*, II (enero 1938), 25. Though it had been Ramírez' policy to remove rural teachers who spoke an Indian tongue from their own linguistic territory, Yucatan teachers apparently escaped mass transferals and were thus able to put bilingual education into effect locally before it received national sanction. Private interview, September 1970.

[15] Vicente Lombardo Toledano, *El Problema de la Educación en México: Puntos de vista y proposiciones del Comité de Educación de la Confederación Regional Obrera Mexicana* (México, 1924), p. 7. Lombardo Toledano called for a unification of liberal-democratic and socialist educational theories during the latter part of the 1920's. He believed it was impossible for education to be neutral in regard to the vital interests of the

social classes, and therefore, it could be fully effective only when a unified program of a definite orientation moved directly toward a single aim. Lombardo Toledano himself preferred a socialist orientation, though many of his suggestions for the improvement of Mexico's educational system were not in the form of a program as such, but in the shape of practical and theoretical remedies to specific problems. Robert Paul Millon, *Vicente Lombardo Toledano: Mexican Marxist* (Chapel Hill, 1966), pp. 18-19. Though it is admittedly very difficult to prove a direct influence of the ideology of one nation on another country's policy-makers, there is consistent evidence to show that Cárdenas supported Lombardo Toledano's *Confederación de Trabajadores Mexicanos* and the influence of this Communist-oriented group on the CROM's proposals for improvements in Mexico's educational system; Howard F. Cline, *The United States and Mexico* (New York, 1963), pp. 222-25. See also William Cameron Townsend, *Lázaro Cárdenas: Mexican Democrat* (Ann Arbor, 1952), pp. 124, 129. The influence of socialist educational policy and Joseph Stalin's positive view of the role of diverse languages in the "little nations" of the state is directly indicated by the quotations of educators in national education reviews and by the acceptance of Russian socialists as advisers to members of the federal educational bureaucracy; see, for example, Peraza, *Revista de Educación*, II (enero 1938), 22-26; Miguel Othón de Mendizábal, "El Problema social de las lenguas indígenas," *Revista de Educación*, II (noviembre 1938), 9-13; Siegfried Askinasy, *México Indigena: Observaciones sobre Algunos Problemas de México* (México, 1939), foreword and pp. 240-67.

[16] Lombardo Toledano, pp. 7-8.

[17] *Ibid.*, p. 9.

[18] *Ibid.* The dissertation, *Geografía de las lenguas de la Sierra de Puebla*, was completed in 1931.

[19] *La Educación Pública*, III, 511. A history of the relationship between Lombardo Toledano and Cárdenas is given by Cline, as is a full discussion of the agrarian and cooperative movements of the Six Year Plan of Cárdenas' platform. The general upheavals—social, economic, agrarian, diplomatic, and political—cannot be discussed here, but must be recognized as providing the background against which leaders such as Lombardo Toledano and Cárdenas moved in their formulation of educational policies which would improve the living conditions of poor workers and Indians in the nation; Cline, pp. 217-18, 224-60.

[20] Chávez Orozco, pp. 77-81; Sánchez, p. 104; George F. Kneller, *The Education of the Mexican Nation* (New York, 1951), pp. 53-67; a more complete coverage of the philosophy of socialist education is offered in George C. Booth, *Mexico's School-Made Society* (Stanford, 1941), pp. 9-25; and Luiz Sánchez Pontón, *Hacia la Escuela Socialista: La Reforma Educacional en México* (México, 1935).

[21] Joseph Stalin, *Marxism and the National and Colonial Question* (New York, 1934), p. 6.

²² *Ibid.*, p. 58. See also Joseph Stalin, *Marxism and the National Question* (New York, 1942), p. 56. For a full list of the objectives of the Communist Party in Soviet Russia with regard to the "non-great Russian peoples," see E. Koutaissoff, "Literacy and the Place of Russian in the Non-Slav Republics of the U.S.S.R.," *Soviet Studies*, III (October 1951), 113-30.

²³ Ruiz, p. 51. For an indication of the Mexicans' familiarity with Soviet methods of integrating minorities, see Miguel Othón de Mendizábal, "El problema de las nacionalidades oprimadas y su resolución en la U.R.S.S." *Obras Completas* (6 vols.; México, 1946), IV, 389-99.

²⁴ Othón de Mendizábal, *Revista de Educación*, II, 10-12. For a recent consideration of the evolution of Mexican integration policies in the 1930's see Gonzalo Aguirre Beltrán, "Indigenismo en México: confrontación de problemas," *Anuario Indigenista* (diciembre 1970), 292.

²⁵ It is ironic that North American linguists and anthropologists exported theoretical arguments to support bilingual education in Indian integration programs before these ideas gained acceptance in the U.S. During this period, John Collier, U.S. Commissioner of Indian Affairs, tried to inject an acceptance of cultural diversity in national Indian policy, but the U.S. then maintained a dominant national ideology of ethnic homogeneity and hence, total cultural assimilation through the direct method. For a comparison of the major features of national Indian policy in the U.S. and Mexico, see Edward H. Spicer, "National Policy in Mexico and the United States as a Factor in the Process of Indian Integration," unpublished paper given before Society for Applied Anthropology, April 1969. See also Othón de Mendizábal, *Revista de Educación*, II, 13. A survey of articles published in this journal, issued by the Mexican Ministry of Public Education from 1937-1939, shows that at least one-third of the articles published dealt with Indian education and reflected the influence of the socialist system on the authors' proposals for bilingual education; see, for example, J. Martínez Aguilar, "El Bilingüismo en la Escuela," *Revista de Educación*, IV (julio 1939), 7-8. For a brief history of the formation of the Polytechnic Institute under the Department of Education, see Townsend, pp. 124-25.

²⁶ Wallis and Bennett, p. 64; private interview, September 1970. Ignacio M. del Castillo, "La Alfabetización en lenguas indígenas: El projecto tarasco," *América Indígena*, V (abril 1945), 145. This article is an extensive survey of accomplishments made by linguists and anthropologists in the study of Indian languages, and it covers in detail the progress of the work of these social scientists in Indian education during the 1930's; *ibid.*, 139-51. Some evidence of the intensity of the debate over bilingual education versus the direct method is found in accounts by individual linguists active in the preparation of bilingual education materials during the late 1930's; these accounts appear with frequency in the publication, *Revista de Educación*. Each education official argued against the direct method of teaching and emphasized arguments for the psychological and sociological benefits of bilingual instruction. See, for example, Carlos Basauri (Chief of the Depart-

ment of Indian Education), "El Estudio de las Lenguas Autóctonas: Base de la pedagogía indígena," *Revista de Educación*, I (agosto 1937), 22-23; Luis Alvarez Barret, (Assistant Chief of the Office of Primary Teaching in the States and Territories and later sub-director of rural education), "La Enseñanza Rural: Las lenguas indígenas, instrumento de los indios para promover su cultura," *Revista de Educación*, II (febrero 1938), 18-22. This last is a long reply to a "Prof. Francisco Antúnez," who had published a letter in *El Nacional* promoting the direct method of teaching the national language. The most extensive review of the entire issue and its history in Mexico is found in Carlos Basauri, "El Problema del bilingüismo y la educación en México," *Revista de Educación*, II (diciembre 1938), 6-11.

[27] "Resoluciones aprobadas por la III Conferencia Interamericana de Educación," *Revista de Educación*, I (octubre 1937), 39.

[28] Angel M. Corzo, *Ideario de Maestro Indoamericano: Por el espíritu del indio se forjará la nueva cultura de america y su grandeza* (México, 1938).

[29] *Ibid.*, pp. 33-34; Townsend, pp. 321; private interview, September 1970.

[30] Basauri, *Revista de Educación*, I, 22. It is significant that acknowledgement was made of the great need for trained linguists in Mexico, and the linguistics curriculum of the *Escuela Nacional de Ciencias Biológicas* was directed toward the scientific preparation of alphabets for the Indian languages and the utilization of these in the nation's literacy program; *La Educación Pública*, II, 565-68. Individual departments of the National University and the National Polytechnic Institute also put their staff members to work preparing materials for teaching Otomi, Tarascan, and Chinantec, languages which not only used more consonants and vowels than Spanish, but also tones, implosives, and other phonemes not easily represented in writing. Kenneth L. Pike, "Cuadro para la transcripción fonética a las lenguas indígenas," *Revista de Educación*, II (diciembre 1938), 12-16.

[31] Askinasy, pp. 259-60; Mauricio Swadesh, *Orientaciones lingüísticas para maestros en zonas indígenas: una serie de conferencias* (México, 1940), pp. 14-16.

[32] Townsend, pp. 319-26.

[33] Departamento de asuntos indígenas, *Memoria de la Primera Asamblea de Filólogos y Lingüistas* (México, 1940), pp. 41-42. Among those attending the Assembly were North American linguists Mauricio Swadesh, Norman McQuown, Kenneth Pike, and William Cameron Townsend; Mexicans included A. Barrera Vásquez, Wigberto Jiménez Moreno, and Miguel Othón de Mendizábal.

[34] *Ibid.*, p. 72. Townsend's psychophonemic method for preparing primers is summarized by Elaine Mielke Townsend, "Accelerating Literacy by Piecemeal Digestion of the Alphabet," *Language Learning*, III (July 1948), 9-17.

[35] Parra, "Las grandes tendencias," *Bibliografía Indigenista*, p. xlvii.

[36] Aguirre Beltrán, *Teoría y práctica*, p. 64. For the methods and principles behind Swadesh's methods of teaching, see Mauricio Swadesh, *Orientaciones lingüísticas* and *La nueva filología* (2nd ed.; México, 1968), pp. 67-199.

[37] Ignacio M. del Castillo, *América Indígena*, V (abril 1945), 139, 147-49.

[38] Comas, *Antropología Social*, pp. 48-49.

[39] Inaugural address to the First Inter-American Indigenist Congress, delivered by President Cárdenas, April 5, 1940, reprinted in *Partido de la Revolución Mexicana, Cárdenas Habla* (México, 1940), pp. 270-73.

[40] Comas, *Antropología Social*, p. 49. A summary of the Congress' program is found in Boletín num. 1, Departamento de asuntos indígenas, *Primer Congreso Indigenista Interamericano* (Pátzcuaro, Michoacán, 1940), pp. 27-29.

[41] Gamio, *Forjando Patria*, p. 23.

[42] Comas, *Antropología Social*, pp. 49-50.

[43] Manuel Gamio, *Consideraciones sobre el Problema Indígena* (México, 1966), pp. 25-39, 60-63, 175-79; John Collier, "¿Indianismo vs. Racism?" *América Indígena*, V (julio 1945), 241-46; and Alfonso Caso et al., *Realidades y Proyectos: 16 años de trabajo* (Memorias del Instituto Nacional Indigenista, vol. X; México, 1964), pp. 11-13.

[44] Private interview, April 1969. For the concern during the 1940's of anthropologists and linguists to remove their methods and policies from an identification with political ideology, see Gamio, *Consideraciones*, pp. 99-102, 124-27; Sol Tax, "Anthropology and Administration," *América Indígena*, V (enero 1945), 21-33. For an interpretive view of the contributions of Cárdenas' administration to Indian education, see Ramón G. Bonfil, "El Esfuerzo Educativo en favor de los Indígenas," *Revista Mexicana de Educación*, I, num. 4 (noviembre 1940), 325-33. This journal was published for a short time in 1940 by the *Sociedad Mexicana de Pedagogía*. Many of the contributors were education officials active during Cárdenas' administration, and the major purpose of the journal seems to have been a defense of socialist educational tenets. Many of the articles devoted to Indian education underscored the importance of recent pedagogical advances in Mexico's schools for Indians; see, for example, León Díaz Cárdenas, "Crítica Panorámica y Sintética de las Actividades Educativas en el Pasado Sexenio," *Revista Mexicana de Educación*, I, num. 4 (noviembre 1940), 356-67. These writers lamented that achievements in Indian education were not statistically convincing to the new administration. Actually, the educational progress of the nation during Cárdenas' term was commendable: federal expenditures for education and the number of rural schools, teachers, and students had more than doubled; Kneller, p. 54. However, the negative effect of the "self-styled Marxists" who had become identified with the Ministry of Education, and

the haphazard pattern of successful projects allowed politicians to overlook education statistics and to point to deficiencies in economic and industrial growth; Ruiz, p. 62. For Avila Camacho's decided emphasis on economic development, see his campaign speeches, Mexican Revolutionary Party, *The Second Six Year Plan, 1941-46* (Mexico, 1946), pp. 9-13, 143.

CHAPTER SEVEN

[1] Secretaría de Educación Pública, *Teoría y Aplicación de la Reforma Educativa* (México, 1963), p. 17.

[2] Octavio Véjar Vásquez, *Hacia Una Escuela de Unidad Nacional: Discursos* (México, 1944), pp. 24-25, 49, 83. Luis Sánchez Pontón was the first appointee as Minister of Education, but conservatives, fearful of his socialist bent, urged Avila Camacho to replace him after he had been in office only ten months. Castillo, p. 422.

[3] Raj Narain, *Education for Literacy: Its Nature, Function and Dynamics* (Allahabad, India, 1958), p. 178; Majorie Medary, *Each One Teach One: Frank Laubach, Friend to Millions* (New York, 1954), pp. 103-06.

[4] Véjar Vásquez, pp. 26-29, 97.

[5] Ruiz, pp. 73-76. For a detailed narrative of the tactics Véjar Vásquez employed to push his reactionary cultural and educational policies, see Betty Kirk, *Covering the Mexican Front* (Norman, Okla., 1942), pp. 150-55.

[6] Address delivered by Avila Camacho, October 29, 1939, quoted in *Second Six Year Plan*, p. 9. See also excerpts of the President's speech made before Congress December 26, 1941, quoted in Kirk, p. 148.

[7] See section VI of *Second Six Year Plan*, pp. 98-102. Examples of communication between policy-makers and social scientists may be found in issues of *Boletín Indigenista* throughout the 1940's; see, for example, "Address by Señor Ing. Guillermo Liera," *Boletín Indigenista*, IV (junio 1944), 97-99.

[8] Luis Alvarez Barret, a staunch defender of bilingual education who frequently expressed his views in *Revista Mexicana de Educación*, a socialist-oriented journal, was sub-director of rural education in 1940. Others who had identified themselves strongly with the bilingual method also held minor positions of authority in the Ministry of Education and the Department of Indian Affairs; the advisory council of the latter agency, appointed February 17, 1941, consisted of Alfonso Caso, Daniel F. Rubín de la Borbolla (a major spokesman at the First Assembly of Philologists and Linguists), Guillermo Bonilla (long active in rural education, especially the Cultural Missions) and Ramón G. Bonfil (an ardent supporter of bilingual education); Departamento de asuntos indígenas, *Memoria, 1941-42* (México, 1942), p. 125.

[9] The ideological framework for the admission of social science tenets to official education policy is provided in the revised Article 3 of the constitution; see those portions reprinted in *Teoría y Aplicación*, pp. 17-20.

¹⁰ *Second Six Year Plan*, pp. 98-100. For the recommendations of the Inter-American Indigenist Institute which correspond to specific articles of the Plan, see Parra, "Las grandes tendencias," *Bibliografía Indigenista*, pp. xlvii-xlviii.

¹¹ Ruiz, p. 165; personal interview, April 1969.

¹² Narain, p. 189; "El Instituto de Alfabetización en Lenguas Indígenas," *Boletín Indigenista*, V (junio 1945), 163, 161, 172.

¹³ Narain, pp. 190-96.

¹⁴ A full account of the activities of the Institute for Literacy in the Indigenous Languages in the 1940-46 literacy campaign is given by Angélica Castro de la Fuente, "La alfabetización en lenguas indígenas y los promotores culturales," *A William Cameron Townsend en el vigésimoquinto aniversario del Instituto Lingüístico de Verano* (México, 1961), pp. 233-36.

¹⁵ Aguirre Beltrán, *Teoría y práctica*, pp. 65-66.

¹⁶ The volumes of *América Indígena* and *Boletín Indigenista* for this period provide a running commentary on social science projects sponsored by the government and involving the cooperation of anthropologists in Indian improvement programs.

¹⁷ "Homage by the Chamber of Deputies to the Indian Population," *Boletín Indigenista*, III (marzo 1943), 41.

¹⁸ Speech by Guillermo Liera, General Secretary of the Department of Indian Affairs, cited in *Boletín Indigenista*, III (junio 1943), 103.

¹⁹ Ramón G. Bonfil, "Sobre la Educación Indígena," *Revista Mexicana de Educación*, II, num. 2 (febrero 1941), 109-10.

²⁰ Jaime Torres Bodet, *Educación mexicana: Discursos, entrevistas, mensajes* (México, 1944), p. 196.

²¹ *Ibid.*, p. 197. Torres Bodet himself checked over and revised the Spanish portion of bilingual texts prepared by the Institute for Literacy in the Indigenous Languages; Castro de la Fuente, *A William Cameron Townsend*, p. 234. The success of this program is suggested by these figures: in 1946, the total number of textbooks in Maya was 150,000; in Otomi, 50,000; in Tarascan, 25,000; and in Nahua and Nahuatl, 200,000; "Campaign to Eliminate Illiteracy amongst Indian Population," *Boletín Indigenista*, VI (septiembre 1946), 243.

²² *Boletín Indigenista*, II (junio 1942), 19.

²³ "Personality study of the Indian Child," *Boletín Indigenista*, III (marzo 1943), 11-13. "Continued progress on the personality study in Tepotzlan," *Boletín Indigenista*, IV (marzo 1944), 9-11.

²⁴ Letter from Gonzalo Aguirre Beltrán to Manuel Gamio, March 6, 1947, *Boletín Indigenista*, VII (marzo 1947), 40-50.

²⁵ The new Minister's views may be found in his *Diez Discursos sobre Educación: Programa Educativo del Lic. Miguel Alemán* (México, 1947).

For a somewhat pessimistic summary of the Alemán administration's view of the role of rural schools written by a long-time rural-school educator, see Castillo, pp. 433-41. See also Ruiz, p. 87.

[26] Castillo, pp. 439-40. A brief account of the project is given by Alfonso Villa Rojas in his introduction to *Los Mazatecos y el problema indígena de la cuenca del Papaloapan* (Memorias del Instituto Nacional Indigenista, Vol. VII; México, 1955), pp. 13-14.

[27] Kneller, pp. 72-73; Aguirre Beltrán, *Teoría y práctica*, pp. 54, 71.

[28] Ruiz, p. 152; Comas, *Antropología Social*, p. 39.

[29] Gual Vidal, pp. 15-16; Villa Rojas, pp. 27-29.

[30] Caso et al., *Realidades y Proyectos*, p. 9.

[31] Alfonso Caso, cited by Parra, "Las grandes tendencias," *Bibliografía Indigenista*, p. lxii. The importance of certain changing emphases in Indian education is born out by Caso's careful wording. He specifically denounced the view of the Indian problem as racial, a tenet of rudimentary instruction; he also refuted the point of view that it was an "individual problem," a basic justification for Véjar Vásquez' Indian education program.

[32] *Ibid*. His comments on the use of language as a criterion for the placement of individuals in a category called *indios* reflect the long and serious discussions which had centered on the question of how to determine *indios* in the national census. See, for example, Lombardo Toledano, p. 7; Gamio, *Consideraciones*, pp. 15-24.

[33] Aguirre Beltrán, *Teoría y práctica*, p. 68; ¿*Qué es el I.N.I.?* (México, 1955), p. 13.

[34] For an extended discussion of the organization of INI, see Caso et al., *Realidades y Proyectos*, pp. 15-16. See also Antonio García, "Teoría y política del indigenismo," *América Indígena*, XI (octubre 1951), 283. For a discussion of the contributions of Alfonso Caso to the development of applied anthropology in indigenism, see Jose E. Iturriaga, "*Introducción*," in Alfonso Caso, *Discursos* (México, 1958), pp. 8-9, and scattered essays in *Homenaje al Doctor Alfonso Caso* (México, 1951).

[35] Gual Vidal, pp. 15-16.

[36] Alfonso Caso, cited by Parra, "Las grandes tendencias," *Bibliografía Indigenista*, pp. xliii-xliv. For a full discussion of the rationale behind the Regional Coordinating Centers, see Gonzalo Aguirre Beltrán, "Integración Regional," *Los Centros Coordinadores* (México, 1962), pp. 24-49 *et passim*; ¿*Que es el I.N.I.?*, pp. 39-49 *et passim* and anexo 5, pp. 81-87.

[37] A 1906 state law for the "improvement and protection" of the Tarahumaras is reprinted in Comas, *Ensayos*, pp. 66-70.

[38] Private interview, September 1970; Mariano Samayoa, "Comunidades de promoción indígena," *Boletín Indigenista*, XI (septiembre 1951), 240-44.

[39] A composite evaluation of the rural school during the 1950's is offered by Ruiz, pp. 196-215. For criticisms which particularly set recent developments in rural education against the accomplishments of Narciso Bassols and Cárdenas, see Guillermo Montaño, "La educación rural," in Leonardo Gómez Navas et al., *La educación: historia, obstaculos, perspectivas* (México, 1967), pp. 65-92.

[40] Aguirre Beltrán, *Los Centros Coordinadores,* pp. 38-44.

[41] Directions to the *promotores culturales* using these bilingual primers emphasized that the reading materials considered the regional characteristics and the interests, needs, and familiar customs of the children. A primer prepared for the Purepecha language stressed both in simple story form and in pictures the family, animals, daily activities, and fiestas of the area before moving to a two-page introduction of Mexican national heroes—Hidalgo, Juárez, and Madero; *Juchari uandkuecha* [our language], (México, 1965).

[42] Aguirre Beltrán, *Teoría y práctica,* pp. 84-85. The philosophy of INI with regard to bringing the national culture to the indigenous populations through education is reviewed by Gonzalo Aguirre Beltrán and Ricardo Pozas, "Instituciones indígenas en el México actual," *Métodos y Resultados,* pp. 245-57.

[43] UNESCO, *Learn and Live* (Paris, 1951), pp. 7-11. For an evaluation of INI's bilingual approach by a member of CREFAL, see Raul Ponce, "Alfabetización en lengua Mixteca," *Boletín Informativo* (noviembre 1964), 10-12.

[44] Parra, "Las grandes tendencias," *Bibliografía Indigenista,* pp. lxiv-lxv. For a summary of the plan, see *ibid.,* lxv-lxvi. The laws creating the Centers are found in *¿Que es el I.N.I.?,* pp. 87-92.

[45] Caso et al., *Realidades,* pp. 15-19.

[46] Angélica Castro de la Fuente, a pioneer of the Institute of Literacy for Monolingual Indians, provides a summary of the problems literacy personnel faced in their work among the Otomi of the Mezquital Valley, *A William Cameron Townsend,* pp. 239-48. Juan Comas, sent by the National University in 1956 to evaluate the Indian Patrimony of the Mezquital Valley, reported that by this date the bilingual method was favored and successfully used by the promoters. "Report of Dr. Juan Comas on a visit to the Indian Patrimony of the Mezquital Valley, October 10-19, 1956," *Boletín Indigenista,* XVI (diciembre 1956), 345-53.

[47] In an effort to remedy the lack of training among development program personnel, the Institute of Anthropology and History, under which the National School of Anthropology operated, initiated in 1952 special courses designed to train investigators and directors for the Coordinating Centers. *¿Que es el I.N.I.?,* p. 27. See Alfonso Caso's letter sent to the director of the National School of Anthropology in January of 1951, which explains the rationale for the founding of the Section of Applied Social Anthropology; *ibid.,* p. 73-77.

⁴⁸ Mauricio Swadesh, "La educación indígena en los centros del Instituto Nacional Indigenista: informe de visitas hechas en febrero-junio de 1956," typescript copy; private interview, April 1969.

⁴⁹ Isabel H. de Pozas y Ricardo Pozas, *Del monolingüismo indígena al bilingüismo en lengua nacional: Una experiencia educativa del Centro Coordinador Indigenista del Papaloapan* (Oaxaca, 1956).

⁵⁰ UNESCO, *The Use of Vernacular Languages in Education* (Paris, 1953), pp. 76-86.

⁵¹ In the midst of INI's reevaluation of the bilingual method, Juan Comas recapitulated arguments for and against the method in his article, "La lengua vernácula y el bilingüismo en la educación," *América Indígena*, XVI (abril 1956), 93-109. Comas drew heavily on the summary of the UNESCO conference; *Use of Vernacular*, pp. 72-75.

⁵² Census figures are drawn from Dirección General de Estadística, 7° *Census de Población*, 1950 Resumen General (Mexico, 1952). For a specific discussion of marginalism in the population in 1950, see Pablo González Casanova, *La democracia en México* (Mexico, 1965), pp. 72-82. In their 1952 report to Ruiz Cortines, Aguirre Beltrán and Parra had emphasized the fact that because of the interrelatedness of culture, language was but one indication of an entire range of economic, health, and education habits which could not be ignored in integral change programs; Aguirre Beltrán and Parra, cited by Parra, "Las grandes tendencias," *Bibliografía Indigenista*, p. lxv.

⁵³ Gonzalo Aguirre Beltrán, *El proceso de aculturación* (México, 1957), pp. 140-42.

⁵⁴ José Angel Ceniceros, *Nuestra Constitución Política y la Educación Mexicana* (México: disertación ante la junta nacional de educación normal en la Cuidad de México, 7 octubre 1954), pp. 25-27.

⁵⁵ José Angel Ceniceros, cited in *Consejo Nacional Técnico de la Educación* (México, 1958), p. 8.

⁵⁶ Ceniceros, *Nuestra Constitución*, p. 28.

⁵⁷ Ceniceros, cited in *Consejo Nacional*, p. 13.

Chapter Eight

¹ Adolfo López Mateos, "Discurso pronunciado . . . en la Universidad Nacional Mayor de San Marcos, Peru, 3 de febrero de 1960," printed in *La Lucha por la Tierra*, ed. Silvano Barba Gonzales (México, 1966), p. 161.

² Adolfo López Mateos, "Al pueblo de Chiapas, 15 de diciembre, 1957," printed in *Pensamiento y Programa* (México, 1961), p. 65. For an elaboration of the role of education in the government's integral program for the indigenous population and education's contribution to national unity, see Adolfo López Mateos, *Pensamiento en Acción* (3 vols.; México, 1962), III, 147-54.

[3] Gamio, *Forjando patria*, p. 325.

[4] Aguirre Beltrán, "Integración Regional," in *Los Centros Coordinadores*, pp. 25-49. An extensive development of this theory by Aguirre Beltrán is found in his *Regiones de Refugio* (Mexico, 1967).

[5] Gonzalo Aguirre Beltrán, *El Proceso de Aculturación*, p. 126.

[6] Secretaria de Educación Pública, *VI Asamblea Nacional Plenaria: La coordinación y la ampliación de la obra cultural y educativa en beneficio de la población indígena* (Vol. IV, Biblioteca del Consejo Nacional Técnico de la Educación; México, 1964), p. 85. See also *Atlatl*, no. 2 (April-June 1970), p. 49; Yolando Lastra, "Literacy," *Ibero American and Caribbean Linguistics*, Vol. IV of *Current Issues in Linguistics*, ed. Thomas A. Sebeok (10 vols.; The Hague, 1968), p. 446.

[7] The extent of cooperation between INI and the Secretary of Public Education in 1964 is graphically related in Caso et al., *Realidades y Proyectos*, 6 maps preceding p. 55. By 1964, there were six Coordinating Centers; in 1969, there were ten; *ibid.*; Alfonso Villa Rojas, "Resultados de la orientación antropológica en la educación indígena del México actual," paper delivered before the Society for Applied Anthropology, Mexico City, April 1969.

[8] Gustavo Díaz Ordaz, "Justicia social," *Ideas políticas del Presidente Gustavo Díaz Ordaz*, ed. Roberto Amores (México, 1966), p. 229.

[9] *Ibid.*, pp. 228-31.

[10] Pablo González Casanova, *La democracia en México*, Ch. V. For a theoretical discussion of the relationships between democracy and development pertinent to González Casanova's book, see Lucian W. Pye, "Introduction," *Political Culture and Political Development*, ed. Lucian W. Pye and Sidney Verba (Princeton, 1965), pp. 3-26.

[11] González Casanova, p. 99.

[12] Personal correspondence, Daniel Cazes, March 1969; personal interviews, Mexico City, April 1969; position paper, students of National School of Anthropology and History, April 1969. Guillermo Bonfil Batalla, "Reflexiones sobre la política indigenista y el centralismo gubernamental en México," paper delivered before the Society for Applied Anthropology, Mexico City, April 1969. For a summary of the viewpoints expressed by "the new departure" group of anthropologists, see Arturo Warman et al., *De ese que llaman antropología mexicana* (México, 1970); for a debate between the professional anthropologists Gonzalo Aguirre Beltrán and Angel Palerm, see "Indigenismo en México-Confrontación de problemas," *Anuario Indigenista*, XXX (diciembre 1970), 277-306.

[13] Rodolfo Stavenhagen, "Clases, colonialismo, y aculturación," in Othón de Mendizabal et al., *Ensayos sobre las clases sociales en México* (México, 1968), pp. 89-150.

[14] Elsie Rockwell and Margarita Nolasco, "El Instituto de Investiga-

ción y Integración Social del Estado de Oaxaca," *América Indígena* XXX (octubre 1970), 119-23.

[15] Luis Echeverría Alvarez, quoted in *Hispano*, 10 de mayo, 1971, p. 26. The general direction of Echeverría's policy as indicated in his speeches and those of his cabinet may be found in *Hispano*, 14 de diciembre, 1970, pp. 32-34; *Hispano*, 22 de febrero, 1971, pp. 33-35. See especially Echeverría's letter to the governors, reprinted in *Hispano*, 4 de junio, 1971, pp. 34-35. See also economic essay on Mexico, *New York Times*, February 21, 1971, Section 3, pp. 1, 11.

[16] "'Plan Echeverria', obras públicas," *Hispano*, 10 de mayo, 1971, pp. 30-33.

[17] Minister of Agrarian Affairs and Colonization, quoted in *Hispano*, 14 de junio, 1971, pp. 15-16.

[18] *Hispano*, 14 de diciembre, 1970, p. 33.

[19] *Ibid.*, pp. 45-47; *Hispano*, 28 de dicembre, 1970, pp. 6-13.

[20] Gonzalo Aguirre Beltrán, *Anuario Indigenista*, XXX (diciembre 1970), 284-85; see also Aguirre Beltrán's review of Warman et al., *Anuario Indigenista*, XXX (diciembre 1970), 322-40.

[21] See especially Margarita Nolasco in Warman et al.; Rodolfo Stavenhagen, "Decolonializing Applied Social Sciences," paper delivered before the Society for Applied Anthropology, Miami, Fla., April 1971.

[22] Bravo Ahuja quoted in "Chiapas da el Primer Paso en la Reforma Educativa," Clipping File, Velasco, SIL, July 1971.

[23] Evangelina Arana de Swadesh, "Los programas educativos para las zonas indígenas," typescript copy dated March 23, 1971, p. 10; private interview, August 1971.

[24] Relative and absolute figures are drawn from: Direccion General de Estadistica, 6° *Censo de Poblacion, 1940: Resumen General* (México, 1943); 7° *Censo de Poblacion, 1950: Resumen General* (México, 1952); 8° *Censo General de Poblacion, 1960: Resumen General* (México, 1962); 9° *Censo General de Poblacion, 1970: Resumen de las principales caracteristicas por entidad federativa* (México, noviembre 1970).

[25] These conclusions are based on the assumption that certain factors such as changes in birth rate, migration, death rate, and inaccuracies in the collection of data have remained relatively constant. The assumption for the latter is probably never safe for census data reflecting linguistic status; at what point an individual's grasp of a second language entitles him to be termed "bilingual" is a troublesome question for linguists as well as census takers. See, for example Richard A. Diebold, Jr. "Incipient Bilingualism," *Language*, XXXVII (January 1960), 97-112. Diebold has, however, pointed out that Mexican census materials since 1930 have ranked in both quantity and general quality of sociological data collected with those of the United States. According to Stanley Lieberson's suggestions for checking the validity

of available census data on language, the Mexican census stands out as the most reputable in Latin America; "Language Questions in Censuses," *Explorations in Sociolinguistics*, ed. Stanley Lieberson (Bloomington, 1967), pp. 134-51. However, in spite of these favorable judgments, James W. Wilkie, an historian who used the census data of the twentieth century to compile a Poverty Index for the Mexican states, has questioned the reliability of the figures on the population speaking exclusively an Indian tongue in 1950; James W. Wilkie, *The Mexican Revolution: Federal Expenditure and Social Change since 1910* (Berkeley, 1967), pp. 212-15. The "politics of expediency" seem to account for Wilkie's evaluation. According to Ramon Beteta (Oral History Interview with James and Edna Wilkie, December 17, 1964), the Statistical Agency had some of its funds diverted to meet the expenses of the 1950 presidential campaign of the official party. Wilkie therefore adjusted the monolingual Indian speakers figures by assuming that the decrease in Indian monolingual speakers was approximately proportional to the decrease in illiteracy between 1940 and 1960. Wilkie's adjusted percentages for monolinguals in 1950 are: Chiapas 17.0, Guerrero 11.3, Hidalgo 13.2, México 4.1, Michoacán 1.5, Oaxaca 21.8, Puebla 9.8, San Luis Potosí 5.7, Veracruz 6.4, Yucatan 16.3.

[26] Karl Deutsch, *Nationalism and Social Communication* (Cambridge, Mass., 1953), pp. 99-100.

[27] This conclusion has been drawn after a survey of the projects reported in issues of *América Indígena* and *Boletín Indigenista* between 1948 and 1970; for a summary of the locations of centers in the states containing the greatest number of Indian-language speakers, see Caso et al., *Realidades y Proyectos*, pp. 27-28.

[28] Oscar Lewis, "Mexico Since Cárdenas," *Social Change in Latin America Today*, ed. Richard N. Adams et al. (New York, 1960), pp. 289-90. A discussion of this prediction by Lewis and general social change implications of the retention of indigenous tongues is provided by Julio de la Fuente, "El Cambio Social y la Movilidad Indígena," *Educación, antropología y desarrollo*, pp. 280-81.

[29] Swadesh, *La nueva filología*, pp. 62-66.

[30] The investigation was based on figures which indicated the percentage of the population of these ten states which retained the Indian languages and a composite percentage of Indianism, based on the percentage of the population pursuing selected Indian customs of food and dress. A rank correlation analysis to show the measure of the degree of association between "Indianism" and Indian language retention gives support to an hypothesis that there is no significant positive correlation between these two characteristics. The rank order correlation coefficient for 1950 proves to be .345; for 1960, it is .042. For a level of significance at the 5% level, a coefficient of .648 is required.

[31] If, on these grounds, Yucatan is omitted from the calculations, the rank correlation coefficient is .775 for 1950 and .700 for 1960, indicating a

sizable relationship between the two characteristics. For a level of significance at the 5% level, a correlation coefficient of .683 is required.

CHAPTER NINE

[1] Bohuslav Havránek, "The Functional Differentiation of the Standard Language," *A Prague School Reader on Esthetics, Literary Structure, and Style*, ed. Paul L. Garvin (Washington, 1964), pp. 14-15.

[2] Linguists of the Prague School have proposed the term *intellectualization* for the adaptation of a standard language "to the goal of making possible precise and rigorous, if necessary abstract, statements, capable of expressing the continuity and complexity of thought, that is, to reinforce the intellectual side of speech." *Ibid.*, p. 6. Members of the religious hierarchy in New Spain frequently commented on this characteristic of Nahuatl, comparing favorably its competence in technical and esthetic expression with that of Latin.

[3] Academia Mexicana correspondiente de la Española, *Anuario 1954* (Mexico, 1954), p. 8.

[4] Enrique C. Rébsamen, "El Fonetismo," *México intellectual*, XXIII (abril 30, 1900), 217-22. This pedagogical journal, published from 1889 to 1900 by a group of prominent educators, includes frequent references to the need to standardize Mexican Spanish and to insure the enforcement of the norm through the schools. Enrique C. Rébsamen, a Swiss educator who began a normal school in Veracruz and tried to influence teacher-training methods in Mexico, wrote a Spanish grammar book, and his *Método Rébsamen de Escritura-Lectura & Guía del Maestro* for the teaching of reading and writing were strongly supported by contributors to *México intellectual*.

[5] Though certainly statistical figures on that portion of the population which spoke only Indian tongues in the nineteenth century are highly unreliable, they indicate how decision-makers viewed the statistical proportions of their problem. According to the 1895 census, 16.60% of Mexico's population represented monolingual Indian language speakers; Moisés González Navarro, "Instituciones indígenas en México independiente," *Métodos y Resultados*, p. 136.

[6] This comment is attributed to "Soc. A. Caso" in Antoñio Luna Arroyo, *El Problema de la Educación Pública en México* (México, 1931), pp. 50-51.

[7] Implicit in suggestions for the active involvement of Indian groups in a quest for economic and social opportunities is a new activist role for anthropologists. Some suggest it has become their duty to help the Indians initiate changes to alter the colonized-colonizer system of relationships; see, for example, Agustín Romano, "¿Nueva tendencia ideológica de la antropología mexicana?", *Anuario Indigenista*, XXX (diciembre 1970), 75-84.

[8] Gonzalo Aguirre Beltrán, "La comunidad en el pensamiento de Alfonso Caso," typescript manuscript, dated April 15, 1969, p. 14.

⁹ The treatment of language planning in developed nations has been handled by Shepard B. Clough, *A History of the Flemish Movement in Belgium* and Einer Haugen, *Language Conflict and Language Planning: The Case of Modern Norwegian*. Joshua Fishman has set forth the characteristics of new developing nations in his concluding essay, "Language Problems and Types of Political and Sociocultural Integration; A Conceptual Postscript," *Language Problems of Developing Nations*, pp. 491-98.

¹⁰ Articles devoted to localized situations in language planning within the nations of Africa and Asia are brought together by Joshua Fishman in *Language Problems of Developing Nations*. A full-length study of an old developing nation, that is, one which inherited separate languages linked with great religions, is offered by Jyotirindra Das Gupta, *Language Conflict and National Development: Group Politics and National Language Policy in India* (Berkeley, 1970).

¹¹ Haugen proposed these principles or processes at the outset of his case study of language planning in Norway; Haugen, pp. 16-26.

¹² Martín Luis Guzmán, *Academia: Tradición. Independencia. Libertad* (México, 1959). Guzmán, who proposed the changes in the statutes of the Association of Academies of the Spanish Language which would give the Hispanic American institutions greater freedom from Madrid's Royal Academy, provides a limited account of the debates of the two congresses. The records of the debates and press reactions to these are helpful, though they have been chosen to support the editor's own interpretations of the antecedents and consequences of the debates.

¹³ José Vasconcelos, cited by Martín Luis Guzmán in "El Verdadero Concepto de la Hispanidad," *Academia*, p. 87. A list of the members of the Mexican Academy and the way they voted on the proposal is provided; *ibid.*, pp. 110-12.

¹⁴ Vasconcelos (and possibly other opponents of the move for more freedom from the *Real Academia*), cited by Martín Luis Guzmán, "El Verdadero Concepto de la Hispanidad," *Academia*, p. 89.

¹⁵ *Ibid.*, pp. 90-91.

¹⁶ Speech by Franciso Monterde, president of the Mexican Academy of Spanish, quoted in *Hispano*, 10 de mayo, 1971, p. 22.

¹⁷ Juan M. Lope Blanch, "Presentación," *Cuestionario provisional para el estudio coordinado de la norma lingüística culta de las principales ciudades de Iberoamérica y de la Península Ibérica* (México, 1968), pp. 1-6. New textbooks will record the characteristic norm for use both within the Latin American nations and in language instruction in other nations. Cooperating in the gathering, recording, and analysis of data are professionals from the Center of Spanish Linguistics of the National University of Mexico and the Center of Linguistic and Literary Studies of the College of Mexico.

¹⁸ See, for example, Leovigildo Islas Escarcega, *Vocabulario Campesino Nacional: Objeciones y ampliaciones al vocabulario agricola nacional* (México, 1935).

[19] A thorough treatment of the presence of *Nahuatlismos* in the present Spanish vocabulary, the general character of incorporation of Nahuatl vocabulary in Mexican Spanish, and the phonetic evolution of Nahuatl words which have been Castilianized is found in José Ignacio Dávila Garibi, *Del Nahuatl al Español* (Tacubaya, D. F., 1939). For an examination of Nahuatl influence on the Spanish of Mexico City, see Juan M. Lope Blanch, *El Lexico Indígena en el Español de México*.

[20] Cosio Villegas, *Historia Moderna de México: La República Restaurada. La Vida Social*, p. 81.

[21] *The New York Times*, December 7, 1969, p. 53. Though Mexicans have eyed with disfavor the incorporation of English words into Mexican Spanish, this phenomenon has been judged as especially frequent for scientific lexical items. For an early account of the Mexican view of the influence of English on Mexican Spanish, see Francisco Castillo Nájera, *Breves Consideraciones Sobre el Español que se habla en México* (New York, 1963).

[22] The Colombian delegate to the first Hispano-American Congress of Lexicography, Antoñio Leon Rey, cited in *The New York Times*, December 7, 1969, p. 53.

[23] Daniel Rubín de la Borbolla, "Prólogo," Departamento de asuntos indígenas, *Memoria de la Primera Asamblea de Filólogos y Lingüistas*, p. viii.

[24] "Thèses présentées au Premier Congrès des philologues slaves," in *A Prague School Reader in Linguistics*, ed. Josef Vachek (Bloomington, 1967), p. 33. The theoretical contributions of Prague School linguists for this discussion are drawn primarily from the article cited above plus the following selections also included in the *Prague School Reader:* Karel Horálek, "La fonction de la 'structure des fonctions' de la langue," pp. 421-25; and Bohuslav Havránek, "Zum Problem der Norm in der heutigen Sprachwissenschaft und Sprachkultur," pp. 413-21. The latter linguist suggests that linguistic uniformity achieved through the dissemination of widespread classic literary writings in Greek and Latin in ancient and medieval periods was accomplished at the expense of intrasocietal communication. The literary function of language was highly restricted within political entities, but increased in efficiency across national boundaries through the use of codes restricted primarily to elites in all nations.

[25] Joshua A. Fishman, "Language Maintenance and Language Shift as a Field of Inquiry," *Linguistics, An International Review*, IX (November 1964), 32-70.

[26] Fishman and others have pointed out that functions of language imply a motivational-purposive interpretation of speech. There has been an increasing diversification of terms for functions of speech since the early suggestions of Edward Sapir and J. R. Firth in the 1920's and 1930's [Edward Sapir, *Language: An Introduction to the Study of Speech* (New York, 1921) and J. R. Firth, *Tongues of Men and Speech* (London, 1964; *Tongues of Men* originally published in 1937; *Speech* in 1930)]. Dell Hymes

terms functions of speech as expressive, directive, poetic, contextual, referential, metalingual, and contact; Dell H. Hymes, "The Ethnography of Speaking," *Anthropology and Human Behavior*, eds. Thomas Gladwin and William C. Sturtevant (Washington, 1962), pp. 13-53.

[27] Linguists have been especially concerned with the need to separate attitudes toward the speaking collectivity from attitudes directed toward objective linguistic characteristics. Perhaps the most effective examination of attitudes in bilingual situations has been done by Wallace Lambert in Canada; see, for example, W. E. Lambert, R. C. Gardner, R. Olton, and K. Tunstall, "A Study of the Roles of Attitudes and Motivation in Second-Language Learning" *Readings in the Sociology of Language*, pp. 473-91; and Wallace E. Lambert, "A Social Psychology of Bilingualism," *Journal of Social Issues*, XXIII (April 1967), 91-108.

[28] Private interview, April 1969.

[29] Viola Waterhouse, "Learning a second language first," *International Journal of American Linguistics*, XV (April 1949), 106-09.

[30] A. Richard Diebold, Jr., "Bilingualism and Biculturalism in a Huave Community," (unpublished Ph.D. dissertation, Yale University, 1961). Many of the most important of Diebold's findings are incorporated in his "Incipient Bilingualism," *Language*, XXXVII, 97-112.

[31] Diebold, "Bilingualism and Biculturalism," pp. 75, 80-82.

[32] Joshua Fishman has proposed that bilingualism with diglossia frequently characterizes those communities in which roles are clearly differentiated for functional varieties of speech. Joshua A. Fishman, "Bilingualism With and Without Diglossia; Diglossia With and Without Bilingualism," *Journal of Social Issues*, XXIII (April 1967), 31-32. *Diglossia* is a term originally proposed by Charles Ferguson ["Diglossia," *Word*, XV (September 1959), 325-40] to mean "two or more varieties of the same language used by some speakers under different circumstances." However, the term has been expanded to include societies which are multilingual and use separate dialects or functionally differentiated languages.

[33] Uriel Weinreich, *Languages in Contact* (The Hague, 1967), p. 99.

[34] Garvin and Mathiot, "Urbanization of the Guaraní Language," *Readings in the Sociology of Language*, pp. 369-70.

[35] Ethel E. Wallis, "Sociolinguistics in Relation to Mezquital Transition Education," *Estudios Antropológicos*, p. 528.

[36] Dell H. Hymes, "Two Types of Linguistic Relativity," *Sociolinguistics*, p. 125. There is very little research in any area of the social sciences on the correlation between regularities in the cultural processes and functions of language, but there is, for example, some support for the thesis that the advanced status of the Zapotecs at the time of the Conquest and their consequent maintenance of a status position among the Indian groups in Mexico have contributed to the maintenance of their language and even to the development of bilingualism in Zapotec and another Indian tongue; *ibid.*, p. 126; Diebold, "Bilingualism and Biculturalism," p. 66.

[37] Linguists and other social scientists agree that the effectiveness of a nation in international political actions is increased if the social unity of the nation minimizes internal differences and maximizes external ones. The nation's superimposing of a common language on speakers of different dialects or languages is merely one way to increase social unity within a nation. A national language is thus functionally defined as "a superimposed norm used by speakers whose first and ordinary language may be different." Einar Haugen, "Dialect, Language, Nation," *American Anthropologist*, LXVIII (August 1966), 927. Karl W. Deutsch, a political scientist, has proposed the term *social mobilization* to describe "an overall process of change, which happens to substantial parts of the population in countries which are moving from traditional to modern ways of life." Karl W. Deutsch, "Social Mobilization and Political Development," *The American Political Science Review*, LV (September 1961), 493. The expansion of this idea and the concepts which Deutsch originally bracketed together in this process of historical change have been expanded by Deutsch and other members of his profession interested in the process of nation building. Deutsch's discussion of the role of language assimilation in mobilization is in his *Nationalism and Social Communication*, pp. 98-100. Later expansions appear in selected essays in *Nation-Building*, eds. Karl W. Deutsch and William J. Foltz (New York, 1963). Deutsch's original presentation of his concept of mobilization was made in his study of the development of nationalism through the opening of channels of communication to transmit information from political-control centers. Basic to this mobilization is the learning of the national language by unassimilated members of the population. There have been few attempts to follow up Deutsch's suggestions by examining how mobilization through language assimilation has been viewed by national decision-makers in developing nations; for one examination of this issue, see Jyotirindra Das Gupta and John J. Gumperz, "Language, Communication, and Control in North India," *Language Problems of Developing Nations*, pp. 151-66.

[38] The issue of the political potency of anthropologists in developing nations has been examined primarily by anthropologists themselves; see, for example, Richard N. Adams, "La ética y el antropólogo social en América Latina," *América Indígena*, XXVIII (enero 1968), 273-90. Adams examines the dilemma of anthropologists who must depend on governmental favor and funding to achieve their aims in national contexts, and he points out that in numerous Latin American nations, anthropologists have not been able to continue their projects or their influence through shifts in political administrations.

[39] Political scientists have proposed that political elites are legitimated by their "endowment and/or evocation of sacred values of the system" and that within developing nations, these "sacred values" are modernization and nationalism; Lester G. Seligman, "Elite Recruitment and Political Development," *Journal of Politics*, XXVI (August 1964), 613. Hence, the research potential of the study of anthropologists as decision-making elites in developing nations is suggested by the fact that in Latin America, especially, anthropologists have frequently played the role of change agents in favor of

introducing to the Indian populations modern methods of improving their economies and means of improving contact opportunities between the Indians and the national culture.

[40] Eric R. Wolf, "Aspects of Group Relations in a Complex Society: Mexico," *American Anthropologist,* LXVIII (December 1956), 1066. There are numerous research implications for merging the suggested approaches of Wolf and other anthropologists to the study of complex societies and linguists' theories of varying functions of language in domains of aggregative behavior. For example, J. Clyde Mitchell's delineation of structural and categorical relationships and personal networks provides concepts into which linguists could fit their models of language and social setting at the level of the individual community; J. Clyde Mitchell, "Theoretical Orientations in African Urban Studies," *The Social Anthropology of Complex Societies,* ed. Michael Banton (A. S. A. Monographs 4; London, 1966), 51-55; and Dell Hymes, "Models of the Interaction of Language and Social Setting," *Journal of Social Issues,* XXIII (April 1967), 8-28.

[41] At the close of his comments on "Linguistics and Language Planning," at a conference held in 1964, Einar Haugen cautioned, "lest it be thought that we are proposing either that linguistics be identified with LP [language planning], or that LP needs only employ linguists in its project, I hasten to add in conclusion that linguistics is *necessary* but not *sufficient.* In so far as LP is a kind of language politics, it needs the insights of *political science* concerning the art of what is possible and the ways of winning the consent of the governed." *Sociolinguistics,* p. 67.

[42] Gamio's 1916 plans for a bureau of anthropology became a reality in the 1920's; the views of social scientists of the Carapan program were institutionalized in Cárdenas' Department of Indian Affairs; the Tarascan Project expanded into a national literacy campaign. The proposals of the Patzcuaro conference were fulfilled in the founding of INI; there are indications the new departure's plea for decentralization will be met in the coming decade. For an example of the influence a single small academic group exerted on the institutionalization of bilingual education, see the editorial written by Mariano Silva y Aceves, director of the Mexican Institute of Linguistic Investigations; *Investigaciones Lingüísticas,* I (agosto 1933), 1-2, and scattered articles which appeared in the remaining three issues published.

[43] Robert J. Di Pietro provides a schematic summary of bilingualism, which may be helpful in determining correlations between the Mexican case and other national situations which might merit the kind of national language planning Mexico's decision-makers have employed. Robert J. Di Pietro, "Bilingualism," *Ibero American and Caribbean Linguistics,* pp. 399-414.

Bibliography

BIBLIOGRAPHY

Since the theoretical foundations and research implications of language policy in a developing nation touch numerous disciplines, this bibliography is organized to facilitate the reader's further investigation of social science theories not fully explained in the text. Materials relevant to pedagogical and linguistic aspects of language policy are identified under "Language Planning and Politics." "Social Change and Policy Process" sources relate directly to social science perspectives on modernization and social change in complex societies. Otherwise, all primary and secondary materials from which the history of language policy in Mexico has been drawn are identified as "Mexican History."

Primary Materials: The published literature on Indian history prior to the Conquest is extensive and is adequately compiled in bibliographies of the nine volumes of the *Handbook of Middle American Indians*. Chroniclers of the Conquest, both lay and ecclesiastical, provide details of early colonial Indian life and descriptions of pre-Conquest culture. Collections of published documents for colonial history, especially those of García Icazbalceta, Puga, and Encinas, supplement data provided in the *Recopilación de leyes*. In the Archivo General de la Nación, the ramos of General de parte, Indios, Civil, Clero regular y secular, Hospital de Jesús, and Cédulas Reales furnish a portion of this book's documentation for the early colonial period. For the first century after Independence, journals and periodicals, such as *Gazeta de Literatura, Gazetas de México,* and *La Libertad,* provide evaluations of Indian life and of conflicts between partisans of the creole ideology and early indigenists. Published documents of the federal government of Mexico and the writings of government officials provide data on administrative decisions and the processes of policy planning in both the nineteenth and twentieth centuries. Decision-makers and local change agents at the in-put level provided personal correspondence and interviews. Specific statements are not attributed to individuals in the text; however, tapes and interview notes are available to qualified scholars. Only the items which are cited in the text or which have particular direct bearing to the text are included in this bibliography. For a more complete review of published materials on social change and language policy throughout Mexico's history, one may consult Caso et al., *Métodos y Resultados de la Política Indigenista*, Parra and Jiménez Moreno, *Bibliografía Indigenista de México y Centroamerica (1850-1950)*, or bibliographies of the *Handbook of Middle American Indians*. *Hispanic American Historical Review* has been abbreviated to *HAHR*, Universidad Nacional Autónoma Mexicana to UNAM, Secretaria de Educación Pública to SEP, Departamento de publicidad y propaganda to DAP, Instituto Nacional Indigenista to INI, Instituto Indigenista Interamericano to III.

Language Planning and Politics

GENERAL

Alatis, James E. (ed.). *Bilingualism and Language Contact: Anthropological, Linguistic, Psychological, and Sociological Aspects. Languages and Linguistics.* Georgetown University Monograph Series, No. 23.

Bright, William (ed.). *Sociolinguistics*. The Hague: Mouton & Co., 1966.

Capell, A. *Studies in Socio-Linguistics*. The Hague: Mouton & Co., 1966.

Clough, Shephard B. *A History of the Flemish Movement in Belgium*. New York: Richard R. Smith, 1930.

Das Gupta, Jyotirindra. *Language Conflict and National Development: Group Politics and National Language Policy in India.* Berkeley: University of California, 1970.

Deutsch, Karl W. "The Trend of European Nationalism: the Language Aspect," *American Political Science Review*, XXXVI (June 1942), 533-41.

Ferguson, Charles A. "Diglossia," *Word*, XV (September 1959), 325-40.

———. "Directions in Sociolinguistics: Report on an Interdisciplinary Seminar," *SSRC Items*, XIX (March 1965), 1-4.

———, and Gumperz, John J. "Introduction, Linguistic Diversity in South Asia," *International Journal of American Linguistics*, XXVI (January 1960), 1-18.

Firth, J. R. *Tongues of Men and Speech*. London: Oxford University Press, 1964.

Fishman, Joshua A. "Language Maintenance and Language Shift as a Field of Inquiry," *Linguistics, an International Review*, IX (November 1964), 32-70.

―――. "Sociolinguistic Perspectives on the Study of Bilingualism," *Linguistics, an International Review*, XXXIX (May 1968), 21-49.

―――. "Varieties of Ethnicity and Varieties of Language Consciousness," *Languages and Linguistics*. Ed. Charles W. Kreidler. Georgetown University Monograph Series, No. 18, pp. 69-79.

――― (ed.). *Readings in the Sociology of Language*. The Hague: Mouton & Co., 1968.

―――, Ferguson, Charles A., and Das Gupta, Jyotirindra (eds.). *Language Problems of Developing Nations*. New York: John Wiley & Sons, 1968.

Garvin, Paul L. "Literacy as a Problem in Language and Culture," *Languages and Linguistics*. Ed. Hugo Mueller. Georgetown University Monograph Series, No. 7, 117-29.

――― (ed.). *A Prague School Reader on Esthetics, Literary Structure, and Style*. Washington, D.C.: Georgetown University Press, 1964.

Goody, Jack (ed.). *Literacy in Traditional Societies*. Cambridge: University Press, 1968.

Greenberg, Joseph H. "The Measure of Linguistic Diversity," *Language*, XXXII (January 1956), 109-15.

Gumperz, John J. "Linguistic Repertoires, Grammars and Second Language Instruction," *Languages and Linguistics*. Ed. Charles W. Kreidler. Georgetown University Monograph Series, No. 18, pp. 81-90.

―――, and Hymes, Dell (eds.). *The Ethnography of Communication*. Special Publication, *American Anthropologist*, LXVI, No. 6, Part 2 (December 1964).

Haugen, Einar. *Bilingualism in the Americas: A Bibliography and Research Guide*. American Dialect Society, No. 26. University of Alabama, 1956.

―――. "Dialect, Language, Nation," *American Anthropologist*, LXVIII (August 1966), 922-35.

―――. *Language Conflict and Language Planning: The Case of Modern Norwegian*. Cambridge: Harvard University Press, 1966.

―――. Review of V. Tauli, *Introduction to a theory of language planning*. *Language*, XLV (December 1969), 939-49.

Hymes, Dell H. "The Ethnography of Speaking," *Anthropology and Human Behavior*. Ed. Thomas Gladwin and William C. Sturtevant. Washington: Anthropological Society, 1962, pp. 13-53.

―――. "Functions of Speech: An Evolutionary Approach," *Anthropology and Education*. Ed. Frederick C. Gruber. Philadelphia: University of Pennsylvania Press, 1961, pp. 55-83.

―――. "Pidginization and Creolization of Languages: Their Social Contexts," *SSRC Items*, XXII (June 1968), 13-18.

――― (ed.). *Language in Culture and Society*. New York: Harper & Row, 1964.

Jernudd, Björn H. Review of E. Haugen, *Language Conflict and Language Planning. Language,* XLVII (June 1971), 490-93.

Koutaissoff, E. "Literacy and the Place of Russian in the Non-Slav Republics of the U.S.S.R.," *Soviet Studies,* III (October 1951), 113-30.

Le Page, R. B. *The National Language Question: Linguistic Problems of Newly Independent States.* London: Oxford University Press, 1964.

Lieberson, Stanley. "Bilingualism in Montreal: A Demographic Analysis," *American Journal of Sociology,* LXXI (July 1965), 10-25.

——— (ed.). *Explorations in Sociolinguistics.* Bloomington: Indiana University Press, 1967.

Macnamara, John. *Bilingualism and Primary Education: A Study of Irish Experience.* Edinburgh: University Press, 1966.

——— (ed.). *Problems of Bilingualism. The Journal of Social Issues,* XXIII (April 1967), entire issue.

"Multilingualism and Socio-Cultural Organization." *Anthropological Linguistics,* IV (January 1962), entire issue.

Ray, Punya Sloka. *Language Standardization: Studies in Prescriptive Linguistics.* The Hague: Mouton & Co., 1963.

Rice, Frank (ed.). *Study of the role of second languages in Asia, Africa, and Latin America.* Washington, D.C.: Center for Applied Linguistics, 1962.

Sapir, Edward. *Language: An Introduction to the Study of Speech.* New York: Harcourt, Brace and World, 1921.

Tauli, Valter. *Introduction to a theory of language planning.* Uppsala: Acta Universitatis Upsaliensis, 1968.

———. "Practical Linguistics: The Theory of Language Planning," *Proceedings of the 9th International Congress of Linguists.* Ed. Horace J. Lunt. The Hague: Mouton & Co., 1964.

Townsend, Elaine Mielke. "Accelerating literacy by piecemeal digestion of the alphabet," *Language Learning,* III (July 1948), 9-17.

UNESCO. *The Use of Vernacular Languages in Education.* Paris: UNESCO, 1953.

Vachek, Josef (ed.). *A Prague School Reader in Linguistics.* Bloomington: Indiana University Press, 1967.

Vildomec, Verobej. *Multilingualism.* Netherlands: A. W. Sythoff-Leyden, 1963.

Weinreich, Uriel. *Languages in Contact.* The Hague: Mouton & Co., 1967.

LATIN AMERICAN

Amado, Alonso. *Castellano, español, idioma nacional. Historia espiritual de tres nombres.* 2d ed. Buenos Aires: Losada, 1949.

Aramburu, Julio. *Voces de Supervivencia Indígena.* Buenos Aires: Emec Editores, 1944.

Bénédict, Gastón. *La Enseñanza Viva de las Lenguas Vivas por el Método Directo Progresivo.* Trans. Juvencio López Vásquez. México: Imprenta Universitaria, 1953.

Castillo Nájera, Francisco. *Breves Consideraciones sobre el Español que se habla en México.* New York: Instituto de las Españas, 1936.

Cuestionario provisional para el estudio coordinado de la norma lingüística culta de las principales ciudades de Iberoamérica y de la Península Ibérica. México: Comisión de lingüística y dialectología iberoamericanas del pilei oficina internacional de información y observación de español, 1968.

Dávila Garibi, José Ignacio. *Del Nahuatl al Español.* Tacubaya, D.F.: Instituto Panamericano de Geografía e Historia, 1939.

Darío, Rubio. *Los llamados Mexicanismos.* México: Imp. Franco-Mexicana, 1917.

Diebold, A. Richard, Jr. "Bilingualism and Biculturalism in a Huave Community." Unpublished Doctoral Dissertation, Yale University, 1961.

———. "Incipient Bilingualism," *Language,* XXXVII (January 1961), 97-112.

———. "A laboratory for language contact," *Anthropological Linguistics,* IV (January 1962), 41-51.

Gomez, Ricardo. *La nueva acentuación ortográfica según la Real Academia Española, formulada en reglas sencillas y faciles.* México, 1885.

Henriquez Urena, Pedro (ed.). *El español en Mejico, los Estados Unidos, y la América Central.* Buenos Aires: Instituto de Filologia, Universidad de Buenos Aires, 1938.

Ibero American and Caribbean Linguistics. Vol. IV of *Current Issues in Linguistics.* Ed. Thomas A. Sebeok. 10 vols. The Hague: Mouton & Co., 1968.

Islas Escarcega, Leovigildo. *Vocabulario Campesino Nacional: Objeciones y ampliaciones al vocabulario agricola nacional.* México: Instituto de investigaciones lingüísticas, 1935.

Lebrija, Antonio de. *Gramática Castellana.* Reproducción Phototypique de l'édition princeps, 1492. Halle, A. S., 1909.

Lope Blanch, Juan M. *El Lexico Indígena en el Español de México.* Jornadas 63. México: El Colegio de México, 1969.

López Vasquez, Juvencio. *Didáctica de las Lenguas Vivas.* México: UNAM, 1958.

Mesa Redonda Sobre el Monolingüismo Quechua y Aymara y la educación en el Peru. Documentos Regionales de la Etnohistoria Andina, No. 2. Lima, Peru: Casa de la Cultura, 1966.

Modiano, Nancy. "Bilingual education for children of linguistic minorities," *América Indígena*, XXVIII (Segundo trimestre, 1968), 405-14.

McQuown, Norman A. (ed.). *History of Studies in Middle American Linguistics*. Vol. V of *Handbook of Middle American Indians*. Ed. Robert Wauchope. 9 vols. Austin: University of Texas, 1967.

———. "Indian and Ladino Bilingualism: sociocultural and linguistic contrasts in Chiapas, Mexico." *Languages and Linguistics*. Georgetown University Monograph Series, No. 15, pp. 85-106.

———. Review of *Cartillas Maya-Español, Otomi-Español, Nahuatl-Español*. *Boletín Bibliografico de Antropologia Americana*, IX (1946), 263-5.

The New York Times, December 7, 1969, p. 53.

Nichols, Madaline W. *A Bibliographical Guide to Materials on American Spanish*. Cambridge: Harvard University Press, 1941.

Reyes, Alfonso. *Nuestra Lengua*. México: SEP, 1959.

Rubin, Joan. *National Bilingualism in Paraguay*. The Hague: Mouton & Co., 1968.

Swadesh, Mauricio. "Observaciones del Conflicto Fonético en Personas Bilingües," *Acta Antropológica*, II (noviembre 1960), 37-45.

Uribe Villegas, Oscar. "La situación sociolingüística de México como marco de la condición indígena," *Revista Mexicana de Sociología*, XXXI (octubre-diciembre 1969), 1019-26.

———. "Problemas metodológicos de raíz sociolingüística," *Revista Mexicana de Sociología*, XXXI (enero-marzo 1969), 109-28.

Vivó, Jorge A. *Razas y lenguas indígenas de México: su distribución geográfica*. Publication No. 52. México: Instituto Panamericano de Geografía e Historia, 1941.

Waterhouse, Viola. "Learning a second language first," *International Journal of American Linguistics*, XV (April 1949), 106-09.

Social Change and Policy Process

Adams, Richard. "La ética y el antropólogo social en América Latina," *América Indígena*, XXVIII (enero-marzo 1968), 273-90.

Almond, Gabriel A. and Coleman, James S. (eds.). *The Politics of the Developing Areas*. Princeton: Princeton University Press, 1960.

———, and Verba, Sidney (eds.). *The Civic Culture: Political Attitudes and Democracy in Five Nations*. Princeton: Princeton University Press, 1963.

Banton, Michael (ed.). *The Social Anthropology of Complex Societies*. A. S. A. Monographs 4. London: Tavistock Publications, 1966.

Beals, Ralph L., Redfield, Robert, and Tax, Sol. "Anthropological research problems with reference to the contemporary peoples of Mexico and Guatemala," *American Anthropologist*, XLV (January 1943), 1-21.

BIBLIOGRAPHY

Bonfil Batalla, Guillermo. "Conservative Thought in Applied Anthropology: A Critique," *Human Organization,* XXV (Summer 1966), 89-92.

Deutsch, Karl W. *Nationalism and Social Communication.* New York: John Wiley & Sons, 1953.

———. *The Nerves of Government.* New York: Free Press, 1966.

———. "Social Mobilization and Political Development," *American Political Science Review,* LV (September 1961), 493-506.

———, and Foltz, William J. (eds.). *Nation-Building.* New York: Atherton Press, 1963.

Diégues, Manuel, Jr. and Wood, Bryce (eds.). *Social Science in Latin America.* New York: Columbia University Press, 1967.

Finkle, Jason L. and Gable, Richard W. (eds.). *Political Development and Social Change.* New York: John Wiley & Sons, 1966.

Jacob, Philip E. and Toscano, James V. (eds.). *The Integration of Political Communities.* Philadelphia: J. P. Lippincott Co., 1964.

Lasswell, Harold D., Leites, Nathan, and Associates. *Language of Politics.* New York: George W. Stewart, 1949.

Lowi, Theodore J. "American Business, Public Policy, Case-Studies, and Political Theory," *World Politics,* XVI (July 1964), 677-715.

Morse, Richard M. "Language as a Key to Latin American Historiography," *The Americas,* XI (1955), 517-38.

Pye, Lucian W. (ed.). *Communications and Political Development.* Princeton: Princeton University Press, 1963.

———, and Verba, Sidney (eds.). *Political Culture and Political Development.* Princeton: Princeton University Press, 1965.

Seligman, Lester G. "Elite Recruitment and Political Development," *Journal of Politics,* XXVI (August 1964), 612-26.

Smith, T. Alexander. "Toward a Comparative Theory of the Policy-Process," *Comparative Politics,* II (July 1969), 498-515.

Steward, Julian H. "Acculturation studies in Latin America: some needs and problems," *American Anthropologist,* XLV (March 1943), 198-204.

———. "Prediction and Planning in Culture Change," *Human Organization,* XVIII (Spring 1959), 5-6.

"Symposium on Values in Action," *Human Organization,* XVII (Spring 1958), entire issue.

Tax, Sol, Wagley, Charles, and Gillin, John. "Research needs in the field of modern Latin American culture," *American Anthropologist,* LI (January 1949), 149-54.

Wagley, Charles (ed.). *Social Science Research on Latin America.* New York: Columbia University Press, 1964.

———, and Harris, Marvin. *Minorities in the New World.* New York: Columbia University Press, 1958.

Whitaker, Arthur P. and Jordan, David C. *Nationalism in Contemporary Latin America*. New York: Free Press, 1966.

Wolf, Eric R. "Aspects of Group Relations in a Complex Society: Mexico," *American Anthropologist*, LVIII (December 1956), 1965-78.

Mexican History

INTERVIEWS

Gonzalo Aguirre Beltrán, Mexico City, April, 1969.
Fernando Cámara, Mexico City, April, 1969.
Alfonso Caso, Mexico City, April, 1969.
Munro S. Edmonson, New Orleans, La., November, 1968.
Joseph Grimes, Mexico, April, 1969.
Andrés Iduarte, New York, March, 1971.
Juan M. Lope Blanch, Mexico City, July, 1969.
Rodolfo Stavenhagen, Miami, Florida, April, 1971.
Evangelina Arana Swadesh, Mexico City, April, 1969.
William Cameron Townsend, Waxhaw, N. C.
Alfonso Villa Rojas, Mexico City, April, 1969.

PERIODICALS

América Indígena. III, 1941-1971.
Anuario Indigenista. III.
Atlatl. 1970.
Boletín Indigenista. III, 1941-61.
Boletín Informativo. 1964.
Boletín de la Sociedad Mexicana de Geografía y Estadística. 1860-1908.
Boletín de la Sociedad Indianista Mexicana. 1911-13.
Boletín del Archivo general de la nación. 1930-60.
Hispano Americano. 1970-71.
Investigaciones Lingüísticas. Mexican Institute of Linguistic Investigations, 1933-38.
La Libertad. 1880-83.
Mexico intelectual: Revista pedagógica y científico-literaria. 1889-1900. 26 vols.
Revista de Educación. Asociación mexicana de profesores de enseñanza secundaria, 1933-35.
Revista de Educación. SEP, 1937-39.
Revista mexicana de educación. Sociedad mexicana de pedagogía, 1940-41.

BIBLIOGRAPHY

PRIMARY MATERIALS

Contemporary materials which reflect policies and practices related to language planning by anthropologists, educators, and politicians have been classified as primary sources.

Academia Mexicana Correspondiente de la Española. *Anuario, 1954*. México, 1954.

Aguirre Beltrán, Gonzalo. "Política indigenista en América Latina." Paper given before the Society of Applied Anthropology, Mexico, April 1969.

———. *El Proceso de Aculturación*. México: UNAM, 1957.

———. *Regiones de Refugio*. Ediciones especiales, 46. México: III, 1967.

———. *Teoría y práctica de la educación indígena*. Mexico: INI, 1953.

———. *La Universidad Latinoamericana y otros ensayos*. Biblioteca de la Facultad de Filosofía y Letras, num. 10. Xalapa: Universidad Veracruzana, 1961.

Alamán, Lucas. *Historia de Méjico desde los primeros movimientos que prepararon su independencia en el año de 1808 hasta la época presente*. 5 vols. México, 1849-52.

Alvarez Barret, Luis. "La política de educación indígena de la Revolución Mexicana." Typescript copy.

Alvear Acevedo, Carlos. *La Educación y la Ley: La Legislación en Materia Educativa en el México Independiente*. México: Editorial Jus, 1963.

Antecedentes, actas, debates y resoluciones del Congreso nacional de educación primaria reunido en la capital de la república en el mes del centenario. México: Tipografía económica, 1910.

Askinasy, Siegfried. *México Indígena: Observaciones sobre Algunos Problemas de México*. México: Imprenta "Cosmos," 1939.

Benaduci, Lorenzo Boturini. *Catalogo del Museo historico Indiano*. Madrid, 1746.

———. *Idea de una nueva historia general de la America Septentrional*. Madrid, 1746.

Beristáin de Souza, José Mariano (ed.). *Biblioteca hispano americana setentrional*. 3 vols. 2d ed. Amecameca, 1883.

Bonfil Batalla, Guillermo. "Reflexiones sobre la política indigenista y el centralismo gubernamental en México." Paper given before the Society for Applied Anthropology, Mexico, April 1969.

Bonilla y Segura, Guillermo. *Report on the Cultural Missions of Mexico*. Washington: U.S. Government Printing Office, 1945.

Carranza, Joseph María. *Discurso sobre el establecimiento de una escuela pública gratuita de primeras letras, y christiana educación de los niños pobres*. México, 1778.

Casahonde, Jorge. *Cómo debe el escuela fomentar el espíritu de maestros.* México: Congreso Nacional de Maestros, 1929.

Caso, Alfonso. *Discursos.* México: Imprenta Universitaria, 1958.

———, et al. *Métodos y Resultados de la Política Indigenista en México.* (Memorias del Instituto Nacional Indigenista, Vol. VI.) México, 1954.

———, et al. *Realidades y Proyectos: 16 años de trabajo.* (Memorias del Instituto Nacional Indigenista, Vol. X.) México, 1964.

Castillo Negrete, Emilio del (ed.). *Galería de oradores de México en el siglo XIX.* 3 vols. México, 1877-80.

Cedulario americano del siglo XVIII. Ed. Antonio Muro Orejón. (Consejo Superior de Investigaciones Científicas, XCIX. Sevilla: Escuela de Estudios Hispanoamericanos, 1956.

Cédulas Reales. México: Archivo General de la Nación.

Ceniceros, José Angel. *Educación y Mexicanidad: Discursos, páginas cívicas.* México, 1957.

———. *Nuestra Constitución Política y la Educación Mexicana.* México: disertación ante la junta nacional de educación normal en la Ciudad de México, 7 octubre, 1954.

Cervantes de Salazar, Francisco. *Crónica de la nueva españa.* Madrid: Tipografía de la "Revista de Archivos," 1914.

Chávez Orozco, Luis. *La escuela mexicana y la sociedad mexicana.* México: Editorial Orientaciones, 1940.

Clavigero, Francisco Javier. *Historia Antigua de México.* 4 vols. México: Editorial Porrua, 1945.

Comas, Juan. *La antropología social aplicada en México: trayectoria y antología.* Serie, Antropología Social, I. México: III, 1964.

———. *Ensayos sobre Indigenismo.* México: III, 1953.

Committee on Cultural Relations with Latin America. Personal papers of participant Rene Sebring Smith, Long Beach, California.

———. *The Seminar in Mexico: A Co-operative Study of Mexican Life and Culture.* Fourth Annual Session, Mexico City, July 13-August 3, 1929.

Cook, Katherine M. *The House of the People: An Account of Mexico's New Schools of Action.* Washington: U.S. Government Printing Office, 1932.

Cortés, Hernán. *Cartas y relaciones de Hernán Cortés al emperador Carlos V.* Ed. Pascual de Gayangos. Paris, 1866.

Corzo, Angel M. *Ideario de Maestro Indoamericano: Por el espíritu del indio se forjará la nueva cultura de américa y su grandeza.* México: DAPP, 1938.

Cronica de la Orden de N.P.S. Augustin en las Provincias de la nueva españa en quatro edades desde el año de 1533 hasta el de 1592. México, 1624.

Cronicas de Michoacán. Biblioteca del estudiante universitario, No. 12. México: UNAM, 1940.

Cuevas, P. Mariano. *Documentos inéditos del siglo XVI para la historia de México.* México: Museo Nacional de Arqueología, Historia y Etnología, 1914.

Dávila, Padilla, Agustín. *Historia de la fŭndacion y discŭrso de la provincia, de Santiago de México, de la orden de Predicadores por las vidas de sus varones insignes y casos notables de Nueva España.* Brusselas, 1625.

Departamento de asuntos indígenas. *Memoria . . . 1941-42.* México, 1942.

―――. *Memoria de la Primera Asamblea de Filólogos y Lingüistas.* México, 1940.

―――. *Primer Congreso Indigenista Interamericano.* Boletín num. 1. Pátzcuaro, Michoacán, 1940.

Diario de México. México, 1805-12.

Díaz Covarrubias, José. *La Instrucción Pública en México.* México, 1875.

Díaz del Castillo, Bernal. *The Discovery and Conquest of Mexico 1517-1521.* Trans. A. P. Maudslay. New York: Farrar, Straus and Cudahy, 1956.

Díaz Ordaz, Gustavo. *Ideas Políticas del Presidente Gustavo Díaz Ordaz.* Ed. Roberto Amores. México: Editorial Ruta, 1966.

Dirección General de Estadística. *6° Censo de Población, 1940. Resumen General.* México, 1943.

―――. *7° Censo de Población, 1950. Resumen General.* México, 1952.

―――. *8° Censo General de Población, 1960. Resumen General.* México, 1962.

―――. *9° Censo General de Población, 1970. Resumen de las principales caracteristicas por entidad federativa.* México, noviembre 1970.

Dublan, Manuel y Lozano, José María (eds.). *Legislación mexicana: colección completa de las disposiciones legislativas expedidas desde la independencia de la república.* 19 vols. México, 1876.

E.A.D. *Los Indios quieren ser libres y lo serán con justicia.* México, 1829.

Encinas, Diego de. *Cedulario indiano.* 4 vols. Madrid: Ediciones Cultura Hispanica, 1946.

Estudios Antropológicos publicados en homenaje al doctor Manuel Gamio. México, 1956.

Fernández de Lizardi, José Joaquín. *El Pensador Mexicano.* Biblioteca del estudiante universitario, No. 15. México: UNAM, 1940.

―――. *El Periquillo Sarniento.* México: Editorial Stylo, 1942.

Fernández MacGregor, Genaro (ed.). *Vasconcelos.* México: SEP, 1942.

Fuente, Julio de la. *Educación, antropología y desarrollo de la comunidad.* México: INI, 1964.

Gamio, Manuel. *Consideraciones Sobre el Problema Indígena.* Serie, Antropología Social, II. México: III, 1966.

―――. *Forjando Patria (Pro Nacionalismo).* México: Libería de Porrúa Hermanos, 1916.

―――. *Introduction, Synthesis and Conclusions of the Work, The Population of the Valley of Teotihuacán.* México, 1922.

Gante, Pedro de. *Cartilla para enseñar a leer.* Facsimile reproduction of Huntington Library's copy printed by Pedro Ocharte. Mexico City, 1569; México: Academia Mexicana de la Educación, 1959.

García, Génaro y Pereyra, Carlos (eds.). *Documentos inéditos o muy raros para la historia de Mexico.* 36 vols. México, 1905-11.

García Granados, Ricardo. *La Constitución de 1857 y las leyes de Reforma en Mexico.* México, 1906.

García Icazbalceta, Joaquín (ed.). *Apuntes para un catálogo de escritores en lenguas indígenas de América.* México, 1866.

―――. *Bibliografía mexicana del siglo XVI. Catálogo razonado de libros impresos en México de 1539 a 1600, con biografías de autores y otras ilustraciones.* Ed. Agustín Millares Carlo. México: Fondo de Cultura Económica, 1954.

―――. *Biografía de D. Fr. Juan de Zumárraga, Primer Obispo y Arzobispo de Méjico.* Ed. M. Aguilar. Madrid: Marques de Urquijo, 1929.

――― (ed.). *Cartas de Religiosos de Nueva España.* México, 1836.

――― (ed.). *Códice Franciscano,* Vol. II of *Nueva colección de documentos para la historia de México.* 5 vols. México: Salvador Chavez Hayhoe, 1941.

――― (ed.). *Códice Mendieta,* Vol. IV of *Nueva colección de documentos para la historia de México.* 5 vols. México, 1892.

―――. *La instrucción pública en la cuidad de México durante el siglo XVI.* México, 1893.

―――. *Opúsculos varios.* 2 vols. México, 1896.

―――. *Vocabulario de mexicanismos, comprobado con ejemplos y comparado con los de otros paises hispano-americanos. Propónese además algunas adiciones y enmiendas a la ultima edición (12^a) del diccionario de la academia.* México, 1899.

Gazeta de Literatura. Ed. Jose Antonio de Alzate y Ramirez. México, 1788-1795.

Gazetas de México compiendo de noticias de Nueva España. México, 1784-1800.

Gleason Galicia, Rubén. *Las estadísticas y censos de México: su organización y estado actual.* México: UNAM, 1968.

Granados y Gálvez, Joseph Joaquín. *Tardes americanas: gobierno gentil y católico: breve y particular noticia de toda la historia indiana: sucesos, casos, notables, y cosas ignorados, desde la entrada de la Gran Nación Tulteca a esta tierra de Anáhuac, hasta los presentes tiempos. Trabajados por un Indio, y un Español.* México, 1778.

Grijalva, Juan de. *Cronica de la Orden de N. P. S. Augustin en las provincias de la nueva españa. En quatro edades desde el año de 1533 hasta el de 1592.* México, 1624, 1924-30.

Gual Vidal, Manuel. *Diez Discursos sobre Educación (Programa educativo del Lic. Miguel Alemán).* México: DAPP, 1947.

Guzmán, Martín Luiz. *Academia: Tradición. Independencia. Libertad.* México: Compañia General de Ediciones, 1959.

——— (ed.). *Escuelas laicas.* México: Empresas Editoriales, 1948.

Herring, Hubert C. and Terrill, Katherine (eds.). *The Genius of Mexico.* New York: Committee on Cultural Relations with Latin America, 1931.

———, and Weinstock, Herbert (eds.). *Renascent Mexico.* New York: Covici Friede, 1935.

Homenaje al Doctor Alfonso Caso. México: Imprenta Nueva Mundo, 1951.

Homenaje a Juan Comas. México: Editorial Libros de México, 1965.

Instituto Nacional Indigenista. *Aprendo a Leer, Cartilla Mixteca.* México, 1959.

———. *Cartilla del Papaloapan.* México, 1965.

———. *Cartilla Tzotzil.* México, n.d.

———. *Los Centros Coordinadores.* México, 1962.

———. *Juchari uandkuecha* [our language] *Nueva Cartilla purépecha.* México, 1965.

———. *¿Qué es el I.N.I.?* México, 1955.

La instrucción pública. Bound collection of materials on education in the states of Mexico in the early nineteenth century. Duke University Library. n.p., n.d.

Iturriaga, José E. *La Estructura Social y Cultura de México.* México: Fondo de Cultura Económica, 1951.

Jiménez T., Aurea Nira. *Analfabetismo.* México: CREFAL, 1955.

Kirk, Betty. *Covering the Mexican Front.* Norman: University of Oklahoma Press, 1942.

Las Casas, Bartolomé de. *Historia de las Indias.* 3 vols. México: Fondo de Cultura Económica, 1951.

Lombardo Toledano, Vicente. *El Problema de la Educación en México: Puntos de vistos y proposiciones del Comité de Educación de la Confederación Regional Obrera Mexicana.* México: Editorial Cultura, 1924.

López de Gómara, Francisco. *Cortés: The Life of the Conqueror by his Secretary.* Trans. Lesley Byrd Simpson. Berkeley: University of California Press, 1964.

López Mateos, Adolfo. *La Lucha por la Tierra.* Ed. Silvano Barba González. México, 1966.

——. *Pensamiento en Acción.* 3 vols. México: Editorial la Justicia, 1962.

——. *Pensamiento y Programa.* México: Editorial la Justicia, 1961.

Lorenzana y Buitrón, Francisco Antonio. *Cartas pastorales, y edictos.* México, 1770.

Lumholtz, Carl. *Unknown Mexico.* 2 vols. New York, 1902.

Luna Arroyo, Antoñio. *El Problema de la Educación Pública en México.* México, 1931.

Mariano Flores, Anselmo. *Distribución Municipal de los Hablantes de Lenguas Indígenas en la República Mexicana.* México: Instituto Nacional de Antropología e Historia, 1963.

Mateos, Juan, A. *Historia parlamentaria de los congresos mexicanos de 1821 a 1857.* 9 vols. México, 1877-86.

Memoria de Justicia é Instrucción Pública presenta la Congreso de la Unión, 8 octubre 1870. México, 1870.

Memoria. . . 1871-73. México, 1873.

Memoria. . . 1876-77. México, 1877.

Memoria. . . 1878-81. México, 1881.

Memoria. . . 1902. México, 1902.

Mendez Bravo, A. *La escuela rural Mejicana: lo que Mejico espera de sus maestros.* Santiago de Chile: Imprenta Lagunas, 1929.

Mendieta, Jerónimo de. *Historia Eclesiástica Indiana,* Vol. III of *Nueva colección de documentos para la historia de México.* Ed. Joaquín García Icazbalceta. 5 vols. México, 1870.

Mexican Constitution of 1917 Compared with the Constitution of 1857. Trans. H. N. Branch. Supplement to *The Annals of the American Academy of Political and Social Science.* May 1917.

Mexican Revolutionary Party. *The Second Six-Year Plan, 1941-46.* Mexico, 1946.

The Mexican Year Book 1909-10. Mexico: Department of Finance, 1911.

Miñano García, Max H. *La educación rural en México.* México: SEP, 1945.

Molina Enríquez, Andrés. *Los grandes problemas nacionales.* México, 1909.

Mora, José María Luis. *Ensayos, Ideas y Retratos.* Biblioteca del estudiante universitario, No. 25. México: UNAM, 1941.

—— (ed.). *Obras sueltas.* 2d ed. México: Editorial Porrua, 1963.

Morelos y Pavón, José María. *La Abispa de Chilpancingo Escrita para perpetuar la memoria del Primer Congreso instalado alli el día 12 de septiembre de 1813.* México, 1821.

Motolinía (Toribio de Benavente). *Historia de los Indios de la Nueva España*, Vol. I of *Colección de documentos para la historia de México*. Ed. Joaquín García Icazbalceta. México, 1858.

Muñoz, Maurillo. *Mixteca, Nahua-Tlapaneca*. (Memorias del Instituto Nacional Indigenista, Vol. IX.) México, 1963.

Nahmed, Salomon. *Los Mixes*. (Memorias del Instituto Nacional Indigenista, Vol. XI.) México, 1965.

Olivera de V., Mercedes and Sánchez, Blanca. *Distribución Actual de las Lenguas Indígenas de México, 1964*. México: Instituto Nacional de Antropología e Historia, 1965.

Othón de Mendizábal, Miguel. *Obras completas*. 6 vols. México: Talleres Graficos de la Nación, 1946.

Palavicini, Feliz F. *Historia de la constitución de 1917*. 2 vols. México: Editorial Porrua, 1938.

———. *Problemas de Educación*. Valencia: F. Sempere y Compañia, 1910.

Pani, Alberto J. *La Higiene en México*. México: Imprente de J. Ballescá, 1916.

Parra, Manuel Germán y Jiménez Moreno, Wigberto (eds.). *Bibliografía indigenista de México y Centroamérica (1850-1950)*. (Memorias del Instituto Nacional Indigenista, Vol. IV.) México, 1954.

Partido de la Revolución Mexicana. *Cárdenas Habla*. México: La Impresora, 1940.

Pérez de Guzmán y Gallo, D. Juan. *Memorias de Academia Española*. Madrid: Establecimiento Tipográfico de Fortanet, 1920.

Pimentel, Francisco. *Memoria sobre las causas que han originado la situación actual de la raza indígena de Mexico y medios de remediaria*. México, 1864.

Plancarte, Francisco M. *El Problema Indígena Tarahumara*. (Memorias del Instituto Nacional Indigenista, Vol. V.) México, 1954.

Pomar, Juan Bautista. *Relación de Tezcoco* in *Relaciones de Texcoco y de la Nueva España*. Ed. Joaquín García Icazbalceta. México: Editorial Salvador Chavez Hayhoe, n.d.

Portes Gil, Emilio. *The Mexican School and the Peasantry*. Mexico: Press of Ministry of Foreign Relations, 1936.

"La posición de los estudiantes de la escuela nacional de antropología e historia de México ante los problemas de cambio social." Position paper circulated at meetings of Society for Applied Anthropology, Mexico City, April, 1969.

Pozas, Isabel H. de y Ricardo Pozas. *Del monolingüismo indígena al bilingüismo en lengua nacional: Una experiencia educativa del Centro Coordinador Indigenista del Papaloapan*. Oaxaca: Nuevo Paso Nacional, 1956.

Puga, Vasco de. *Provisiones, cédulas, instrucciones para el gobierno de la Nueva España.* 2 vols. México, 1878-9.

Puig Casauranc, J. M. *La Educación Pública en México a tráves de los Mensajes Presidenciales desde la Consumación de la Independencia hasta nuestros Dias.* México: SEP, 1926.

Ramírez, Ignacio. *Obras de Ignacio Ramírez.* 2 vols. México, 1889.

Ramos Arizpe, Miguel. *Discursos, Memorias e Informes.* Biblioteca del estudiante universitario, No. 36. México: UNAM, 1940.

Recopilación de leyes de los reynos de las Indias. 3 vols. Madrid: Consejo de la hispanidad, 1943.

Rodríguez y Cos, José Miguel. *Iniciativas presentadas pro . . . ante la Comisión Nacional del Centenario de la Independencia, a fin de consolidar, por medio de la educación pública, el espíritu de la nacionalidad mexicana, é incorporar á esta á la raza indígena, y celebrar dignamente el 80° ániversario del nacimiento de C. General Porfirio Díaz.* México, 1907.

Romero García, Fernando (ed.). *Diario de los Debates del Congreso Constituyente.* México: Imprenta de la Camara de Diputados, 1922.

Rosa, Agustín de la. *La instrucción en México durante su dependencia de España.* Guadalajara, 1888.

Sáenz, Moisés. *Carapan, bosquejo de una experiencia.* Lima, Peru: Librería e imprenta Gil, 1936.

———. *Escuelas Federales en la Sierra de Puebla: Informe sobre la visita a las escuelas federales en la Sierra de Puebla.* Publicaciones de SEP, Tomo XV, num. 5. México, 1927.

———. *México integro.* Lima: Imp. Torres Aguirre, 1939.

———. *Reseña de la educación pública en México en 1927.* México: SEP, 1928.

———, and Priestley, Herbert I. *Some Mexican Problems: Lectures on the Harris Foundation, 1926.* Chicago: University of Chicago Press, 1926.

Sahagún, Bernardino de. *Historia general de las cosas de Nueva España.* Ed. Carlos María de Bustamante. 3 vols. México, 1830.

Salazar, Juan B. *Bases of the Socialist Secondary School, A Plan submitted to the Institute of Socialist Orientation, Secretariat of Public Education, June, 1935.* Trans. Francisco Olave. México, 1936.

Sánchez, George I. *Mexico: A Revolution by Education.* New York: Viking Press, 1936.

Sánchez Pontón, Luiz. *Hacia la Escuela Socialista: La Reforma Educacional en México.* México: Editorial Patria, 1935.

Secretaría de Educación Pública. *Acción Educativa del Gobierno Federal del 1 de septiembre de 1954 al 31 de agosto de 1955.* México, 1955.

———. *VI Asamblea Nacional de Educación, reunida en México del 11 al 22 de agosto, inclusive, problemas que se sometieron a su estudio y conclusiones aprobados.* México, 1930.

———. *VI Asamblea Nacional Plenaria: La coordinación y la ampliación de la obra cultural y educativa en beneficio de la población indigena.* Vol. IV. Biblioteca del Consejo Nacional Técnico de la Educacion. México, 1964.

———. *La Casa del Estudiante Indígena: 16 meses de labor en un experimento psicológico colectivo con indios, febrero de 1926-junio de 1927.* México, 1927.

———. *Cinco años de labor educativa del gobierno de méxico.* México, 1963.

———. *Consejo Nacional Técnico de la Educación.* México, 1958.

———. *La Educación Pública en México, desde el 1 de diciembre de 1934 hasta el 30 de noviembre de 1940.* 3 vols. México, 1941.

———. *El esfuerzo educativo en México.* 1924-28. 2 vols. México, 1928.

———. *Gómez Farías y la Reforma Educativa de 1833.* México, 1933.

———. *Memoria . . . 1936-37.* México, 1937.

———. *Memoria . . . 1939-41.* México, 1941.

———. *Memoria . . . 1947-48.* México, 1948.

———. *Memoria . . . 1948-49.* México, 1949.

———. *Memoria . . . 1949-50.* México, 1950.

———. *Memoria . . . 1950-52.* México, 1952.

———. *Las Misiones Culturales, 1932-1933.* México, 1933.

———. *El Movimiento Educativo en México.* México, 1922.

———. *Teoría y Aplicación de la Reforma Educativa.* México: Instituto Federal de Capacitación del Magisterio, 1963.

Secretaría de Estado y del despacho de Justicia é Instrucción Pública. *Memoria.* México, 1844.

———. *Breve noticia de los Establecimientos de Instrucción dependientes de la. . . .* México, 1900.

Seis Años de Gobierno al Servicio de México, 1934-40. México: La Nacional Impresora, 1940.

Sierra, Justo. *Discursos.* México: Herrero Hermanos Sucesores, 1919.

———. *Justo Sierra, Educación e Historia.* Ed. Abreu Gomez. Washington: Unión Panamericana, n.d.

———. *Obras Completas del Maestro Justo Sierra.* Vol. VIII. *La Educación Nacional: Artículos, Actuaciones y Documentos.* Ed. Agustín Yañez. México: UNAM, 1949.

Simpson, Lesley Byrd (ed. and trans.). *The Laws of Burgos.* San Francisco: John Howell Books, 1960.

Solórzana y Pereyra, Juan de. *Política Indiana.* 5 vols. Madrid: Ibero-Americana de Publicaciones, 1930.

Stalin, Joseph. *Marxism and the National and Colonial Question.* New York: International Publishers, 1934.

———. *Marxism and the National Question.* New York: International Publishers, 1942.

Stavenhagen, Rodolfo. "Decolonializing Applied Social Sciences." Paper delivered before the Society for Applied Anthropology. Miami, Fla., April 1971.

Summer Institute of Linguistics. Clipping File "Velasco."

Swadesh, Evangelina Arana de. "Los programas educativos para las zonas indígenas." Typescript copy, March 23, 1971.

Swadesh, Mauricio. "La educación indígena en los centros del Instituto Nacional Indigenist: informe de visitas hechas en febrero-junio de 1956." Typescript copy.

———. *La nueva filología.* 2d ed. México, 1968.

———. *Orientaciones lingüísticas para maestros en zonas indígenas: una serie de conferencias.* México: Departamento de asuntos indígenas, 1940.

Torres Bodet, Jaime. *Educación mexicana: Discursos, entrevistas, mensajes.* México: SEP, 1944.

Torres Quintero, Gregorio. *La instrucción rudimentaria en la república.* México: Museo Nacional de Arqueología, Historia y Etnología, 1913.

———. *México, hacia el fin del virreinato español: antecedentes sociológicos del pueblo mexicano.* México: Librería de la Vda. de Ch. Bouret, 1921.

Townsend, William Cameron. Letter to Luis Alvarez Barret, Sub-Director General, Rural Education. Typescript copy, April 15, 1940.

Tozzer, Alfred M. (ed. and trans.). *Landa's Relación de las Cosas de Yucatan.* Papers of the Peabody Museum of American Archaeology and Ethnology, Vol. XVIII. Cambridge, Mass.: Harvard University, 1941.

UNESCO. *Learn and Live.* Paris: UNESCO Press, 1951.

UNAM. *Memoria del Primer Congreso de Escuelas Preparatorias de la República.* México, 1922.

Vargas Martínez, Ubaldo. *Morelos: Siervo de la Nación.* 2d ed. México: Editorial Porrua, 1966.

Vasconcelos, José. *De Robinson a Odiseo.* Madrid: M. Aguilar, 1935.

———. *La raza cósmica: Misión de la raza iberoamericana, Argentina y Brazil.* México: Espasa-Calpe Mexicana, 1948.

———, and Gamio, Manuel. *Aspects of Mexican Civilization.* Chicago: University of Chicago Press, 1926.

Véjar Vásquez, Octavio. *Hacia una Escuela de Unidad Nacional: Discursos.* México: SEP, 1944.

Velasco Ceballos, Rómulo. *La Administración de d. frey Antonio María de Bucareli y Ursúa.* 2 vols. México: Publicaciones del Archivo General de la Nación. Tomos XXIX-XXX, 1936.

———— (ed.). *La Alfabetización en la Nueva España: Leyes, Cedulas Reales, Ordenanzas, Bandos, Pastoral y Otros Documentos.* México: SEP, 1945.

Villa Rojas, Alfonso. *Los Mazatecos y el problema indígena de la cuenca del Papaloapan.* (Memorias del Instituto Nacional Indigenista, Vol. VII.) México, 1955.

————. "Resultados de la orientación antropológica en la educación indígena del México actual." Paper delivered before the Society for Applied Anthropology, Mexico City, April, 1969.

Wallis, Ethel E. and Bennett, Mary A. *Two Thousand Tongues to Go: True-Life Adventures of the Wycliffe Bible Translators Throughout the World Today.* New York: Harper & Row, 1964.

Warman, Arturo et al. *De ese que llaman antropología Mexicana.* México: Editorial Nuestro Tiempo, 1970.

A William Cameron Townsend en el vigésimoquinto aniversario del Instituto Lingüístico de Verano. México, 1961.

Zavala, Lorenzo de. *Ensayo histórico de las revoluciones de Mégico, desde 1808 hasta 1830.* 2 vols. Paris, 1831 (Vol. I). Nueva York, 1832 (Vol. II).

Zayas Enríquez, Rafael de. *La rendición de una raza: estudio sociológico.* Veracruz, 1887.

SECONDARY SOURCES

Adams, Richard et al. *Social Change in Latin America Today.* New York: Vintage Books, 1960.

Barranco, Manuel. *Mexico: Its Educational Problems: Suggestions for Their Solution.* New York: Teachers College Press, 1915.

Bobb, Bernard E. *The Viceregency of Antonio Maria Bucareli in New Spain. 1771-1779.* "Texas Pan American Series." Austin: University of Texas Press, 1962.

Bolton, Herbert Eugene. "The Mission as a Frontier Institution in the Spanish-American Colonies," *American Historical Review,* XXIII (October 1917), 42-61.

————. *Rim of Christendom: A Biography of Eusebio Francisco Kino, Pacific Coast Pioneer.* New York: Macmillan Company, 1936.

————. *The Spanish Borderlands.* "Chronicles of America." New Haven: Yale University Press, 1921.

Booth, George C. *Mexico's School-Made Society.* Stanford, Calif.: Stanford University Press, 1941.

Brandenburg, Frank. *The Making of Modern Mexico.* Englewood Cliffs, N. J.: Prentice-Hall, 1964.

Bravo Ugarte, José. *La educación en México (. . .-1965).* México: Editorial Jus, 1966.

Cámara Barbachano, Fernando. "El mestizaje en México: Planteamiento sobre problemáticas socio-culturales," *Revista de Indias,* nums. 95-96 (enero-junio 1958), 27-86.

Cantón Rosado, Francisco. *Historia de la instrucción pública en Yucatan desde el siglo XVI hasta fines del siglo XIX.* México: SEP, 1943.

Castillo, Isidro. *México y su Revolución Educativa.* México: Academia Mexicana de la educación, 1965.

Castro, Eusebio. "Trayectoria ideológica de la educación en México." *Historia Mexicana, IV* (octubre-diciembre 1954), 200-08.

Chávez, Ezequiel A. *El Primero de los Grandes Educadores de la América— Fray Pedro de Gante.* México: Imprenta Mundial, 1934.

Cline, Howard F. *Mexico, Revolution to Evolution: 1940-1960.* New York: Oxford University Press, 1963.

―――. *The United States and Mexico.* Revised edition. New York: Atheneum, 1963.

Cockcroft, James D. *Intellectual Precursors of the Mexican Revolution 1910-1913.* Latin American Monographs, No. 14. Austin: University of Texas Press, 1968.

Cosio Villegas, Daniel. *Historia Moderna de México: La República Restaurado. La Vida Social.* México: Editorial Hermes, n.d.

Cuevas, P. Mariano. *Historia de la Iglesia en México.* 5 vols. Tlalpam, D. F.: Imprenta del Asilo "Patricio Sanz," 1921-1926.

La Cultura. Vol. IV. *México: cincuenta años de Revolución.* México: Fondo de Cultura Económica, 1962.

Dabbs, Jack Autrey. *The French Army in Mexico, 1861-1867: A Study in Military Government.* The Hague: Mouton & Co., 1963.

Decorme, Gerard. *La Obra de los Jesuitas Mexicanos durante la época colonial 1572-1757.* 2 vols. México: José Porrus e Hijos, 1941.

Delmez, Albert J. "The Positivist Philosophy in Mexican Education, 1867-1873," *The Americas,* VI (July 1949), 32-44.

Dunne, Peter Masten. *Pioneer Jesuits in Northern Mexico.* Berkeley: University of California Press, 1944.

Ebaugh, Cameron Duncan. *The National System of Education in Mexico.* "Johns Hopkins University Studies in Education," No. 16 Baltimore: Johns Hopkins University Press, 1931.

Elliott, J. H. *Imperial Spain 1469-1716*. New York: St. Martin's Press, 1963.

Gibson, Charles. *The Aztecs Under Spanish Rule: A History of the Indians of the Valley of Mexico 1519-1810*. Stanford: Stanford University Press, 1964.

———. *Spain in America*. The New America Nation Series. New York: Harper & Row, 1966.

Gómez Navas, Leonardo et al. *La educación: historia, obstáculos, perspectivas*. México: Editorial Nuestro Tiempo, 1967.

———. *Política Educativa de México I*. México: Editorial Patria, 1968.

González Casanova, Pablo. *La democracia en México*. 2d ed. México: Ediciones ERA, 1967.

Gonzáles Navarro, Moisés. "El mestizaje mexicano en el periodo nacional," *Revista Mexicana de Sociología*, XXX (enero-marzo, 1968), 35-42.

Gonzales Obregón, Luis. *Don José Joaquín Fernández de Lizardi (El Pensador Mexicano). Apuntes Biográficos y Bibliográficos*. México, 1888.

Gringoire, Pedro. "El 'Protestanismo' del Mora," *Historia Mexicana*, III (1953), 328-66.

Hale, Charles A. "José María Luis Mora and the Structure of Mexican Liberalism," *HAHR*, XLV (May 1965), 196-227.

———. *Mexican Liberalism in the Age of Mora, 1821-1853*. New Haven: Yale University Press, 1968.

Hanke, Lewis. *Aristotle and the American Indians: A Study in Race Prejudice in the Modern World*. London: Hollis & Carter, 1959.

———. "The Requerimiento and its Interpreters," *Revista de historia de América*, I (Mexico, 1938), 25-34.

———. *The Spanish Struggle for Justice in the Conquest of America*. Philadelphia: University of Pennsylvania Press, 1949.

Helps, Arthur. *The Spanish Conquest in America and its Relation to the History of Slavery and to the Government of the Colonies*. New York: AMS Press, Inc., 1966.

Horowitz, Irving Louis (ed.). *Masses in Latin America*. New York: Oxford University Press, 1970.

Jacobsen, Jerome Vicent. *Educational Foundations of the Jesuits in 16th Century New Spain*. Berkeley: University of California Press, 1938.

Kneller, George F. *The Education of the Mexican Nation*. New York: Columbia University Press, 1951.

Lanning, John Tate. *The Eighteenth-Century Enlightenment in the University of San Carlos de Guatemala*. Ithaca: Cornell University Press, 1956.

Larroyo, Francisco. *Historia Comparada de la Educación en México*. México: Editorial Porrua, 1947.

Lewis, Oscar. *Life in a Mexican Village: Tepoztlan Restudied*. Urbana: University of Illinois, 1951.

Mason, J. Alden (ed.). *The Maya and Their Neighbors*. New York: D. Appleton-Century Co., 1940.

Mecham, J. Lloyd. "The Origins of Federalism in Mexico," *HAHR*, XVIII (May 1938), 164-82.

Medary, Marjorie. *Each One Teach One: Frank Laubach, Friend to Millions*. New York: Longmans, Green and Co., 1954.

Merriman, Roger Bigelow. *Philip the Prudent*, Vol. IV: *The Rise of the Spanish Empire in the Old World and in the New*. New York: The Macmillan Company, 1934.

Millan, Verna Carleton. *Mexico Reborn*. Boston: Houghton, 1939.

Millon, Robert Paul. *Vicente Lombardo Toledano: Mexican Marxist*. Chapel Hill: University of North Carolina, 1966.

Narain, Raj. *Education for Literacy: Its Nature, Function and Dynamics*. Allahabad, India: Garga Press, 1958.

Nash, Manning (ed.). *Social Anthropology*. Vol. VI of *Handbook of Middle American Indians*. Ed. Robert Wauchope. 9 vols. Austin: University of Texas Press, 1967.

New York Times. February 21, 1971, Section 3, pp. 1, 11.

Othón de Mendizábal, Miguel et al. *Ensayos sobre las clases sociales en México*. México: Editorial Nuestro Tiempo, 1968.

Padden, Robert C. *The Hummingbird and the Hawk: Conquest and Sovereignty in the Valley of Mexico 1503-1541*. New York: Harper & Row, 1967.

Peterson, Frederick. *Ancient Mexico: An Introduction to the Pre-Hispanic Cultures*. New York: Capricorn Books, 1959.

Powell, T. G. "Mexican Intellectuals and the Indian Question, 1876-1911," *HAHR*, XLVIII (February 1968), 19-36.

Prescott, William H. *History of the Conquest of Mexico and History of the Conquest of Peru*. New York: Random House, n.d.

Ricard, Robert. *The Spiritual Conquest of Mexico: An Essay on the Apostolate and the Evangelizing Methods of the Mendicant Orders in New Spain: 1523-1572*. Trans. Lesley Byrd Simpson. Berkeley: University of California Press, 1966.

Romanell, Patrick. *Making of the Mexican Mind: A Study in Recent Mexican Thought*. Lincoln: University of Nebraska Press, 1952.

Ross, Stanley R. (ed.). *Is the Mexican Revolution Dead?* New York: Alfred A. Knopf, 1966.

Ruiz, Ramón Eduardo. *Mexico: The Challenge of Poverty and Illiteracy.* San Marino, California: Huntington Library, 1963.

Schoenhals, Louise. "Mexican Experiments in Rural and Primary Education: 1921-1930," *HAHR*, XLIV (February 1964), 22-43.

Scholes, Walter V. *Mexican Politics During the Juárez Regime 1855-1872.* Columbia: University of Missouri Studies, 1957.

Simpson. Lesley Byrd. *The Encomienda in New Spain: The Beginning of Spanish Mexico.* Berkeley: University of California Press, 1950.

Smith, Justin. *The War with Mexico.* 2 vols. New York: Macmillan, 1919.

Spicer, Edward H. "National Policy in Mexico and the United States as a Factor in the Process of Indian Integration." Unpublished paper given before Society for Applied Anthropology, April 1969.

Stabb, Martin S. *In Quest of Indentity: Patterns in the Spanish American Essay of Ideas, 1890-1960.* Chapel Hill: University of North Carolina Press, 1967.

———. "Indigenism and Racism in Mexican Thought," *Journal of Inter-American Studies*, I (October 1959), 405-25.

Strode, Hudson. *Timeless Mexico.* New York: Harcourt, Brace, & Co., 1944.

Tannenbaum, Frank. *Peace by Revolution: Mexico After 1910.* New York: Columbia University Press, 1933.

Torre Revello, José. "Algunos libros de caligrafía usados en México en el siglo XVII," *Historia Mexicana*, V (octubre-diciembre 1955), 220-27.

Townsend, William Cameron. *Lázaro Cárdenas: Mexican Democrat.* Ann Arbor: George Wahr Publishing Co., 1952.

Turner, Frederick C. *The Dynamic of Mexican Nationalism.* Chapel Hill: University of North Carolina Press, 1968.

Valdez Padilla, Miguel Oscar. *Política indigenista: elementos para el desarrollo de las comunidades indígenas de México.* México: UNAM, 1968.

Vázquez de Knauth, Josefina. *Nacionalismo y educación en México.* México: El Colegio de México, 1970.

Villoro, Luis. *Los Grandes Momentos del Indigenismo en México.* México: El Colegio de México, 1950.

Whetten, Nathan L. *Rural Mexico.* Chicago: University of Chicago Press, 1948.

Wilkie, James W. *The Mexican Revolution: Federal Expenditure and Social Change since 1910.* Berkeley: University of California Press, 1967.

Wilson, Irma. *Mexico, A Century of Educational Thought.* New York: Hispanic Institute, 1941.

Wolf, Eric. *Sons of the Shaking Earth: The People of Mexico and Guatemala*

—*Their Land, History, and Culture.* Phoenix Books. Chicago: University of Chicago Press, 1959.

Zavala, Silvio. "Sobre la Política Lingüística del Imperio Español en América," *Cuadernos Americanos,* XXVII, No. 3 (May-June 1946).

Zea, Leopoldo. *Del liberalismo a la revolución en la educación mexicana.* México: Talleres Gráficos de la Nación, 1956.

―――. "Hacía un nuevo liberalismo en la educación," *Historia Mexicana,* V (abril-junio 1956), 528-48.

―――. *The Latin-American Mind.* Trans. James H. Abbott and Lowell Dunham. Norman: University of Oklahoma Press, 1963.

Zepeda Rincón, Tomás. *La instrucción pública en la Nueva España en el siglo XVI.* México: UNAM, 1933.

Index

Abad y Queipo, Manuel, 59
Academy of Language. *See* Mexican Academy of Language
Acculturation
    evaluation of, as indigenist goal, 148-49, 152-57, 188-89
    of Indians, as national goal, 72-73, 85-87, 96-98
    levels of, 136-37, 154
    under incorporation programs, 103-6, 132, 185-86
    views of, underlying bilingual education, 110-19, 143, 202
    See also Castilianization; Integration
Acolhuaque, 3, 4
Agriculture
    development of, as modernization goal, 158-59, 170-72, 188-89, 197
    influence of, on language, 117, 195
    modern techniques of, in integral education, 88, 117, 137, 148-49, 153, 185, 188
Aguirre Beltrán, Gonzalo, 132, 141
    as director of INI, 159-61, 189
Alcalá, University of, 6, 31
Alemán, Miguel, 131-38, 140
Alvarez Barret, Luis, 111, 115

Alzate y Ramírez, José Antonio, 53
América Indígena, 121, 160
American Bible Society, 67
Anthropology, applied
    in community projects, 129-31
    early proposals for, in indigenism, 84, 120-22
    evaluation of political role of, 142-43, 155-58, 160-61
    Mexican view of, 106-7
    in regional development, 132, 136-39
Aquilar, Jerónimo de (Spanish interpreter), 10-11
Assembly of Philologists and Linguists 116-19, 127, 138
Assimilation, 152, 170-72, 202
    See also Castilianization, Incorporation
Augustinians, 14, 20, 28
    geographic distribution of, 22-23
Avila Camacho, Manuel, 123-131, 132, 170
Aztec, 9, 63, 65, 73
    empire, 1, 11, 16, 22-23
    Indians, 28, 32
    official language policy, 1, 3-4, 24-26, 177-79

Baranda, Joaquín, 72, 74, 97

Barreda, Gabino, 71
Barrera Vásquez, Alfredo, 118, 139, 146
Basauri, Carlos, 104, 111
Bassols, Narciso, 96, 103, 110, 112, 140
Belmar, Francisco, 76-77
Benítez, Fernando, 160
Bilingual education, 132, 159, 186
  and bicultural agents, 94, 138-39, 172, 187-88
  early proposals for, 68, 69-71, 102, 105, 107-12, 189, 196
  endorsed by Ministry of Public Education, 153
  in literacy campaign, 127-30, 153-54
  influence of, beyond Mexico, 113-14, 128, 139-40, 146-47
  within INI's indigenism movement, 135, 146-48, 161-63, 173, 202
  need for, 100, 105
  opposition to, 113, 121-22, 124, 143-46
  and textbook preparation, 104, 130, 133
  See also Institute of Literacy for Monolingual Indians; Linguistics; Literacy
Bilingualism, 121, 123, 181
  maintenance and shift factors in, 116-17, 198-200
  semi-permanent functional status of, given official recognition, 164, 170, 189-90
  Spanish-Nahuatl, 195
  statistical measures of, 163-70
  as a technique in Indian education, 186-87
  as a transitional status, 111, 149, 154, 173, 188-89, 202
Bonfil, Ramón, 159
Bourbon kings
  policies of, 44-53, 97
Bravo Ahuja, Gloria Ruíz de, 158
Bravo Ahuja, Victor, 157-60
British and Foreign Bible Society, 67
Bucareli, Antonio María, 50-52
Bulnes, Francisco, 74

Bureau of Anthropology and Regional Populations, 85-86
Burgos, Laws of, 7-8, 12-14, 38

Cabrera, Luis, 93, 121
Cacique, 4, 10;
  definition of, 9
Calles, Plutarco Elías, 89, 94
Carapan Project, 103-5, 139, 140, 145, 186
Cárdenas, Lázaro, 122, 123
  organization of Department of Indian Affairs, 106-7, 131
  Socialist education under, 109, 121
  support of bilingual education, 112, 114-16, 120, 140, 170, 201
Carranza, Venustiano, 85, 93
Casa del estudiante indígena, 103, 138
  establishment of, 94-95
  influence of, 95-96, 97, 185-86
Casa del pueblo, 88, 91, 92, 132
Caso, Alfonso, 159, 183
  contributions of, to theory of indigenism, 133-34, 136
  and National Institute of Anthropology and History, 111, 122, 127
  and political influence, 122, 127, 141, 189
Castellanos, Abraham, 76
Castilianization
  identification with Christianization, 5-8, 12-14, 19-20, 36, 179-82, 200
  Indian resistance to, 40, 52-53, 172
  during Isabella's rule of Castile, 5-7, 179
  in national era, 145, 162, 196
  for unification of Castilian empire, 37-40, 48-49
  See also Direct method
Cédulas Reales
  1550: Schools to teach Castilian to the Indians (Charles V), 18-21, 26, 28, 38, 39
  1551: Indians to congregate in villages (Charles V), 34

1565: Missionaries to learn language of Indians under their charge (Philip II), 26, 28
1570: Nahuatl official language of New Spain's Indians (Philip II), 26-28
1574: Requirements for appointment to ecclesiastical office (Philip II), 27
1578: Language requirements for parish appointments (Philip II), 27
1580: Nahuatl instruction in University (Philip II), 27
1603: Language prerequisites for parish assignment (Philip III), 35
1612: "Houses of correction" for Indian girls to proscribe use of Indian tongues (Philip III), 37
1618: Reissue of 1603 decree (Philip III), 35
1619: Removal of clergy from parish assignment for failure to learn indigenous tongues (Philip III), 35-36
1627: Indigenous language instruction in University (Philip IV), 36
1634: Castilian official tongue for education and administration of Indians (Philip IV), 37-38, 39
1686: Lay and religious officials to implement Castilianization (Charles II), 39-40
1690: Preference in selection of administrators for Indian villages to be given to those speaking Spanish (Charles II) 41
1691: Organization and support of village schools to teach Spanish (Charles II) 41, 46
1693: Lay officials to force Indians to attend school (Charles II), 41
1770: Review of Castilianization and renewed emphasis of Bourbon Crown's language policy (Charles III), 48-50, 51

1772: Establishment of seminary to train Indians to teach Spanish in their communities (Charles III), 51
1778: Provision of village schools to teach Spanish (Charles III), 51-52
Ceniceros, José Angel, 148-50
Centers of Indigenous Education, 95, 97
Centralization
  arguments favoring, 106, 114-15, 119-21, 130-35
  through INI, 121-22, 135-39, 187
  within Mexican Academy of Language, 192-93
  struggles resulting from, 140-42, 148-49, 155-57, 189
Chalca, 3
Charles V, King of Spain (1516-1556), 42
  1526 ruling on interpreters, 12
  1535 order for education of Indians, 28
  New Laws of 1542, 13-14
  1550 orders to spread Castilian, 18-21, 28, 38, 39
  1551 ruling on *congregaciones*, 34
Charles II (1665-1700), 44, 46, 200
  1686-1691 decrees reviewing language policy and ordering village schools to teach Castilian, 39-41, 181-82
Charles III (1759-1788), 44
  1770 order reviewing Castilianization and Christianization, 47-54, 182
  1770-1778 orders supporting Indian primary schools and colegio, 51-52
Charles IV (1788-1808), 58
Chávez Orozco, Luis, 111, 115, 116
Chontal, 3, 22, 196
Christianization
  beyond central Mexico, 21-25, 31-35, 45
  evaluation of, 47, 52-53
  language techniques of, 15-19, 23-30, 34, 180

Christianization—*continued*
   linked with Castilianization, 19-21, 35-38, 179-81, 200
   methods of, compared with Soviet language policy, 110-11
Científicos, 79
   definition of, 74
Cisneros, Francisco Jiménez de, 5-6, 15, 21, 180
Codification
   of Castilian (peninsular), 54-55
   of Latin American Spanish, 194
   of Mexican Spanish, 181, 192-94
Congregaciones, 42
   definition of, 34
Congress of Chilpancingo, 60
Congress of Instruction (First), 72-73
Conservatism, 68, 69
   interpretation of, 58
   under Santa Anna, 66-67
Constitution of 1812 (Spain), 61
Constitution of 1824, 60-61
Constitution of 1857, 67, 68
Constitution of 1917, 85, 97, 126
   Article 3, 85, 109, 123, 125, 149
   Article 31, 85
   1921 Amendment, 86, 183
Cordova, Hernandez de, 9
Cortés, Hernán, 1, 3, 177, 180
   and Indian conversion program, 13-14, 16-18, 42
   and interpreters, 9-11, 47
Cosmes, Francisco G., 74
Council of Indigenous Languages, 118, 127-28, 139
CREFAL (Regional Center of Fundamental Education for Latin America), 139-40
creole priests
   and competition with peninsula-born priests, 35, 46-50, 53
Creoles (*criollos*), 90, 97, 151, 182
   and concept of nationality, 63-64, 68
   definition of, 35
   and estimation of language, 55, 67, 74, 189
   as a social class, 42, 57, 59, 61, 75, 81, 85, 191

CROM (*Confederación Regional Obrera Mexicana*), 108
Cruz, Rodrigo de la, 19, 23
Cuauhtémoc, 73, 182
Cultural missions, 91, 99, 116
   Department of, 88, 106, 124
Culture
   dualistic, of Mexico, 73-74, 157
   equation of, with standard, 99-100, 108-9, 186-87
   and group identity, 7-8, 134, 138-39, 153, 183-85, 200
   as key to economic status, 147-48, 172-75
   language as an index of, 3-6, 30-31, 37-38, 43, 53-55, 93, 181-82

Decentralization
   of social change programs and language policy, 143, 160-63
   official programs under, 157-60, 189-91
Department of Indian Affairs
   and bilingual education, 112, 116, 118-19, 130, 184
   establishment of, 105-07
   in National Literacy Campaign, 127-29, 135
   replacement of, by Office of Indian Affairs, 131
Deutsch, Karl, 170
Diario de México, 54
Díaz, Porfirio, 74, 180
   view of, on Indians, 75-79
Díaz de Léon, Jésus, 77, 121
Díaz del Castillo, Bernal, 4, 11
Díaz Ordaz, Gustavo, 154-55
Dictionary (ies)
   of Americanisms, 66, 196
   for Indian languages, 113, 118
   of Royal Spanish Academy, 55, 183
Diebold, A. Richard, Jr., 198-99
Diglossia, 199
Direct method, 54, 86, 95, 143, 164, 184
   definition of, 92-93
   evaluation of, 145-46, 161-63
   opposition to, 101, 116-17, 135

INDEX

in rural school programs, 91-92, 96, 102, 138, 143, 185-86, 196, 201
Dominicans, 14, 20, 30-31
geographic distribution of, 22-23

Echeverría Alvarez, Luis, 158-62, 172, 189
Economy
of Aztec tributary system, 3-4, 177-79
and educational opportunities, 69, 100, 126, 156-57
and language policy, 107-9, 114, 116-17, 146-50, 161-63, 197
and regional development, 131, 136-39, 142, 151-60, 187-89
Education
colonial higher, 27-31, 46, 53-54, 58
colonial primary, 24, 27, 31-33, 39-42, 46, 50-53, 58, 182
cultural goals of, 7-8, 12-14, 57-59, 61-64, 78-81, 87-88, 99-100
elite, early national, 60-67, 180
primary, early national, 61-64, 68, 72-76
public system of, 66-67, 85, 97-98, 194
reform in 1970's, 158-60, 189-90
See also Rudimentary instruction, Rural schools
Elaboration and language planning, 195-96
Elites
in colonial Spanish society, 53-55, 191-92
in Indian society, 14, 19, 44-46, 51
intellectuals as, 98, 201-02
national political, 145, 152, 155, 158, 162, 202
sociocultural influence of, 57-59, 81, 148, 182, 193-94
Encomenderos, 38
and Castilian language policy, 8, 11-14, 181
definition of, 8
English, 70

Federalism, 60, 72
Ferdinand V, the Catholic, King of Castile (1474-1504), 5, 8
Fernández de Lizardi, José Joaquín, 58-59
Fishman, Joshua, 198
Franciscans, 14, 33
geographic distribution of, 21-23, 31
in Indian education, 16-19, 29-31
and support of Nahuatl, 19-20, 24-32, 180
training and linguistic techniques of, 5, 18
Francisco (Indian interpreter, 1517-19), 9-10
French, 54, 70
Fuente, Julio de la, 105, 111, 132

Gálvez, José de, 51
Gamio, Manuel, 135, 152
and Teotihuacán regional program, 86, 90, 186
theoretical contributions of, to applied anthropology, 120-21
views of, on education, 84-87, 96, 100, 106, 119
Gante, Pedro de, 16, 18, 28
García Icazbalceta, Joaquín, 74
Gazeta de Literatura, 53-54
Gómez Farías, Valentín, 63-65, 68
González Casanova, Pablo, (linguist), 104
González Casanova, Pablo (political sociologist), 155-56
Grammar(s)
to codify Castilian, 66
by colonial clergy, 6, 18
for national literacy programs, 113, 135
of Nebrija, 6, 25, 54
Grijalva, Juan de, 9, 10
Gual Vidal, Manuel, 132-33
Guerrero, Vincente, 62

Haugen, Einar, 192-96
Henry, Jules, 105, 111
Hispanization. *See* Castilianization
House of the Indian Student. *See* Casa del Estudiante Indígena

House of the People. *See* Casa del Pueblo
Huastec, 22

Incorporation
  evaluation of, 94-106, 114, 116-17, 120, 188
  goals of, 87-92, 184-86, 196, 201
Indigenism
  as distinct from Indianism, 120-22
  evaluation of, 148-50, 155-58, 160-63, 169-72, 188-90, 200-02
  in literacy campaign, 129-31
  in regional development, 133-36, 140, 151-55
INI. *See* National Indigenist Institute
Institute for Literacy in the Indigenous Languages. *See* Institute of Literacy for Monolingual Indians
Institute of Hispano-American Lexicography, 195
Institute of Investigation and Social Integration, 157-58
Institute of Literacy for Monolingual Indians
  early history of, 127, 132-33
  methods and successes of, 135, 142, 187
Integration
  definition of, 99, 114
  evaluation of, 148-50, 152-53, 155-57
  and language policy, 100, 103, 172-75, 195-96
  need for, 107
  in program of indigenism, 117, 119
  and regional development, 133, 136-37, 187-89
  theoretical basis for, 134-37
  See also Indigenism
Inter-American Conference of Education (Third), 113
Inter-American Indigenist Congress
  First, 120-22, 127, 133, 134, 138
  Second, 134

Inter-American Indigenist Institute, 121, 129, 146, 159
Inter-Amereican Scientific Conference (Seventh), 112
International Americanist Conference (Eighth), 120
Interpreters, 101
  in Aztec empire, 1, 4, 175-77
  in Conquest, 9-12, 15-16
  in Christianization, 16-18, 33
  in established Colonial empire, 21, 44, 47-49
  See also Naguatlatos
Isabella I, the Catholic, Queen of Castile (1474-1504), 21, 38
  and language policy, 1, 5-8
Iriarte, Juan de, 54
Ixtlilxochitl, Fernando de Alva, 4, 16

Jesuits, 31-32, 51, 62
Juárez, Benito, 67, 69
Julian (Indian interpreter, 1517), 9

La Celestina (1499), 7
Ladino
  definition of, 43
Lancasterian schools, 64, 68, 124
Landa, Diego de, 33
Language functions, general, 69-71, 136, 161-63
  effects of bilingualism on, 172-73, 190, 197-98
  theories of, 197-200
Language functions, specific
  poetic expression (Latin) 25, (Nahuatl) 4, 25, (Spanish) 66
  prestige (Indian, in general) 97, (Latin) 30-31, (Nahuatl) 3, 199, (Spanish) 88-90
  scientific expression (Latin) 4-5, 179, (Nahuatl), 4-5, 178-79, (Spanish) 193-94
  separatist (Nahuatl) 197, (Spanish) 53-55
  socioeconomic status (Nahuatl) 3, 190, (Spanish) 45-46, 77, 116-17
  unifying (Nahuatl) 177-79, (Spanish) 20-21, 38-39, 52, 59, 76-79, 93, 181-82

workaday technical (Nahuatl) 25, 178-79, (Spanish) 78, 181, 197
Language policy
authority in determining, 47-49, 140-41, 161-63, 180-81
authority in implementing, 40-44, 51-53, 76-79, 85, 144
goals of colonial, 19-21, 37-41
goals of national, 72-74, 116-19, 135, 147-50, 161, 164
See also Bilingual education, Castilianization, Direct method
Las Casas, Bartolomé de, 13, 42
Latin, 54, 59, 65
in Colegio de Santa Cruz de Tlatelolco, 28-31
as a literacy tool, 28, 32
in New World conversion program, 8, 15, 24-25, 33
in Spain, 6
as a standard language in Europe, 4, 5, 179
Lathrop, Maxwell, 112, 118, 128-29
Laubach, Frank, 124
Law of Compulsory Instruction, 72, 75
Lewis, Oscar, 171
Liberalism
and education, 63-65, 68, 69
interpretation of, 58
Linguistics
and analyses of Indian languages, 76-77, 101-3, 111-19, 145-46
early friars' approach to, 17-18, 180
and literacy programs, 127-29, 135, 146, 153-54
and teacher training, 88-89, 113-14, 117
See also Bilingual education
Literacy
in Indian tongues, 27-29, 33-34, 37, 67-68, 100-2, 107-10, 124, 126-27, 143-44
as key to economic shift, 82-84, 147-49, 187-88
motivations for, 106, 116-17
in national modernization program, 126, 152

See also Bilingual education, National Literacy Campaign
Lizardi. *See* Fernández de Lizardi
Lombardo Toledano, Vincente, 108-10
Lope Blanch, Juan M., 194
López, Jerónimo, 30
López Mateos, Adolfo, 151-54
Lorenzana y Buitrón, Antonio, 47-49, 51, 182

Malinche (Doña Marina), 11
Marginals
Indians and mestizos as, 136-37, 146, 148-50, 152-53
and internal colonialism, 155-58
Marqués de Croix, 48, 50, 51
Mass communication and sociopolitical mobilization, 152, 158-59
Maximilian of Austria, Archduke Ferdinand, 67-68, 189
Maya, 69, 70, 107, 195
bilingual education program for, 112, 128, 135
in Christianization program, 32
use of, by early interpreters, 9-11
Melchior (Indian interpreter, 1517), 9-10
Mendicant Orders, 6, 15
See also Regulars *and specific orders*
Mendieta, Jerónimo de, 4, 22-23, 25-26, 178
Mendizábal, Miguel Othón de, 104
and Soviet language policy, 111
Mendoza, Antonio de, 28
Mestizo(s), 73, 90, 105, 195
cultural characteristics of, 148-49, 163
definition of, 41
as exploiters of Indians, 153, 156-57, 172
in integration program, 136, 151-53, 188
Mexican, synonym for national, 89-90
as a social class, 43, 61, 148-49

Mestizoization
  definition of, 151
  linked with indigenism, 152-53
Mexica, 1, 3, 4, 11
Mexican Academy of Language (Mexican Academy of Spanish), 182-83
  debates in, during 1951 and 1956, 192-94
  founded, 74
  proposed, 65-67
Mexican Indianist Society
  and language policy, 76, 77, 83, 183
Mexican Institute of Linguistic Studies, 112, 114
Mexican Society of Anthropology, 134
Mexican Society of Geography and Statistics, 76
Mexico, University of (UNAM), 27, 36, 65, 86, 112, 134
Michoacán, 22, 59, 106, 120, 140
  Archbishop of, 42
  bilingual materials for, 128-29
  site of Carapan, 103
  site of Tarascan Project, 112, 118-19, 127
Ministry of Public Education, 103, 115, 124, 187, 189
  goals of, 87, 149-50
  organization of, 86-87, 119, 131-32, 154, 159-60
  policies of, 139, 140-41
  socialist orientation of, 109, 121, 186
  support of bilingual education by, 153
Missionaries. *See* Augustinians, Christianization, Dominicans, Franciscans
Mitla, 73
Mixtec, 3, 22, 40, 112, 141
Modernization
  and economic development, 126, 154, 200
  in the Mexican pattern, 152-56, 162, 170
  role of language standardization in, 191, 194
Molina, Alonso de, 18

Molina Enríquez, Andrés, 81, 152
Montezuma, 4, 11
Mora, José María Luis, 63-65, 67, 68, 84
Morelos, José María, 60
Motolinía (Toribio de Benavente), 17, 30

Naguatlatos
  in Christianization, 21, 23
  in colonial civil affairs, 44
  definition of, 12
  effect of, on colonial language policy, 12, 14, 179-80
Nahua, 3, 112, 128-29, 135
Nahuatl, 9, 11, 18, 21, 43, 54, 112
  in Aztec empire, 1, 3, 23, 177-79
  in bilingual education, 68-70, 135, 197
  and Christianization, 18, 27-29, 180-81
  in early national education, 65, 67
  estimation of, as standard language, 4-5, 25-26, 177-79
  influence of, on Spanish language, 195
  as post-Conquest "universal language" of Indians, 19, 23-27, 180
  transcription of, in Roman alphabet, 16-17, 27-29
National Indigenist Institution (INI)
  bureaucratization within, 140-42
  in era of decentralization, 159-60, 170, 173, 187, 189, 202
  organization of, 121, 133-35, 154
  reassessment of, 143-50
  regional organizations of, 136-39
National Institute of Anthropology and History, 107, 111, 122, 127, 134
National language
  and national mestizo identity, 73, 86, 88-92, 148-49, 154, 170, 186-87
  and national socialization, 100-101, 106, 113-19
  and pluralistic decision-making, 158-63, 202-03

INDEX 297

selection of, 72-74, 182-84, 190-92
statistical measure of speakers of, 163-74
as unifying force, 76-79, 81-83, 149-52, 157, 183-84
See also Standardization
National Literacy Campaign, 87, 124, 132, 143, 170, 187
bilingual method in, 127-29, 153-54
National Museum of Archaeology, Ethnology, and History, 73, 189
National Polytechnic Institute, 111, 125, 134
National Preparatory School, 71
National Technical Council of Education, 149-50
National unity
cultural identity and, 61-68, 73-74, 82-83, 129-30, 149-50
and language policy, 69-71, 76-79, 121-22, 123-25, 151-52, 196, 197-203
and pluralistic culture characteristics, 156-57, 160-63, 183-84
and school systems, 183-84
Nebrija, Elio Antonio de, 6, 25, 54, 179
New Galicia, 23-24
New Laws of 1542, 13-14
Normal schools, 72, 74, 91, 96, 184

Oaxaca, 48, 67, 105, 132, 160
bishop of, 40, 47
Chontal speakers of, 198
Coordinating Center in, 141
Institute of Investigation and Social Integration of, 157-58
Jesuit seminary in, 32
linguists in, 112
province of, 25
valley of, 22, 24-25, 26, 195
Obregón, Alvaro, 86
Office of Indian Affairs, 131-32, 137-38, 142
Otomi, 22, 23, 65, 70, 156
bilingual materials for, 112, 128-30, 135
functions of, 197, 199

linguistic independence of speakers of, 32
Patrimonio Indígena among, 142-43
in tributary system of Aztecs, 3

Palavicini, Félix F., 85
Pani, Alberto, 82-83
Papaloapan
Flood Control Project, 132-33, 137
Regional Coordinating Center, 141, 145
Parra, Manuel Germán, 141
Partido Nacional Revolucionario (National Revolutionary Party) *See* Six Year Plan of PNR
Patrimonio Indígena (Indian Patrimony), 142
Peninsulares, 46, 49, 55
definition of, 42
Peru, 120, 193, 203
Philip II (1556-98), 21
1570-1592 orders in support of Nahuatl in Christianization, 26-28, 35, 181
Philip III (1598-1621)
1599 order to priests to learn Indian tongues, 35-36
1603, 1618 orders in support of 1599 ruling, 35, 37
1612 order to establish "houses of correction," 37
Philip IV (1621-65)
1627 order supporting Indian tongues in University, 36
1634 order to spread Castilian, 37-39
Pike, Kenneth, 112, 115, 146
Plan of Iguala, 60
Polyglots, 21-22, 26
Ponce, Alonso, 24
Popoloca, 3
Popular Evolutionary Party, 82
Positivists, 77, 83, 89
education views of, 68-69, 71, 74, 79, 183
Pozas, Ricardo and Isabel, 145-46
Prague School of Linguistics, 178, 197

Promotores culturales, 138, 142-44, 149, 188, 197
Puig Casauranc, José Manuel, 94

Quiroga, Vasco de, 31, 140

Race(s)
  Aztec, synonym for Indians, 63
  as basis for discrimination against Indians, 72-75, 122, 134, 149
  fusion of, to achieve national unity, 89-90, 152
  Mexican, synonym for nation, 89
Ramírez, Ignacio, 69-71, 84
Ramírez, Rafael
  and Indian education, 88, 95
  language policy of, 91-92, 100, 102-3
Ramos Arizpe, Miguel, 59
Reconquista: definition of, 5
Recopilación de leyes, 39
  See also Cédulas Reales
Redfield, Robert, 111
Real Academia Española. See Royal Spanish Academy
Regional Coordinating Centers
  cooperation of, with other agencies, 142, 154
  language policy of, 143-44, 170-72, 196-97
  organization and administration of, 137-39, 141, 188
Regulars
  in Christianization, 23, 27, 180, 182, 200
  definition of, 21
  See also Augustinians, Dominicans, Franciscans
Requerimiento, 9
  definition of, 8
Revolution of 1910, 81, 84, 102
  impact on education, 86, 93, 98, 116, 170
  influence on views of Indians, 89, 185, 200
Rodríguez Puebla, Juan, 62-63
Rojas, Mariano Jacobo, 68, 189
Royal Spanish Academy (*Real Academia Española*)
  duties of, 55, 193
  influence of, in Mexico, 55, 66
  Mexican associate institution of, 74, 182, 192-93
  See also Mexican Academy of Language
Rudimentary instruction
  evaluation of, 94, 106, 116-17
  goals of, 82, 85, 88
  Law of, 82-83, 93, 97, 185, 196
  status of, in 1914, 85
Ruiz Cortines, Adolfo, 138, 140-41, 149, 153
Rural schools, 90, 92, 94, 96-97, 184
  administration of, 86, 154
  decline of, 132
  Department of, 88, 103, 105
  evaluation of, 99, 103
  failures of teachers in, 100, 101, 143
  language policy of, 135, 138, 147, 185
  pre-primary, 82
  number of, in 1930, 91
  See also Rudimentary instruction

Sáenz, Moisés, 94, 116
  and Carapan, 103-6, 139, 140, 145
  evaluation of language policy, 101-3
  theory of incorporation, 89-92
  theory of socialization, 186
Sahagún, Bernardino de, 28-29, 110, 178
Samayoa, Mariano, 138
San Francisco, Escuela de, 17
San Gregorio Collegio, 31, 51, 62
Santa Anna, Antonio López de, 66-67, 97
Seculars, 23, 27, 31, 180
  definition of, 21
Segregation policies
  in colonial New Spain, 42-44, 45, 53
Sierra, Justo
  as influence on education, 75, 84, 89, 97, 125
  view of, on language policy, 77-78, 183-84
Silva y Aceves, Mariano, 112

Six Year Plan of PNR, 109, 124, 126-27
Socialism, 109-10, 123
See also Soviet Union
Solórzana y Pereyra, Juan de, 38, 44
Soviet Union (Russia)
language policy of, 106-11, 123, 125, 183
Spelling reform, 183
Stalin, Joseph, 109-10, 123, 161
Standardization
of Castilian in Isabella's reign, 6-7, 177-79
of Castilian in New Spain, 55
comparison of, in developed and developing nations, 190-91
of Indian languages, 162-63
of Nahuatl, 4-5, 23, 25-26
of Spanish in Mexican nation, 65-66, 74, 183-85, 192-94
Statistics
and measures of monolingualism and bilingualism (1920) 89, (1950) 147, (1940-1970) 163-70
use of, in policy-making, 76, 107, 147, 163-74
Student movement (1968), 156-57
Summer Institute of Linguistics, 103, 112, 115, 118, 146
and bilingual method, 135, 139, 145
cooperation with other agencies, 111-12, 139, 154
influence on Cárdenas, 116
See also Townsend, William Cameron
Swadesh, Evangelina Arana de, 160
Swadesh, Mauricio, 105, 118, 128
evaluation of language policy, 143-46, 172-73
Tabascans, 13
Tannenbaum, Frank, 102-3
Tarahumara, 112, 138
Tarascan, 103, 104, 106, 112
bilingual materials for, 128, 135
linguistic independence of, speakers, 22-23, 177

Tarascan Project, 124, 141, 143, 153
community orientation of, 131
linguistic methods of, 145-46
organization of, 118-19, 127
Tax, Sol, 111
Tenochtitlán, 3-4
Teotihuacán, 73, 86, 90, 186
Tepaneca, 3
Tepoztlan, 58, 68, 131
Testera, Jacobo de, 33
Texcoco
cultural capital of Axtec empire, 4, 16, 178
site of Escuela de San Francisco, 17-18
Tlatelolco, Colegio de Santa Cruz, 28, 30-31, 110
attempts to revive, in eighteenth century, 44-46
Torres Bodet, Jaime
as Minister of Education, 125-28, 130, 132, 139, 141, 151
and UNESCO, 128, 139-40
Torres Quintero, Gregorio, 82, 83, 92, 145
Totonac, 3, 22, 112, 135
Townsend, William Cameron
and Cárdenas, 112, 140
and establishment of Summer Institute of Linguistics, 103
and recognition of need for linguists in integration program, 101-2
role of, in early bilingual education, 112, 115-17
Translators. See Interpreters
Tzeltal-Tzotzil area, 137

UNESCO, 128, 139-40
support of vernaculars, 146-47
Urbanization, 151-53, 156-59, 170, 188

Vasconcelos, José, 97, 99, 124, 125, 132
and development of rural education, 86-87
language policy of, 87-89, 184, 193

Vasconcelos, José—*continued*
   theory of incorporation of, 89-92, 186
Véjar Vásquez, Octavio, 123-27
Velasco, Luis de, 21
Vera Estañol, Jorge, 82
Villalpando, Luis de, 33
Villaurrutia, Jacobo, 54

Wallis, Ethel, 199
Weinreich, Uriel, 199

Xochimilca, 3

Yucatan, 9, 10, 84, 103, 129
   bilingual method in, 107, 128-29
   correlation between language and Indian traits in, 173-75
   Indian opposition to friars in, 32-33
   regionalism of, recognized, 84, 102-03

Zapata, Emilio, 89
Zapotec, 22, 70, 130, 156, 199
Zavala, Lorenzo de, 61
Zayas Enríquez, Rafael de, 75
Zumárraga, Juan de, 28-29

O'Toole Library
Withdrawn

O'Toole Library
Withdrawn